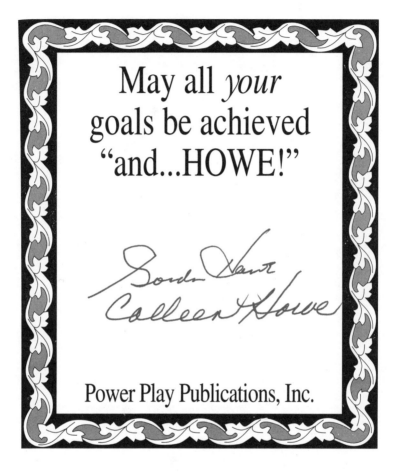

May all *your* goals be achieved "and...HOWE!"

Power Play Publications, Inc.

and...HOWE!

and...HOWE!

An authorized autobiography
by Gordie and Colleen Howe
with Tom DeLisle

Power Play Publications, Inc.
Traverse City, Michigan
49686

Library of Congress Catalog Card Number: 95-92430

Power Play Publications, Inc.
Traverse City, Michigan

ISBN 0-9647149-0-6

2 3 4 5 6 7 8 9 96

CONTENTS

CONTENTS, CONTINUED

Marty, Mark, and Dr. Murray Howe (Number 15)

FOREWORD
by Dr. Murray Howe

This is going to be fun. The story of Mr. and Mrs. Hockey® and their brood of little draft choices is one of my favorites. This may sound funny, coming from one of the Howe kids, but I am truly a Howe fan. So for the next ten minutes, kick back, grab a tuna-fish sandwich and some Vernors, and enjoy a glimpse into the Howe family from someone who's been there.

What is it like to be in a famous family? Well, the answer is, it depends on the family. In my case, it's like a triple-dip chocolate almond ice cream on a sugar cone: unbeatable. My parents supply the chocolate.

Take my dad for instance. Sure he managed to dislodge a few players' faces from their heads with one hand, while casually scoring with the other, but any super-human athlete with superior genetic material could do that. That's not why we named our first-born son after him. It's because of the man inside.

He's the guy who signed autographs for twenty rambunctious little-leaguers who happened to corner him in Baskin-Robbins while he was visiting a teenage Marty Howe behind the counter; then Mr. Hockey® bought them all ice-cream. He's the guy who chased a purse-snatcher on foot, then in a car, then on foot again, until the would-be criminal gave up the goods in exhaustion. Just another day for Gordie Howe at the mall.

He's the guy who would sign autographs at Olympia for hours after the game, handing each signature to me and telling the

1

fan "Get HIS autograph. HE's the really famous one." No one was sure what I was famous for, but they looked long and hard at my signature (which of course no one could decipher, coming from a future physician). And most of the young fans came away proudly sporting a pen mark on their nose or a crumpled shirt from when Mr. Hockey lifted them up "by their ears."

Gordie Howe is also obsessed with helping people. After cleaning his windshield at the gas station, he often moves on to clean the windshield of the next car over. Now THAT turns heads, even if no one recognizes him. When he comes to visit, I usually save a few projects for him to do; otherwise he'll cut down one of my favorite trees or rearrange the furniture. And he does every task with a vengeance. Ask him to wrap a package, and it will require explosives to open it.

Thank God he never hit me. Or even yelled at me. He didn't have to. Since I didn't feel like dying young, I tried to stay on his good side. That's pretty easy, since he doesn't have a bad side. He would go out of his way to invite us to do whatever he was doing, even though we were likely to slow him down. "Murray, how bout comin' down to the rink with me?" he'd ask. Or more frequently, "Mur, c'mon and help me shovel the drive." Hmm. "Well, no, that's okay Dad." I hated to give him a complex, but it's hard to keep up with a compulsive helper. He wore me out.

While Gordie Howe is a great helper, he is an even more outstanding father. Everything that he does, he does with his children in mind. If you ever hear him speak, he always makes a point to include every one of the kids. "My son, Murray, the doctor; and my lovely daughter, Cathy, couldn't be here today;" he'd begin. "But Mark, number four on the Red Wings; and Marty, coach of the Motor City Mustangs; are happy to be here today at the Owosso County Livestock Auction." If he starts including the nine grandchildren, there's gonna be some mighty long speeches. But, because of the man that he is, he'll do it anyway. Kids are his number one priority.

He's the guy who dragged his whole family around with him on every vacation he ever took; which made for some pretty interesting experiences. "Hey, let's go say 'Hi' to Jackie Gleason!" he said as we walked the course at Inverrary. "Okay" I said, trying to remember exactly who Jackie Gleason was. So we talked about classic cars with ol' Jackie in his garage. And we talked about travel with the Osmond brothers in their pajamas (Cathy's first love). We shook paws with "Gentle Ben," the long-forgotten movie star bear. And even more dangerously, we rendezvoused in the golf course with then President Gerald Ford. While I wasn't exactly Republican, nor a Donny Osmond fan, it was still pretty exciting stuff for a twelve-year-old.

But, while Mr. Hockey will rub his kids' elbows with the stars, he hardly considers himself one. A woman saw him signing an autograph for a fan recently. After the fan left, she excitedly approached him and asked, "Are you somebody famous?" "No," he replied, "I just used to baby-sit him." "Oh," she said, and walked away satisfied that she wasn't missing out on anything big. Mr. Hockey goes out of his way to assure that every person he meets goes away satisfied. Because that's who he is.

What about Mom? Sure, she's run for Congress, written a couple of books, headed a few corporations, and chaired a foundation or two—any high-powered, idea-generating, philanthropic visionary can do that. But that's not why I named my wife after her. Actually, that was just a coincidence. Who is Colleen J. Howe?

She's the one who likes to anonymously pick up the tab of

perfect strangers at restaurants just to see their reactions. And she was the one who gift-wrapped a kitten for our neighbors whose pet had died, leaving the feline on their door-step, complete with an anonymous note signed with paw prints. She's also the one who suggested I invite the neighborhood bully to my birthday party. "Mom, are you crazy?" I protested. I pictured him hurling a soccer ball at my head while blowing out the candles. Well, that didn't happen. Not only was the party a success, but I became the bully's best friend. Smart lady, that Colleen Howe.

Her motto is: Why not? "The boys don't have a junior A hockey team to play on in Detroit, why not make one ourselves?" So she did. "Dad, Marty, and Mark needed an agent to negotiate their contracts and endorsements. Why not me?" she thought, not waiting for an answer. Hey, you can't beat her commission fee. "Why not write a book about our family?" Voila! Believe me, once she gets an idea, she will make it come to life. And she has lots of ideas.

She's also the one who sacrifices herself totally for others. Like letting go of her youngest (guess who?) at the tender age of thirteen, to help him pursue his dream of playing professional hockey. She would not allow her own needs to interfere with what she knew was best for her son. And, like making sure that all the kids had a friend to bring along on family trips "up North," no matter how much chaos or extra pounds of food it required. And, in perhaps her most challenging role, she's the one who says "no" when my dad cannot fulfill someone's request. She sacrifices her own image, out of love and respect, for my dad's.

She comes complete with a sack full of valuable lessons designed to guide a person through adulthood. "Oh, you want to drink beer like the big guys?" she inquired. Presto, I got my own mug for the home beer tap. "Just let me know when you're having

4

some, and it's off limits to your friends!" she added. I kept my part of the bargain, she kept hers. By age twelve, beer had lost its mystique, and I had earned her trust. One of my most memorable lessons came during a Wings' game, when I could not persuade some fellow ten-year-olds that I was Gordie Howe's son. I didn't want to push the issue, but when one of the boys insisted he was Bobby Hull's son, that meant war. "Okay" I said smugly to the infidels, "I'll go up to Mrs. Howe and she'll tell you who I am." No one was more surprised than I when she said "Go away little boy, I don't even know you." The boys exploded into laughter and walked away, too late to notice Mrs. Howe's grin beneath the facade. Embarrassed, I sulked for two days before I got the message. It doesn't matter what others think about you; it only matters what you think about yourself.

Colleen Howe loves to plant dreams. Leave St. Nick's cap in the fireplace for you to find Christmas morning. Help you pick out that one special bracelet for your grade school sweetheart. String holiday lights around the backyard rink to create the perfect "Winter-wonderland." And always, always, always include others in the opportunities that come along. Like, writing a foreword for a book, for instance.

Speaking about including everyone, my work is not complete without talking about the Howe kids. Marty, my oldest brother, spent most of his youth chasing me, chasing girls, and trying to out-do Mark on the ice rink. Of course, Marty never considered the fact that he was superior to Mark in almost every sport EXCEPT hockey. Life is cruel.

Marty has two gifts, both compliments of my dad. One, all he needs in life is his wife, Mary, a scuba tank, and a fishing pole. Two, he can design and build anything 3-dimensional at warp speed. And once it is built, it will require a bomb to dismantle it.

5

While I may have many more years of formal education, Marty posseses an enviable wit, wisdom, and intelligence. Plus, he no longer chases me.

Mark, the second Howe to be the oldest active NHL player, has dedicated his whole life to hockey and to his family. He is the most unselfish person I know. Midway through high school, he GAVE me his customized van, so that I could do important things, like see how many cheerleaders I could stuff in it at one time. Then he GAVE me his moto-cross bike so that I could scare myself to death all summer long. Meanwhile, he would drag me along to the golf course, on his dates, and even drive out of his way to take me to school in his hot wheels. He could have easily just dumped me at the bus stop. Mark makes being a little brother fun; even when I'm thirty-four.

Cathy carries the curse of two x chromosomes. In any other family that's no big deal; but when you are a Howe, it doesn't make sense to have two x chromosomes, because you only need one to play hockey, and that's all the Howes are supposed to do. Cathy was blessed with incredible athletic ability, academic potential, and good-looks to match. She was the only cheerleader who could beat the guys in arm-wrestling.

Unfortunately, no one in the media seemed to notice Cathy because she didn't play hockey. I, on the other hand, played hockey and got noticed. The media overlooked the fact that I had to be the most mediocre Howe to ever lace up a pair of blades. Life was, once again, cruel. But Cathy finally discovered the one thing she could do that none of the Howe boys could: be a mom. And since then, she and her husband, Wade, have raised a pair of beautiful daughters, Jaime and Jade, who openly prefer horses over hockey pucks.

And as for me, "the little guy" as my dad calls me, my

family is my life, just as I have learned from Mom and Dad. My wife, Colleen, and I have been blessed with one beautiful daughter, Meaghan, and three boisterous boys, Gordie, Corey and Sean. They are all good-looking, like their mom, and outrageous, like their dad.

MY Colleen was actually supposed to be named after my Dad (she was born during the Red Wings playoffs in 1961). Of course, that extra x chromosome squelched that. And I'm sure glad she got that chromosome, too. It would've been embarrassing for me to marry someone named Gordie.

The lives of Gordie and Colleen Howe are extraordinary. But what makes them extraordinary in my eyes has nothing to do with hockey goals or award certificates. It's their unending dedication to their children, their family, their friends, and their community. That's what life is all about. There's lots more to say, but I have another brain C.A.T. scan to read. So you'll just have to go on without me. Take it away Mom and Dad.

DEDICATION

Creating "*and...HOWE!*" has taken on many meanings for us—beyond turning out a book. It is also the celebration of the launch of a new corporate dimension to our lives, Power Play Publications, Inc. It is also our inaugural literary project.

Through several months of preparing text and selecting photographs, we were constantly reminded of the many people, places, and experiences that were a part of our story, and that have touched our lives.

There are friends, or sometimes strangers, who brought meaning to our lives by helping us, without ever knowing how much it meant.

There are our children and grandchildren, who have brought us so much joy, of whom we are so proud.

There are our parents, grandparents, and even great grandparents, who loved, guided and coveted us; as well as giving us the building blocks of strength and character we have today. Our roots truly shaped our lives.

There are even those who brought us disappointment and injustice; they, too, are part of what developed our patience, strength and willingness to forgive.

There are the numerous corporations, outside of hockey, who enabled us to create a better life for ourselves. They gave us the opportunity and the confidence of knowing there was really a life after hockey. They provided us with supplemental income and treated us with deep respect, in spite of the fact we had not dedicated our entire lives to them.

There are the media personalities who, with few exceptions, also became a part of our lives over the years, in the sense of honesty, trust, and mutual respect.

There are the fans who were with us everyday, somehow. They still are everywhere we go, as well as in our daily stacks of mail. We've saved their letters since the 1950's, they provide an incredible documentation of history in our lives.

There is the support team for Power Play International, Inc., Power Play Publications, Inc. and the Howe Foundation. Our staff and associates aid and guide us, as well as dedicate themselves to our growth, development, and success.

There are the friends with whom we remain especially close, even when we are not always together. What we shared with them will forever remain in our hearts and our memories.

This book is dedicated to each and everyone of the above, as well as you, the reader! Through these pages, our mission is to have you get to know us and know what we represent.

Gordie and Colleen

PREFACE
By Tom DeLisle

The reminiscences, observations, and opinions of the Howe family presented in this book are taken from over sixty-seven hours of taped interviews and conversations with Gordie and Colleen Howe and their children, Marty, Mark, Cathy and Murray.

In playing any of those recordings, the listener is struck by the frequency of laughter heard from the Howes. They are a family with an unusual and often-voiced sense of humor. Colleen and Gordie, in particular, display the sort of earthy and sometimes even dark comic sense you might expect from a couple who have spent a half century dealing with the harsh and sometimes heartbreaking realities of athletic life.

Gordie's sense of humor has always been one of his ways to overcome adversity, disappointment, and fear. Colleen, a more serious person, had to learn to view family and business on the lighter side. This made otherwise taxing situations far less stressful. Living with Gordie continuously taught her the value of a sense of humor.

INTRODUCTION
By Tom DeLisle

Gordie Howe has the mind of an engineer; Colleen Howe has the mind of a master engineer. Her self-described streams of energy and stamina do not come in bursts. They are constant and apparently unending, like the power and constancy of a rapid river. She is an ebullient and non-stop communicator, and a voracious consumer of, and commentator on, the developments and trends of contemporary life. She sleeps very little, concentrates always, and spends probably three-quarters of her vast waking hours on the telephone—pushing, pulling, schmoozing, directing twenty projects a day, and staying up-to-date with the personal and professional news of the Howe clan. No business dealing is too big or too small to be left to others. Typical back-to-back phone calls for Colleen might be from Gary Bettman, president of the National Hockey League, followed by a call to Gary Kosch, the manager of the new Gordie Howe Tavern and Eatery in Traverse City, informing him that the Howe memorabilia throughout the interior has to go out on loan for a show she and Gordie are doing. Yes, it will be returned by Friday! Thanks Gary!

She is at once imposing and soft, hilarious and serious, dreaming cosmic visions and laboring over minute points. She is as comfortable being a laser-beamed businesswoman as she is in her role as the most doting grandma on the planet. Like her husband, she is an amazing mix of contrasts and ironies. There are few, if any, mysteries about the Howes. They are the most old-fashioned and decent of people, in every good connotation those terms imply. Yet for a couple as down-to-earth, even common, as Colleen and Gordie are, they seem always to be inhabiting a spot all their own, somehow quite unlike any duo you have ever encountered. If you tried to ascribe their unique presence to either Gordie's understated charisma or Colleen's zeal for life, you would surely decide it must be a combination of the two.

A story about Colleen: In late March of 1995, the Howes accompanied their son, Marty, to the press party given at the Joe Louis Arena in Detroit to announce that he would be coaching the new Motor City Mustangs in the professional Roller Hockey International League. It was a day in which Marty, predictably, had to share the spotlight with his dad who, at almost sixty-seven was named as the team's tenth, and last, draft choice in a clever publicity move by Mustang management.

Being the full-time mom she is, Colleen would sneak up a side aisle to take distant snapshots as Marty spoke from the front table to the media. Red Wings Shawn Burr and Dino Ciccarelli, part-owners of the Mustangs, were in attendance, along with other Red Wing players who had just completed a practice session on the Joe Louis Arena ice. Son Mark, who had suggested Marty for the coaching position, was in the room, and playfully introduced his mother to teammate Darren McCarty: "I'd like you to meet Gordie's wife." Colleen, jokingly referring to Mark's crack, but revealing also a touch of her own business philosophy, laughingly said afterwards "He'll be sorry for that. I always get 'em back. I'm worse than Gordie. I get their number and get even with them later." Her husband, of course, is legendary and notorious in hockey history for settling scores and aggressively repaying transgressors.

In the course of the afternoon spent at Joe Louis, Colleen and Gordie met and mixed with the new Mustang owners, Red Wings owner, Mike Ilitch, Roller Hockey International league president and former Montreal star, Ralph Backstrom, media bigshots, and current Red Wing coaches and players. All were greeted enthusiastically by the Howes, and it was obvious that all were charmed, if not thrilled, to be in the presence of the Howe family. Tellingly, however, the most genuine and affectionate greetings and embraces of the day were shared by Gordie and specifically Colleen with the arena laborers who hovered near the edges of the fancy party. Veteran employees who had worked at the old Olympia Arena were greeted like longlost family, and their delight in seeing the Howes again was obviously tangible and deeply heartfelt.

A reference in my notebook from that day says: "Colleen VERY tight with the workers around the Joe Louis Arena. Hugs. They approach her from all over to say 'hi.' Custodians, blue collar people. Olympia vets. Interesting contrast to the bigwigs. Very telling."

There was an affection shown between these people and both Howes that cannot be faked. And the happy greetings and embraces occurred well in the shadows of the bright lights that had been set up for the press conference. It was no show, by Colleen and Gordie or the workers, but a series of affecting reunions. If someone were to ask me to illustrate the sincerity and goodness of this most unusual couple, and Mrs. Howe especially, I would refer to the scene I witnessed that day.

GORDIE: We were out in Phoenix, having a great time at a golf outing that featured a lot of different sports stars. Joe Dimaggio was there, Ernie Banks, Curt Flood, Boomer Geoffrion,

Wilt the Stilt. There were all kinds of stars and entertainers.

They were holding a silent auction to raise money, and one of the items you could bid on was a great painting of Joe Dimaggio that Curt Flood had done. It was a great painting. I had no idea that Curt, a great outfielder like Joe, could also paint. I knew he had changed the laws of baseball by challenging free agency. And Joe Dimaggio is just, well, he's Joe Dimaggio. I wanted to bid on this portrait, but I figured there wasn't enough money in the world to buy it. It was just beautiful. I told this to Colleen, and she said, "Well, I'm going to bid on it anyway." I said, "Be my guest."

I had talked to Joe at lunch, and he said he really liked the painting too, and wanted to bid on it himself, but he thought it would look funny if he did. If he bid too low, he would look cheap. And if he got it, it might seem strange that he bought his own portrait.

At the auction that night, they announced that "The winner is...Colleen Howe." And I looked and I said, "How much did she bid?" I still don't know as of today. I don't want to know.

COLLEEN: I never told him. It was $2,500 FOR CHARITY!

GORDIE: Colleen went up to get the painting, with a big smile on her face. Everybody gave her a big hand when she got up there. She had told me when she put in her bid, "If I win we'll have to get Joe to sign it." So, she called on Joe to come up to the podium, and I thought she would have him sign it there for us. So when Joe goes to center stage, and Colleen says to the crowd, "This is such a magnificent picture, and Gordie and I would love to have it in our home, but I think it should belong to only one person." Then she gave it to Joe.

Well, it was a great thing to do, but I went bilingual.

"What the hell did she do that for?" It was funny, because I really wanted it. I can see that painting now. And she looked me right in the eye and said "Don't you realize that the art of giving is to give something you truly would like to keep for yourself." And I said, "Yeah, and boy, did we give."

Joe was stunned and surprised. It really wiped him out. He said nothing like that had ever happened to him. But that's Colleen, she does those kinds of things. That's the kind of person she is, loving to surprise someone.

INTRODUCTION
By Gordie and Colleen Howe

As Gordie and I embarked on this *and...HOWE!*
publication we wanted to accomplish several ideals. One of
them was to have you enjoy what you read in these pages.
Next was to be certain that, for all intents and purposes, we
opened our world and intimate thoughts to you. As well, we
wanted you to laugh a little but at the same time understand
that we, just as you, have our serious and hurting times. We
intended, most of all, to have you know us as people, rather
than celebrities, who think you're pretty special. For that
reason we have attempted to keep this book as native to our
way of speaking and thinking as possible. It was our intent to
move away from some of the traditional methodology of
reaching out to a reader. We wanted you to feel as though we
were sitting across from you and telling you this story
ourselves. This applies also to the chapters on Marty, Mark,
Cathy, and Murray. You'll sense a more personal touch with
them through their own words.

Lastly, we wanted to make certain that everyone who
acquires one of the *and...HOWE!* books has the opportunity to
get it autographed whether or not they are able to see us on
tour. Just follow our directions in the back of this book on the
page entitled, "Book Plate Offer."

CHAPTER ONE

HE SAID HIS NAME WAS GORDIE

COLLEEN: I've often thought about my destiny, or what God had in store for a girl from Detroit who knew nothing about hockey, had never seen a hockey game, who lived nearby where Gordie Howe was living, and Gordie came to watch her bowl. That was the moment in time when we first met. I couldn't possibly know what was really happening, that my whole future was about to begin!

He was a handsome guy from Saskatoon, Saskatchewan. I had never even heard of Saskatchewan at that point in my life. It was the spring of 1951. Gordie had received a very serious head injury in the playoffs the year before, an injury that nearly killed him. I was in high school when that happened, and I remember the very morning I was ready to run out the door and jump over the fence and head for MacKenzie High School when I heard my stepfather at the table talking about this hockey player that was almost killed in last night's game.

And I thought, how awful! Of course I had no idea what that person, Gordie Howe, was to mean in my life someday. Probably it's a good thing that we don't know our destiny, that we can't see how something that we might regard as not important would someday be so crucial to our lives. Had Gordie died, my whole life could have been changed dramatically. But that wasn't my destiny—or Gordie's.

So was it chance or destiny, that we met? Perhaps Gordie

felt that someday he would meet someone he liked in Detroit. Probably most of his family believed that he would come home to Saskatoon and meet someone there. There certainly were a lot of opportunities for Gordie to meet women, and why we were meant to find each other we'll never know, but then Gordie says, "It was blue jeans." Colleen questions, "Blue jeans?" Gordie responds, "Yeah. You wore them! You were at your best when you released the bowling ball."

COLLEEN: I was bowling one evening with my team at the Lucky Strike Bowling Lanes near the Olympia. As shy as Gordie was, he made the effort to come over and talk to me and offer me a ride home which, when I think of it now, was probably very difficult for him to do. He just was not that outgoing a person, and not really a worldly kind of individual. Guys weren't necessarily worldly at that time. Even though they were famous hockey players, they didn't have either the money or the opportunity to be worldly. That's why they were doing simple things like bowling at a neighborhood recreation center."

It was frustrating, because I had my family's car that night and had to refuse Gordie's offer of a ride home. I really was disappointed, because I thought, 'Oh that guy is *so* good looking and nice, and now I might never see him again. I wonder who he is?' He said his name was Gordie, but it didn't mean anything to me because I was not a hockey fan and didn't recognize him as *the Gordie*, Detroit's famous player.

GORDIE: What she didn't know was that there was a guy in love with her before she even met him. I used to watch her at the bowling alley a lot, and I finally got the manager there to give me her phone number. It was something to meet with this girl. I had waited several weeks before I approached her. Was that being shy or showing respect? I guess it was a combination of both.

COLLEEN: As it turned out, he persevered and now having my telephone, he started calling me. We talked by the hours. We became phone friends. We got to know each other, but I didn't have any idea what he did for a living. We would talk for three or four hours a night. I really enjoyed visiting with him. He was so nice. He was so mature. Gordie had a maturity that was well beyond that of someone who was only twenty-three at the time. Plus, he was so sincere. He also showed a great deal of respect for his parents and family.

My mother used to ask who this fellow was I'd talk to on the phone every night. I told her that his name was Gordie. He is such a great guy, and he comes from Canada. I also knew all about his mother and father, that he had eight brothers and sisters and that he lived in Saskatchewan. And my mother suggested that I invite him to our home. I believe it was because she wanted to use the phone.

GORDIE: When did you find out what I did for a living?

COLLEEN: I think it wasn't until you took me to meet Ted and Pat Lindsay, on our first date, several weeks after we were phone pals. It was at the restaurant bar, owned by mutual friends of my parents, Ronnie and Jess Sellers. The Sellers called my family to tell them who you were besides a guy named Gordie.

GORDIE: That's why, when I met your dad, he knew who I was.

COLLEEN: And I made the connection—that Gordie was *the Gordie Howe*, the star player for the Red Wings my father had been talking about at the kitchen table that fateful morning. He talked about that poor guy they had rushed to the hospital after he was so badly hurt in the game. All the while I was out of there to get to school.

Finally we went out on our first date, and I think it took a lot of courage for him to ask me.

GORDIE: It took so long because I had to save up my money.

COLLEEN: We went to the Michigan Theater in downtown Detroit. I can't remember the movie. I think I was too smitten at the time.

GORDIE: I didn't see it, either!

COLLEEN: But I do remember holding hands with him, and thinking 'Oh my God! This guy is so romantic!' Then he took me to Carl's Chop House for dinner, and I found it interesting that everyone there seemed to know him. "Hi Gordie...hey Gordie!" And I thought, 'Gosh, he knows everyone.' Gordie said he wanted me to meet some women friends of his, so we went to Sellers Restaurant and Lounge, and met Ted and Pat, who were engaged at the time. That was typical of Gordie. He wanted me to meet his friends and get their approval.

As the evening went on, I was beginning to realize that these fellows did something very important and they were really celebrities in Detroit. Everyone fussed over them and wanted their autographs. I guess they took it for granted, everyone knew who they were, including me.

GORDIE: Do you remember when I brought you home the night before I left to go back to Saskatoon? We were out quite late...

COLLEEN: Yes, until about three in the morning, and I had to work that day!

GORDIE: I never even went to sleep that night either. I went home, packed and left about six in the morning for the two-day drive to Saskatoon. When I did get her home that night and I opened the front door to let her in, there was this little room off to the side and I could see her dad in there at his desk. He had just smashed his new car. And I thought, oh cripes, he does not look happy. I went to kiss her goodnight, and she said, "No, come on in. Say hello." So Colleen introduced me, and I remember he said, "Gordie, it's nice to know you."

COLLEEN: Just as we started dating, Gordie took a trip to Florida with Ted, Marty Pavelich, and Red Kelly. And shortly after that Gordie had to leave to go back to Canada. He was in the U.S. on a temporary visa, and he would not be allowed back in the U.S. except for visits. So we wrote each other every day while they were down in Florida, and we dated back in Detroit before he left the country to go home to Saskatoon.

GORDIE: I went back home each summer and played semi-pro baseball in Saskatoon. I think Colleen thought she had a live one when I asked her (and it was on the first or second date), how old do you think someone should be before they get married?

COLLEEN: I always wondered why you ever asked me that question.

GORDIE: Maybe I had an idea that you had too many guys banging at your door. Maybe I was dropping a hint to slow down some of the other guys you dated.

COLLEEN: We found out early how much we thought alike, and I immediately had strong feelings for him. I also had this romantic inclination toward him, because he was a pretty sexy looking guy.

GORDIE: Hmm. You didn't tell me that!

COLLEEN: I even remember what he had on the first time I met him. He had a leather jacket, a suede kind of western coat. It looked like something he bought out West. He was very handsome. He still is. I have to watch him, even now. Can't leave him out too much alone.

We were separated for the summers during the years that

21

we dated, because Gordie went back to his home town, Saskatoon. So, the chances of us actually having a courtship and a continuing relationship was always jeopardized. Absence offered a great chance of us not ending up together, had we not been so much in love. Gordie always tells the story about the summer he wanted to go fishing at Lake Waskesiu in the Prince Albert National Park. We used to write each other almost every day, but this time I didn't hear from him for a long period of time. I really thought he had forgotten about me. I was really lovesick over him. There was a great deal of love there, and my mother was very upset with me hanging around the house. She told me that I shouldn't stay around the house like this. "You've got to get out with your friends again, and you've got to be with other people. If Gordie does care about you, you'll hear from him."

So, I started to listen to her advice and I even met another individual who thought he was in love with me, but it wasn't the same. When I had heard nothing from Gordie, I guess I just felt that it was over, that I was never going to see him again. Then training camp time arrived and Gordie returned from the lake and fishing, and he called me. That was the moment in time when I realized that nothing or no one else mattered and, for me, it was just a matter of being with Gordie.

He had been fishing and golfing at the lake, and he explained it was such a remote area that they didn't have a post office there and that's why he didn't send any mail. I was just dying when I didn't hear from him. Years later, after we got married, we went up to Lake Waskesiu, and the first thing I saw was a post office! I said, "Oh look, they have a post office now." Well, he'd forgotten about what had happened because he said, "They've always had a post office here." Oh! Sure!

GORDIE: I've never told her this, but basically I was shy

22

to write. I couldn't express my feelings in writing. And to be honest, I couldn't spell that well and I didn't want to look like a donkey. When I did write her, I wrote with a dictionary beside me. It's hard to say "I love you" through the dictionary. I didn't have a dictionary at the lake, so I told her there was no post office up there. I got caught later on that one. My Mom knew how I felt about her. I didn't have a picture of us together, so I took a picture of her and a picture of me, and put them next to each other in the house at Saskatoon. My mother said "I think Gordie has found a girl."

COLLEEN: He never told me about the dictionary. This is the first I've ever heard that. All this time I just figured it was, well, out of sight, out of mind. I know Gordie was shocked when he came back to Detroit and he found that I thought we weren't going to see each other anymore.

When Gordie was a child, he was called "doughhead" because he had trouble reading. People said some cruel, cruel things to Gordie. I know that Marty and Cathy had problems with a mild form of dyslexia, and Gordie, we suspect, was also dyslexic as a child. We've found that it's most commonly passed on from the male parent. People had never heard of dyslexia when he was growing up. And for him to try to read in front of a class and be laughed at, it was so painful for him. And he was so much bigger than the other kids, so he was called a big dummy.

People who know Gordie know what a great and unusual intelligence he has. He's very bright, but to some people he was a big dummy because he had trouble reading and spelling. In fact, one of the hockey players said something like that to Gordie in public, "you big dummy." I can't remember where it happened, but I know Gordie got mad. He's slow to anger, but just don't get him angry. He's like his mother in so many ways, I don't think I ever saw her angry. But he's like his dad if you get him mad. He has a lot of personal pride, and it's not too smart to call him names.

GORDIE: I think I was the only guy in hockey history who once got a standing ovation and a standing boo in the Montreal Forum within two minutes. I scored a goal, I think it was my 600th, and they gave me a nice ovation. Then my thumb caught J.C. Tremblay, of the Canadiens, on his cheekbone, and put it out of place for a little while. He went down in a heap on the ice and, boy, the standing boo took right over. It was really funny, what a change of heart.

Purely accidental? Well. I'll tell you what happened. I had been doing television work on the playoffs the year before, the Wings weren't playing. And Dick Duff of Montreal was playing bridge with some guys on an off-day, I guess, and I was watching him, and he "finessed," which is a strategic move. So I said "That was a great play." And J.C. overheard that, and he said "what would a dummy like you know about it?" Well, that wasn't a bright thing to say. I told him that I had played a couple of hands of bridge with Charles Goren, who was known as the leading player in the world. So I felt I knew the game pretty damn well. I told J.C. "I've probably forgotten more about this game than you'll ever know." And a couple of other words were exchanged. And I said, "Let me put it this way. Something will happen to you some game. And when that happens, remember this moment, will ya?"

I said "This is not a threat. Just a promise to mark down in your book." And when that occurred the next year, and he was laying on the ice, rolling around, and they took him off, Dick Duff came by and said to me, "Ask him if he remembers..."

It was totally uncalled for, J.C. saying that to me. I thought it was, anyway. My memory is good.

COLLEEN: Something brings you together in life. In our case, a lot of things had to happen. And when you add it all up, and the great distance that we grew up from each other, two different countries, you have to think it was destiny.

GORDIE: What about my dad and mother? My dad was born in Wisconsin. And he heard about the Homesteader's Act where you could go up into Saskatchewan and whatever piece of property you worked, it was yours, free. He crossed the border, they pointed at him, said "Okay, you're a Canadian. Keep going." They were trying to populate the prairie. So he made his move. He used to be a track star, he was a great runner. He was used to moving fast.

My mother was born in Germany, right at the Polish and German border. She was separated from her family, and was passed from family to family as a worker. Her grandfather found her. He was the local coffin maker and he also worked burying victims of plague. People would come to his house, knock on the door, and hand my mother, a child herself, their dead children. She was tough, tough stock, my mom. Later, her mother found her again. They came to get her to take her with them to Canada. And they ended up in Windsor, of all places, right across the river from Detroit.

Mum took a job there as a housekeeper. Her family went on without her, then came back again later to tell her they were going out west. She ended up going with them to Saskatchewan, where she met Dad and they got married. They had kids of their own. There were eleven, but a pair of twins died. And my grandfather had five offspring from a second marriage. His wife died, so Mum had to take care of fourteen kids in all.

And she had to feed us with love, because there wasn't

much food.

COLLEEN: Our backgrounds parallel in a way. There was a lot of moving involved in my childhood, also. My father, at twenty-eight, was a musician. He played during the Big Band era at the Grande Ballroom in Detroit. And my mother was very young, only seventeen, when she met and married my father. But my mother made the big decision to leave my father, because their lifestyles and ideals were worlds apart. He had some problems with drinking and philandering, and she decided that was not going to be a part of her life. Instead of putting me up for adoption, she leaned on the help of her mother and my Great Aunt, Elsie, who this year is one hundred years old and lives in North Carolina near our daughter, Cathy.

We lived in the downtown section of Detroit, along Vernor Highway, Cass, and Peterboro. And even though we were going through the Depression, not unlike Gordie's family, we didn't realize we were poor. It seems like everyone, then, was the so-called poor. I don't remember going hungry. And I know Gordie's family was always fed, even when it was hard to provide. People were pioneers then, and they really took care of each other.

My childhood was split between Detroit and Sanilac County near Sandusky, in the Thumb area of Michigan. My great-grandfather, Samuel Ford, born in Mt. Hope, Ontario, later immigrated to a farm in Sandusky where I spent my pre-school years with Aunt Elsie. There was no central heating in the house. We just had a big wood stove to keep us warm. I would sleep in the little attic area with my great-aunt, under these big warm comforters. The construction on those old-time houses wasn't very good, so once in a while we would wake up in the morning with snow on our bed. But this is not a terrible memory to me. It was something that was pretty humorous. We made the best of things. We would laugh about it. And I had the whole run of that little farm. If I wanted a carrot, I would go and take it; versus Gordie, when he wanted a carrot once in a while...

GORDIE: I'd steal it! Or kohlrabi. (It's like a turnip.) They are really tasty. And there was this crabby old guy in our neighborhood who used to sit on his porch in his rocker, watching his garden. And we would have two guys walk down past his house, and he would stare at them, to keep his eye on them. While he was doing that, we'd go around the side and lasso the kohlrabi with a rope. Just throw it over the top of them, and pull 'em right over. It was fun. Tasted good, too. He rarely saw us. I can't believe some of the things I did when he was gone.

COLLEEN: Gordie was from a large family, and I was an only child. When I was school age, I lived with my mother and my great aunt. Then my world changed when my great aunt and my uncle Hughie were married, and I moved with them. This allowed my mother to work and support me. I was really their child until I was twelve years old, when my mother remarried and I gained my stepfather, Budd Joffa, whom I loved very much. He and my mother later divorced, and I hope that through this book I'll be able to find him. I've lost all track of him. If you don't have someone's social security number, it's very difficult to locate them. He was very good to me, and I would really like to see him again some day.

It's a blessing that my grandmother is still alive. I said to Gordie, "You notice that all the women outlive the men in our family!" All kidding aside, I had great support from these people in my life. My mother, I think, feels very badly that she couldn't spend more time with me, and I tell her that she shouldn't feel like that, because I completely understand. It was because of her that I had the kind of environment I did. I don't remember being poor. I just remember being cared for and loved.

The biggest thing that happened to me was when I lived upstairs at my grandmother's house on Springwells Avenue in Detroit. I had a friend across the street whose name was Marjorie Brushart. She had a real large family, and I liked to be around people with large families. (Maybe that was another thing I liked about Gordie, like "Oh boy, you have a whole bunch of sisters and brothers and I don't have those.") I had my own room, but they used to sleep five to a room, which I thought was wonderful.

Marjorie and her family always went to church, and one Sunday they asked me to go with them. That was a big turning point in my life. It became a real treat for me to go to Fort Street Presbyterian church in downtown Detroit. (It's still there and quite famous.) My life was really guided by that church, up to the time Gordie and I were married. I really feel the strengths and characteristics I have in my life come from the people who raised me, and from the influences that I had from Dr. Ratz and Rev. MacDougell during my formative years.

I'd go to church camp all summer. It was what I lived for, besides all those people who cared for me. I spent wonderful times with them as a child, being somewhat spoiled by all these great-aunts who had this one child, this little blond girl that they made clothes for and dressed up. And in a way, I was like Gordie, in that I was very comfortable being around older people. When I sew or do anything creative or domestic, I owe it all to these folks. And I think that helped me as a homemaker, as a mom and as a wife. These were people who were just so solid and loving that I felt I was loved by the whole world. I always was made to feel that way—until I got into hockey.

When you look at Gordie, there is a reason why he is of the ilk that he is. His environment and his family had so much to do with who he is, what his feelings are about life, his nature, his strengths. When I think of his father, I remember what an incredibly proud man he was.

GORDIE: Proud, but he could be a mean sucker when he wanted to. Not to us kids, to other people. He would fight for us. We didn't have a hell of a lot. I bought Mum and Dad a new home, I think it was around 1950 or '51, after I had some success in Detroit. The biggest fear I had when I joined the Red Wings was that somebody would come and see where I lived. I was scared that the guys might stop by. It was an old house, with an outside john. And as soon as I got enough money we put in plumbing. In fact, I was barbecuing something one day when my dad said "What in the hell is the world coming to? We used to cook indoors and go to the bathroom outdoors." He was such a funny guy.

Yes, he was a proud guy, too. I wanted Dad to put the house I bought in my name so I could pay for the taxes, and then write them off as a deduction. But he wouldn't do it. It would have been an injury to his pride, the old bugger. So I told my Mum, "If I send you any money, don't share it with that old coot!"

COLLEEN: In my estimation, Gordie is really a combination of the best of his mother and father. He got the characteristics from each of them that gave him the qualities that he needed to succeed and survive in hockey. He's a proud guy, too. He has a quiet nature, though as time passes he is growing to be more of an advocate in helping others, like being one of seven who fought for the former players' pension dollars recovery. When he played, there was no way you could survive in those days if you were outspoken or an advocate for something. It's hardly popular to be team rep, even today. There's a chance you get labeled as a trouble maker.

Gordie's always had this great tolerance that his mother had, of being able to have such strength of character and, at the same time, be able to cope with so much and never let anyone know exactly what was happening inside.

GORDIE: As we've mentioned before about destiny, I was playing golf in a tournament in Owosso, Michigan, and there was a party that was held later. So Colleen and Mum and Dad met me there at the Owosso Country Club. This was just before I retired from the Red Wings. We were there, and the music was going, and I looked at Colleen and said, "Isn't that amazing? I was just thinking, I have never danced with my mother." And she said, "Well, there's no time like the present. Why don't you ask her now?"

So I asked Mum, and we got up, and we started to dance. And everybody else cleared the floor; it was strictly our floor. They stood around us and applauded. And we danced, and when the music was over we bowed and everybody laughed. Then, it was just a week later that we were burying her. We just had that one time.

GORDIE: What was the best time of my life? It was when I started dating Colleen. Dating her gave me something. I used to do the dumbest things. I'd walk up to the bowling alley and watch people bowl. My entertainment was going over there and watching. I'd especially go on Monday nights, because Colleen Joffa used to be the bowler. Or I'd just go downtown on Woodward and sit and watch people. Finally I sought out a lot of people to help me meet this very attractive blond girl. I was asking for somebody who knew her, so I could do it the proper way. I think it was Joe Evans who ran the place, and he gave me the introduction. So I met Colleen, and she gave me a feeling that at last I knew somebody who was worth it, that there was a whole different world out there. She changed everything for me.

COLLEEN: I have kept all of Gordie's and any of my letters he saved from when we first met, and from the summers when we wrote back and forth to each other. I haven't looked at them in years. But I know they're something that our kids will enjoy someday. They will be able to really tell something about us, and how we really were in those times.

FIRST LETTERS FROM GORDIE TO COLLEEN

From Hollywood and Dania, Florida — Postmarked April, 1951.
Excerpts from letters addressed to Colleen Joffa, 9375 Kentucky, Detroit 4, Michigan (Sent shortly after they first met).

April 15 from Hollywood, Florida
Dear Colleen:
Hello honey, well we're not there as yet but already I've found out you can miss someone even though you know them but for a few days.
Love, Gord

———————

April 17 from Hollywood, Florida
...As soon as we get our tans we all intend to catch a few big fish. I'm really looking forward to that as I love to fish. There's only one thing I like more this last week and that's a little girl in Detroit.
Love, Gordie

———————

April 19 from Hollywood Beach, Florida
Hello love,
...All I can think of right now is as I've always thought for the

past few days and that is "I wish you were down here also."
Goodnight for now, dear.
Love, Gordon

April 20th from Hollywood, Florida
...We intend leaving here the night of the 26th so we will be in Saturday sometime. I hope to stay awhile and spend a few days with you if I can. I would love to spend as many more nights with you as I can before heading for home. So how about telling everyone you are out some place starting the night of Saturday the 28th...
As always,
Love, Gordie

April 23 from Hollywood Beach, Florida (with a newspaper clipping from the Saskatoon paper and a picture of a blizzard)
...I really enjoyed my fish as we ate about 6:00 and I hadn't anything to eat, and believe it or not all I had was one beer all day. So you and I seem to be in the same boat, but that's the way I like it. 'Cause I think the world of the girl in my boat with me.
Love and stuff, Gordon

LETTERS SENT FROM GORDIE TO COLLEEN IN THE SPRING AND SUMMER OF 1952 FROM SASKATOON
First letter is to Colleen vacationing in Miami Beach
May 9, 1952
Dearest Colleen,

Hi love. Sorry I haven't written long before this and while I'm at it, I better say I'm double sorry because we go into the woods tomorrow and seeing as we have to walk six miles carrying food and all, I won't be coming out each day to mail a letter. So this short note will let you know that I received your two wonderful letters which I was very happy to receive as I too have missed you more than you'll know.

...Well love it's getting on and we're due out of here at 4:30 in the morning. So I'll leave you with the thought in your mind that there's a fisherman up north who is missing you like crazy.
As ever,
Love and all, Gord

June 14, 1952
Hi dear,

Once again I have heard three sweet words from you which I should use more often and that is, "I miss you." They sound awful good to me coming from such a sweet young lady as you and again I say I should use them much more often. But the truth is I don't know too much of sweet words so just give me time as I am a comer.
Love Gordie

June 16, 1952
Hello dear,

Guess what — little Gord received not one but two very nice letters from you today which is setting a pace I really can't hold up to, but believe me it is awful nice.
It sounds like you're having yourself one wonderful time this summer which is very nice. I only wish I were there with you to enjoy your company and to see all the nice places and also to enjoy the sun as it's something we haven't seen out here for the last week.
Love, Gordon

June 28, 1952

I sure wish you weren't so darn far away so I could run down to see you on weekends. But as it is, it takes me a week's driving to get there and back. It would be nice if you also lived right here. Seeing as I'm dreaming, I might just as well go all out. As it is, I'll just have to go on missing you until I get the call from Adams.

And also, I don't know as yet just where I'll be staying in Detroit because, as I said before, Adams would like to see me back with Ma Shaw and the boys.

Well dear, it's needless to say that I miss you. Of course there's joy in hearing from you all the time, but it's not like the real thing as you well know.

As always, Love Gord

July 3, 1952
Dear Colleen,

First on order is the thought of the day. "Love me or leave me, or let me be lonely, my love is your love to share with you only, I'd rather be lonely than happy with somebody new." This song just finished playing so I thought it a good way to let someone know they have been missed by a farm boy.
Love, Gordie

July 23, 1952
Dear Colleen,

Hello dear. Well at long last they sent me home from the lake long enough to have a little party for my brother Vern and his family, and so I could get a letter off to you to let you know all is well and that I miss and enjoy your letters very much.
Love, Gordon

CHAPTER TWO

WE HAD ALL THE RIGHT THINGS

GORDIE: When I was eight, nine and ten years old, I used to deliver pamphlets in town for Livergrandt's, a local grocery store. They paid me 35 cents a day. I'd get my money, and put it in my hiding place at home. Eventually, I got my total up to around three dollars one year, and that was my Christmas money.

The first thing I wanted to do was get Mum something special. I gave it some thought, and came up with the idea of a little egg beater, one of those old-timers with double prongs that you'd hold and whip up the eggs. I went to a store downtown, probably the Five & Dime, and I got one for her. I was standing in line to pay for it with my brother, Vic, and one of my friends, and a guy who worked in the store kicked us out! I said, "but..." And the guy said, "No buts. You kids have been in the way, you shouldn't be hanging around here. Get on out of here." So I figured, all right then, great. Now, I've got my three dollars AND an egg beater. I've got my first present and I still have my money.

Then I remember we went to Bernie's Hardware. We went in, and I got a really nice hunting knife for my Dad. I think it cost two dollars, which was a lot of money then. I thought, boy, my Dad's really gonna like this. So...AGAIN something happened. We bounced our way into the line to pay for it, and some shopper got mad and complained. So the clerk said, "Young man, you're bothering the customers. Will you please get out?" So I said, "fine," and I'm thinking well, the hell with you. So we went out, and now I've got the knife, an egg beater, and I've STILL got three bucks! I figured I'm doin' pretty good.

Then, when we were going home, we walked by this lot where we used to play ball and they were selling Christmas trees. We started looking around, and I noticed the guy who was selling the trees would, every now and then, look at one, then throw it out. Well, I went to the pile where the reject trees were, looked around, and pulled one out. It was small enough that I could carry it home. So now, I've got a tree, a knife, the egg beater and all of my money.

I know it sounds like shoplifting, but in all honesty, I got thrown out of everywhere. And we weren't raising hell, we were just kids, you know, just touching everything, wondering what to buy. And I'm sure we were dressed like bag boys anyway, so we must have made people nervous. I told my parents how I got everything. My Dad laughed, but my Mom was concerned I might have gotten myself in trouble. Heck, it was the best shopping I ever did in my life.

COLLEEN: Gordie's shopping experience is not dissimilar to a time when we were living in Lathrup Village, Michigan, and our son, Murray and his little friend, Mindy Lymperis, decided to wander down to the corner drugstore. They had been there many times. It was where we could charge things, and Murray had never seen us pay for anything. They had so much fun gathering all the little toys their arms could handle, and gleefully headed for home with all of their new things; all free.

Just about this time, Mrs. Lymperis and I are looking frantically for the five-year-olds, who we thought were in our yard playing. Someone said they saw the children walking toward the drugstore, so I jumped in the car and headed in that direction. And then I spotted them, loaded down with as many toys as they could carry. I pulled over to the curb, so relieved to see them, but astonished at how they could carry so many things.

They were so happy to have all these new things; so it was not good news when I told them they had to return them to the drugstore owner because they weren't paid for. We all piled in the car with the goods and returned everything with great apology. The druggist was very understanding and we all laughed when Murray told us how he always saw me just take things and not give anyone money for them. The druggist also remarked how the "little people" could so easily go unnoticed between the aisles, especially when he was busy.

Each of the children got to pick one item from their returns, then I gave them the money for it, and they experienced for the first time how you pay for things.

As I drove home with two happy, safe, and smarter kids, I reflected to when I was ten, and with a friend, had taken a tube of lipstick from a dime store counter and left out the door. Then the horror began. Every minute I imagined someone was going to find out I had done this and I would be put behind bars in a juvenile detention home. I anguished when someone knocked on the door, thinking it was the police coming to get me. I didn't know where to hide the tube so my parents wouldn't find it. I finally put it in my pocket, went back to the store and put it back where I got it. Even that was scary for fear someone would see me with it in my hand. But it was over and I was feeling like I was born again, free of the terrible guilt and fear.

GORDIE: There's an old story which Alan Thicke tells, that says "Gordie's from Saskatoon, way out on the prairie. That place is so flat you can sit on your front porch and watch your dog run away for three straight days."

It was so cold out there in the winter, 35 and 40 degrees below zero sometimes. We'd be going early in the morning to play a hockey game prior to school. I used to stick my head out the door and you could hear the crunch of footsteps in the snow. You could even tell if someone was coming, and about how far away they were. A fella by the name of Vernon "Wimpy" Jones played for King George school, and I was the goalie. I used to walk to his place, and then we'd walk together. But when I got to his house, his dad would make me bring my pads in to thaw them out. They'd be stiffer than a board. Then I'd hold them in front of my face to break the wind, or I'd walk with a newspaper to protect my face. God, it was cold.

We kept the house heated with wood and coal. We'd have a big block of coal that would go in and we'd fire it up, then when we'd go to bed it would be nice and warm. But you always kept your socks on because when the fire went out it would get cold. The frost was everywhere, and if your hand was damp you best keep it away from the window, or anything metal. You've heard the old stories when kids would lick something cold and their lips or tongues would get stuck? It happened, believe me.

Being an old house, there'd be a lot of cold air coming in our windows, so Dad would take plastic and staple it around the windows or stuff felt along the edges on the inside. He used to work like crazy to keep the cold out.

I remember one year, we made our own skis. We got some lumber, and somebody showed us how to cut it, water them down, warp 'em and put a little tip on. Then we'd nail on rubber or rubber bands, and make an elastic binding for our toes. Then we'd slide our toes into the holder and pull the rubber band back around our heel. We'd ski down the river bank, which was the only hill we had in the city. We even built a little jump. And after one or two jumps, you'd have to go make yourself another pair of skis.

On a few occasions we'd go around with snowshoes. You talk about deep snow, I'll swear that at the railroad tracks out in the country, you could almost touch the telephone wires, that's how high it got. We had some snowstorms when I was a kid that, if they came in from the East, the snow would block the whole front of the house. You couldn't go in or out of the house through the front door. We'd have to go out the back, and try to dig through to the front door. You'd kick out about seven or eight feet of snow. It was amazing.

You know, I look back and I think, those were hardy people who established their homes out there. People used to walk to work in a blizzard. You know it's cold when you come out of the house, and you see the smoke from the wood fires going straight up in the air, like two-by-four columns, right on up into the sky. It was so damn cold even the smoke was trying to get out of town as fast as it could.

There was no running water in the area where we lived. The city water used to be a tap on every other block. We used a 45-gallon drum that always had to be filled to hold the water. We kept the water drum outside, on an open porch, and in the winter we'd put it inside to keep the water from freezing. My brothers conned me one time. They told me I was very strong, and so I was the one most capable of hauling this water up the hill to our house without any other kid helping. I must have been pretty stupid to believe them, but lifting and carrying those heavy pails was something that helped me with hockey. I also developed good leg strength from hauling the water up the sandy soil we had there. It was uphill-going for about half a city block. I found out damn fast you couldn't fill that thing all the way up and carry it. You'd fill it up a half or a third, go back and dip the water pail and carry up some more.

It used to drive me crazy at times, when Dad would take some of that water every now and then and pour it on the garden. It turned out I wasn't hauling for us, but for the garden.

Bathing was not the most common thing in families like ours in those days. When I did take baths, I did it at school. They had big tubs at school. And our teacher, knowing darn well what our situation was, would mark off the kids who could take baths at certain times. I remember there were four shower heads in there. I thought that was really something. It was a luxury for us. In Saskatoon in those days, from anywhere around L Street down, the streets in the lower part of the alphabet, no one had running water. In the better area, people even had paved roads. Those were considered the high mucky-muck people.

You could skate anywhere for miles on the roads. If we had heavy rains, or an early snowfall, and water would go down in the gullies or sloughs, and into ponds, we had all these areas to skate on. The Hudson Bay slough went out to about the airport, which was four miles or more. We'd walk about three blocks from my house to it, and skate the entire length of the slough. We learn where the ponds were by knowing where the bluffs were. Most of them had little ponds in between them, so we'd go to these hills and there'd be a nice sheet of ice. We'd play until we cut it up or, if the ice was thin, it would get a little rubbery. The water would start to follow your tracks. So you'd have to take off your skates and go to the next pond. We used to walk across the countryside quite a bit doing that.

When the river froze, high winds would keep it pretty clear of snow. Boy, we could skate to the next city if we wanted to. We used to play hockey by going up to what was called the Grand Trunk Bridge and we'd play in between the piers. It was good ice there, too as a rule.

My Dad used to keep my skates sharpened with a file. Then he'd get very ingenious, with his ability as a mechanic. He drilled and made a little frame that he hooked onto the washing machine. He put a belt on the flywheel of the washing machine that set up and turned a stone. He would cross cut the blade with it, rather than what they do now, where they run parallel to the skate. It would go "RRRRRR!" so loud that you had to get the heck out of there when you heard him start it up. As far as I was concerned, he did a good job of creating a way for us to have our skates sharpened.

We were skating on all kinds of outdoor ice. We'd grab onto the back of a bus and let it pull us all over the country. We called it "trailing." Then the drivers got a little wise to us, and started putting cinders on the road. That was the end of our trailing. Heck, we'd sit behind them, like we were skiing. In the daytime the sun or friction from traffic would melt down the top of the roads, then at night it would freeze up, and we'd have a great path again.

I doubt that Dad ever had a pair of skates on in his life. He'd tell stories that he'd skated. But no, I don't think so. In fact, other than on TV, I don't think my Dad ever saw me play more than ten times in his life. We didn't have much money, so he sometimes couldn't afford to go away to see me play. When the fans honored me one night in Detroit, in 1959, it was the first time he ever saw me play. That was my thirteenth year into a career, more than twice the average time of a hockey career.

We used to make what, in those days, was sort of a homemade bow and arrow. The arrowheads we remade from shingles. We could fire those things out of sight. We used them mostly for goofing around, but you could hunt with them. In order to get shingles, we'd go to old buildings. There was this one old farm that, to us, looked very vacant. About five of us, my brothers and some friends, went up on the barn roof and were picking out the best shingles when all of a sudden a rifle shot—pyoo-BANG!—blew a shingle into splinters. We dropped off the back end of that barn and were going ninety miles an hour before we knew it. We were running like crazy, and came to the railroad and its big fence. We were small enough that we were able to dive under it. But this guy was still on our trail. So we ran through this culvert, while a couple of guys went over the top of it when another bullet rattled—bang!—off the gravel behind us. This guy was quite serious. He was mad, losing those shingles. Thank goodness there were a lot of bluffs, with little patches of trees. When we got to the first one, we laid down there to see where he was. It was then he put rifle shots into two of those bluffs, one not far away. He *was* mad. He was shooting right into them. So we made ground, I'll tell ya. We got the heck out of there. It scared the hell out of us, but we were laughing at the same time. Geez, we didn't know someone lived on the property. We thought we were taking shingles from an abandoned barn. Then we find out we're taking it from a barn that a guy owned and was still using. We never went near there again.

We never meant any harm. It was just a place we thought was empty. I'll tell ya, I'll never forget the long drop from the roof at the other end of that barn. It had been easy going up, because we went up through the belly of the barn, through the hayloft, and just swung out over the top and we were on the roof. But coming down demanded a quick departure. We slid down, and then hung as far as we could and then dropped. It was funny, but scary at the same time. The guy probably was shooting a .22 rifle. I didn't get close enough to find out for sure. And I think he succeeded in doing what he wanted to do—frightening the living heck out of us.

In those days you couldn't afford anything. And one time I did something with the same group of guys that really scared me. I only did it that once, because it wasn't worth it. I guess it bothered me.

The deal was, we staged a dummy fight in back of Livergrandt's store. And guys were cheering us on. I was one of the dummy fighters, going at it like crazy, pretending we were serious. We were fighting like heck, and when they got nosey and came out to look at us, somebody ran in the store and stole a pound of butter. We used it to have a corn roast. We went out to some cornfield and helped ourselves, got a few head of corn, then cooked it up, boiled 'em up over a fire. This time was special, 'cause we had the butter there. It worked pretty good. Borrowing from farmers was pretty common in those days. We'd get carrots and potatoes out of some farm garden. We loved those. My family had an acre ourselves for a garden. You'd use some for your own family and sell the rest door to door.

The kind of things, like taking that butter, scared me. And I think I learned a lesson. There was a fellow from Saskatoon, a pretty good hockey player, and what he did was, since he needed a shoelace in a hurry, he took a wire hanger, straightened it out, and put a hook at the end. Then he went in a store and took a lace off the wall, but he got caught. That little lace kept him out of the U.S., because later when he went to get his green card, the theft was on his record. He couldn't go anywhere. So knowing about what happened to him scared the living daylights out of me.

The butter deal was the end of my career as a juvenile delinquent.

I remember the first time I realized I had any strength was

when I threw a snowball at a guy who pushed my brother, Vic, off a teeter-totter. I was on the other end, and I had a sore butt when I got up off the ground myself. This guy was a grade-eighter and I was just a grade three kid. So, I just packed up a snowball with some little cinders in it, and hit him right in the head. They had to dig cinders out of this kid's eye for about an hour. It didn't hurt him, except for the irritation, and he had to wear an eye patch.

Later, after he had found out who had done it, he came to get me when I was in the school washroom. He was a big guy. I had good size, but I was a lot younger, and this guy was so big he looked like my Dad. He hauled off and swung at me, trying to hit me in the head. But I jumped in the air, and he hit me in the chest. And it didn't hurt. I remember I had a leather jacket on, and it didn't hurt at all. Then I just automatically swung back, and I hit him in the same eye I hit before. He grabbed at his eye, and it was all over. And I figured "God, this Howe is tough." Nobody ever bothered me after that. It worked out pretty good. I got off with my life.

I remember Dad buying our first radio. It was one of those round-shaped ones. It only stood about eighteen inches. He got it when I was about six or seven. It was really exciting to hear it. It's funny, I can still see that dang thing. It was brown wood and only had three knobs on it. It was rounded off at the top, like the spire of a church. And, along with that, we got a record player, one that you had to wind up. We used to play all those old tunes.

I remember listening to hockey games on that radio. Foster Hewitt. He had that line about..."hello hockey fans in Canada and our armed forces in Newfoundland," or something like that. For a while, as a kid, I thought Newfoundland was overseas.

Before we got our radio, we used to go to the home of

some friends and we'd listen to "Lights Out," that really spooky radio show. Oh God, that was funny. It was scary, and I remember the guy's voice..."Ha ha ha..." And there'd be big screams on that show, and when the door was opened for us to go home after it was over, we'd run like deer. We had a block to go and we'd just streak for home. If somebody even touched my foot while that show was on, I'd be out the door and gone. Nobody could have caught me.

We used to go to the movies on Saturday mornings when I was a kid, but only when we'd earned enough money to go. We'd walk downtown about a mile and a half to the Roxy theater, that's where Emile Francis' wife, Em, used to work. We'd pay five cents and sit there for three hours. There was the Lone Ranger, and we'd watch that twice. "Hi-Yo, Silver!" Whatever cartoons or movies were on, we couldn't care less, we were at the movies. On Friday nights they used to have a show outdoors in a parking lot and they'd have this little platform and give away peanuts. This was for a church, and I used to go there. They'd feed us, and talk to the kids. Then they'd have other kids get up and say something and quote the Bible. That's when I'd leave. I was afraid I'd have to read.

I remember we were walking back one night, crossing the tracks to go home, and some hobo sitting on a flat-bed train car made a remark about my sister. A guy with him jumped off that car and started for us and, hell, you couldn't have caught us with a rocket. It's funny how you remember those things. It was scary! Later, two of us went back and fired about eight rounds of rocks at 'em. And then ran again.

When I was a kid, I often ate oatmeal three times a day, because of the lack of food. For milk, my Dad used to buy dry Carnation powder and we'd add about a gallon of water to it. It was not very good!

So when I was around seven or eight, the doctor said I had spinal problems, that my back wasn't strong enough because I wasn't getting the proper nutrition. I remember he said that if I got hit hard enough in the back, I might never walk again. So to strengthen my back, he had me hang like a monkey from the doortop. I'd get on there, and my mother would take the chair away, and I'd swing at my hips as long as I could, trying to straighten out my spine. Also, I had to take iodine pills for a goiter; they were big as marbles. They were so big I used to eat them between a piece of bread.

I have some back problems now, but they're not related to my childhood. My back is basically strong. In fact, if Mark had my back, he'd be an All-Star. The muscles pull from time to time, and it went out on me recently. I was doing too much snow shoveling and lifting. That must be why trainers always say to cool off a horse after a run. Instead, I jumped in the car right after my work, and drove for about an hour straight. My back just went into spasms. But, after some stretching, it went away quickly.

Both my parents played musical instruments. Dad played the fiddle, and Mum played the guitar. She played chords, and he played the melody. He also would call at the barn dance square dancing events. Mum tried to teach me some chords, but fat hands and lack of talent were my two drawbacks. Mum had an old six-string Spanish guitar and Dad had a raggedy old fiddle. They didn't play much at home, just when they'd go out to a function. As the family grew, I think they played a lot less; they did it more in their early married days.

I remember that nobody at our house dared touch the radio when a group called the Islanders were on in those days. They were out of Prince Edward Island, a great group. And the lead guy was a tremendous fiddler. That was Dad's program. (All this was back when young people used to play games for their own entertainment.)

My sister-in-law, Amelia, lived at our home when my brother, Vern, was at war. She talks about when I used to go through the catalogues. I'd say "When I become a professional, I will buy different things," and then, I used to add them up. It used to come to some high figures.

I always wanted to get things for Mum. Everything she could use. She had nothing back then. No plumbing. No iron. No range. Nothing. It was just—well, you didn't realize how hard you had it. Mum grew up during the days when she was just lucky to be alive. One of the things she loved to do was fish. God, she could fish all day long. She could fish in a bathtub. I got her a pole one time and put her name on it. She loved it.

My dad hated the water. One day, he and his buddy were out on a boat. They had had a couple of cold ones, and they were acting up. They were fishing right at a cutoff, where the water goes from three feet to about eighteen feet deep. And whatever they were doing, they turned the boat over. Dad was scared of water, and I guess he was hanging on for dear life. I don't think he could swim. And the guy said, "I will go for help, Ab," and he took off. My dad was holding on and holding on. He was getting tired, and it was getting harder to hold on. Then he got too tired, slipped off the bottom side of the boat...and his feet hit bottom. He had been hanging on like mad for about a half hour in three feet of water.

I remember some of the things I did with my dad. I went hunting with him a few times, and he liked a drink every now and then. He'd carry a little flask with him. He said it was in case of snakebite. So every once in a while, he'd yell "snakebite!" and

47

take a snort.

He was a real outdoors man, a very tough individual. And strong, my God. When he was young, he used to hunt coyotes for the bounty on them. The bounty was because the coyotes out there would kill off livestock. One time, he had no money, so he couldn't afford to buy any bullets to hunt coyotes. So he went riding across the countryside trying to find some kind of work when, suddenly, he saw a coyote. Well, he put his horse into full gallop, and ran the damn thing down. He leaned over in the saddle, grabbed the coyote by the leg, and cut its tendon so it couldn't bite the horse or run. He threw it down, got off the horse and ran and got a fence post, and finished it off. He skinned it and got his money and came home a rich man. He used that money to buy bullets, so he could go coyote hunting again.

I know he used to talk about that horse. It was a roan, and it was known as a killer horse; it would kill a man. They were going to put it away because it was dangerous, and my dad said "No, I'll take it." And he used that horse and hunted with it and never had a problem.

One real talent of my Dad's was he could run like a deer. He was a great athlete, a tremendous runner. He was about exactly my size, but I never inherited a bit of his speed. None whatsoever. But, otherwise, I guess I resemble my dad quite a bit, both in looks and sense of humor. I walked into a room last year out in Saskatoon, and my sister was standing there and she said, "Jesus, look at Gordie. He's the spittin' image of the old guy."

The house I was born in was in Floral, Saskatchewan. I think the back wall was a dirt wall. I was only about five days old when we moved out of there into Saskatoon. A lot of people have me playing hockey in Floral, but that's pretty hard to do at five days old. I've been back to see that house. It's a very little place, the back of it was built into a hill. It was made of wood. And when I looked into it, there were two beds and the only thing for mattresses were newspapers piled on them. Who was living there then, when I went back to see it, I don't know. Maybe some guy looking for a place just to lie down or something. It was dark and dingy. Very small. It was easy to see that, my parents, who had come up there on that Homesteader's Act, were pioneers, and lived a life of poverty and struggle.

I remember one time scaring Mum out of her wits. We were playing in someone's garage, one that had a dirt floor. I remember being on top of something, like an old pirate's chest. As I was standing there, I was pretending to be like Tarzan. I pounded my chest—"aaa-eee-aaa!"—as I leaped up to grab for this crossbar. I was going to swing from there to grab a second one. Well, I grabbed it, but I kind of overshot my mark, and as I went for the second one, my head hit it first. I went straight down—boom—right on my head, landing on my forehead. I was out, cold. Somebody ran home and got my mother, who was just a half a block away. They said, "Gordie's dead." She came running down and she told me later, "God, you sure looked like you were dead, too."

I was out for twenty-four hours, and woke up in the hospital. I couldn't understand where I was. I had to go to the bathroom, so I got up and wandered around. I couldn't figure out where I was or how I got there. Now, we had an outside john at our house, and if it was cold out, we used to go in a bottle. So I'm walking around, looking for the bottle in the hospital. Luckily, a nurse came in and said, "Do you have to go to the bathroom?" and took me to it. I was about eight at the time. That's what I get for watching all those Tarzan movies. The thing that did make me mad was that I missed playing in my hockey game during the time

I was unconscious.

I probably raised more hell than I should have. There was a family who lived near us. They were miserable; real miserable. As far as they were concerned, nobody could have fun. As kids, we went out and made our own little golf hole near our house. We cut the grass as best we could, and then put a little sand on it, made it smooth, and that was our number one hole. And we put a hole in it, so we could play a little golf. This was when I was only in grade two. All of a sudden, the police show up and tell us we can't do that. This couple had called the police on us for making our own little course. And anything else we would do the police would be over again saying, "you can't do that" and, "you can't play ball." It was really annoying, because we weren't bothering them at all.

So, one day I had witnessed the burning of some tires. Boy, did it make vicious smoke. So we all waited until the wind was just right, and we piled up quite a few old tires. I don't know how many there were. We had some gasoline, and we poured it on the tires. When we figured the wind was just right, we lit the pile. I guess you could say we were mean little buggers. But, oh, we were laughing like crazy. That black smoke went straight to their house. Boy, it was something. Of course, we ran around the other way when they came out of the house. They were trying to put the fire out, and they couldn't. Geez, we were laughing. And nobody knew who did it. I'm sure we were suspected, but nobody said a word.

On Halloween, we would take a couple of pails of water and put a line across them, and ring the doorbell at some guy's house, then run like hell and get a distance away. So the guy would come to the door. We would call him a few names, and when he took a run at us, the pails would wrap around him and he'd trip and get hit with all that water. God, it was beautiful.

When I was still at Westmount School, which was the first and second grade, I used to have a little route to school known only to Gordie Howe. Back then they used to have Beehive Corn Syrup and I collected the labels. If you sent away for them, you would get a picture of the hockey player of your choice. They were nice pictures, and a pretty good size, about six by four. I'd say I did pretty well collecting those labels out of people's garbage on my delivery route. With only 120 hockey players in the league, I had 180 pictures. Every time you sent one to Toronto and they didn't have the player you wanted, you'd get a Turk Broda back. He was Toronto's goalie when I was a kid. He started with them around 1935 or '36. So I could peddle Turk Broda, trade him to other kids. It's ironic when you think that I ended up scoring my first goal in the NHL against Turk in 1946. My favorite player at that particular time, because of the name, was Syd Howe of the Red Wings.

But talk about enterprising. When I found a Beehive Corn Syrup label in somebody's garbage, I'd go to the house and make it a point to ask if I could have the label off their new can. And if they didn't want to give it to me then, I'd ask them "Would you please hold it for me?" And they would. I'd go back there about two or three weeks later and they had my can, and the label. I used to send away for my hockey pictures, but I used to have to do odd jobs to get money to send for them. I guess we were using three-cent stamps, so I had to get money for that.

I would do odd jobs whenever I could, like deliver those pamphlets of the price listings for Livergrandt's. And I'd have to cover about a six square-block area. In those days the mailbox wasn't on the street, so I had to put the pamphlet in a slit in the door or just bang on the door and hand it to someone. I'd prefer a lot of times to bang on the door. It was 30 below zero. You'd want to be invited in. So they'd ask me in and give me something to drink, and talk to me. People knew me, because I played with a lot of the kids around there. I did that all winter.

In the summer, I was strong enough and big enough to handle Livergrandt's bike, and I'd deliver the smaller groceries. It was a tough thing to do, because we lived in such sandy soil, and to ride a bike in that is a little tough; but that was basically how I made summer money. Another way we found to make money, and as an animal lover I have to say we didn't do it with any joy, was taking care of a little varmint out there on the prairie called a gopher. It's a rat with a fuzzy tail, and a fancy name. They used to eat the crops, and the farmers were always very anxious to get rid of them. So we used to get one cent a tail. We had our little slingshots and different ways of taking care of those little varmints. Then we'd get all their tails together and collect our money. We'd go out to 13 Mile and 32nd Street and turn the tails in, which is about a ten-mile walk out of town. The reason for the bounty on these little things was not only what they'd eat, but when they got out of hand, the farmers had to poison them. And when you're poisoning an area where you're growing food which will be consumed by humans later on, it's not the best thing in the world to do.

I remember this particular farmer, I don't recall what his name was, but he used to bring us a meal. He'd give us sandwiches and lemonade and feed us when we'd show up there on Fridays and Saturdays. I know we went up as high as one hundred or more of those tails sometimes. And that dollar-something would get us each popcorn and maybe five-cent candy bars and five cents for the movie. Of course, I could go to the movies another way and save that money. Sometimes I'd sneak in the back door. We'd have one guy pay to go in, and then he'd open the back door and we'd all sneak in. I know it sounds terrible now, because of what we have in the present day world, but when there's nine in the family and very little money to go around, you learn to do things like that to survive. Every penny was worth something to us. It all counted.

I used to snare rabbits and make mitts of them. I learned to sew in grade three and I put that to good use. They taught me how you take the needle and you wrap the thread in a circle and run it down to a knot right on the dead end. That was pretty fancy. So, it was a combination of things that we used to do to get by, and we learned things that came in handy. But then as I grew a little older and, as I was improving in strength, I went to work with my father on a part-time basis pouring concrete sidewalks throughout Saskatoon.

When I first started to skate, it was hard to be a good skater without tight-fitting good skates. That's why they called me awkward. In the modern-day world, I guess the word would be "klutz." And I did have a nickname for a while when I was a kid. They called me "Doughhead." Of course, as soon as I got big enough, they stopped calling me that, because they found out I didn't take to that very much. I had a lot of pride. My mother recalled it years later, and she talked about the problems I had. I had trouble in school, and I failed grade three, and that really hurt me. I was in tears for two days over it. I went to summer school and I devoted a lot of time in that school to learning something, because I sure wasn't lazy, but I couldn't spell very well. I always had a difficult time with that. Some people have the ability to do it very easily. But, I always had trouble with words, and I never talked to people much about it. But, for the first time in my life, I really took a liking to school when a teacher, a fellow by the name of Mr. R. H. Trickey took a liking to me. What a difference that made. He would assist me and help me with the problems I had, and just pats on the back would mean a hell of a lot more to me than a grade.

I've done crossword puzzles all my adult life to try to help my spelling and word usage. I used to do them all the time when I was playing hockey and traveling so much. I've found my own name in crosswords quite a few times. It's quite a thrill. I've seen Bobby Orr and myself. I can spell his name easily, but sometimes I have trouble with my own. Too many damn letters. Four.

I had a lot of friends when I was a kid, and we did everything together. We went from hockey, to football, to soccer, and then to baseball. We all loved playing baseball together. One day, we were playing, dressed in whatever clothes we had because we didn't have any kind of uniforms. Two cars pulled up, and ten or eleven kids jumped out. And we thought, oh hell, look at this. They looked so nice. They had all these nice shirts, and real gloves and everything. And this one guy said to us "Do you guys want to play?" I said, "Yeah, we'll play." We kicked the living hell out of them. We had some really fine ballplayers. Somebody who was there watching us play came over and talked to us, and they got us uniforms with pullover shirts, and we put the initials of our school on them. So that's how we got started as ballplayers.

When I was about ten or eleven, I did other enterprising things to make money. I saved my money, and bought a big fishing pole and put a reel on it so I could extend my reach. So, I became a very efficient fisherman. I'd catch ten or twenty fish a day, and run them over to the Chinese restaurant in town, bang on the door, and sell them for five or ten cents a fish. That was good money. I sold a lot of fish. Once I caught an eleven-pound pike when I just had a little cane pole. I was fishing near some guy who pointed and said "Why don't you try and catch that big one over there?" So I just threw my hook in there. I was using a piece of beefheart, and the pike hit it. I yanked it up, but I broke the rod, so I'm grabbing the string, and I got it near me and I pulled out a knife and stabbed it. It was a hell of a fight. I finally got it out, and I was so excited I rode on my bike to go show my dad. He took it home and chopped it up, and that's what we ate for a while.

When I went back to Saskatoon one year with Colleen, she said, "Let's go to the Chinese restaurant where you used to sell the fish." So, we went in and damned if the original owner wasn't in there. Now, he knows me as Gordie Howe from hockey. But I said, "You may not remember me from many years ago. Remember the little guy that used to sell you fish?" Oh, he was surprised. We had a good time. I said "You cheap bugger, you could have paid me more."

When I was about twelve or thirteen, I caddied in Saskatoon at the city golf course, to make money. I liked doing that, because I really loved golf and golf courses. But geez, one time I really goofed up. The Intercontinental Packing Company, now called Olympic Packing, was owned by a fellow named Mr. Mendel. One day he came out to golf, and I caddied for him. Every time he swung at the ball, it made me laugh, because he was so heavy. I just couldn't stop. He was so big, and he just looked so funny swinging at the ball, so every time he swung, I laughed. He turned to me and said, "Are you laughing at me?" "No sir." He said, "Then, why are you laughing?" And I said, "I just enjoy everything." Hell, I was stuck for an intelligent response, but I still could not stop laughing. I just said, "I'm sorry, sir. I'm not laughing AT you." And I'm thinking "Oh, you dummy! You won't get paid THIS day."

So he turns to me and says "Can you play golf?" I said,

"yes," and he invited me to try one hole. I smacked it down the center, hitting it really well. When we got to the green, he said he had a lot of trouble with the greens on that course, so I said "Well, I play a lot here, so I can help you." So I plumbed the green for him. He asked me what I was doing, and I said I was using a plumb line to test the alignment of the green. I said "The line's about four inches to the left of the hole." So, he tried it and made the putt. He said "That's very good, how does that work?" So I explained a plumb line to him, and how you use your strong eye to determine how the green's laid out, how the ball will break. I had read about this in a golf magazine at the golf course.

It ended up that he was very nice to me, and I caddied often for him. Sometime later he offered to help me get a scholarship so I could take up golfing, but by then I was too serious about hockey.

On the far end of town, they had the Grand Trunk Railroad bridge. We used to go over the bridge to get to the golf course. I think this happened when I was in grade eight. Somebody got the fancy idea that we should write our names out on the steel structure of the bridge, which is probably about 160 feet above the ground. In order to do it, we put a rope around a railroad tie at the top of the bridge and dropped it down with a weight on the end of it. Then the guys would go over the edge and walk on the girders. Somebody would swing the rope over to them until they grabbed it. Then, you'd be like Tarzan, swing over and grab another girder that was away from everything, a self-supporting one. You'd write your name on it, and then swing back to the original girder, grab it, and crawl back up. The drop was about 140 feet if you slipped.

The police found out about it, and they knew all of us. Guess we should have written somebody else's names. They got a hold of us, and this one policeman said, "My God, kids. What are you trying to do?"

I did some rough things. I was looking for golf balls one day out in an area off the golf course near a sanitarium. I got cold and sat down with a couple of friends, and we were going to warm ourselves with a little fire. One of the kids got a whole bunch of dry grass and we lit it. Well, it started going like hell, and all of a sudden we had a 30-foot wall of flame. Now, we're trying to put it out, but there's no way. So we ran like hell, went over to the railroad, pulled the alarm, and kept right on going. As I said, I did some risky things.

We didn't have much during the Depression, but we weren't conscious of being poor. We were rich with friendship. We had so much. There was so little, but so much.

I was aware that somebody had more, but the people who had more, shared. People shared a lot then. It was a different kind of country. People cared a lot more. And, if somebody needed help, they got it.

I really think I had a great childhood. As I say, we didn't have a lot, but we had all the right things.

CHAPTER THREE

IT'S THE BEST GAME I'VE EVER PLAYED

COLLEEN: Marty has a quiet nature, like Gordie...but look out! This guy that we used to call Mr. Messy at home now has become Mr. Perfection. He measures twice and cuts once. He's really such a good craftsman, his tools are all special. He puts them away and defies you to touch them. So there's hope for anybody who has a kid that's messy, because it's amazing how they change as adults.

Marty was in real estate in Connecticut. He felt there was a lull in real estate values there, so he decided that he would take the time to apprentice with various builders to learn the building process. He restores old homes and does fabulous home improvements. He totally remodeled our studio in Traverse City, previously known as the "House from Hell." Marty has diverse talents, such as scuba diving, fishing, business and coaching. His current passion is with the Motor City Mustangs of the Roller Hockey International roller hockey league. He was selected to coach the Eastern All Star teams this season.

GORDIE: Marty's a quiet type, full of passion for whatever he does.

MARTY: My carpentry experiences emanated from renovating older homes. My grandfather Mulvaney used to do a lot of woodwork and Mark and I actually helped him build a house in Traverse City. He pointed us in the right direction, popping in some nails and carrying wood for him. I've always enjoyed it. It promotes self-confidence and makes you proud of your accomplishments. When you're done, it's something you can look at and see the result of your work.

My coaching debut began in Flint, Michigan with the "Flint Bulldogs" of the recently formed, Colonial Hockey League. The Bulldogs were in Flint for one year and there were many challenges. The owner got the fans so mad that they wouldn't come to the arena. He took the position that because he was spending so much money keeping the team in Flint, the people should come to the games for his efforts, and he said so in the papers. I don't know if he meant it or if he was hoping that the fans would get mad and come to the games just to yell at him. It was a terrible situation that ended up with the franchise relocating to Utica, New York.

I like coaching. The most enjoyable part is interacting with the players. I receive tremendous self-satisfaction out of seeing a player improve his playing capability. If I can reward players something from which they could benefit and improve, that's what I like to accomplish. But in Utica it was hard having to worry about lack of capital, along with the worry about the team making a profit, and all the bottom line factors when all I should have my attention on is icing a good team and winning. I'd probably be a better coach for an American league team, a place where they're improving players and always concentrating on win, win, win. The idea should be to develop players so they can move up to the NHL while providing good sports entertainment and talent for the fans in that city. In situations like Flint and some of the other minor league teams, you're forced to win or you don't draw, and if you don't draw, you're not going to have a team.

Currently, I'm the Head Coach and recently named General Manager of the Motor City Mustangs of the Roller

Hockey International League. We have a 24-game season, and play in downtown Detroit at Cobo Arena. In-line hockey is in its third year and so it's a relatively new league, but I really think it is the wave of the future. The structured seasons are established so they don't overlap between ice hockey and the roller hockey so some players are able to have jobs year round. If you go anywhere in the streets, there are thousands and thousands of kids getting into in-line skates each year. I can even see leagues operational year round, playing hockey and not even needing ice. Because of the non-ice conditions necessary for the playing surface, in-line has created a more affordable, as well as a more convenient, sport.

Roller hockey is very similar to ice hockey. There are a few different rules, because we have no blue lines, just the center ice line, which is the offside line, and the game is played four-on-four with three forwards and one defenseman. This creates a faster game, with more shooting and, of course, more scoring. The checking's there, but there's no fighting allowed. If you fight, you get ejected from the game and suspended. If you initiate the fight, the other team is awarded a penalty shot. So it's easy to see the league really frowns on the boxing aspect of the game. I'm sure there's always going to be a fight or two and someone will get suspended during the year, but the rules are really set up to discourage fighting.

With a four-on-four concept, you need even more skilled players. The local IHL ice hockey team, the Vipers, sent us a couple of players. I believe that their coach, Rick Dudley, is looking for them to, perhaps, gain a few more puck-handling skills or improve their eye-hand coordination and work on their conditioning year round.

I've had several coaches: the ones I've enjoyed working for were guys like George Armstrong, Bill Dineen and Gerry

Cheevers. Coaches that don't come in and scream, yell, kick buckets, and become irate. They give you confidence by playing you and by patting you on the back when you do something right. I take that approach more than one of screaming, cursing, and yelling. Although I can get upset sometimes, it takes me quite a while to reach that point. But, like Gordie, when I do, I really get upset. But most of the time I'll sit down with my players and review game videos, which gives me a chance to show them where they erred and mistakes occurred. They clearly see what they're doing and don't do it again. They learn and profit from their mistakes.

At the time I decided to quit hockey as a player and I was playing with Hartford, I had a couple of years remaining on my contract. I could have probably played another two, three, or even four years. My career was stagnant. They were going to send me to the minor league team at Binghamton and I was probably going to only be developing the younger players there, which wasn't my job. In my heart I wanted to play a game for the Red Wings. So, I went up to ask Emile Francis if he'd try to move me to Detroit. That ended up being a big mistake, because I think I got the Whalers mad at me. He kept me until the end in the training camp, but I didn't play any exhibition games, and I was sent to Binghamton with no explanation or plan in mind.

In Emile's mind, he probably had me pegged for helping develop his players. I think those were his plans for me and I probably threw a wrench into it. When I did report to Binghamton (I believe we were in Rochester playing an exhibition game), I must have gotten scored on about four times. I just found my heart wasn't really in the game, and I became discouraged. I had gone to the minors before and been upset about it, but when I put on my blades, went out there and played, I forgot all about what was bothering me. I played my game to the best of my ability, and then worried about other things later. But that was the first time I was sent down, and it was the first time I ever played without my heart being in what I was doing. It was also the last game I ever played. That night I called Emile, talked to my wife Mary, and said, "I'm coming home, this is it. Hockey isn't enjoyable anymore."

It wasn't really that hard to give up the game. At that point, if I still had any desire to go and play, I could have reversed things and stayed in Binghamton, I would have played. Probably I would've been called up to Hartford for my thirteen or fourteen games during the season, and that would have continued.

Looking back at the challenges of getting established into a new field, since I retired, I most likely should have played those two more years; but at that point, I just wasn't happy. I've played with guys who felt like that, just did not put out the effort for the team, and I didn't like them for it. I didn't want my teammates to think of me that way either. I have too much respect for myself and my fellow players to do something like that; so I told the club I was leaving, and they arranged a buyout.

My best hockey experiences as a player were with Mark and my Dad, playing in Houston, Toronto, and Boston. I played on three straight championship teams. The first two years at Houston, we won the Avco Cup, the WHA championship. And my last year in juniors, when I was with the Toronto Marlboros with Mark, we won the Memorial Cup championship. I also enjoyed the year I was in Boston, playing for the Bruins. I don't know if I had a great year, but I played very consistently and did what they asked of me.

Playing in Detroit was my dream, because my dad had played there. We were born there, and all of our personal and hockey development was there. When we played for Olympia Agencies, we always had Red Wing uniforms, and I liked that. In fact, it was almost odd when I first went to Toronto and played for the Marlboros. I was wearing that blue and white, and it seemed strange. It was the first time I wasn't wearing red and white.

I actually came close to getting back to Detroit. The year I played for Boston, I was on loan from Hartford. Larry Pleau said they were sending me to camp in Binghamton and not inviting me to camp in Hartford. I asked if I could work out a deal for myself with another club. Larry told me he didn't have time but if I could find a team to go to he would pay half my salary. At that point, I called Detroit and ended up working out a deal that I could go to Detroit's camp. And I felt even if I went down to their team at Adirondack, I was a good enough caliber of player that I would have a good chance to get called up at some point during the season. This would have fulfilled what I wanted to accomplish at that point in my life. That was the year, though, that Mike and Marian Ilitch bought the team and changed some of their personnel and my deal went sour for reasons not explained to me.

It was close to the beginning of training camp, so I scrambled and made a few more phone calls. Harry Sinden called from Boston and he worked out an agreement for me to go to their camp. I think he had me pegged for the minors, too, but Gerry Cheevers was really my kind of coach. He knew I'd work effectively for him, and picked me for the Bruins squad. He works with you and lets you build confidence. In fact, I was mainly paired with Brad Park and it turned out well for both of us. I was like his legs for him at that point. He would do the stick handling, and I would go chase the puck. The whole team played that way and we were a closely knit group of guys who worked together.

Brad gave me a lot of help. For example, I used to skate

like mad into the corner, get the puck, then turn around and take a look to see where I was going to go. And Brad said, "No, you've got to be looking around before you get to the corner, so you know where you're going to go when you get there." He was very good that way.

Besides Brad, I also got defensive coaching from Doug Harvey when we were in Houston, the first year in 1973. I think Doug was someone that you could learn from by watching, but he wasn't that good at verbalizing information. He taught one valuable thing to me. Every day he made me go behind the net, pick up a puck and take a backhand shot around the boards. I would do this ten times in a row. It helped me immensely, because my back hand shot was pretty bad at that point. I was a defenseman and I had to be able to pass effectively either way. What Doug had me do was very helpful to me during my whole career.

When we were kids, Mark was the hockey fanatic in our family. I wasn't all that interested; I liked girls, track, fishing, and football. Mark was all hockey. He'd go to practice with my dad and skate around while the team dressed. He collected sticks and he knew all the stats on every player in the NHL. He lived and breathed hockey. I loved many sports, but I think probably football was my favorite. My dad and mom never really guided or pushed us into any particular sport. They always made sure we had equipment, support and transportation. Since my dad was gone most of the time during the hockey season, he really didn't have a chance to coach us. He was playing, we were playing, and we were all over the place as a family. We've always been a close-knit family and after the season, he'd try to take Mark and me fishing in Canada. The pilot would drop us off on the shore and we'd stay there a week, just catching fish. That's probably how I got hooked on fishing, one of my most favorite pastimes.

It's funny the situations that stick in your mind about your hockey related experiences...This happened in the early '80s, maybe around '83 or '84. I had been sent down to Binghamton, and Ulfie Samuelsson was going to be my defense partner my first night there. People who follow the NHL and AHL now know that Ulfie was kind of disliked by the other teams. I had no idea what was going on, but I found out that he was a target of some of the other players that night.

Jack Brownschidle was another defenseman on that team. He came up to me and said before the game "I don't know if you know it, but Ulfie cut one of these guys on this team in the last game. He gave him about thirty stitches." I guess it was a pretty bad gash. This was in Ulfie's rookie year, after he had just come to the team from Sweden.

I thanked Jack. I was glad to find out this information. If something happened, I could be prepared for the worst. I figured Nova Scotia would be running at Samuelsson all night long. The first kind of odd thing that happened was that their team didn't come out of the dressing room on time. That was unusual, but I didn't think anything about it. Finally, they came out about four or five minutes late. Even that didn't mean anything. I dismissed it and went on with the warm-up. Then, I noticed as they were skating out, they all had their helmets on. Even then I thought that maybe their coach was playing some psychological game. It was strange, because usually some guys are standing around looking at their reflection in the glass or fixing their hair. Then a little light went on in my head and I thought, something is wrong here. Meanwhile, I'm standing at the blue line, we're going through normal routine, guys are taking shots and passing the pucks out. When suddenly this player from Nova Scotia goes skating by me at what looked like eighty miles an hour. I spun around, and as I did, I saw the rest of the team coming at us. I said, "Oh no, just what I needed, first day back in the minors and here comes trouble. We're going to have a brawl in warm-up, of all things." I'd never had a brawl in warm-up, even in juniors, so I thought, welcome to the minors, Marty.

Now, this is an all out gang fight, all over the ice, and it goes on what seemed like forever. Occasionally it would break up for a second, then somebody would start another battle and all hell would break loose. It seemed ten guys went after Ulfie behind the net. It was a big pile-up, there were skates and blades in the air, sticks were flying everywhere. Even the coaches were fighting. The Nova Scotia assistant coach was really a big buy and he came up behind our coach, ripped his jacket in half and pinned him up against the glass. The referees weren't even dressed to go on the ice yet, so they were up in the stands in their underwear taking notes, writing down who's doing what. They can't do anything without their equipment on. The police were notified. After about twenty minutes or so of this, the police walked out on the ice to break it up. But when they'd walk up to somebody on the ice (very carefully) and break up a little fight, then four other fights would start. They'd get over to another fight when the guys they just left would start fighting again. Nothing was working! I saw the police go into a huddle. They reappeared with two large german shepherd police dogs. They were huge, beautiful dogs. The police must have been figuring that these dogs would stop it, so they let the dogs out on the ice. Well, the dogs got out there, but they froze. They just stopped in their tracks when they hit the ice. Their legs went out on them, and they started sliding around. Their legs were all stiff, and they had funny looks on their faces. They sat up straight and instead of running at the fighting players, they started sniffing at the ice and pawing at it and stuff. Now the police are all scratching their heads, they don't know what to do. It looked funny, but the players couldn't really laugh, not while someone was punching them in the head. So the players just kept going at it. It went on for maybe another five minutes or so, and then the coaches finally came out and broke it up. The dogs were still standing there. They couldn't move.

I was fortunate in that fight. Archie Henderson of Nova Scotia had grabbed me and, well, I don't think Archie would mind if anybody called him a goon, because he was a goon. He was a pretty tough guy, and I guess I was blessed he wasn't in the mood for fighting that night. He grabbed me right away, and said "don't grab my jersey...just watch." So we just stood there, and watched. I didn't hold him, but he had hold of my jersey, so we just skated around like that.

The funny thing was, after all that fighting, Ulfie came out of it just fine. He's a strong kid; built like a brick. We started the game and I think three guys on each team got kicked out by the referees. Welcome to the minors!

As someone who's coached and played in the minors, I know the hardest adjustment comes in the mental part of the game. The biggest thing is anticipation. I think if there's one major difference between the major and minor leagues, it's that guys can anticipate and know where the puck is going to be before the play happens. The most talented players have that ability.

Physically, you find some pretty tough guys in the minors. When I was coaching in Utica, I had a lot of college Division Three players, and they had an idea that fighting was glamorous. Their attitude was—they've seen these guys fight, and they want to go fight because they didn't fight in college. I was shaking my head at this thinking. I figured that this was going to be like the slaughtering of the lambs, which it was. I was to the point of feeling sorry for these guys, getting cut and beaten up so badly. I've never seen so much blood in one year. I felt sorry for them because they just didn't know any better. I was trying to teach them that if you're going to get punched like that, at least fall down, or hold on to them, or at least bury your head in your chest so you don't get your face punched. A lot of guys learned the hard way, by experience.

It's strange that I didn't fight much in my professional career, but when I was a kid in Detroit, playing for the Olympia Agencies, I used to fight a lot. Even in school, I used to fight all the time. I was sort of a bully growing up. It used to be the cool thing to do. You get the two biggest guys at recess and you go fight. I got challenged a lot, and maybe being Gordie Howe's son had a lot to do with it. I enjoyed it at the time, I was one of those guys who'd get in a fight and later couldn't remember what I did. I'd kind of lose it in the heat of a battle. My temper is sort of famous in our family. I've changed quite a bit now. Age slows you down. When I used to have a pretty short wick, I'd blow up at almost anything.

MARK: I remember the time Marty got in a fight at school and got suspended. It was funny, because he always took the bus home, and I always ran or rode my bike. That would give me an extra 15 minutes to play ball hockey. That's why I did it, I didn't want to waste time on the bus.

But I got home one day and he's sitting at the kitchen table. I said "What's going on? What happened, what are you doing home?" He just said "shhh." And I said "What do you mean, shhh?" And right then Mom comes in the room and she's steaming, "He got in a fight at school. I guess he broke the boy's nose and got suspended for three days." So I thought it was a good idea to go downstairs.

About a half hour later, Dad got home from practice and Mom's very concerned about this situation. I went up to the kitchen on my way to go play hockey out in the driveway, and I stopped in the kitchen because Dad was talking to Marty. Mom was upstairs. Dad said, "Well, what happened, Marty?" Marty said, "This guy in music class was cutting down the Red Wings and making fun of you, saying what a jerk you are. He wouldn't stop. I couldn't take it anymore, and I turned around and punched him."

Dad looks around a little bit, taps Marty on the shoulder, and whispers "Way to go."

I remember going outside to play and saying to myself, "Yeah...way to go."

MARTY: I had a run-in with George Bolin, the new owner of the team in Houston, in our last year there when a new management took over and they were hassling us. We were all at a meeting and my mom did all our negotiating and was speaking for all of us. Normally we wouldn't even be in the room, but for some reason, they wanted us there. I guess it was to appeal to splitting up the Howes. Prior to this meeting, Mother had gone through months of negotiation with the Aeros in order for Mark, Dad and I to renew our contracts, and remain in Houston. Most of these meetings had broken down because of some good ole' boy attitudes. My mom decided to reach out to Bill McFarland, then WHA President, to preside at this gathering and mediate the situation. He did little or nothing to help the parties together and let George Bolin, and his caustic attitude, run the show. It was the beginning of the end of our term in Houston. A few weeks before, the Aeros had asked their players to defer their next paychecks because the team was in dire financial straits. Since our contracts already called for deferred compensation, however, they already owed us back wages. Basically they wanted us to bankroll the team, but the players who agreed to it never got paid their salaries nor their players dollars. Ours was recovered through my mother's negotiations with the Whalers agreeing to include it in our ten-year agreement. In this meeting, Bolin was just belittling my mother, griping, bitching and moaning about her and calling her names. I could tell my mom was starting to get a little more than upset, but no one was doing anything about it. Well, have you ever seen how the little hairs on your neck go up? And on the top of your head? Well, I was really hot. I figured the hell with this, I stood up and said a few things to Bolin—that we had had enough and he could take his contract and put it where the sun doesn't shine. That's what I told him, probably in words not that nice.

GORDIE: They'd reneged on our contracts two or three times already. In these negotiations, Colleen finally got up and left. They were treating her with no respect whatsoever. It was a real good ole' boy technique. Bolin and some of the other owners tried to make another offer, and Marty said, "Why don't you write it down on real soft paper and then shove it up your butt," and then left the room; right after Colleen had done the same, feeling she didn't need this abuse.

After that, Bolin held Marty's next check in the front office. They sent word that Marty could only get his check if he went up and apologized. Marty told them, "If I come up there, you won't like me because it won't be to apologize."

MARTY: I was upset. Unfortunately, we loved Houston, and I would have loved to have stayed there. Of course, at that point, you could tell the organization wasn't going anywhere. I don't like to burn bridges, but that was probably one I torched. Their financial situation was not good while Bolin kept saying he was trying to get us to sacrifice for our own good. It was all a bunch of bull.

My mom was actually the disciplinarian in our house and she gave us most of our family values. When my dad was there, he spent as much time with us as he could, particularly in the summer after the season, taking us fishing and doing family things. We were always busy as kids, involved in sports that were mainly people-oriented team sports. The only sport I played that wasn't team-oriented was when I ran track. That involves a team, but most of it is individual competition. I used to run the 100-yard dash and the 220, and I used to do a little bit of the high jump and the long jump. I think I ran 23.2 in the 220 and I used to run a 10.2 in the 100-yard dash. I was good enough to set some school records (which may still stand).

Being Gordie's kid, you always cope with some negative comments, like 'you'll never be as good as your old man.' And, of course, I never expected to be. It was probably the comment I heard most often. You get challenged on the ice, you get compared everywhere in your life to Gordie. But, I think all the good points always out-weighed the bad. When you know what a good person my dad is, it doesn't bother you. The positives are always there.

And my mom? Well, she's the conversationalist. Besides that, she's always benevolent. In the lean times for me, she's always come around and helped out. She's very intelligent, as well as dedicated. I don't know how she does it, when she only gets a couple of hours of sleep a night. She's a workaholic type who loves what she does and is proud of it. She's kind-hearted, almost too much so, and is always doing things for family and friends. She tends to go a little overboard with giving, but that's not a fault.

71

Dad's got the most patience of any person I've ever met, as long as he's not on hockey skates. As soon as he puts on those blades he is not the same person he is off the ice. He'd cut you in practice just as soon as look at you. In fact, when we played together, he cut more guys in practice then he cut in regular games.

When a player held onto his stick, most guys would pull it away and skate away, but as soon as Gordie skated away, the stick would come right back at you. So, either you ducked real fast or you were going to have a stick in your face. God, he almost got me several times. Yeah, he was terrible, he didn't care who it was. And if you saw him going into a corner with two guys, just leave him in there, cause he has no qualms on checking whoever is near him. He's going to come out of there with a puck one way or another, and that's the way he played. But off the ice, he would take all the abuse that people gave him. He doesn't react to abuse most of the time. As for me, it would only take a couple of idiotic remarks and it would be hard to control my temper. Gordie could just let it roll off his back and not let it bother him. He has that kind of special nature. He always tries to sign every autograph request. He'll stay there for hours and hours. He's been doing this as long as I can remember, but it's hard for him now with his arthritis condition throughout his wrists and hands. Yet, you see the amount of time he sits there and signs autographs at some of his appearances. I don't know how he does it, except for the fact that he loves people. I think that the biggest reason of why people are drawn to him is because he spends time with them and genuinely is a fun and sincere person.

We called him "Dad" all the time; until we turned pro and played on the same team in Houston. Then, when we would say "Dad" to him, he wouldn't even acknowledge us. He would act like he hadn't heard it, even when we were off the ice. I think it was because he didn't want to be called "Dad." It may have embarrassed him or he was not used to it. We quickly found out if we didn't call him Gordie, he did not acknowledge us. I guess the only time we called him Dad after that time was when he got hurt.

Gordie's so strong that he could do amazing things on the ice. However, he only got in one fight when we played together. Normally he just dinged guys over the head with a stick. I found that out quickly. It was actually during my first pro game. The weather was hot and the ice was awful. There was cement and ruts, there was barely any ice. The first shift, our line started the game and this suicidal player came out and went right up against Gordie at the face off. He just dropped his gloves and said, "Come on, Howe!" Gordie didn't even blink. He hit that guy right square between the eyes with his stick. The guy wasn't wearing a helmet. He went down like a ton of bricks, holding his hands on his head where blood was squirting. Gordie received five minutes and the other player got two minutes for delaying the game, because he dropped his gloves. Wow, I thought. Is this what it's going to be like in pro hockey? As soon as his penalty was up, Gordie came back out and the rotation was right for him to stay on the ice. He skated up for a face-off again, and another guy came up to him from their team, another victim off the bench wanting to get even. This guy steps back a step, doesn't drop his stick, but he says, "Come on, Howe."

I'm thinking...wow, didn't he see what happened to the first guy? Again, Gordie didn't even flinch, and he hit this guy right over the head with his stick again, right between the eyes in the forehead. He didn't even know what hit him. He'd hit guys there all the time and giving them three to five stitches every time he did it. I could never understand it. If I hit a guy over the head,

I wouldn't know if it was going to kill him or not or even cut him, but Gordie was a skilled practitioner.

Five or six games later, I realized that Gordie was consistent with this strategy. It wasn't like it just happened once. I said to him, "We're all hockey players, and they're hockey players. We're doing the same thing. We're trying to make a living, so how can you do that to them?" He said "I just want to cut 'em a little. I know how hard I hit 'em. I'm only going to give them about three stitches." I never had that touch or feel, but that's the control he had with a stick. He was a master at it. It made you real happy to know he was on *your* team.

I think Gordie knew what he was doing, because when he was on the ice he got so much room out there. The opposition wouldn't go anywhere near him—and I don't blame them. Everyone talks about his elbows, but it really wasn't the elbows he used when I was his teammate. It was the surgery he performed with his stick.

One night we had a bench-clearing brawl in Houston. It was towards the end of our shift, and a fight started. I turned around and a guy was right there, so I grabbed him by the chest and fell backwards. This was another one of those long fights. Now I've got this guy on top of me, and I'm holding on to his arms and, of course, he's saying things like "let my arm go, I won't hit you." I'm thinking, oh right! I'll just let go. No way. The fight went on, then it would break up after about five minutes. Then one of our players would sucker punch somebody and it would start all over again. This went on three or four times, lasting a good fifteen minutes. The whole time I'm still with the same player and he's still on top of me. We're not punching or anything, I'm just holding onto his arm so he can't move. Well, the brawl finally broke up and our captain, Teddy Taylor, came over and tapped him on the shoulder. "The fight's over, let him up." The guy just turned around with a smirk and believe it or not, he had a toothpick in his mouth. I remember that so clearly. He just turned around to Teddy and said, "I'm not doing anything." And he wouldn't get off me.

GORDIE: Teddy Taylor tapped the guy, and said "Okay, that's enough." And the guy used some very uncomplimentary remarks about Taylor, and Teddy was gonna take care of this guy then and there but all of a sudden somebody took a whack at somebody else and back into the pile everybody went. So I get into the fight for a while and get hold of a few people. After that settled down, I saw this guy was still on top of Marty.

MARTY: Gordie skated over and said the same thing, "Okay, let him up." This guy says the same thing to Gordie that he said to our captain. So Gordie merely reached over and stuck two of his fingers up this guy's nose. Gordie's little finger is about the size of my thumb, so this guy's nose was just about as wide as his face was with those two fingers in there. When Gordie did this, he lifted that guy right up in the air with his two fingers. Suddenly, this player was getting up as fast as he could, because it looked like it was pretty painful. He's waving his arms and he's dancing on his toes, yelling "I'm up, I'm up, I'm up!" That was one time I was grateful Gordie saved me. At that point, my arms felt like rocks. They were so tight from holding onto this guy. But that's Dad, he's such a strong equalizer.

GORDIE: I had gone over to say merely, "Okay, it's all over." But then I got some kind of uncomplimentary remarks. So I went over the top of him with my index finger and the middle one, and I stuck them right in his nostrils and I lifted. I don't know why I did it. But when I pulled him up, I said "Up, you so-and-so." And up he came. He came off Marty in a big hurry.

75

Marty said later, "You should have seen the look on that guy's face."

MARTY: I contemplated attending college and playing football. However, in my sophmore year of high school, fate intervened. I was playing on the varsity football squad, and our hockey team that year was, I think, 72-1. But, we were scheduled one day to play the hockey team that beat us, and so I asked the football coach if it would be all right if I missed practice. Usually, there was never a conflict between football practice and my hockey games. I really wanted to play the hockey game, but I figured if I missed football practice, my coach wouldn't play me the next game or he'd do something to punish me. Instead, he said, "If you don't show up for practice, your equipment won't be in your locker tomorrow." So that was it for my football career. I was devastated. My mother was pretty upset as well, since she believes there are too many restrictions, rules and regulations that create drawbacks for youngsters in sports. She thinks working things out to offer youngsters further exposure is what programs should offer.

Looking back, however, it was the best thing that ever happened to me, because it was the next year that Tommy Smythe signed me to play junior hockey with the Toronto Marlboros. If I hadn't gone to Toronto, I probably wouldn't have played pro hockey, because I tripled my development in those two years. The organization was exceptional and I was fortunate to have George Armstrong as a coach and Frank Bonello as a general manager.

I didn't know what to expect in Toronto. I wasn't sure I'd make the team. To this day, I'm not quite certain why they kept me. I guess I went out and hit anything that moved; that was something they liked. I wouldn't back down from anything and I could skate. I could always skate, but my puck-handling skills were dismal. I was one of those tall, skinny kids who was awkward; the kind a coach looks at and says "you're a defense man." I think it took me about a year-and-a-half before I could even lift the puck. So, for those kids who are out there going to hockey school to improve, there is hope.

GORDIE: Mark was the exceptional skater in the family. When we were in Houston, Mark, Marty, and I had a race one day thinking Mark would win. I was third, and Marty was first. It surprised the heck out of Mark and me. Now we had a new leader.

I got too much credit when we all played together. I think the boys were the ones who deserved the praise. They were the ones who earned their ability to be drafted and had to prove themselves. One of my favorite memories was the night at the Sam Houston Coliseum when I was behind the net. I fell and as I was going down I managed to throw the puck out in front of the goalie, then I fell into the mesh of the net. Well, the shot went into the net while I was down on the ice, and the puck was literally only about two inches from my nose as it hit the mesh. I was thinking "Great, that's another one for Mark." I got up and I could see this big smile on Marty's face. It was his first goal, and I was in on it. What a tremendous feeling.

MARTY: There weren't many pro players coming out of the states in those days, but there was exceptionally good talent in the Detroit area. We had the advantage of playing against many Canadian teams. I played with many of the same players during my early years with the Teamster 299 and Roostertail Teams. I think there were only two years that Mark and I didn't play together on the same team. One was the year I was in the midget division, and the other was when I went to the Marlies. Mark remained with the Junior Red Wings in Detroit playing for the

U.S. Olympic team in Sapporo. He was the youngest player to play for the U.S.A. Hockey Club.

It was important to my mom for us to play together, because then she'd only have to drive us to one place. In fact, she was pretty darn happy when I got my driver's license, since that was when Murray started to play hockey, too, and Cathy had so many activities of her own. Mom and Dad got me a car and said, "There you go. Now you can drive yourself." But Mom still got to every game she could manage. I don't know how many thousands of miles Mom put on the family car, taking us all over Canada. Our Coach, Jim Chapman, arranged for us to play about 100-110 games a year. In our Detroit Parks and Recreation League there would only be about 25-30 games, so all other games were traveling for exhibition games. We'd usually be some place in Ontario every weekend playing a team. We owe a lot to those Canadian teams who played us and gave us such great competition.

In my first year in Toronto, I came back to Detroit for the Christmas holidays and there was a fund raiser game against the Detroit Jr. Red Wings and the U.S. Olympic team. I was only going to play one period. So, I drove from Toronto that day and arrived in Detroit just minutes before the game started at the Olympia. I dressed and played. With about a minute left in the first period, a player got hurt, and came to the bench. I quickly jumped over the boards onto the ice to replace him. The puck was in their end, so I chased one of their players back into their end. When I got to him, he was just about two-and-a-half, maybe three feet away. I just skated up to him with my hands to the side to block any pass out, and the puck just went straight up, hitting me directly in the cheekbone below my eye. I spun around and fell down. I couldn't feel anything on the whole side of my face. In hockey you soon find out that when you get hurt and you go numb, something bad is happening. I said, "Oh, great!" And as I hit the ice I heard the buzzer sound, so I knew there were only a few seconds remaining in the period. If I would have just stayed on the bench instead of being a hero by jumping onto the ice, my injury would never have happened. Instead, I fractured my cheekbone in three places, and it required surgery. The puck had also cut me below the eye, which was stitched after the game. But the doctor felt it should be checked so Mom and I went to the hospital for what we thought was a routine cautionary exam. Instead, I was scheduled for plastic surgery immediately. The surgeons put wires through the initial cut, and wired two cheekbone fractures. Then, they cut another incision in my eyebrow and wired together the bone at the temple.

The next day I was still in the hospital, with both my eyes swollen shut. I couldn't see a thing. I was in there about five days. This was over what, I thought, would be my Christmas holiday. Great holiday! Not even one person from the Red Wings who requested my services for the game ever came to see me or even asked how I was doing. In fact, the Marlies took care of all the medical bills. Then, when I returned to Toronto, the Marlies fitted me up with a cage to protect my face, and I wore that cage for the rest of the season. My face stayed numb for about a year. The feeling finally came back, slowly. Sometimes when I ate my food, I could taste blood. That's how I knew I had bitten my cheek. Part of it is still numb, but most of the feeling has returned.

When I first started playing, I used to run at everything that moved. I think in my first year I separated my shoulder about five times. Usually that was because somebody ducked, and I'd end up playing Mr. Torpedo man, running head first into the boards, one time jamming my neck. That was the worst thing I've done in hockey. When you attempt a forceful check on a player, but they duck on you, you'll likely injure yourself on the boards I'm certain it was in one of those situations that I fractured my vertebra—even though I didn't know it at the time. You play through injuries when they're not checked out. In my case, my muscle structure held the bone together and I was fortunate that the bone healed in that position.

The way I found out that I had a fracture was when I was going to have my wisdom teeth out at the hospital. They did a series of x-rays on my teeth and because the surgery also required a chest x-ray, they noticed that one of my vertebra had been fractured. The doctor asked me when I'd had a diving accident. I said, "I've never been in a diving accident." Then he showed me this fracture in my neck, that I had never known existed. My mom is always very concerned about situations like mine, and in fact, was instrumental in creating a series of on-going symposiums at the University of Connecticut Health Centers with President Dr. John Di Biaggio. The programs were aimed at the prevention and care of youngsters in sports by informing coaches, trainers, and teachers of the necessary treatment and care of the injured. I was just lucky. Occasionally, my back will ache if I'm driving for a long time. I have my wife Mary, crack my back and that makes it feel better.

I busted the other cheekbone when I took the butt end of a stick in the face from Robbie Ftorek. I've injured my knee, not requiring surgery. Then my wrist was broken quite badly, and was probably the worst injury I remember.

I was playing in Springfield, Massachusetts. It was the first year I was sent to the minors. I was in a corner and waiting for a teammate to get in the open. (There's one thing about playing in the NHL that's different from the minors. Players don't play their position like they should. They don't clear out of the area and get to the spot they're supposed to be so you can get the puck up to them. That's what anticipation is all about.) I waited a little too long for someone to get in the open so I could give him the puck. If you give him a pass when he's not looking, he's just going to get nailed. Just then, Chris Nilan was coming across the ice, and whenever he's out there, you know he's going to try to take a run at you. I was thinking, I'm going to fix this guy. So, I made that pass and came around with one arm to hit Chris as hard as I could in the chest. When I did that, it felt like my arm just cracked in half and fell off. Really, it was like somebody took the front part of my arm, cracked it, and just moved it back up towards the elbow. My arm was about four inches shorter than it should have been.

So, that was another body part that went numb right away. I didn't know I broke my arm at first. I got up and tried to pick the hockey stick up with my glove, and the stick fell right out. I looked down and I noticed my arm was a lot shorter than normal. I returned to the bench and I couldn't get my glove off. The trainer removed it, I looked down, and part of my arm was laying over top of the other part. Both bones were broken, and the muscles had contracted and pulled my hand back.

Then, when I saw what had happened to me, I stood up and I kicked the boards and ended up breaking my toe. It was a bad night...to say the least!

Chris came up to me later, and said it wasn't a dirty hit, and it wasn't. It was a clean hit. I thought I was going to fix *him*, right? It just didn't work out according to my plan.

GORDIE: I remember the first Pee Wee tournament I went to in Quebec City, when Marty and Mark were playing. I had a day off and rushed up there to join Colleen and the kids after they had arrived. We were watching the Roostertail's game when one of the opposing players put a stick across Marty's throat. He raked Marty with it, put a burn across the side of his face from his ear down to his Adam's apple. The game went on with no penalty and our team eventually lost the game.

After the final buzzer, when the two teams were shaking hands, Marty hit the kid who hurt him. There was a bit of a flare-up, and Colleen was concerned about the entire incident. This was at a time when there were stories in the papers about kids playing under a lot of pressure, that maybe there were too many demands on youngsters, causing them to overreact with anger. I went down to the locker room to find out what had happened. When I got there, Mark and most of the team were crying because they had lost. That was their way. I looked at Marty, standing there with a big grin on his face. He never got overly upset about losing, but this time he was actually smiling. He said, "I can't cry because it's the best game I ever played."

So I said "What happened?" Marty said "See this, Dad?" And there was this big ugly red mark on his face and neck. "That guy did that to me in the first period, and I told him 'I'll get you before the night's over.' So when I was shaking hands with those guys and I saw the number on his arm, I let him have it."

MARTY: It was quite a while ago, but I do remember it because I never really reacted like that after a game. But, the player had gotten me in the neck, and I was trying to retaliate but I couldn't ever get back at him during the game. The only time I really caught up with him was in the final handshaking ceremony, so I suckered him. We were out of time and I knew we weren't playing this team again, ever, in my life, so I had to do it then or never do it.

GORDIE: I said I understood and left the locker room. I

82

walked out, and there was Colleen. She was truly concerned at what had happened. She felt this was a marvelous tournament, and there was a goodwill aspect of relationships between the Canadian and U.S. teams that she didn't want to see damaged. Many people were paying a lot of attention and homage to the Howe family. She asked, "Well, what happened?" I said, "It's okay. He kept a promise he made."

It was funny, Red Storey, the former NHL ref and a good friend, had worked the game. He came up to me afterwards and laughingly said, "Oh no! Do we have to look forward to ANOTHER generation of Howes acting like that?"

MARTY: I get more upset about losing games today as a coach, than I ever did as a player. I think when you're playing there's something you can do about it, but when you're coaching, you find yourself wishing you could get out there and do it yourself. It's more frustrating! I take defeat harder now than I did when I was playing. When we were growing up, we used to lose a lot. As we progressed in our careers, into the bantam and midget divisions, we started winning more than we were losing. After a while we were rarely losing. We had great coaches like Carl Lindstrom, Pete McGonigal and Jim Chapman. Still, I took those fewer losses in stride; I figured we were going to come back and do well the next time. We always made it to the nationals and most of the time we won. We became accustomed to winning. We played on very strong teams, with extremely talented players, able to compete with the Canadian teams.

I'm similar to my dad in that I'm pretty easy going and quiet. I don't talk a whole lot, nor does Gordie. I'm not as patient with the public as Gordie. Besides, nobody's as good as Gordie.

Gordie's amazing when you think about it. Even when he's had a lack of sleep on the trips that he goes on, he's still so patient.

Every place he goes somebody wants to have dinner with him, and keep him up late exchanging stories with him: He'll get in late, awaken for an early flight to some other destination, and repeat the same scenario.

He's not a twenty year-old, so I don't know how he does it with the lack of sleep he gets. But, you can tell when he's really tired. He gets big bags under his eyes and he'll do some yawning. Even when he's tired, he's still nice to people, even if they're rude to him. I can't go that far. I have limits.

Dad's very smart and witty, and most of that is self-taught. When he grew up, I don't think education was that much of a priority in his life. His lack of education probably bothers him now. I would have loved to have gone to college, that was one thing I wanted before I went into pro hockey. I am still an extremely poor reader. I was diagnosed as having dyslexia. My mom used to take me to a clinic, and they'd go through all those tests and give me reading drills. When you have visual problems, you look at sentences and you'll skip back and forth so you're not fluid in your reading. When you're like that, you don't like to read. Some people and teachers will just label you as a bad reader. I was fortunate that a third grade teacher recognized my handicap and contacted my mother. The reading clinic therapy improved my reading ability.

Perhaps my dad had a mild dyslexia; we suspect his mother did as well. I always think about Eddie Shack, when the topic of reading comes up, because Eddie, who has had a reading problem for years, always says, "I don't need to know how to read as long as I know how to count!" (Money, that is.)

I get along with my brothers and my sister very well, even though Cathy used to tell on us all the time. "Oh, Marty did this or Mark did that," and we used to threaten—we're going to kill you if you say anything. First thing you know—"mommy, mommy, Marty said he's going to kill me."

I don't see the family all that much because we live in different states. Lately, I've seen Murray more, because I've built a deck and remodeled his house for him. As we were growing up, with Murray and Cathy, there was a four-year age difference. We wouldn't have any of the same friends, and I think we used to tease Murray a lot and he used to hide from me. He was the reader in the family. He used to consume books. He'd just read all the time and play with his toy soldiers. He'd find a quiet place to get away from us so he could read and not have the war zone he created, destroyed.

I think my mother gets a bad rap because she has firm convictions. It's like any agent, lawyer or manager who represents their clients. When she's fighting for the Howes, she has to be even stronger. If it wasn't for her courage and fortitude, we wouldn't have done half the things we accomplished. She's the one who has her name on the line and is responsible; which often makes you unpopular—more so if you're a woman. She works harder than anyone I know, doing things for us and others. People don't understand what she's done for her family and others. She's made my Dad's career and life so much more fruitful, and continuously helps her family whenever possible.

I think Gordie is Gordie, and everybody knows him. I don't know if it's true or not, but I believe in my heart that when he went to the WHA, Gordie may have gotten black-balled by the NHL for awhile. I don't think the hard feelings are there anymore, but I think at one point they existed.

I think he got the cold shoulder from some people. They needed to blame someone for what they created themselves. Gordie would be an ideal ambassador or a representative for NHL clubs, but no one has ever made him an offer. I think some people forget the things he did for the game of hockey and the NHL. The fact that my mother and dad are all but removed from hockey, allows them freedom they've never experienced before. They are much more in control of themselves.

I used to love to watch Bobby Orr, another star removed from the game and on his own. He had such speed, and he had strength, too. With his acceleration, he just took control of the game. There aren't too many players you can say that about. He was fun and exciting to watch. When I was younger, Bill Gadsby was probably my favorite player. He was always tough. He was aggressive, and he'd fall in front of pucks with his face or whatever it took to keep the opponent from scoring. He was a true and dedicated competitor. I used to watch him and try to emulate him in my game.

But I've gotta rate Gordie number one. When I was a kid, sitting in the stands at Olympia, the few times I did go to a Red Wings game, I never appreciated what Dad did or how magnificent he was. It's when you play *with* him, you're right there and you experience it firsthand. You realize he's pretty awesome. I'll say this: You don't want to play against him.

"I've always had great respect for Colleen and Gordie. As good as Gordie was on the ice, he has surpassed that off the ice as a human being."
— Bobby Orr

CHAPTER FOUR

SLOW DOWN, DAMN YOU

GORDIE: When you talk about hockey today, you see the kids mostly playing indoors, in very nice arenas. I was talking to some young fellows today, and I asked them "Have you ever shot a tennis ball?" And they said, "No, just a puck." So I was telling them the benefits of playing ball hockey on the road, or in a drive. What you create by doing that, basically, is a bouncing puck. It forces you to be light of hand to control it. I told them it taught me a tremendous amount of skill and dexterity.

I told them I used to practice that as a kid. Whenever I went anywhere, I was stickhandling down the road. And from the time I got my first pair of skates, I don't know if it was the challenge, and I don't even know if I thought I could do well at hockey, but I found it so exciting. Boy, you'd jump on the ice and you'd feel like a million dollars. Then later on, when I got a little bigger, I could skate on the interlocking ponds or sloughs there in Saskatoon, and I could go anywhere, for miles, all the way out to the airport. Suddenly the whole city was my backyard.

We could play hockey all day. Imagine a twelve-hour game. You'd play all day, go home and eat, come back and say "Who's winning?" I think hockey was a means of companionship to all of us, as kids. You don't have to say a whole lot. You just go out and play, have fun, and stay out of trouble.

The story has been told before, but the first pair of skates I got came about as a result of my mother's kindness. Mum had a little cup and she kept whatever change she had in there. And one day some lady came to the door, I think my mother recognized her. This was during the Depression, when there was little or no money and no jobs. My dad did have some jobs, because he could work with his hands and do so many mechanical things. And when this woman came to our door, I believe she was trying to get milk money for her family. My mother gave her some, and the lady gave Mum what she had in a gunny sack. It was like an old potato sack.

My mother came over with the sack, and I remember sitting down and waiting, because we had no idea what was in the sack. She dumped the sack over and, among some other things, there were skates in side. The skates were a little big for a five or six-year-old when this happened; but my sister, Edna, who's passed away now, and I just looked at those skates with big smiles.

Edna grabbed one skate, and I grabbed the other one and we ran out into the backyard. We had patches of ice outside where the snow would melt and then freeze in the garden. Everybody had a garden then, corn patches, potato patches, you name it. Edna and I were pushing ourselves across this ice on one skate. We'd run like hell and glide across the ice. We were having a great time. We did this every day until one day she got cold and went in the house to get warm. I followed her in and when she took the skate off, I put it on and she never saw it again.

That was when, all of a sudden, my backyard was replaced by the whole city, because I could really get around on skates. We used to get in behind the buses, we'd hang on to the bumpers and just ride for hours. The drivers didn't like that, so every now and then, they'd stop and chase us. That didn't deter us.

I even had street shoes with blades on them. I remember this was a period when my dad was on relief, and he'd take me down for a new pair of shoes. I'd take my old shoes off and put on the new ones. My dad would take the old shoes and put metal blades on them, so I had a street shoe with a straight blade. As soon as Dad would put them on my shoes, away I'd go. Geez, they made great skates!

One time I was skating with a friend of mine, Frank Sheddon, on the sloughs. We'd skate along, walk over the roads, and skate some more. Sometimes the slough area would be four or five feet deep. This day my buddy Frank is in that area and the ice starts turning soft and flexible. That's when, as you're skating, water starts accumulating under and you had to get by it. You'd have to skate like crazy. Then suddenly I heard—splash! That's when Frank fell through the ice and for a second he was in over his head. It was freezing cold, too. He got out all right, but we had about a mile to go to get home. We were both scared.

Have you ever seen a clothesline in a high wind, with a pair of body underwear flying stiff as a board? That was how Frank looked. He was awfully sick after that; probably had pneumonia. He was just a frozen body by the time we got home.

The next day, I went over to ask how he was doing. And Mr. Sheddon, who was a real nice man, asked me if I was going out for the Red Wing Pee Wee hockey team. I said, "Well, I don't have the equipment." He went in and got me all of Frank's bags and equipment and said, "Here, use these. See if you can make the team." So I did make the team, and he let me keep some of Frank's things. The skates I got to use were nickel plated. My first nickel-plated skates! They were beautiful. I was just flying with those blades. I'd never skated with anything so nice in my entire life. Half the time I was skating, I was jumping up in the air just so I could look down and see them. I'm sure Mr. Sheddon never knew what he did for me, and I've never forgotten it.

When we used to skate on the river as kids, we did something foolish. In the winter, the ice companies used to cut big chunks of ice out of the river to sell for people's ice boxes. They'd use a big saw, like lumberjacks use, cut the ice in blocks, pull 'em out of the water and put 'em on the wagon in sawdust to keep 'em until the summer. I think you'd put a 50 pound chunk of ice in the old ice boxes in order to keep milk and food from spoiling.

After the men cut the ice blocks, but before they'd get pulled out, we'd skate like hell toward that area. When we got up to them, we'd skate over all the loose blocks. These blocks were bobbing around in the water, and we'd have to go stepping over them real fast. Oh, those guys would scream and holler at us. If one of us fell, of course, we would have been in real trouble. We drove those men crazy, but they could never catch us.

According to my Dad, Vic was always the better hockey player, better than me. He was so funny. And Vern, my oldest brother, was the best of us all, so Dad said. It wasn't until Dad was old, on his death bed, that he finally gave me more credit. He was kidding me, and said, "Aw, I saw a few games on television. I guess you were better than your brothers."

Vern was the best mechanic in the family. He would help Dad out a lot while "yours truly" would be sitting there handing Dad different socket wrenches and screwdrivers, while I watched the guys skate or play ball. He'd ask for a three-quarter socket, and I'd hand him a screwdriver. And he'd poke his head out and say "Go play your damn ball."

My father has been depicted by some people as being so rough and tough, but God, he was also so helpful to me. When I was at King George school, I used to shoot a puck and a ball at the side of our house for hours at a time. We had a shingled veranda, which ran about halfway or two-thirds the way around the house. It was a great target, and I'd sit back and fire away; breaking a lot of shingles. The veranda was getting down to the bare plank boards. My dad came out of the house one day and looked at it. "Come here," he said, "we're going to do something." And he took me by the hand and we walked down to the Quaker Oats mill. When railroad grain cars would come in there, they had big plywood stoppers on the doors. So we picked up a couple of them and Dad carried them home. He leaned one up against the house, and put the other one on the driveway, and said "Now, shoot to your heart's content." He didn't get mad at me or give me a kick in the rear end. He helped me out, and I think of that when people say that he was mean. They obviously never knew him.

Oh, he was a powerful man. He wouldn't take any guff from anybody. And he told me not to, either. We were playing pool one night at a tavern, when I was a bit older, and this guy kept bumping Dad's hand every time he was about to shoot. Dad never hit with his fists, he hit with the butt of his hand. He drilled this guy alongside the jaw, and his whole body cleared the end of the table. The owner of the place said "Ab, you better get out of here, I think you killed him." It turned out the guy was okay, but he was out for a while. But that was Dad. "Don't take guff from anybody."

And he said if I wanted to play hockey, to do my best and not complain. And if I couldn't do the job, don't cry about it, just quit. Well, he was talking to the wrong guy about quitting.

There was a man named Adams who lived about a mile from us, and we'd go to his place to play ball hockey. My dad used to do some work with Mr. Adams because he was in construction. And he had a rink he built in his yard that we used to play on. He put chicken wire around it that went up about twenty feet. This was so that nothing flew out of it. It was about eighty feet long, and maybe thirty feet wide. The nets were extremely small, and we'd play there all day long. That was where I learned to stickhandle and hand-eye coordination. Mr Adams had cut out a section of the wire located over the window to the house! When those dang tennis balls would get frozen they would really hurt, so all we had to do was rap on the window, and Mrs. Adams would throw a new tennis ball out to us. We'd throw the old one in for her to thaw it out in the kitchen.

I remember at that place he also had built a horseshoe pit. And he and my dad were good horseshoe players, even to the point that they used to play at night. The only way to see was to wire light bulbs to the top of the horseshoe pegs, and they used to throw at night. They very seldom would break a bulb. They were pretty darn good.

I think the most teams I ever played for at one time was five. I played for as many teams as I could, I just loved to play. Let's see, I played on our school team. There was a mercantile league that the business people put together. I would play regularly scheduled Pee Wees and Bantams with my age group as I got older. I played on a church team, and I played on a team for pick-up games. I would just change sweaters, and go from one team to the other. I went looking for teams. I wanted to play as much as I could. I probably started playing that much when I was around ten or eleven. Five teams at once, boy that was fun. It's unfortunate that so many rules and regulations prohibit or hinder children's ability to have more exposure to do more of what they love.

It's always been said, and it's true, that I ate my meals with my skates on. That's a fact. Mum would spread newspapers over the linoleum floor in our house so I didn't have to take off my skates to eat. I'd skate down the ice on the ruts in the road to home whenever I got hungry or cold. I'd go home, get warmed up, eat, and go right back out to play more.

We could skate on the roads because we had gravel roads with four ruts in them from the cars. With the heavy snow, the roads were always covered, and during the day the top of the snow would melt a little bit then re-freeze as nice sheets of ice. So you just stepped out onto those roads. Hell, I could skate anywhere. We'd play after school every day, and on weekends we'd go from early morning to late night.

When I was playing goaltender for King George School, in order to improve myself, I'd sit under a lamp post at night and let the guys shoot at me. And I had no mask. And no jock. That meant I had to be *very* fast, especially on the low shots.

When I was a goaltender and first started playing indoors, we used to play in this really cold rink. We would walk to the rink, and the guys would light matches to try and thaw out my pads. Winky Smith was a neighbor, and he and I used to walk to the games together. His uncle was blind, and he'd walk down to the games with us sometimes, too. It was amazing. He'd come down and watch the games. That's what he always said. Actually, he'd just listen, and there'd be enough people talking about what was going on that he could sit there and enjoy it.

When we played for some of those different teams, we used to have to get our parents' signatures, a signature from our school, and one from a church in order to play. It was a way of trying to discipline us. We would go to the Salvation Army Hall and attend their services to get their signatures as church signatures. We'd be in the middle of the service, and they'd stop to announce, "We have four young men who are due on the ice very shortly"—and we were out of there.

I even did duty with the Salvation Army band to qualify for a team. I was tapping drums with them, trying to keep time with the music. Then we sang, and that was the thing that killed me. I was not the outgoing type where I could perform, and I couldn't read in front of people. That *really* bothered me. One of the churches had me read in front of everybody, and that was the last time I attended. It would embarrass the heck out of me, and the other kids always laughed at me.

As a kid, I played all different hockey positions. For a while I was a goaltender, but could play defense and forward anytime. When I went to Winnipeg, to the New York Rangers camp when I was fifteen, the guy handing out the equipment asked, "What position do you play?" I said "All of 'em." He said, "Are you a smart aleck?" I said, "No sir, I've played goalie, defense, and forward." He said, "Okay, we'll make the question easy. What would you *like* to play?" So I said, "defense." I didn't know why, I just figured I was a good defenseman. So, I had my first pro tryout on defense.

People have written that I'm naturally ambidextrous, but the reason I could shoot the puck with both hands is because I started playing goalie as a kid. The only thing I could find to use as a catching glove was a first-baseman's mitt that went on my left hand. Now, I was a right-handed shot, but because I didn't have a catching glove to wear on my right hand, I had to become a left-hand shooting goaltender. I had to hold the stick with my right hand and keep my left hand free to catch the puck. And I learned to shoot the puck from the left as a goalie, clearing it up the ice and into the corners. And since I shot right-handed when I wasn't playing goalie, I developed a shot from both sides. I didn't even know I was doing it for a long while, switching hands to shoot from either side. It was Jack Adams who brought it to my attention at my first Red Wing training camp. I had gone in on the goalie during practice, switched hands and scored. And he called me over and said "What are you doing?" I said, "What's that, sir?" He said "You shoot both ways." I said, "I do?" I had no idea I was doing it. Here I was training myself for hockey, setting myself up for the game, and I didn't even know it. And it all goes back to being a goaltender as a kid and not being able to get a catching glove for my right hand.

At the old Saskatoon Arena, which my dad helped build, there were two small dressing rooms that the players could squeeze into. As a kid, I would wait outside the arena, and when refreshments would come for the players, beer and pop to be delivered to the dressing rooms, I'd volunteer to help. That way I could get in the rink and see the games. That was how I first encountered Sid Abel. He played for Moose Jaw, and he let me carry his skates into the arena one time. The players were always pretty nice to us when he walked into the dressing rooms.

Sometimes we'd cause trouble to get in the rink. There was an old tractor that they'd keep outside the rink, and we'd start it up and run it up against the building. We were little farm boys, and we'd been on tractors before and knew they didn't have a key to start some of them. That thing would be banging against the arena, chugging away like hell, and the wheels would be going and going and just digging a hole. Then, when the maintenance guy would come running out to stop it, we'd run inside. And eight of us would see the game.

Ab Welsh was my hero in those days. He played for Saskatoon, on the senior team, and he took me in the dressing room one day, and I got the autographs of all the players. And he asked, "Which way do you shoot, kid?" I said "right, sir." He said "good" and handed me a stick. Boy, that meant a heck of a lot to me. I came out of there about fifteen feet tall. He didn't know it, but he made a friend for life that day. I guess that was about the first new stick I ever had. It was a beautiful stick. It was a lie seven. And I think that had a great influence on me, because that's the lie I used throughout my career. I remember when I met up with Sid, I saw he took a rasp and rounded off the heel and toe of his stick so that he could pull in the puck when it was close to his feet and shoot it. So I learned from him, too, just by watching.

When we played hockey as kids, we'd do anything to keep our sticks usable. We'd glue it, tape it and tack a little metal on it. We did everything since we couldn't afford sticks. They would wear down from playing in the street and get real thin. Sometimes it would end up that we were playing with a toothpick. It was heartbreaking when they'd break.

One day I became a hero to my friends. There was a big fight in a pro game at the arena, everybody on both teams was in it. When everyone wasn't looking, I ran down to the bench and stole all the sticks. I grabbed them all and went home. I was just a kid, but I was big enough to carry all of them. Nobody noticed me because everybody was watching or was in the big fight. I gave them to my buddies, because we didn't have sticks. "You a left? Here you go." Actually, most of them were straight-bladed in those days, so it didn't matter much. It was brutal that I did that and I can't believe it was me taking something like that. I was trying to survive, I guess. And maybe it's why I give so much time, money and other things away to people today. Oh yeah, that was brutal. I don't believe I did that.

I was a kid determined to get my uniform. We had nothing, but we rink rats would get some of the lesser stuff that other players threw away. When equipment got too cut up and looked too bad, it was thrown out as junk. Sometimes I took the stuff that had been thrown out, used by other rink rats, and thrown away again. I'd pick it up and take it home. I'd sew the heck out of gloves, out of any kind of equipment, and use it.

Quite often, I played with magazines wrapped around my shins. And if there was anything else you could get in there, you'd put it in. I'd find shin pads that were like bamboo poles and were all ripped, and pieces would be missing, but who cared? You put it all around your legs and put rubber bands around the pants to hold it all together. A lot of us played that way. As a matter of fact, when I was a goalie, I only had these partial shin pads with just a little bit of padding. One of the senior hockey players was shooting at me, but he kept it low. I was making saves, and I cringed at a couple of kicks. He came in and said "What do you have underneath that?" I said "nothing." He went in and gave me a pair of shin pads to wear underneath so he wouldn't hurt me. That's how I went on to learn to play goal. It was a valuable hockey learning experience, being a goaltender. But going against the big guys in goal is where I learned how and when to shoot the puck. You have to think of the puck as having eyes. What it sees is totally different than what you see as the shooter. You try to envision the net and the goaltender as a target from where the puck is positioned rather than from where you're viewing it. When you're in a slump, all you look at is the goalie. When you're hot, all you look at are the empty spaces all around him (or her!).

Another way I got hockey gear was from various local people who helped me. A fellow by the name of Rolley Howes had a hardware store in town, and he took a liking to me, I guess. His store sold sporting goods. Mum bought me a hockey stick there, for my birthday. He said, "Young man, if you score a hat trick, or get a total of three points in the next game, I'll give you a pair of hockey gloves." I said "a cheap pair?" I was just joking, but he said "No, no, you'll get the best." We used to count the number of rolls of the back on the gloves to determine how nice the gloves were. Five rolls was the ultimate. The cheap gloves didn't have any rolls, just one big solid piece. And when you got gloves with rolls, wow! You could wear those gloves to school.

He had seen how we dressed. We played in regular street pants, and we'd slip the pads underneath them and put the rubber bands on. So Rolley knew we needed equipment. I think we were playing another town in a playoff game, and I got twelve points in the game, four goals and eight assists, I believe. So he said, "You exceeded the limits a little. We'll throw in a pair of shin pads, too." And, when the gloves had four rolls on them it was really getting exciting.

One time in school hockey, playing for King George School, we had a game that I recall. My brother Vic and I were on the school team. We went down to the city arena; they weren't very good. We only played forty minutes. I made quite a few goals. And the guy calling the game, the referee, came over to me and said, "If you don't take a rest, I'm going to give you a penalty." I guess it doesn't sound too sportsmanlike.

Actually, I was the coach, because the teacher left the team in my hands. He said, "You can handle 'em." We only had ten or eleven guys, so I made three lines and three defenses and kept rotating everybody, and I stayed out there the whole time. I didn't want to come off. I was having a ball!

When I got back to school, Mr. Trickey called me into his office. Mr. Trickey was our coach, and he used to tell me when I said I wanted to get out of the nets, that I'd never make it out of Saskatoon unless I played goalie. Yeah, so for twenty some years afterward I used to send him letters. And he'd make a point whenever I was in Saskatoon, to show up to see me and we'd laugh about it. We became pretty close friends.

Anyway, I remember when he called me in after that game, he had me sit down. And he said, "Okay, our boys are back. How did we do today?" And I stood up and said, "King George won, sir, the score was sixteen to zero!" He said, "sixteen to zero. You really poured it on." And I said, "Yes, sir." "Well, who got all the goals?" And I said, "Vic and I." "Vic and you?" And I said, "Yeah, Vic got one."

So I got a lecture. He did not think that was very nice. Even though I told him that, unlike other games, I did sit out some of the time. He said, "You did?" And I said, "Yes, sir." So he said, "Very good." I didn't tell him it was because the referee told me if I didn't, I'd end up in the penalty box.

My first big All-Star game during the time I played for King George was when I was a goalie. We won our championship with me in the net. Because they only picked two players from each school for the All Star team, I was the back-up goalie. We were losing three to nothing at the end of five minutes so they pulled the first goalie and put me in. And I think we won six to four or something like that. That was my first big game in Saskatoon. We played at a rink that held around 4,000 and it was packed. You couldn't get into the building. It was the All Star game between the East and West school districts of Saskatoon. The Saskatchewan River in town was the dividing line between east and west. I was around thirteen or fourteen years old, and had such a good record as a goalie. That was when he told me I should stay in net. As I had been told, "Otherwise I'd never get out of Saskatoon."

Mr. Trickey was very good to me. I remember that was the first year that I started to enjoy school, and it was because of him.

Isn't it something, what a teacher can do?

And I remember, it was a macho thing at school if you could kick a football up on top of the building. I was one of the kids who could get it that high. I'd nail that sucker up there, and the janitor would have to go up and get it. Then what they did was make you write twenty pages of history as a punishment. So I said I'd write pages 150 to 170. So Mr. Trickey said, "Now let's see. Before I even check the pages, let me guess that you wrote out page 150 to page 170." And I said to myself, "How did he know?" Well, he knew because most of those pages were pictures. He was wise to me. I'm sure he had heard those page numbers before.

As Marty and Mark did when they were young, I often played in leagues with guys that were a lot older. During the war, the Saskatoon senior club would run a few guys short, and they'd ask me and some of my friends to play for them at various times. I was probably fourteen or so at the time. We played in a town one night where the crowd was throwing stuff at us, spitting at us. I thought, oh, this is fun, because I'd never played in front of a crowd, other than in Pee Wee hockey. We were winning, and the other team couldn't keep up with us, so they decided to show a little muscle. Then a big fight broke out, and the fans started coming out on the ice and THEY got into it. Beautiful! I can't remember his name, but one of the veterans on the team grabbed me and put me behind him. He said, "Kid, stay there. And if anybody gets by me, you hit him on the head." Well, when I'm scared I listen very carefully!

So there's fighting going on everywhere, and this guy comes around the veteran, and I take my stick and—BANG—I nail him right in the head and down he goes. As he was crumpled there on the ice, I look and see a yellow stripe on his pants. That means one thing, RCMP...Royal Canadian Mounted Police. And the veteran looked at me and says, "Oh God! That was the wrong guy! Let's get out of here." I guess I knocked him out. I thought after that they'd be after me to put me in jail, but no one ever came to get me.

When I was fourteen, I got to play on a team from Saskatoon in a town game against the Bentley brothers, Max and Doug, who were from Delisle, Saskatchewan (they were very famous there). The business people sponsored us as a local club. I was big for my age, and this was sort of an exhibition game in which I was playing against men. Three of the Bentley brothers were playing in the NHL that season. They were all great athletes, I played baseball with quite a few of them later on.

Well, that was one of those nights when I could have skated forever. You know, you're young and you're fresh and you're full of excitement just playing against great players like the Bentleys. I remember I got a couple of goals, and we had them down four to nothing. I was flying along when all of a sudden I got speared, right in the belly, from Doug Bentley, who played for the Black Hawks. He had to be ten or twelve years older than me. I went down with a big "ohhhh." I'm sucking wind when Max looks down at me and says, "Slow down, damn you."

It was years later when I was once again playing against Doug, only in the NHL. He was still with Chicago and I was with the Red Wings. One night I drilled him and when he went down, I leaned over and said, "Slow down, damn you." We talked about it later, and he got a big kick out of it. It shows that you never know what's going to become of kids that you play against and you hurt.

That was how I had my understanding with Harry Watson. He was from Saskatoon, and started out in the NHL around 1940. I got a chance to play against him one time when he played for the

Number Four Air Base in Saskatoon while he was in the service during the war. I was around fourteen or fifteen at the time, and it was another one of those times where I felt like I could skate all day. After the game he came and asked my name. I was excited that he was interested in me. That was a sign I had impressed him.

Then about four years later, when I was in my first year with the Red Wings, and we were playing against Toronto I found myself opposite this same guy, Harry Watson, who was a big left-winger. He went into the corner with me early in the game, and he said, "Look out, Gordie!" I thought, boy, that's rare. Why would he be warning me? He threw the puck out, I looked at him but I didn't say anything. Maybe a period or two later, I'm in a position where he's got his head down, and I said "Look out, Mr. Watson!" And he slowed up, and we held the puck with our skates to get a whistle. He looked at me and said "We're gonna get along just fine." And that was a very unusual relationship between two players—you don't hurt me and I won't hurt you!

My first training camp was in 1944. I went into Winnipeg, Manitoba with the New York Rangers. Contrary to common belief—that I was so shy I left training or not good enough to make the team and they sent me home—are not accurate. The management did take me upstairs to talk to me. They wanted me to go to the Notre Dame School in Wilcox, Saskatchewan outside Regina where I could work further on my hockey skills. They also wanted me to sign a 'C' form, which would have automatically made me a New York Ranger. The first thought I had was, I'm not Catholic. And the second thought was, I'd be going to a regimental school awfully far from home. Heck, I decided I'd rather go home, and that's what I did. I *was* very lonely at the Winnipeg camp. That's when Alf Pike, a New York Ranger veteran, gave me some guidance. He'd get me in the food line at the hotel so I could be sure to get something to eat. I was so backward then, I'd just sit in the background and watch everyone else. When you're in a strange environment, most people feel awkward. I'd never been out of Saskatoon, except to play one game in Regina, Saskatchewan about one hundred miles away.

The first day I went over to the rink, the Rangers gave me equipment which consisted of a lot of things I'd never seen or put on before. I decided to watch Alf Pike put on a garter belt. I had never owned one of these. I was used to wearing any equipment I had right under my street pants. I didn't even have a cup protector until I was much older. It was discarded in a dressing room by some rink rats in Saskatoon, the kids who always hung around the rink and got the best of anything thrown away. What they didn't want they left behind for the kids like me. I sewed the jock strap together and taped up the broken plastic cup that went inside it. Obviously, I felt grateful for this find, because I even had to play *goalie* without a cup protector.

There were a lot of brawls in those days. When my brother Vern played, he used to be the main instigator in most of the fights. He wasn't that big, but he could hit like a sledgehammer. He got into a few problems in the league he was in. This was before any of the bench brawling fighters were being fined. If there was a fight, the whole team joined in. As a young man, I didn't get in that many brawls. I was usually playing with guys much older than I was, so I was smart enough to stay out of it.

I was a big kid. I was six feet tall at fifteen years-old, and hovered around 200 pounds at the same age. Then my growth stopped suddenly, and I played all my career at six feet in height. I always joke that I'm not that tall now because I've lost some of my hair. My weight also remained the same throughout my playing years. I was usually between 196 and 204 pounds.

Compared to the size of players in hockey now, I was one of the top five big guys in the league. On the current Red Wings team, I'd be right in the middle in terms of size. I'm smaller than at least half of the current players. It's amazing how much bigger some of the pros are today, such as Eric Lindros and Mario Lemieux. But size doesn't mean a hell of a lot if a guy doesn't have heart or guts. Just look at Dino Ciccarelli on the current Red Wings team. He takes on guys when he practically has to use a springboard to hit them in the chin. Scouts are always looking for size though; and, since I was big as a kid, size was one of the reasons that probably got me the invitation to my first pro training camp.

The following year, Fred Pinckney, a Red Wings scout, asked me if I'd like to go to the Red Wings camp. I said, "Where is it?" and he told me it was in Windsor, Ontario, outside of Detroit. I asked who else was going, and he said there were about eighteen of my friends. Well, that perked my interest to go with them. I thought, "Oh great, I'll be with guys I know." What Fred Pinckney did for me was buy me a whole outfit of clothing. There was a coat, jacket, pants, and shoes. It was the first suit I ever owned. He even bought me a nice hat, too, but I used it as a tip for the porter on the train. I figured he could use that fedora. I sure didn't want it. As we rode on the train to Windsor, Ontario, I thought I was on top of the world, being a part of the Red Wings Camp for the first time.

It wasn't my dad telling me to sign with the Red Wings, which is another old fable. There was also a false story about Dad getting money to steer me to the Red Wings. My Dad was never in on my going to the Red Wings Camp. When I knew my friends were going there, I wanted to be with them.

The Wings signed me and assigned me to their Junior Club in Galt, Ontario. It was the first time I felt deceived by Detroit at the early age of sixteen. They told me after I got to camp that I couldn't play any games there, only practice. Murray Armstrong, an old New York Americans defenseman, was the coach. He said I had the option of going back to Saskatchewan and playing, or I could stay there in Galt and practice with the team every day. By staying I'd be registered as an easterner, he told me, and be able to play hockey in the east. It was just that they couldn't get me an automatic transfer from the west to the east because of my age. This is what I was told, but it wasn't the whole story.

The fact is, there was a limit of three players permitted to make that transfer in one year and the Red Wings already had transferred three players. Apparently, the selection for third player had been between Terry Cavanaugh, who went on to become the Mayor of Edmonton, and me. Terry was chosen because he was older, and a left wing. They thought he would be the better of the two of us. They chose him over me, and put him in the lineup while I only practiced all season. As I recall, I played one game as a Junior, and that was for the Galt Red Wings, in Windsor, right across the river from Detroit. It was an exhibition game. I got their attention, and they liked me because I hit somebody and knocked them out. I thought, they're impressed! But they still couldn't let me play. It was unfortunate, because I sat out the whole year. The plus was that I got in about one hundred practices.

I ended up leaving school while I was in Galt. I was away from home, and I intended to go to the local high school there to continue my education. Then I remember walking up to the school with my brand new textbooks, with the intention of taking these courses. Everyone was saying hello to each other, while I was standing there like an awkward stranger. It was then that I decided to give my notebook away to someone. I, then, walked down to the nearby railroad tracks. When I came to the first big factory I saw, I went inside. It was the Galt Metal Industries Company, and I told them I wanted a job.

The person at the plant asked me for the name of somebody to vouch for me, and I gave them the name of an official with the hockey club. They phoned this person who told them that if I wanted to work, let me work. So the company gave me a job. This was in 1944, and World War II was still on. They trained me to make shrouds for the air cooling system of the Mosquito Bomber. I did all the measuring for the patterns. I did some spot welding while I was there. Then they sent me over to Plant 2 as an inspector. I was getting up in the world. There I had to put these pieces in a vice. These were trench mortar shells. My job was to turn the air up, and ream out all the burrs from the shells. I was pretty good at it. I also had a micrometer in order to take readings. I didn't know enough about micrometers, so I couldn't read it. So I just scratched it where the line should be. I enjoyed doing that work. As an inspector, I'd close down a machine if it wasn't working right. Imagine somebody throwing a mortar in a tube if the fins were wrong. You'd probably lose a couple of your men. I knew it was very important that I properly measure. I'd just keep walking all day around the plant, feeling good about being a responsible employee.

I never knew how much women could swear until I worked in that plant during the war. I worked the entire year I was with the Galt club. I'd work, then go down to the rink, practice with the team, and then go home. I was satisfied, but I think the club should have insisted that I go to school. I know it was my decision not to go to school, but what does a sixteen year old understand about the ramifications of a decision like that? I feel now they should have given me better guidance and made certain I got my schooling.

Galt management said they wanted to do something for me, and I told them I would like to have a Red Wings jacket. I didn't have many clothes anyway, and that would be my main, number one gear. I asked Jack Adams about it, and he said that would be no problem. I waited, but never got a jacket for an entire year.

I wanted that jacket so bad all the time I was in Galt. I remember that quite a few times I walked down to the railroad station by myself. I knew when the Red Wings' train would be coming through town traveling to games. I'd just wait there for them. I figured that if they stopped for anything, I'd go aboard and see if I could ask Adams about my jacket, but the train never stopped. They went rolling right on through every time. I'd just walk back home.

I came back to training camp in 1945, and Adams told me they were going to turn me pro and send me to Omaha. I was now seventeen, and it sounded great. I would get $2,350 for the year. It was then I reminded him that I never got the jacket he had promised me. He chuckled and told me not to worry about it, and that he'd see that I got a jacket. Guess what? I never got it *that* year either.

It was the following year, when I was assigned to the Red Wings, the big club, that I said, "Mr. Adams, it has been two years now and I haven't got my jacket yet." He then told me to go downtown to get a couple of them and sign for it. I was so thrilled and went downtown with Marty Pavelich and Ted Lindsay, and bought one with big heavy slit pockets. It was smooth, like satin on the outside, with leather sleeves and an alpaca lining. It had a big "D" with "Red Wings" written on it. It looked like the most beautiful jacket in the world.

I also saw my first NHL game in Toronto, when I was with the Galt Red Wings. We used to play on Sunday, so the club took us to Toronto on a Saturday night and got us in the doors. I remember being in the stands and watching a guy named Cowley, a centerman for Boston. He was really impressive. He skated down the ice and made this real quick movement to his left. He caught Turk Broda moving and fired the puck from the blue line and scored. I said, "What a fantastic goal." I can still see it! I remember as I watched that game, how I was looking for all the guys whose pictures I'd collected.

I was very impressed with the speed and power of the NHL game. The atmosphere was unbelievable—and so exciting! All those people crowded in there. I never saw such a big crowd. We were way up top in the standing room area. I could have cared less, I was so thrilled just to be there.

Somehow I got stranded after that game. The guy who gave me the ride to the rink told me to meet him at the "Honey Dew" restaurant. Heck, there were about eight "Honey Dew" restaurants around the Toronto area. I didn't know which one was the right one. At one o'clock in the morning, I still hadn't located him. I had no money, I'm in Toronto, I'm sixteen and my home is in Galt, Ontario. I guess he was with some woman. But there I was looking for him for my ride home. I felt abandoned. I remember that as vividly as the game. Not knowing what else to do, I went back to the arena and someone let me inside. I was freezing, hungry, and didn't know what to do. I sat there in a corner. Then, at about 1:30 a.m. my ride showed up. I never liked him again.

I felt very good about myself, and about my chances to someday play in the NHL. I was confident! I could see success. I went to training camp with the Red Wings in Windsor and, during a game, I had come down on Jack Stewart and Bill Quackenbush, their two best defensemen. I went through the middle and scored left-handed on Harry Lumley. The puck got away from me at one point so I reached over left-handed, shot it, and in it went. That's when Jack Adams called me over and said, "What's your name?" And I said, "Howe." "Are you related to this man over here?" he asked pointing to Syd Howe, a star with the Wings for quite a while. (I had collected his picture, too.) I responded with a "No." Then they brought Syd over and they took a picture of the two of us. After that, I thought that there was a big chance for me in hockey. When I skated, I watched people and everything they did. And I would try to stay with the fastest guy on the ice, I could keep up most of the time.

I would always ask questions. I was a student of the game. I remember one of the old senior players taking the time to show me how to shoot a puck when the puck is a fully, extended arm length and stick length away from me. He'd bring it in toward him and fire it away with a little wrist shot. I wasn't totally aware of what I was doing, but I practiced it until it was refined.

In fact, as I think back, I worked hard during most of my life to prepare myself for the next hockey season. Early on, I worked a lot with my dad. One of the things my father did all his life was work with his hands. He was powerful! I saw him lift things I wouldn't even attempt. I think he could lift more than me. With all that training he put me through, I could lift five cement bags at once. I guess they weighed 94.6 or 96.4 pounds each. I'd grab them, kitty-corner, from a bended knee position. My hands were strong enough that I could grip them, lift them, turn around, take a step and put them on the wagon. My Dad would always brag about how much I could lift, so I could never embarrass him by dropping the bags. I paid the price for this pride by having to undergo a hernia operation the first year in Omaha.

I tried to build up the strength in my hands, too. It pays off in most sports. I could hit a baseball and a golf ball a long way. The strength I developed always improved my ability to be better than the next guy.

I knew enough to build up my strength to play hockey. I even selected a certain job if I knew it would help my physical development.

I became aware of my body building needs. I knew strength and power had to be important, because every time I heard people talking about a hockey game, they'd talk about how strong this guy or that guy was. That made me even more aware. Strength was noticed by everyone.

The first job that I had which involved my Dad, was working on what was known as a "Crocker Dam." The crew would go off shore to ten feet of water, and they would cut through the ice, and pile drive timbers into a 30-foot square into the river bed. They'd pump out water so the men could build an intake on the river bed, and would then attach pipes from the intake to pump city water to the water treatment plant. I worked on those kinds of projects handling some of the concrete. I also worked after school hours and on weekends for some overtime when they were pushed for time to get projects finished. I got used to manual labor because it was nice getting a check. I was fourteen years old then.

Because I was tall and strong, my dad let me run the cement mixer. It took forty-two shovels of gravel for every load. I remember every one. Then I had to put the powdered cement into the mixer and keep water running in there constantly. Since I ran a machine, I received mechanic's wages which was around eighty cents an hour. The rest of the men were making around fifty cents. This pal of mine, Wilf, and I used to bug some of the

110

older workers, because we were always working on conditioning for hockey. When we were digging with shovels to lay new sidewalks where the old wood walks used to be, Wilf and I did it like the shovels were pogo sticks. We'd just bounce on the shovels, and we'd clean out 600-700 feet of area before the other eight guys could clear out a hundred feet. My dad was the foreman, and one day he came along and said, "Look, you guys better slow down." I guess some of the older guys thought we were trying to make them look bad. Sometimes we'd find money underneath the wood sidewalks. We'd put that in a special bucket. Dad would take some of that money and tell us to go down to the corner store and buy some chocolate milk for ourselves as a treat. We'd take a half hour break and come back.

There was a guy my dad once worked with, by the name of "Frenchy." He lived not too far from our house with his wife and kids. Since I was making those extra wages as a mechanic, I asked my dad if he would take and give it to Frenchy, and give me Frenchy's check. I knew I only needed my job for the summer months, but Frenchy needed all the money he could get to feed his family. The gesture worked to the benefit of Wilf and me because in the minds of the workers, we went from the two brats to two really nice kids. It was just a simple gesture that turned our whole summer job around. The older guys really liked us.

My whole attention during those years was directed toward being involved in athletics. I loved to play soccer. Even at the age of seventeen, when I turned professional in hockey, I always went back home and played soccer for the summer. Soccer was great for conditioning. I played the center-half position. I was tall, and pretty strong, and I could kick equally well with both feet, which was something unusual I was told. There were a couple of English exchange students playing with me on the team. One was a center, and the other played an inside right position, while I played inside left. Whenever we'd get penalty kick opportunities, they'd let me take them. I probably had whatever it took to be an ambidextrous kicker. If I had been fully ambidextrous, I'd be able to write left-handed and right-handed, and I can't do that.

When I played golf, the only clubs I used were a three-wood, a five-wood, and a seven-wood. That's all I put in the golf bag, then I started putting a left-handed five-iron in there in case I got in trouble. It came in handy a lot. I did this "three clubs in a bag" technique while playing once in a Detroit tournament. I hit my first shot up against a tree. Next I hit a left-handed five-iron about 155 yards and landed it about six-feet from the hole. It was then that I realized that being able to shoot left and right in golf gave me a real advantage. I used to practice doing this all the time. There was a driving range in Detroit, in the area of Seven Mile and Wyoming; where I used to hit balls by the hour; switching right, then left, right, then left. Most of the people out there had never seen anyone practice this way.

The longest drive I ever hit was about 340 yards. That was measured and marked off at the course we played during our Red Wings training camp at Sault Ste. Marie, Michigan. That shot was hit right-handed!

The first big fight I ever had in a game was in Omaha when I was with the Aksarben (Nebraska spelled backwards) team. It was against a big guy named Harry Dick (true name), a defenseman, who played for Kansas City. I was fairly quick, and I landed about five punches. I was doing pretty good. Meanwhile, I could see his right hand cocking; pulling back, like in a cartoon. Like a machine, he was winding up. And when he threw it, he hit me in the chest and knocked me back about twenty feet. I hit the ice so hard I skidded on my shoulders. The guys ran over to me, and I'm laughing. They asked if I was okay, I said, "Yeah, but did he nail me!" I was excited, and it struck me so funny to think how I must have looked as I flew through the air. Here was this seventeen-year-old idiot out there, enjoying his own embarrassment.

One of the first guys I cut was Tommy Ivan, my first coach. It was in an East-West game and I went into the corner with him and he came out with four stitches in his cheek. The players told me it was a little bit of lumber that caused it! You can believe it!

I didn't date much as a teenager, even when I turned pro. I was only getting $2,300 a year, so how the heck was I going to take a girl out on that? I went out once with a teammate at Omaha named Barry Sullivan. He had a girl that looked like Elizabeth Taylor. She had a friend who would only go out if it was on a double date. That was the only date I had in Omaha. I had just turned seventeen, and only thought about hockey. I wasn't worried about having a social life. I was learning everything I could about hockey. Little did I know, I was only one year away from playing in the NHL.

> *"I've worked with a lot of players but Gordie
> was an easy lad to coach, the type of person
> who was a good listener. He would play any
> way that you wanted, both defensively and
> offensively. A real team player!
> Colleen was a fine girl, a real lady. She was
> always willing to do anything for the club and
> I enjoyed her company."*
> —*Tommy Ivan*

CHAPTER FIVE

WHAT ARE YOUR VALUES
OTHER THAN CARING?

COLLEEN: Through the years, I've done most of the planning in our lives. I especially enjoy developing activities that surprise people, create happiness and gratification or fulfill a need. It's all a part of my life and it's my forte. It's a delight for Gordie, because he always had the security of knowing I was very capable and that I would do whatever had to be done.

I never waited until he got home to resolve a challenge. I fixed it. To a degree, I became the home engineer. Gordie was gone so much of the time that when he did get a chance to be home, he was usually very tired, or he was called to go to an appearance for the club. There was no way for him to come home and take responsibility for anything. Besides I enjoyed planning and organizing our schedules, and being able to see the rewards from it. It's fun to create, develop, manage, and complete projects and reap the satisfaction of having participated in an idea that becomes a reality.

I'm a highly responsible person. I will do whatever has to be done, and people who work with me know that I'm tireless. Gordie saw the benefits of a teammate who could make decisions and make them happen. In many ways, managing a family is like managing a business. At times I felt I could run General Motors. There were so many hats to wear and responsibilities to carry out every day with no days off. The difference was, I was a one-woman show.

GORDIE: People have asked me if I ever felt Colleen was too much in control. I've told them, it's hard to feel that way when I know that Colleen does eighty or ninety percent of the work for our family and business. It's strange they ask me that question when I'm out playing golf, and Colleen is at home in the office, doing every task possible.

COLLEEN: Married couples often ask themselves who's going to be the disciplinarian? Who's going to manage the schedules, the kid's arrangements and so on? If you have two store managers what happens? I know, when it's time to make a decision, they're going to stand around and argue about it if they have a difference of opinion. I never disciplined our kids by saying "Wait til your father gets home." If our children misbehaved, or needed somebody to talk to them, I didn't wait a week, I took care of it then. If you don't take care of things promptly, everyone forgets what it was even all about. I was there full-time with our family, I know. Besides, why did Gordie want to come home, after being away for days or weeks and have his first contact with his family be about what anyone did wrong? He did, of course, know the circumstances and that was generally through the children.

In the years we were first married, I just yearned for the time we could afford two cars. One reason was I would always have to drive Gordie to the Michigan Central Station, which was located almost downtown Detroit on Michigan Avenue. I'd have one infant, and another just fifteen months older that I'd have to dress in clothes and snowsuits to take Gordie to the train. Then, I'd have to pick up Gordie at the station when the team would come back from road trips. They would always get in between two and four in the morning, unless the train was late, which was often. I would get the kids out of bed, dress them, and take them with me in the middle of the night. We only had one car, so it was either do this or I'd never have any transportation while Gordie was gone. We didn't get a second car until about 1960, when we moved out to Lathrup Village, just north of the city. This was after we had our first outside income from our corporate and outside revenue stream.

When Gordie was gone with the car, I would walk everywhere with the kids. That's why I still like to walk today. I've never yearned for extravagant clothes or other material things. (How many dresses and shoes can you wear anyway?) When we were married in 1953, Gordie was making about $7,500. That was not a lot of money, especially for a player who was leading the league in scoring every year and was a first-team All-Star, but there was little that could have been done about it at that time. It was a matter of too many players and too few teams. In retrospect, not making huge dollars may have been a blessing to us in forming our grass roots development. Too much, too fast, too young hasn't always proven to be what creates stable people.

If we had been wealthy, I don't think we would have taken the steps we did to diversify our interests. Nor do I think we would have been as prudent or appreciative of money. We really budgeted and saved. I did the budgeting then, and still do. We were always careful with our spending and plan to also treat ourselves to things, like a vacation to Florida. We learned to be wise with our money. We actually bought our first new home on Stawell Avenue in Detroit. I remember how nervous Gordie was when we signed that mortgage because, prior to this, he had never financed anything he owned. It scared me too, but not for the same reasons. I didn't think about him being injured and maybe losing his job. My thoughts just didn't work in that direction. I only wanted to make sure we had something to show for our money, that we could utilize as an asset. If we paid rent for a house it would leave us with nothing if we moved. The mortgage on our first home looked like the biggest debt we could imagine.

Gordie reflected to that time once, when we were in Hartford and we bought a new car. As we were driving out of the dealership, Gordie said "Do you realize that this car costs more than our first house?" He was right, the house cost $14,000. Marty and Mark were born while we were there, and by the time I was pregnant with Cathy, in 1959, we were a little cramped for space. Knowing we were still planning on other children, it was time to sell.

Being a hockey player can be a very transient job, and that was especially true in the old days. You never knew when you might be uprooted, and there wasn't the kind of money the players get now, so it was very hard to relocate. When I think of some of the hockey couples we knew, who had to move so often, it was not always a very pleasant or secure life for them. It was more like being a gypsy who has to be out of town on a minutes notice in the middle of the night. Some wives just stayed packed, in a sense. I remember listening to a game on the radio with Julie, the wife of Benny Woit, who played on the Red Wings with Gordie. It was a close game, and Benny accidentally put the puck into his own net causing the loss of the game. When this happened Julie got up and left the room, while I listened to the end of the game. I yelled "Julie, where are you?" She said "I'm packing the baby, and I'm packing the bags. I know when he comes home we'll be gone. We're gone." She was upset, and convinced that was the end of Benny in Detroit. She was right, although Jack Adams didn't trade Benny until after the season. We'll never know if that was the reason, but it showed me the kind of pressure we all endured.

GORDIE: I remember Jack Adams took Ted Lindsay and me in a car one day, and drove us to Oshawa. He said, "I want you two to see your next centerman." We watched Alex Delvecchio playing as a junior. Alex was already earmarked for centerman. That move eventually resulted in the trade of Dutch Reibel, who was our center when we won the Cup in 1955. I thought Dutchy was very good and didn't understand all of Jack's reasoning. Unfortunately for Dutch, he was one of those guys whose interest died when they traded him. He went to Chicago in all the many trades that were going on in the '50s. Being traded just kills some people.

In those days the way you knew you were traded was, if you came in for practice and both pair of your skates had been put under the bench, you were gone. Simple as that. They would phone down and tell Lefty Wilson, our trainer, what players were moving. I remember coming in one day, and seeing that five guys had two pair of skates under the bench. I also saw that one of them was Murray Oliver. It really bothered me because he was a friend, so much so that we had named our youngest son after him.

When the players would come into the dressing room they wouldn't always notice their skates right away. They weren't looking. Then Lefty called out five names and said "Jack Adams wants to see you." I remember Murray broke down and cried. It really devastated him. I tried to console him, and said "Murray, as much as you're gonna be missed here, you're going to find new friends in Boston. There are just as many nice guys on every other team, and you'll be okay." In a sense I always felt that when a player had a real problem was when he couldn't be traded. Murray ended up loving Boston and then he got traded from there to Minnesota! It took the heart out of him again, but he ended up enjoying Minnesota, too. In fact he still lives there. It can be

*Colleen, 1951—Bowling championship
awards. You can't beat those hats.*

Colleen 1950—Miss DSR.

Colleen 1951—in blue jeans.

Colleen in her Buster Brown hair cut forever supporting the phone company.

Mommy and me at Belle Isle in Detroit.

Aunt Elsie and Uncle Hughie.

Elsie with me at a vacation cabin July, 1940.

Grandma Viola Marks.

Mother, Margaret, with her dear friend, Ann.

Great grandfather, Samuel Ford, with Grandpa Almon to his left. Taken in Sandusky, Michigan in 1922, with sons Nick and Dan.

*1970—Aunt Elsie and
Uncle Hughie.*

Colleen 1951.

*Howard Mulvaney, my dad, with me
at Gordie Howe Hockeyland,
September, 1965.*

My step father, Budd Joffa, 1953.

Grandpa James Howe's family. Ab is over his right shoulder.

Kate and Ab's wedding day, 1918. Gordie's parents.

Gordie's home in Floral, Saskatchewan, Canada.

King George School soccer squad champs with Mr. Trickey to Gordie's left. Vic Howe in second row on far right.

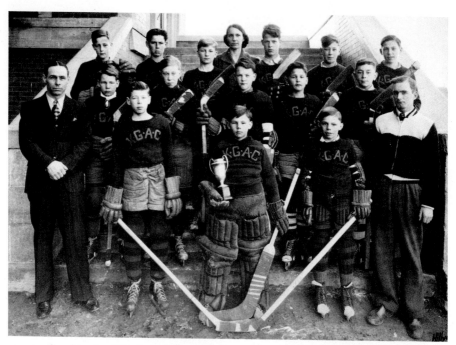

Grade school hockey with a lady for a coach. Mrs. Crawford, in back with Gordie. Mr. Crawford on front left.

Gordie loved fishing at Belleville, Ontario, September, 1952.

Gordie with his first car in Saskatoon, 1948.

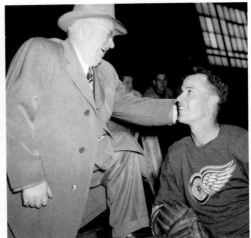

1946—Rookie Howe.   *1947—Jack Adams' new find.*

A budding pro ball player with the Saskatoon
Gems until Adams called it to a halt.

Mid 1960's—All Gordie's family.

Visiting Saskatoon, Saskatchewan 1954.
Kate and Ab with our first born, Marty.

Mary and Marty Howe.

*Teamsters 299, first sponsors for Pee Wee Team
coached by Jack O'Neill and Jim Chapman, 1959.*

Millie and Joe Schoenith, sponsors of the Roostertail Hockey Team.

Marty with Olympia Agencies Junior B team in the Southern Ontario Hockey Association.

"Gee Mom, I love these outdoor rinks." — Mark and Marty, 1960.

Colleen and her boyfriend, Red Storey.

Visiting Marty, a Toronto Marlboro Junior.

Marty, as a Marlboro, playing the remainder of the season with a protective mask, January 20, 1972, Olympia Stadium—Toronto vs. Junior Red Wings.

The Howe's facing off for the first time in Detroit at Cobo Arena, 1973.

Doug Harvey in St. Louis. Marty's defense coach in Houston.

The Whalers', Marty, before he was sent to Binghamton, February, 1984.

Boston Bruins', Marty, doing battle with Mike Foligno.

"I wonder where my career is heading?"—Marty.

*Marty coaching in Flint, Michigan in the
Colonial Hockey League.*

*Marty with fan, Mr. Paquette, when coaching
the Utica Bulldogs of Utica, New York of the
Colonial Hockey League.*

*Marty speaking at the announcement of his coaching position with the
Motor City Mustangs of the Roller Hockey International League.*

Gordie, age seventeen, 1945 Omaha Ak Sar Ben Knights farm system team, with first coach, on right front, Tommy Ivan.

Howe and Howe!, Syd that is! 1946, first training camp.

awful rough! There's not much security in playing hockey or most sports, especially back then. No one heard of multi-year contracts!

COLLEEN: Even with Gordie, being the great player he was, we could never feel security in his job. Especially in Detroit, with a sometimes unpredictable Bruce Norris as an owner, and Jack Adams trading players on a wholesale scale. Gordie found out, years later from Larry Regan, that Jack was mad at Gordie for something one time, for who knows what, and actually called Los Angeles about trading him. They had worked something out, but Jack changed his mind at the last minute. Even though I never put myself through what Julie Woit did, I could empathize with her. Even if someone told these wives how to prepare for a rootless life like hockey, they couldn't really understand the reality of it until they went through the experience.

When I first got to know Gordie, I really didn't realize how much he would be gone. When we were dating, he would go home to Canada in the summertime. But at that time I was working and had other activities and responsibilities to keep my mind off of the space of time. But when we were married there was just the two of us and my life had changed. If Gordie was gone, I'd call a friend and we'd go to a show, but most of my friends were in hockey now and very few stayed in Detroit. I kept busy, taking care of all the fan mail, taking care of the house, the insurance, the bills, taking walks and arranging Gordie's calendar. It wasn't until the kids were born that things changed. That's when all my efforts went to care for and hold a family together. And I realized I had to do a lot of it alone.

In raising the children, I was definitely the tougher parent. Gordie was a great father, yet he recognized that, since he was gone so much, I had to hand down the ground rules for the things that would go on in our home. Basically, our philosophy at home was "You be good to me, and I'll be good to you." Our relationship with the kids was a very reciprocal kind of thing. It was a give and take approach.

We never told our youngsters what time to come home. Never. We'd say, "What time do you think you'll be home?" And they would tell us. This way they were learning to make decisions. I think that was a good way to handle curfews. We respected their judgement and they never named some ridiculous time, or abused the freedom they were given. They would name a reasonable time, and I'd say "Well good, then be home at that time so your dad and I can go to bed and not be worried about you." At the same time, we gave them the same kind of respect. If Gordie and I were going somewhere, we'd let the kids know where we were going and what time we would be home.

Since I was with the children most of the time throughout Gordie's non-stop career, I had to deal with whatever took place, be it a flood, fire, accidents, chauffeuring and any and all arrangements. I couldn't store up the problems or responsibilities until Gordie got back from being on the road. Now, I don't ever believe in spankings, but I did believe in whacking a butt. I think there are a lot of opinions as to what is a spanking. Some people think a spanking is like a beating. I can't remember Gordie ever spanking any of the kids. I remember I shook Cathy one time. She wrote with crayons all over the wall in the hallway. So I grabbed her, and I shook her, and I said "If you ever do that again, you're REALLY gonna get it!" She said she never forgot that, because I really scared her because she never knew what "it" was.

I know Gordie and I haven't always been perfect parents, but I think we've been very good parents, and it has paid off so incredibly. We feel so close to our kids. When we had difficulties, we were able to deal with them. Cathy had the most problems growing up, but you have to remember that she was young at a time when a lot of kids were really rebellious and getting into REAL trouble. I asked her once, "Why is it that you never went off the deep end? Why do you think you were able to straighten your life around when it needed it?" And she responded "Because I could never let you or Dad down. I could never look you and Dad in the eye if I hurt you; and I always knew in my life that no matter what I did, not matter how bad it might be, that you and Dad would still love me." That brings tears to my eyes even as I tell it!

Often I've pondered over the fact that there are two things in life that we get no schooling or learning about except what we pick up from our own families: marriage and child-rearing. I'll be honest, when I first saw Marty, when he was first handed to me after he was born, I said "Oh, my God, you poor little thing. I don't know the first thing about what to do for you." This was a living, baby. And I didn't even know how to feed him. I thought, if he doesn't burp, is he going to die? A lot of this was because I was an only child and wasn't raised around younger siblings. Somehow, I also knew that just like anything else, I'd learn from experience. I told myself, you just pull up your boot straps and try to do the best you can.

Obviously, our house was not a normal kind of household. With Gordie coming and going, and the kids having such an incredible hockey schedule, our schedule and mileage was amazing. Our lives were even more hectic once the kids got in school. I was driving here and there to ever more of their activities. At least with school sports, the athletes get taken to the games on school buses, but with parks and recreation hockey, you have a situation where it's all dependent on the parents. I just accepted the fact that I would be doing this for the rest of my life—being an underpaid, yet dedicated, chauffeur. I didn't regard this as something bad. Actually I enjoyed going and participating in what the kids were doing and watching their games, whether it was hockey, track, football, school, church or whatever. Heck, my problem was that if my kids were doing something that I thought was wonderful, I wanted to shout it to the world. It was always a thrill for me to watch their participation, whether it was Marty and Mark playing hockey, or Cathy doing so well in track, or Murray getting all kinds of honors in school or in plays. After all, what parents wouldn't be proud of their children?

I used to see as many as 200 hockey games a year. Games, not counting practices. During those years, Gordie was playing, and I saw all of his games. Marty and Mark were normally on the same team, there were two years when they weren't. Oh boy! Meanwhile, Murray had started playing on a team. So there were four players on four teams in our family during some years. Imagine what that was like, when I was driving to just about every game, and poor Cathy had to go with us. One night she left me a note on my pillow that said "I am hockey sick." I had to agree. It was laughable in later years when I was into furthering hockey development that someone would comment "What does Colleen Howe know about hockey or hockey talent?" For their information, I saw more practices and games than most scouts in the NHL. I was living hockey all the time. In fact it was a way of life. That's when I got a really good feel for the game. I could tell when goals were about to happen before they did. Loyal fans, ones that have been attending games for years and years, understand what I'm saying. There is a rhythm to hockey that you start to feel, naturally, when you watch it enough. You can sense when a line is moving into a good pattern and you know a goal is about to happen. You also know what to look for when assessing talent in players.

The only thing I didn't like, was that hockey took us away from church, because most of our games were scheduled on Sundays, morning, noon and night. It bothered me because I felt our children weren't getting some of the religious background they deserved. Yet, I have a strong feeling, that it isn't the church that is the cause of people being good people. I feel that the basis of religion has to be in your heart. Beliefs have to be with you all the time. Spending time together also offered a lot of real-life experiences from which our kids were learning during their activities on how to be good people, and to treat others with kindness and respect. We did, however, say our prayers at night.

When we lived in Lathrup Village, to add to our non-stop activities, we put a pool in our backyard. And we really saved our extra dollars to get that pool in there. Gordie was always worried whether or not we could afford any large purchase, and then I'd find some money. I saw this hole in the ground with water in it as another healthy recreational asset and bonding factor for the family. Besides it was a great way to share with and entertain our friends. We always encouraged our children's friends to come to our house, no matter how many there were. In that way, I knew the whereabouts of our kids. When families don't encourage the friends of their children to come around, I think they make a huge mistake, unless of course, the friends destroy the whole house. For those same reasons we bought our first cottage up at Bear Lake in Northern Michigan. It got to the point that the kids would hate to leave their friends behind during the summers, so we brought their friends up, too. Their friends got to know us, and some of them felt just as though they were our kids, too. I think all of this kept our children close to us, because we shared their worlds as much as we could. And we shared our world, and our friends, with our children. We were not socially accepted in some circles because we always wanted to bring our family along. But our motto was, "love me, love my children," and it hasn't changed.

GORDIE: Family came first! Our traditions and our values always centered around family. I vividly remember when I was seventeen, in Omaha, living alone in a rooming house having no place to go for Christmas. Thank goodness our coach, Tommy Ivan, invited all the single guys over for dinner. I thought that was a tremendous gesture. Sid Abel was that way with me when I first joined the Red Wings. He and Gloria would have me over, occasionally, for dinner. That was a tradition that became part of our family, too. At Christmas, Colleen would say "Who are the players with nowhere to go?" and we'd invite them over to our house. What are your values, other than caring? And it makes me proud when I see the same kind of caring from our own kids.

COLLEEN: In being a parent who lives for her family, her best friends, I've pondered, "How can you conceive a child, birth that child, raise the child to be a person you dearly love, and let them get away from you?" Children grow up and then, perhaps, have their own family that you also dearly love. How can a person not continue to have them be a major part of their lives? I'd go to the end of the earth to make certain we have time to see and communicate with our children and grandchildren. If we ever lost those relationships, we'd be losing the part of our lives that gives us the most delight in the world.

Your family is really your legacy, and they should be coveted. We also feel we've been so fortunate to have the people our children have married—Mary with Marty, Ginger with Mark, Wade with Cathy, and Colleen with Murray as part of our family. We feel about them as though they were our very own. A family legacy is so important, more important than a hockey legacy. I don't even think about a legacy in hockey, because if I didn't have that special relationship with my family, the rest of life and then hockey wouldn't mean very much to me.

Let me share with you some very precious letters I wrote to Gordie while living some of the times I've described to you in this chapter. Think of me, when you read them, as a young and very lonesome wife, of a player who is spending a month to six weeks at training camp. Also, a mom who has one new baby, one toddler, and no car; trying to keep up with all of the responsibilities while, at the same time adjusting to the real world of parenting and home engineering. I think you'll get the feeling very quickly.

LETTERS TO MR. GORDON HOWE, C/0 THE DETROIT RED WINGS HOCKEY CLUB, SAULT STE. MARIE, FROM COLLEEN HOWE, 8556 STAWELL, DETROIT, MICHIGAN. (TRAINING CAMP, 1955.)

September 13, 1955
Hi Honey —
Phoned the AAA and Kotcher a while ago and here's the news. The AAA said to be sure to get a bill for the temporary repairs on the car from the Sault dealer so they can reimburse us for the money or pay it if you haven't already. Mr. Kotcher said he would give us these deals:

On a '55 Convertible	*$3,900 minus $1,000 for our car* *$2,900 full price*
On a '55 88 Deluxe	*$3,650 minus $850 for our car* *$2,800 full price*
On a '55 Ninety-eight	*$4,100 minus $1,200 for our car* *$2,900 full price*

125

What do those prices sound like? That's quite a bit of money! Should we wait for a '56 or not? I think so! This means, of course, we don't pay off the house, but it should only take us to next winter. But that should be all right. Miss you lots, Honey, and time seems to drag when you're gone. The kids are good so far and I have no kick coming. Hope you're not too sore from skating. Call me at the end of the week when you decide what you'd like to do. A 98 hardtop would be real nice. What do you think?

Bye for now. Hugs and kisses from your three babies.

I love you, Colleen
P.S. Mark is 19 pounds.

September 15, 1955

Hello honey —

Thought I'd drop you a note to remind you that you have three folks back here in Detroit who are very lonesome for you. One is asleep, the other on my lap bugging me and the last one is writing this letter.

Poor Marty, I feel so sorry for him in the morning. He goes in our room and says, "Where da? Where da?" while he looks all over the bed. He really misses you.

...I scrubbed half the basement and plan to enamel it when it dries. Then I'll do the other half some other day. It's too much in one day.

...Let's go to see about our suits when you get back because it may take quite awhile to make them. They'll have a job on their

hands between your shoulders and my backend.

Well, sweetie, that's the news for now. There's not too much to say. Don't get around much any more. Pat (LINDSAY) said she might get me a car for next week. Maybe. Write if you get a chance. Haven't heard from you yet. Why not? Bye bye.

Love, Colleen and the boys

September 21, 1955

Hello darling —
It has cooled off a bit today and made it a lot easier to sleep so Marty had a real long nap this afternoon. He's been so good since you've been gone.
I called Aunt Elsie to see how the baby is and she said fine. They're going to bring him back Friday evening. Marty looks in his bed and says, "Where Tee-Tee?"
...Read where Goldie (BOB GOLDHAM) still hasn't signed yet. Maybe you'll be the only non-R.C. yet. (???) It won't seem right without Goldie the year he decides to quit.
Lilly gal called yesterday and invited Jake (PAVELICH) and me over for dinner (spaghetti) on Thursday. It'll be nice to get out for a change. Stevie (Carr) said she'd watch Marty so it shouldn't cost me any money. I may have to take a cab, though, unless Jake offers me a ride.
...I called Pat about the car but her mother thinks her granddad wants to use it now. Sure glad I didn't plan on it.
The Munroes (neighbors) have been very nice. They've offered to take me to the store any time I wanted anything. I've gone up

twice with Marty in the wagon alone because I didn't need very much.

...I sent in our house payment for this month and also an extra $1,000. That should cut us down to $4,800 so we're getting it down little by little. We have a little more than $4,900 in our account plus what's in our checking so we're pretty well set for the car and insurance policies for the year.

...How's your cold now honey? That's what you get for kissing those strange girls.

This time you pick out the car and the <u>color</u> so I don't get any complaints. Ha Ha. Just so it isn't green!

That's about all for now, honey, because someone's starting to bug me to play with them. I'll run out to mail this now. I sure miss you — hurry home, but be careful on the road. Bye for now.

I love you, Colleen

September 23, 1955

Hello darling —

Looks as though you fellows might be ushering between periods this season since the Olympia maintenance crew has voted to strike when their contract is up October 1st. They want 50 cents per hour more per shift. Wonder if they'll get it.

...Sure sad because I missed your call tonight...Stevie (Carr) said I missed you by about 10 minutes. Darn it anyway. I love talking to you so much.

Received your two letters today and it's so refreshing to know you miss and love me (and the boys) but mostly me. It's sure tough *to be alone when you're in love. I should have a long discussion with J.A. (JACK ADAMS) some day about the importance of wives at Training Camp. That's a good idea you and Marty have of having us meet you up north. Pretty sneaky, eh what?*

...Carol (Carlin) called and wants me to go to dinner tomorrow evening with her and Pat. We called Jake too but you can tell Marty he's got a real conservative wife 'cause she said the budget won't allow her to go. Besides she's tired of driving all over because everyone is on the west side and she's so far away. I think I'll go though, since I haven't spent any money since you left and don't want to break any records.

Looks like I might have to go to the games with you this winter because Marty and Jake live so far out in Inkster and they come in the expressway. Maybe someone may take a home somewhere near here and we'll arrange something after all. Hope so, because that's such a drag to sit around all that while at the Olympia. Besides the sitter costs too much to waste any time. We can come home to eat a bit more often this year, okay?

Am kind of anxious to meet some of the new wives this year. If the fellows are all nice, I'm sure the gals will be, too. It'll be kind of nice to see some new faces.

Weeded out the garden today and have two huge brush piles to burn when you get home to help me. I don't want to light it when I'm here alone. Also transplanted one of Stevie's rose bushes on the fence on to our fence by the garage. Hope it takes because it's such a pretty one. That Stevie is one of the best! Got down and weeded your patio, too. There were quite a few little weeds sneaking in there to give us some trouble next spring so I gave them the blade. That back corner will be a good place for swings next year. We can get a small load of sand for it so we won't need a sandbox, either. By the way, I watered your grass that's coming

129

up where you tore up the old sandbox.

So you guys are going up to Edmonton now! Fine thing! You save those goals for season games, honey, the ——- with those exhibition deals. Those aren't money-makers anyway.

...Before I close, honey, I want you to know that although I act kind of goofy sometimes, this gal is still as much or more in love with you as the first night we went out together — and that's really a lot. Hurry home, dear.

My love, Colleen

———————

March 25, 1955 (TO GORDIE HOWE, C/O RED WING HOCKEY CLUB, HAMILTON, ONTARIO)

(BEGINNING OF STANLEY CUP PLAYOFFS)

Dear honey, baby sugar doll —
I haven't written you a letter in so long that I thought you might enjoy hearing from your lonely little wifey.

After you left on the bus, Teresa, Bev, Marlene, Irene, Bibs and I went to Harrison's for a sandwich. Just living it up all the time! Then we all went home to our lonely individual abodes to think of our sweet husbands and to wish they were with us instead of being so far away.

...It was a riot this morning — you should have seen it. I got up with the little angels (?) and got them breakfast. Then your sleepy wife tried to grab a little catnap. I slept about 15 minutes and during that time, Marty opened all the jello and pudding packages and poured them all over Mark, who was sitting there eating all he

could cram into this mouth. It took me over an hour to undo what took them a matter of minutes. Then they both went into the tub for a complete shampoo and bath. Wish we would have had some flashbulbs here so I could have taken a shot of the picture that stood before me when I poked my head into the kitchen. The three of us just looked at each other and laughed. (My laughter was a bit on the hysterical side.) All the joys of motherhood!

I don't know how the weather is in Toronto, but right this minute Hal is shoveling eight inches of snow off your sidewalk. What a snow we've had today! I went out twice to knock some of the weight off the shrubs. There was so much snow on the branches, they were breaking and bending right to the ground. I'm going to the grocery store tomorrow on dogsled.

Well, dear, things here are pretty horrible without you. I'm really looking forward to going on our vacation together and as far as I'm concerned, it will be more than a second honeymoon, and much nicer than our first. No arguments! Maybe I can make it up to you for all the little bitching I do sometimes. Also maybe we can make up for some lost time on our love life (you'd go for that, eh?)

Anyway, I'll be very happy to have you home, dear, because I love you more than you'll ever know.

All my love, Colleen
P.S. What do you want for your birthday?

CHAPTER SIX

DON'T SMILE TOO HARD,
YOU'LL GET DIRT IN YOUR TEETH

CATHY: I think some people assume that Dad's this tough, hard-spoken kind of individual, maybe because of his aggressiveness on the ice. They may think that's what he is like off the ice, and of course he's not. People always ask me what is it like to be Gordie Howe's daughter. And I say—well, he's just my dad. I don't know anything different. He's been the guy that has said, "no you can't go out on a date until I meet this boy." Or, "are you sure you want to marry this gentleman?" Or, "have you got your room picked up?" Or he calls from the airport and says, "I'm just blowing through town. How are things going? How are the kids?" But because I've never had any comparison, he's just my father. At home he's quiet, dry-witted, soft-spoken, and thoughtful.

We joke a lot that my dad's hands are so large, and we'd say, boy, if Dad ever smacked me with hands like that. But I look back on my life and never once do I ever remember him spanking us. When the boys used to fight a lot, he'd pick them up each by the napes of their necks and pull them apart, but he never once laid a hand on us. Not once. I bet I've heard him raise his voice probably a handful of times in my entire life. He's like a duck. He just lets things roll off his back. His personality is just this level line. It's real calm. He's a calming influence to be around; but he is a big teaser. He can give the needle to the kids. He can

132

get them going. But being around other celebrities, as I've gotten older, I realize that he's not one thing in public and another thing in private. He carries out who he is at home into his professional life.

GORDIE: I'll tell you about Cathy. We were on the Birthday Tour, and we were at a function. There was quite a crowd, and some guy walked in and asked "What's going on?" Somebody replied "Gordie Howe is signing autographs." Now, Cathy was standing there with a camcorder, taking pictures for us. And the guy says "Oh, does he charge?" And Cathy answered him, "Yeah, it's ten dollars per autograph, but the money goes to charity."

The guy says "Hell, I wouldn't pay no ten bucks for an autograph. It goes to charity? Yeah, sure. I bet." And Cathy says "No, you've got it all wrong. One hundred percent of the money goes to charity." And the guy said "Oh really? Do you know Gordie Howe?" And Cathy said "Oh yeah. I know him real well. I slept with him."

Well, now she's got his attention. The guy looks at her. And she doesn't stop there. "And, I've slept with all three of his sons." The guy must have figured he had a live one, and I guess he took a stride towards her, and Cathy says "Oh Dad?" And I look over and say "Yes, Cathy?" And the guy says "Oh, damn" and walks away. That's Cathy's sense of humor.

Another time, she and I were walking along the beach in Florida, and Cathy is a good-looking girl. We were walking along talking, and somebody said "I think that's Gordie Howe." And somebody with them said "No way, because that's not his wife Colleen." Cathy hears this, and reaches over and taps me on the bum. Then she kisses me on the cheek and says "Oh, Gordie." That little bugger. Oh, did we laugh.

CATHY: Mom was the disciplinarian in our home, but never in a hard way. My relationship with my parents was different than most of my friends' situations. My friends had the attitude, well, just avoid your parents. But with my parents, I never thought about trying to sneak around and avoid them. I mean, they'd put rules on me that left a lot of responsibility with my own self, and I think because they trusted my judgment. I guess Mom must have felt, at some point, like I do with my fifteen year old now. I put a lot of responsibility onto Jaime because I think I understand her well enough to know what kind of decision she's going to make. With Mom and Dad, I always knew that if I had a problem I could call them. I never worried about the repercussions if I made a mistake; I guess that's a comfort zone. My friends used to run around and drink a lot, but my mother said if you want to drink and your friends have permission from their parents, come in the backyard, sit around the pool and drink beer if you want. But if I ever catch you behind the wheel of a car, if I ever hear of you driving drunk, you won't have your car anymore and I won't trust you anymore. And that was reason enough. I wouldn't want to ever let them down.

Around our house we never had much time to get into trouble. The boys' hockey schedules kept us all going, and in high school I was running track. Before that I had thirteen years in the orchestra, through elementary school and secondary school, playing the viola. I guess I got that from my grandparents. My mother's father played with a couple of big bands during the big-band era and my Grandpa and Grandma Howe played fiddle and guitar at square dances. Grandpa used to say to me, "You play the fiddle like I do." And I'd say, "No, I play the viola." But between that and ten years of dance class, Bluebirds, friends, church, and helping Mom, I was always busy.

I think of all of us, I probably put my parents through the most. I was definitely the most rebellious of the bunch. I think any of the gray hairs they have, that weren't caused by age, were primarily caused by me. Marty and Mark were only a year apart in age, then it was four years until I was born. Murray and I were closer in age, but he's one of those brothers that nobody wants for a sibling, because Murray never did anything wrong, and that made me look twice as bad. I was never really hurt about it, because Murray was my best friend growing up. And Marty and Mark kind of paved the way for us being teenagers. By the time I got to that age, Mom already had been through four years of it. She'd say, "Oh I've seen this situation before and I know what to do."

Mom was firm, but never harsh or tough. With Mom, when you asked for something and no was the answer, you didn't ask again. You knew that that was her decision, and that's the way it was. But the good side of that is you always knew where you stood with her. She didn't fluctuate. She didn't change her mind. You were welcome to voice your opinion, but it wasn't going to change what she'd already decided.

It's tough enough to get through your teenage years and to find your individuality as it is, but I guess it can be harder when you have a famous father. I'd find out that maybe some person just liked me because of who my father was, or at another point, who my brothers were. But I size people up pretty quick. I pretty much stick with my intuition. There were times, back then, that I approached Mom and Dad and I said, "You know, I'm feeling this way. Is this really what's going on or am I misunderstanding things?" And they were straight up about it. They said, "No. That's going to happen your whole life because of who your father is. It's just going to happen. It's something that you'll just have to trust your instincts on. You'll learn lessons from it." But, I think the biggest challenge of having a parent who is successful at anything, is trying to prove not only to yourself, but to them, that you can do as well at something, whether it's one field or another. Everyone has to recognize their own accomplishments. I think probably my biggest goal in life was to do that. And then it became my second biggest goal, because what I eventually wanted most was to make sure that I had the same relationship with my children that I had with my parents. I worked hard at it.

And it's interesting how it has worked out. Because the group of people that I'm friends with now, whether it's in business, or whether it's in the horse industry, or whether it's in the fund raising I do, I find I'm around people just like me. People, especially my girlfriends that I am closest to, who all have a similar type of relationship with their parents. And maybe that's our common bond and why we all hit it off and get along so well. So, I'm comfortable around them.

It wasn't always so easy. There were times that I can remember when there were important things going on in my life that my parents couldn't always be present for. There were all the track meets and all the high school recognition ceremonies and this and that, and I'm sure they were at as many as they missed. But the important ones that they missed, at that point, were a big deal to me. And I'd think, if my dad were somebody else—if he were just a regular father and he worked nine to five, he'd be able to be here. And Mom, especially as I got older, was always busy doing stuff for Howe Enterprises or Power Play International. At that time I could understand that most of us kids were grown and she was entitled to her own life, but it's an aggravating situation for a child. It bothered me then, but when I look back on it now, I think it's no big deal.

I'm really kind of a combination of both my parents. Probably overall, I'm more like my mother. I have drive like my mother does. My mother's more driven than my father is. But I get a lot of my compassion from Dad. My weaknesses? I can't pass by a stranded motorist without stopping. My Dad's that kind of a person. My temper is much more like my mother's. I'm much more hot-tempered. I'm much more opinionated than my father is. Water doesn't roll off my back too easily. It gets stuck in my feathers. I get in a dander.

And my brothers, well, they're all goof balls. Marty's the oldest. Marty is the strong, silent type. Marty is funny, more down to earth. He'd rather be quiet, listening to country music, rather than running out on the town and having a lot of fun. He's more laid back. And Mark is driven. In that aspect, I'm a lot like Mark. I'm probably closest with Mark. But Mark's more energetic. Mark doesn't like to sit down, he's got to be in perpetual motion. He's so funny. And Murray. Murray's the humorist of the bunch. Murray goes 100 miles an hour. Murray is into marathons and community involvement and he's a kook, too. With him it's one of those things where all you have to do is call Murray's house and listen to his answering machine, and that will explain Murray in a nut shell. It's so funny because I'll tell Mom when I've had a really bad day, I'll call Murray's house just to listen to his machine and I say, "Yep, life is good, I feel better already." Murray's always got something lighthearted to say. Basically, I think Marty and Mark are probably the tightest in the bunch, and Murray and I were closer when we were younger than we are now. But it's fun, because we may not see each other or talk to each other for six or eight months, maybe even a year. Then we'll get together and it's like I saw them yesterday. And I love my sisters-in-law because they're like sisters, and all my nieces and nephews. We really have a good time together, but we just don't get enough of it.

One of the reasons is that we live in North Carolina, out in the country, in Salisbury. It's where I wanted my kids raised. We were in Charlotte for a while, but it was too busy. I didn't want my kids exposed, if I could avoid it, to too much. Both the kids, Jaime and Jade, are into rodeo. They barrel race horses.

That started when my daughters were in private school and Cathy-the-volunteer-for-everything offered to co-chair an auction and one of the items that was donated was eight horseback-riding lessons. At the end of the evening we were ready to close that table and I kept track of the closing mark. And nobody had bought it, so I bought it. Wade said, "what are you going to do with that?" And I said, "I'll give it to Jaime." This was about three years ago. And I went home, all excited. I couldn't wait to tell her I bought her horseback-riding lessons. She said, "I will never get on a horse, Mother."

So our four-year-old at that point, Jade, said "Well, I want to ride horses." And I thought, oh, this is not going to work. So I called the instructor and I said can you just walk her around the ring for a half hour for the eight lessons? And she said sure, great. Well after the third lesson, I got the older one on the horse and that was the end of it, or the beginning of it. The little one kind of quit riding after those lessons. She was kind of bored and the older one continued on to a category called Western Pleasure, which is ring work and judged strictly on your riding and the horse's ability in the ring.

Jaime did that for a couple of years. Then we met up with a new group of friends, the Tarlton's, through the horse business, and introduced our kids to barrel racing. That was not quite a year ago. I love everything about it. I love being with the horses. I like working them. It's a great group of people. It's a family-oriented sport. It takes up a lot of time. My mother says, "Oh you're going out to the barn again!" It's not like we just go out there, we ride. The kids not only have to train their horses and condition them, but they also have to keep themselves mentally and physically in tune with the horse. They have to run as a team, but Mom didn't realize that until she and Dad were down last November. Thanksgiving was the first time they had seen the kids ride, except on the video I sent. Dad didn't realize they could ride so good. He figured after five months they wouldn't be that far along. The younger one started last June, and has done exceptionally well. We bought her an older, very level-headed horse. But Jaime's horse got very sick one night just before Nationals and died.

I can still remember it. We couldn't get the horse to be calm and she was in excruciating pain. The only time she was calm was when Jaime came over. So we let her lay down. Jaime put her head in her lap and just petted her. The horse stayed calm for a good half hour and then the vet came and told Jaime we're going to have to put her down now. So, he told Jaime, you need to leave. So I got her up and, of course, the minute Jaime walked away, the horse started screaming again. I got her about ten feet away and Jaime passed out cold. So I had to pick her up.

It's a bond. I told Wade, I think because they're larger animals there's this larger aura around them, you know. You can tell what kind of mood they're in the moment you walk up and touch them. That horse was very attached to Jaime and Jaime vice versa, so we took her and packed her up and said, that's okay. We don't need to be here for a week. So I packed the kids up and we went down to Augusta, Georgia, to where the barrel racing nationals are. We spent a week there, and Jaime said, "I'm going to learn how to do this now." And I said, "Great. You have a beautiful big gelding in the barn. We can teach him how to do it." So they run together.

Potentially it's a dangerous sport. I watch a lot of children on horses and I think, now why on God's earth would that parent put that child on that horse? There would be no way for me to do that. I specifically look for a lot of different qualities in a horse. Of the horses that we own, there isn't one that would be lying in the stall that you couldn't walk in and lay down on top of; especially Jade's horse, she's nineteen. Jade can walk to the fence line, where they're out in five acres, and she can yell her horse's name. That horse will be at a full-out run to get to that little child at the gate. Jade will crawl on her bare back. No saddle. No bit. No bridle. No lead line, nothing, and ride her strictly by moving her arms across her neck. But I know that the horse will take care of her.

Any sport is real competitive. In barrel racing the parents stand there and say, now make sure you do this and do that and you turn and you dig and you pull, you know, and you kick. Well, I talk to the horse first and I say, "You just go in and do your best, and take care of my baby." And, as I gaze out in the dirt-filled air in the rings, I always look at my kids and say jokingly, "Don't smile too hard. You'll get dirt in your teeth." And every parent around me says, "Don't you want to tell them to do this or that?" And I reply, "Those kids know their horses. Those horses know those kids. They're either going to go in and do a good job and win or they're not. My coaching them at the last minute isn't going to do it. I want them to relax and catch a breath before they cover about 420-some feet of ground with three barrel spins in 18 seconds."

A lot of times it's easier for me because I watch it through the little video view finder. But sometimes when I'm not videotaping, my heart is in my throat. I saw Jade come up out of her saddle in a full out run and I told her there must have been her guardian angel with her. All of a sudden the horse hit a hole or something, because her neck went down and that kid went— whoop! Popped right back into the saddle. She was riding her horse at a full out run on her neck. And I've seen Jaime come over the front of *her* horse, head first, flip over and land on her feet and I'd just about have a heart attack.

Right now, Jade's standing third for North Carolina and Jaime's standing sixth for North Carolina, that's for the eighteen and under divisions. Jaime's only been racing since October 1994, and Jade started about five months ahead of her.

When Mom and Dad first talked about the idea of my father's 65th Birthday Tour, I wasn't one to raise my hand and say, oh, I'll do it! I ended up organizing it as much as anyone. I think the most difficult part was trying to work with so many different individuals and situations, because we were traveling two days here, two days here, two days here. It was like being with a touring rock band, only worse.

Mom was real busy with other projects, so I kept her posted on a daily basis. I think what I most enjoyed, because I'd been away from hockey and in the south for so long, was watching the recognition on people's faces when they saw Gordie. And he was a trooper, because it took some long hours. We'd be up at four in the morning. I'd have to work. For example, for the first stop in Ottawa, we arrived early in the morning. I had been up since 4:00 a.m.; went all day through press conferences and visiting charities, and so forth; attended a dinner that night; got up early the next morning; and went through another tour of a couple different charity facilities. We had a 6:00 a.m. television show, six o'clock in the morning! We had about four hours of sleep. Went all day. Went to the hockey game. Couldn't get out of the arena because there were so many people waiting outside. They snuck us out and got us back into the hotel. It was about 1:00 a.m.. We were packing up and had to be up at, 4:00 a.m.

Then at 2:30 in the morning, the fire alarm went off at the hotel! Oh, we were so tired at that point. In two days, I had less than six hours of sleep. I was a walking zombie. And Mother comes running in and says, "It's the fire alarm!" I said, "I know, mother. I can hear it." So, I go outside in the hallway and everybody's standing out there. My mother comes running out with my coat on and she says, "you need to grab your coat in case we need to go outside!" And I said, "mother, you're wearing my coat." She said, "Well then grab mine!" And that was the kick off of the tour.

It was kind of fun, so we just stayed up at that point, and they kept us informed. It wasn't a dangerous situation. It was a broken water pipe. I thought, oh boy. Things just have got to go uphill from here. We were so tired. At that point I realized I needed more control of what each city was planning. I was looking two weeks in advance from there, since we had about six cities to cover right away. Then I had a few days at home. But I really enjoyed it. I had a lot of fun.

I think Mom's goal was to raise a half-million dollars to give away to charities, and we raised nearly a million dollars to give to them, which was terrific. That was double our goal. But, it was a long year. At first the project seemed a bit ambitious, but the most difficult part was getting down to those final details. The parking. Who's going to drive and where. Being picked up. Airport schedules. Drive time, you know? Nobody managed to remember that we needed sleep time or changing time in between all these events. We couldn't go from a charity visit right to a black-tie dinner without at least an hour to change and those kind of things weren't calculated. That was my mistake. I learned a lot after the first two weeks. After the first two weeks on the road I thought, oooh. I have a lot of work to do. But it ran smoothly towards the end and the people—the cities themselves were very responsive. Although some of the responses were quite humorous. We got a nay response back from New Jersey and it said Gordie wasn't synonymous with hockey. I felt like replying, how old are you? Maybe they were thinking of another Gordie.

I remember the first year Mark was playing with Detroit, we went to a game. We went out afterwards—someplace across the street from the Renaissance Center. We were eating in the back and these two obnoxious drunks came over to our table just as our food was served. And they were yak, yak, yak, and f-this and f-that, and my husband stands up and says, "I'm sorry. I didn't get a chance to introduce myself. I'm Wade Roskam. I'm Mark's brother-in-law. I'm a minister." And the guy says, "Oops! Time's up," and they were out of there.

But it goes both ways. There are times when Dad's tired and he's irritable and he just wants to be left alone, but you wouldn't know it. He gets to mumbling a little bit. But he doesn't say anything mean. After they leave, he just says, "You'd think that people would realize from looking at me with bags under my eyes, that I was tired and really didn't feel like being invited for a drink some place." He never complains, but I can tell he's tired when he starts rubbing his face and when he crosses his arms a lot.

It's a lot of fun doing things with my parents. We went up to Traverse City for the opening of the Howe Arena a few years ago. We were all going to skate in the grand opening. The press was there, and a pretty good crowd.

GORDIE: It was a great honor in our lives, for all of us, to have the new arena named Howe Arena. And there was this fella by the name of Gil Ziegler that bid the most money, I think around $10,000 or $15,000, to be the first skater at the new rink.

I was there with Colleen, Cathy, Wade and their kids, Jaime and little Jade. And when they brought this man forward to receive his applause and take the first skate, he said "Those who know me know I can't skate. There should only be one man who takes the first skate at this Arena." And he wanted me to do it. It was a terrific gesture.

So we had the whole family put on skates and join me on the ice. As I stepped on the rink, Colleen very wisely handed me little Jade. And I went skating with her, and it was a warm day, so there was mist coming up off the ice. And I'm floating around the ice with this beautiful young lady in my arms, followed by Colleen and the kids skating behind us. And Colleen had them play, "Wind Beneath My Wings," on the loudspeaker. I was about to stop to get Jaime to carry her, too, or at least get her to skate with us, when I looked and saw all these people in the crowd crying.

That's when I went from a hero to a dope real fast. I didn't know what the problem was, and I said to a woman standing there, "God, what happened?" She said "This is sentimental, you big jerk." Everybody was choked up. It was an emotional scene.

CATHY: I think the hardest part of that whole thing for me was when Dad picked up Jade to skate her around the rink. Little Jaime was standing there like she thought she was going to go out there, too, and she looked like—oh, I guess I'm not supposed to go. You know, that little heart. I could just see it in her face later when I watched it on the video, although I didn't see it at the time. All I was thinking was I hadn't skated in five years. "Please God, don't let me fall and embarrass the daylights out of myself in front of anybody who happens to be looking at me instead of at my father" You know, those are the things you think of.

Speaking of videos, a problem with having famous parents is that everybody gives them so much. What do they need for Christmas? You know, what do they need for their birthday? Mom's a lot easier than Dad, because she and I have the same taste. I'll see something and if I like it, that's perfect. We'll buy it. Dad's more difficult. This year we put together a video tape. My camera has all these special effects capabilities, so I played it back in slow motion and I put it to music. Well, Mom called and she was crying. My heart sunk and I thought, oh no, what happened? She said, "I can't talk. Talk to your father" I thought, God! I thought someone had died. Well, it was the video, she had just watched it. She was so touched she couldn't catch her breath to talk. The video was about the horse that Jaime had competed on for so long, there was this real sad song in there about "if I had only known that this was our last walk in the rain." And I had played it under slow motion footage. It's a beautiful video of the two of them. They were both dressed up in the rain and she had all her silver and her gear and the saddle and everything on her. It was the last show they were in together, about three weeks before she colicked and died. Mom showed this video at Mark's and I guess Travis got all emotional, and then Mom started crying, again. Mother got everybody going.

I'm a lot like my mother. I can't stand it when I see somebody smacking their children in public. My husband says, "Don't say anything, Cathy." But it's against my nature. I've got to open my mouth. I'm always butting in and I probably shouldn't, but I can't stand by and do nothing.

COLLEEN: Cathy and I were in Charlotte one day, and

145

we came out into this parking lot. We see this huge guy beating his little boy with a belt. He was so mad at this little kid, he's hitting him with his belt.

Now, you would not want to deal with Cathy and me together. That's a double dose of trouble, believe me. We went right up to this guy told him to stop. His wife was there, and she got into it, telling us "Stay out of it. We'll do anything to this kid we want to." And we said, "Not in front of us, you won't." I tried to settle these people down. "Let's talk. We don't want to get in your business, but you shouldn't do that to that boy." Oh, Cathy was hot. We were both upset. And you think, if they would do that to the child in public, can you imagine what happens to him behind closed doors? Pretty scary.

Well, they just took off. We didn't resolve anything, but at least we got them to stop. Cathy took their license plate and reported them to the police. We knew the police couldn't take any action against them, but we wanted it to be placed on the record.

CATHY: I ran track in high school. I was faster than everybody else in our gym class and our coach said "I really want you on the track team." In the finals every year, it inevitably boiled down to Sandy Gadsby and me. She's Bill Gadsby's daughter, my Dad's former teammate, we're very close to their family. Sandy and I were bosom buddies and it ended up with me in first place and Sandy in second every time. I mean, we used to get the biggest kick out of that because we really enjoyed ourselves. Then, when we moved and I hit high school in Houston, I was recruited for the track team there. I basically was a sprinter.

I ran the anchor leg for the 220 relays, which is now the 200. So I was in the 220 relay, the 440 relay, I ran the 220 and I threw the shotput. And that was a lot of fun until I dropped one on my foot. I broke all the bones in my foot two weeks before district finals. I was out for the rest of the season.

The worst part about it was I was so excited. I'd been on the track team for the whole year. Marty and Mark used to show up quite a bit. Mom and Dad were pretty busy, but it was the first meet my mother was attending. I was so excited. Mom's finally going to come and watch me run. I was all hyped up on the bus and I got there and we were goofing around with the shotputs. Sixteen pound weights were what we warmed up with, and that thing landed on my foot and I thought, I refuse to acknowledge this hurts. It doesn't hurt. And I just ignored it, and it was two hours later, after I had warmed up, ran, stretched, and went to change into my spikes, and I saw my whole sock was covered in blood.

It's been said that the Howes have a high threshold for pain. Maybe it's a lack of brain cells, I don't know. When I delivered Jade, my obstetrician had left town so I had a replacement. When he came in, I was, at that point, in transition. And he said, "You're the only female patient I ever had that was still laughing at this point." Because I was dilated to eight and I still wanted to walk, he said, "you are my worst nightmare of a patient. You are one of these people that are going to be walking down the hall and that baby's going to go BAM and hit the tile floor." And I said, "I can't stand to lie down. I have to walk." And he said, "I don't know how you can walk." I said, "I don't want to lay in that bed." But, I finally followed the doctor's orders.

They have all these gimmicks that they give you to try when you go through Lamaze. My first delivery I didn't go through Lamaze. My delivery was thirty-two hours, and an absolute nightmare in labor. The second one was so fast. She was born within three hours after I started. I was lying there after I got into bed. I had nothing else to think about but the pain, and I was uncomfortable. I kept saying, "Damn, I'm sweating." Wade was there with me, and he would take this sports magazine and fan me. I kept saying "Hit my face, hit my face!" Of course, I meant with the air from the fan. So he hauls off with the magazine and whacks me right in the face! And I looked up at him. I said, "What the hell are you doing?" He said, "Well, you said hit my face." "I meant with the air!" And oh, we laughed so hard. I laughed till I cried. He and I both laughed. I said, "That was your one and only chance. Don't ever do that again. Don't even think about it." The funniest part was, I delivered her within about ten minutes after that. I think it was two or three more contractions and the baby was delivered. They handed me Jade and she was real quiet and they took her away and did all her testing. When they brought her back to me I said, "Well, no, I want Wade to have her," and I handed her to Wade and she started crying. He immediately started to sing, which he did all through my pregnancy. He sang to her and she immediately went silent. (Well, so did the whole room because he's got this incredible voice). And then the next thing I knew, he started laughing and I said, "what?" She had wet all over his hand, so I said, "That's a payback for the slap."

Both Jaime and Jade are runners too. Marty was also a runner in our family, Murray did marathons, Mom a 10K, and Grandpa Howe was apparently a great runner when he was young. He was the only man I ever met who had hands bigger than my father. And Grandma Howe had hands about as big as Dad's. Grandma was big, too. Grandma was very strong; strong not only in spirit, but in physical stature, too.

Jaime ran on the track team last year in high school. It's the first time she did this. She ran the 400, did the long jump, and the one where they hop, skip, and jump—the triple jump. Jaime's legs have a thirty-four inch inseam. My dad has a thirty inch inseam.

Jade holds a record in North Carolina for running a mile in under seven minutes. This was when she was in the first grade. And she walked part of that mile. She said she felt bad for the other kids because they kept saying, slow down, slow down. As a matter of fact, her gym teacher last year came to me after she ran that. She said she just could not believe the way this child could run. She said you really need to enter her in the local Walk/Run Mile. So we agreed to do that.

Well, Jade is prone to severe nosebleeds, for no reason. I think it's sinus problems. But she had one the night before the race, and I said, "Wait." I had real reservations about letting her run because of the amount of blood loss. She was weak. But she said, "No, no, no." She wanted to go. My husband said, "Maybe one of us should run with her." And I said, "Right, like who?" Which one of us could run a seven minute mile? That's a joke.

So we strategically placed ourselves at various points on the route, and one of our neighbors was there running, a guy named Tom who we asked to keep an eye on her. So the gun went off and they went down about 400 yards. They circled through the woods of this park and at that point, I lost sight of her. So I ran towards the end of the mile. Tom was running along with the kids, they were fourth-graders and under, and he said he suddenly saw this little swoosh go by him. She was going so fast that he said "Jade, slow down!" She said, "No, I gotta keep going. I want to get this over with!" He said all he saw was that little pink shirt.

Whoosh! Right by him. And when those kids started coming out, she placed thirteenth out of over 300 children and she was the only child of her age in that top group. I think the rest of the kids were third and fourth graders. She was so tired. She was wiped out. When she got to the end, she said, "Ohh mom." I said, "Honey, I told you not to overdo it." She said, "No, there was no sense in trying to walk." She wanted to get it over with. She's that way about injuries, too. Boy, she won't let you know when she's hurt.

I was living in Kalamazoo. I was eighteen, and a senior in high school. The family of one of the boys I was dating was pretty heavily involved with the Kalamazoo Wings. So, we went to a game, and there was a reception afterwards. Who should be there but Bruce Norris, owner of the Red Wings. He sat all night staring across the room and looking at me. I thought, he must know I'm Gordie and Colleen's daughter. He recognizes me. That was my assumption.

But then he came over and started into this spiel. It must have been some standard come-on of his. I don't know where these lines came from. I'm so young, so much younger than this guy, but he's going on and on. I was astounded. I just stood there and listened because, at that point, it was kind of funny to me. I thought, this guy is such a shmuck. He was trying to impress me with all that he owned and where he'd been and all the places we could go and things we could do and see. Just the two of us. With my date standing five feet from me!

Finally, he mentioned owning the Red Wings, and I said "Well, I'm well aware of that. I'm sure you know my parents, Gordie and Colleen Howe."

I will never forget the look on his face. He was shell-shocked. He stood there, looked, and stared. I don't think he

150

thought I was serious. I said, "I'm Cathy! Yeah. I'm the little girl that used to go to all your Red Wing Christmas parties to see Santa Claus when I couldn't even skate yet." I walked away from there and I went right home. I called Mom. I said, "You will not believe what happened to me tonight."

It was a reception after the game. A cocktail party, needless to say. And I was probably the only woman in the room under twenty-five, or one of a few. His taste, I guess, ran to younger women. His target audience was very limited that night.

When I was young, I used to go down to Olympia to watch the games quite a bit. It was great fun for a kid. I never really considered the possibility of Dad getting hurt. I mean, it was just something you didn't think about, even though it's a contact sport. It isn't a realization at that age. No, I was more interested in seeing the security guard that always ran our section. He was really nice. And I always looked forward to seeing Lydia, the lady that worked in the popcorn concession, right where you came in the main doors downstairs. And I couldn't wait to see Sandy Gadsby. We'd go down and get free cotton candy, too. And we used to go in the Olympia Room, which was the original one. We could go in there and eat between periods, that was our big time. We had our different spots. Then we discovered the copy room. One day we saw somebody pushing a buzzer. The two of us just stood there staring. What's in that room? So we waited until the halls were empty and we snuck down in there and I held Sandy up so she could push the button and the door popped open. It was a copy machine. Boy, did we have fun! We copied our hands and our faces and our feet and our shoes. It was big fun.

And I enjoyed the games. I'm a professional howler and whistler. Jaime says, "Boy, your whistle is so distinctive over anybody else's." I said, "It's from years of cheering for your brothers and your dad. It's from years of standing and screaming and whistling and...Yahhh!"

I went on those hockey trips with Mom and the boys. All of them. Yeah, I particularly remember one trip, I think it was to Fort Wayne, Indiana. I think there were two or three families on this motor home we borrowed. We put all the luggage in the shower. It gave us a lot of room. We had a lot of miles to cover. And I think we were in a traffic jam and we were running late and Mom told everybody to go ahead and get dressed for the game. Well, nobody knew it, but the showerhead was leaking water. All the luggage and hockey gear got wet.

Everything was soaked. In order to dry it off, we had underwear, shirts, jockstraps, and things flapping and flying from the windows of this motor home, trying to dry them as we went down the highway. I can remember Mother said, "Oh, we must look funny." That was one of the fun trips. Yeah, it was a lot of fun and I enjoyed watching the sport then, more than I do now. I watch hockey now, even though I don't see a whole lot of it. We do have a team in Charlotte. I'm much more analytical of the game than emotional about it, unless there's a family member out on the ice. Then I'm more emotional. I'm like, "hey, back off! Watch out! Watch your back! And why isn't that other man covering his man? Why are you covering two?" I scream things like that and my husband looks at me like I've gone nuts.

People ask me about Dad being the greatest player of all time. It's not that his hockey reputation isn't important to me, but I don't think that it's real important to him. He knows what he accomplished. Probably his greatest accomplishment is not the goals and the points, it's what he's done with his life. Who he is and how he has evolved as a person. Sure, it's nice to get recognized for the work that you do, but I don't think he'd be any different if he were never publicly recognized for what he's done. His greater accomplishments are what he's done as a father and as a friend and as a grandfather. And the person that he is has set an example for us, and that's so much more important than what he's done on the ice.

There's always the funny side to Dad. I mean, if he saw us standing down near the ice at Olympia, before the game or even before a face-off, there would suddenly be a stick above you with ice on it. He'd dump ice on you, just his little way of saying hello.

I guess I always had a sense that he was watching me. I could be sitting, talking with somebody, like a friend in high school, and I'd sense that he was looking at us from the bench. Dad always knew when Mom and I were in our seats. Because he'd come out of the locker room after the game and ask, "Where were you the second period?" He knew. And I wouldn't have thought that he had time to think about that as he sat there on the bench. As a parent now, when I'm in the ring, I know my kids are with my husband. I need not worry. But yeah, he was paying attention all the time.

I think his love for what he did is the reason that he was so successful. Not only did he have the physical attributes to be the athlete he is, but I never heard him complain. Never heard him complain he had to leave on a road trip. I never heard him complain about anything.

Maybe he feels that the one thing he really didn't follow through with in his life was education. I have a mild case of dyslexia. I can type about ninety words a minute. But I will write "was" instead of "saw." And if I type "saw," I will read "was." I guess Dad may have the same problem. On the other hand, how much does a professional speller make for a living?

COLLEEN: When our kids were very young, I always told them I had eyes in the back of my head. So one day when they were all piled in our bed after a shower, Cathy started brushing her hair and mine but she kept parting my hair in the back. I asked what she was doing and she said she was trying to find my eyes in the back of my head. I never told her where they were. It was my way of making them think twice, and maybe head off things that would otherwise go on behind my back. The C.I.A. was another thing I told them I represented (Colleen Intelligence Agency, that is!) for which Cathy fully qualifies. (Same initials!) This was more or less verified by her actions when she was on a mission to stop a wrong-doer.

Near her home in Charlotte, construction was going on down the street, thereby creating a parade of work trucks passing her place each day. One in particular always went much too fast. Cathy nicely asked that they slow down, because of the speed limit and the fact that there were many young children crossing the street continuously. The driver and passenger gave her a one-fingered peace sign and accelerated even more.

Then Cathy tried the "sprinkler to the open window" method to get them to slow down, but they yelled some obscenities and drove even faster. At this point, Cathy and a friend came up with a plan to video these jerks while they drove faster, gave fingers out the window as they went by, cursed at Cathy, drank beer on the building site and took their morning toilet break right out in the open.

Then the C.I.A. (Cathy Intelligence Agency) called the building company and spoke to the owner telling him there was a little problem that they'd like to discuss with him. When he came over, they said it would be more helpful to him if he watched what they had on video rather than just trying to explain everything. He watched with disbelief, and told the ladies they would no longer see those two men there again. He apologized and congratulated them on their brilliant video and headed to the job site whereby he made certain those two workmen were not on the job again. All in all, it was a pretty good job of investigative detective work. Go get 'em, Cathy!

CATHY: What have my parents given me? Integrity. From Mom, I've learned to be a little tougher than a lot of people. I've learned that my parents really are living examples of what they wanted us to be. They wanted us to be strong and think for ourselves and care for other people and give of our time and give of ourselves. A classic example with them was the time Murray called me and he was upset. He had decided he didn't want to be a hockey player. He wanted to be a doctor. I said, "And this is a problem? Telling Mom and Dad?" And I chuckled, but for him it really was an emotional struggle.

My parents are just so supportive. Mom once said that even if any of you kids wanted to live on a beach in a shack and be a surfer, or just live in a shack and paint, Dad and her would support us. And they've always been there. I guess I'm pretty lucky in that aspect. They've taught me to be fair with people, not to judge anybody, that it's not our place to judge people. We have no concept about what goes on in the bigger picture beyond ourselves. Especially Dad. Dad doesn't sit and judge other people. He accepts people at face value and I guess one of the biggest lessons I've learned from him is his belief that there are so many good people on this earth, and we should accept people for who they are. If they screw you, walk away. There are too many good people you'll meet to spend time worrying about the ones that aren't. You can't help everybody.

I'm the only one in the family who's been through a divorce. It was probably the most difficult thing I ever had to tell my parents. It came at a point when I was leaving for a vacation. I knew the whole thing was falling apart, and I had a small baby. I remember Mother was so excited, because she said she had the biggest surprise for me. I had confided in Marty about what was going on with my marriage. And he said, "Oh, oh," and I said "What?" He said, "You'll find out tonight." We all went out to dinner and when we came back, Mom had started showing all my wedding pictures on video set to music. As soon as I said, "Oh, you've got to turn this off." I couldn't even watch it. I said to her, "I have to talk to you." And Mom said she knew something was deeply wrong. But she took it pretty good and said she supported me either way. I expected some form of lecture, but she accepted my decision and never passed judgment. She only asked, "What can your father and I do to help you?"

They have taught me by example how much work it takes to make a marriage work. They've been married forty-two years now, and in this day and age, that's rare. But yeah, these are probably their greatest gifts—not to pass judgment on others and to give and to care. And to always realize the importance of family.

"40 years of memories on the ice and off have blessed us with a true friendship."
—Bill & Edna Gadsby, NHL Hall of Famer and wife, dear friends

CHAPTER SEVEN

IT'S A LONG WAY FROM SASKATOON

COLLEEN: Gordie is superhuman when it comes to tolerance. He's just incredible. Sometimes I've asked him, "Why it is he never gets mad. I'll start thinking, get mad, will you! And he'll say, "Okay, when things settle down. We'll talk later." And then, I give up. It drives me crazy at times, because I would really like it if he would just get mad at me. But not Gordie! He's so easy going. So how can you get angry at a guy who won't get angry back?

When he was on the ice, he was so different. Anger was a major outlet for him. He would do things to other players that would shock me. I'd ask "Why did you do that?" It just seemed so unlike his real character. And he replied "If you're going to survive out there, you better make them think you're a little crazy." Well, I believe in his playing days he had them thinking he was a lot crazy.

GORDIE: When I was young, and first came up with the Wings, I used to eat steak in the morning, and eggs in the afternoon, so I wouldn't get sick. That's how nervous I was. I could keep protein down. Then I felt pretty good.

The very first game I played at Olympia in 1946, as a Red Wing, everybody lined up at the blue line. The whole team stood there after they'd warmed up. The ice was not resurfaced. The refs blew the whistle and the two teams just stood at their respective lines and listened to the National Anthem. Then they'd go over to the bench. Jack Adams, our coach, would say "This guy and that guy will start." Those players would skate back on the ice and be ready to go, while the rest would go sit on the bench.

I'm out there with Doc Couture, Pat Lundy, Ted Lindsay and the rest. I'm standing there on the blue line as the anthem is playing. They only played the Star Spangled Banner then, not the Canadian Anthem. I'm making notes in my head, "Let's see...15-2...15-4..." trying to figure out this strange game of cribbage that some of my roommates were trying to teach me at the little space we lived in Windsor, Ontario. After the anthem, I went over to sit on the bench, and Jack yelled, "Sid, Adam Brown, and Howe." And I said, "Me?" Yipes, we were starting and I'm on the first shift. They didn't even give me time to get nervous.

I had a good game and scored a goal. We pulled the goaltender with a minute to go because we were behind three to two, and we tied it up. I figured I'd had a good game, and helped out with my goal. I thought they'd leave me with that line and I'd play a lot from then on, but I never saw the ice again until about twenty games later. I never understood why, but then who could understand Jack?

I remember looking across the line that night at Syl Apps, one of my heroes, and Turk Broda plus a lot of guys I had only heard about and held in high esteem. I remember, also, when we made our first trip to Toronto, the guy who used to take photos for the Bee Hive Corn Syrup cards had me pose for my very first card. While I was there, I looked around and I asked "Is this where Syl Apps and those guys have their pictures taken?" He replied "Yes," and I said "Then you won't have to ask me to smile!"

I didn't have great expectations. I was just hoping that I could last one year. Then I could always say I played in the big league. When I got that first goal I thought, "Okay, now I'm registered in the record books." I remember Adam Brown came over after I scored, and said "You didn't get that, I got it." "Whaaaat," I responded, almost in shock. He kept on arguing with me, then he started laughing. I said "Oh geez, I was gonna go to the President of the league! That was my goal!"

I had an old fellow come up to me with some ancient yellow-toed skates, skates I'd never seen, and say "These used to be your skates." I thought, "Oh, okay," as my heart dropped. These were definitely not my skates, and I didn't want to hurt his feelings. I told him, "If *you* want to say they're mine, okay, they're mine. But *I* can't say it." Another man came up to me recently, with skates with number Nine patches on them. And he said, "I want you to sign this paper that says that you scored your 600th goal while wearing these skates." I responded, "Geez, I can't do that. I don't even know if they're mine." The guy went on, "Well, can you say you scored *some* goal with them?" And I said, "Sure. If they *were* my skates I would have HAD to score some goals in them, or I wouldn't have had a job."

One thing that was different about the game in the early years was how much we used to talk to the referees. Red Storey was one of my favorites. I'd talk to him all the time on the ice. I remember one time, we were playing Boston, and some kid on the Bruins put his stick up and hit me right in the lip. I got mad and grabbed him, but before I did anything I looked over at Red to see if he's going to call a penalty on this guy. Red had the whistle up to his lips, then he pulled it back down. No penalty. He changed his mind.

Now the game continues for a while, and then I get my

chance. I hit this guy with everything I've got, and he's completely laid out on the ice. He's also not breathing too well. While he's lying on the ice, the trainer comes out and kneels over the top of him. Then Red comes alongside of me, and he says to me, real confidentially, "Did you wonder why I didn't blow the whistle?" I said "Yeah, it occurred to me." He said "I knew you'd get him back."

The Red Wings, and all the NHL teams, used to travel by train all the time, back in the '40s and into the '50s. However, the Red Wings were one of the first to fly. Jack Adams had us out to the airport for our first team flight on a flying boat! It was one of those old things with a big bubble on it. We were supposed to take it out for a flight, and for some reason we never made it. There was a problem with the plane, I guess. From the way it looked we figured we were lucky.

Our first Red Wings flights were in DC-3s. They weren't exactly built for comfort, but they were pretty reliable. I was only scared one time. It was at night, we were landing in Montreal, and there was a snowstorm. I remember sitting next to Johnny Wilson. We were bouncing around in the sky. It was solid snow out the window, and they were trying to get this thing down to the ground. I looked at Johnny and said "I'm sweating so much my tie is wet!" I never perspired this much in a game!

While Johnny's looking out the window, trying to see something, I asked "Johnny, can you see anything out there?" He yelled, "Look at that—they're eating dinner!" We were flying so low, that he could see a light on in a farm house, and people sitting around a table.

Then I remember hearing the engines roar as they took the plane back up in the sky again. As we're bouncing around even more, they tell us, "We're gonna try to make one more pass at it."

Well they did and we landed. We got beat, big time, the next night by the Canadiens. It's no wonder, we were thinking about having to make our return flight back to Detroit.

Long before the glass, when I started my career at Olympia, the rink ends used to be lined above the boards with something like old chicken wire. Which did I prefer? As far as getting at any miserable fan, I liked the chicken wire. I used to dip the snow on my stick, and as I'd go by some guy who was lipping off, I'd just tap my stick and the snow would spray all over him. The people around this person would laugh like hell, but "snow-face" would go crazy. Sometimes they'd throw beer at us and anything else that could get through the screen. It was like being right next to the crowd, almost in the stands with them. The chicken wire would give, where the glass didn't, it would bulge in towards the crowd. And because you could really hear what people were saying, it brought the crowd and the players together. The major drawback was that players were cut pretty badly on that wire if it was not kept repaired.

It was sad to see the Olympia when it was starting to be torn down. It looked like cancer had hit it. Going through it for the last time you could see holes in the ceiling. I think even the rats wanted to desert it, but I am sure there were still some big ones there. Colleen opted not to go with me, because she wanted to always remember it as it was throughout all the games and exciting times we spent there. Later, we went back and dedicated a plaque on the site, where they have the Olympia Armory now. Johnny Wilson, Elliott Trumbull, and a few others were there in the parking lot where the Olympia stood. I asked "Where was center ice?" Someone took us out into the parking lot to where it was located. It was a strange feeling. I remembered when I last went into the old dressing room, found the spot where I sat all those years, and sat down on the bench one last time. God, it brought out the emotions.

After it was demolished, I got a brick from the Olympia Stadium. Before then, I went with Elliott Trumbull, former Red Wings PR Director, and a few of the former Red Wings and broadcasters who spent many years in the old Red Barn; when they were planning to tear it down. I asked the construction director if he'd do me a personal favor, if I could have an old clock with a wire cage on the front of it. I had looked at it so many times in my whole career. And he said, "Don't say another word— you've got it." But I never heard from him again. I guess you can't win 'em all!

Then I heard someone was at the stadium with an automatic screw driver and took the doors off the dressing rooms. Murray saw them and said to the guy, "Oh, that's really great, why don't you give my Dad one?" The guy told him, "No way! Screw your dad." Later on this same individual wanted me to sign the doors and Murray said, "Don't sign them, Dad. He's miserable..." I didn't sign them.

I designed my own gear during my career. I never wore suspenders. I didn't like anything pulling on my shoulders. Instead, what I'd do is put the shoulder pads on and just let them lay there. I also used to put two holes in my pants, put a lace through those holes, tie them tight and let my hips hold them in position. We used to wear those big balloon pants, so when you made a quick movement you'd swivel inside them and shift the protective pads. That meant when you'd get hit you'd get charley horses all the time. Players don't get to experience that as much now, because the pants and the pads turn with them. The manufacturer discovered what we were doing to our pants, to keep them from shifting. They also picked up on something smart the Europeans did, which was to put a belt on their pants. The pant makers then made some major adjustments. So today, when players make a move, the pants and pads move with you.

I've only had three teeth knocked out in my career and, oddly enough, it was in the first game I played. After that someone had to come through lumber to get to my mouth. Actually, you get hit in the side of the mouth a lot, so your teeth get chipped or loosened quite often.

The chipped teeth were a problem. I went to a team dentist on Vernor Highway at Jefferson, in Detroit. His equipment was filthy. We never knew, back then, what we were going to be subjected to, but, fortunately, later on we got excellent dental care in Detroit. Dr. Filthy sharpened up my teeth that were chipped, and put Hollywood caps on them. But they all abscessed. Man, I was in so much pain. When I was playing, it hurt so much I couldn't think about the game. They were bleeding and were very inflamed. One night I couldn't deal with it anymore, so I called him about two o'clock in the morning. I said, "Doc, I'm really hurting," and I went over there. He pulled the caps out and did a root canal, while I fell asleep in the chair. I hadn't slept for a long time. Then he decided to pull 'em. Although you know it's part of playing hockey, there are the times when you learn there often *is* a heavy price to pay.

When I was young, I was self conscious about my looks. I didn't want to be seen without teeth, so I used to play the game with my false teeth. The trainer told me that was bad for me, because I could get hit in the mouth and choke on them. But I played with them anyway. I felt better with them in. Finally, when I got old enough, I could go without 'em.

One time I was laughing on the ice when I had my choppers in, and Charlie Rayner's stick hit me in the nose. He was a goaltender, and his stick came up off my stick as I was protecting the puck, and hit me right in the face. Honest to God, my teeth shot out and I grabbed for them and caught them before they hit the ice. Now I'm tucking them in my mouth, kneeling down on the ice, bent over. When my teammates came over, and asked me if I was all right, I'm laughing like hell, saying "I can't get my damn teeth in."

Later on we had a superb dentist with the Red Wings, Dr. Florian Muske. He was the one who took care of permanently repairing my teeth when I retired, after the Red Wings informed me it was too late to do it because I'd lost my dental insurance. Just unbelievable. It was senseless to try to permanently fix my teeth while I was still playing. They could just get busted up again. So Dr. Muske said, "Gordie, I know what the club told you. I'll take care of it," and he did. I've always appreciated what he did for me.

One of the funniest stories I've heard surrounds Dr. Muske who had a brother who was an OB/GYN and strongly resembled Florian.

One evening, in between periods of a Red Wings game, a lady came running up to Florian, very excited to see him and chatting away like a magpie about her family plus other friendly talk. He must have looked at her a bit bewildered and she said, "You do remember me, don't you, Dr. Muske? After all, you did deliver all my children?" Florian politely responded, "Not unless it was by mouth!"

The woman was so embarrassed by the mistaken identity, but they had a big laugh together. Florian often wondered what his brother's response would have been had the situation been reversed.

Another time they met me at the office when I got whacked in the mouth while at an out-of-town exhibition game. By the time I got to Detroit I was in major pain. They stayed with me some long hours that night, until they knew I was okay. Then they made sure I got home okay.

Even though the stories can be funny, Jack Adams was a tough guy. If he ever took a dislike to you, you were gone. It scared the hell out of us. And lots of times he'd get down on a guy who didn't understand why. Sometimes we'd go out and play golf and have a few beers afterwards, say at training camp after practice. Then when you came back with beer on your breath you'd be scared as hell of running into Jack. We had to hide from him all the time.

Colleen and I had a party at our house one year, I think it was 1954 or so. And just to be proper she invited Tommy Ivan, our coach, and Jack and Helen Adams. Well, Tommy said "Thanks, but no. A team party isn't the right place for a coach. It's for the players." He suggested we invite Jack. He said "He won't show up, but it'll make him feel good." Right!

Wouldn't you know, the old bugger was the first guy through the door and acted like the life of the party, posing for pictures with all the wives, and just having the time of his life. Well, I had all this beer for the guys, and we had to keep it hidden in the basement in laundry tubs with ice. When guys would come in, I'd whisper "What you want is down the basement." And they'd sneak down there because we wouldn't drink in front of Jack. That can put a crimp in a party!

I was on a TV show once, and said that lightning put the fear of God in me. The host said, "No, the Good Lord doesn't put fear into anybody." And I said, "Wait a minute, he CONTROLS that lightning, and that scares the hell out of me." And that's the way Jack was. He controlled everything. He used to say, "I may not be right all the time, but I do sign the checks. And that makes me right."

Red Kelly is very intelligent and a real gentleman, although he isn't portrayed that way in a television movie being developed, and that's wrong. Red never said a swear word in his life, except once. I heard him swear once. We went down Cass Avenue, out to a radio station on Jefferson in Detroit. We were coming down Cass from Grand River and the Olympia, and somebody drove through a stop street and hit Red's old Edsel. The guy had the nerve to say to Red, "What the hell are you doing?" And Red said "What the hell do you mean what the hell am I doing?" And I thought, oooh, is Red mad! That was the only time I heard him swear. Normally, he'd say "What the hang do you think you're doing?"

There was a misunderstanding about an event in New York when Red was being honored at The Night of Stars event. I got up to talk about him, saying what a great guy and great hockey player he was. But I said "I feel a little bit responsible for him being traded." And I explained very simply: "When I was captain of the Red Wings I introduced him at a banquet as the perfect example of a guy who would play over pain, play with an injury." Now, I had my own personal rule that if somebody was hurt, I thought we should let the public know. That way they wouldn't get on his butt. I'd rather have five guys on the opposing team taking shots at me than 15,000 hometown fans booing me because they think I'm dogging it on the ice. Then you see a guy lose his heart, and you lose him as a hockey player. At the end of the previous season, I guess it was 1959, the press was on Red's case, saying

"What's wrong with Kelly?" and the fans picked up on that. Well, nobody knew he was playing with a broken foot, trying to help us get in the playoffs. I told the media Red took a needle in his foot before the game, to deaden the pain. I know what that feels like, because I've been there. By the third period that pain-killer had worn off, and then he wasn't the same Red Kelly. It was difficult for him, because he played a lot of his game with his feet. He could control the puck with his skates so well.

And I said at this banquet, "Instead of criticizing Red, we should show him how much we appreciate what he did." Well, a guy in Toronto heard the story, and a Detroit writer wrote it up with the headline "Did They Make Him Play?" I wasn't talking about the club forcing Red to do anything. That wasn't my point. Then one of the guys called up Red, when that story appeared, and asked "Are your bags packed?" Red said, "What are you talking about?" They said, "You better get out and buy yourself a paper." And that was how Red found out he was traded.

That's the kind of thing that could happen. People wonder why you'd be fearful as a hockey player, and there is an example. Red had sacrificed for the team, sacrificed his butt off, and they traded him. When I mentioned the episode in New York, I wasn't making an apology. I was just saying how it all happened. I was trying to pay tribute to Red. Hell, we'd never have won anything without Red. He was one of the most versatile and talented guys ever to play the game, and a real winner. He has the Stanley Cup rings to prove it.

But something unprecedented was set by Red during that trade. He balked, and demanded that the Wings could only trade him to the team of his choice. He got his way, as he headed for Toronto, where he won several Stanley Cups. Good for you, Red!

During the Adams years, you could say one thing and you

would be gone. I remember when Ted Lindsay got traded. I was near Chicago with Fred Huber, the team's radio announcer, when it happened. Marty Pavelich had heard about it, and broke the story around town. The press descended on Jack like vultures. It was a huge story. So Jack called out to find Huber, to take care of some of the public relations problems. I got the call, and Adams asked me to find Huber, then he said to me "And by the way, Gordie, that so-called friend of yours, Marty Pavelich, will never ever wear a Red Wing uniform again." That was it, just for telling people what he had heard. Was I concerned about my security? Yes!

I remember the Wings used to have a yearly break-up party at the end of the season, at a steakhouse in downriver Detroit. And one year, when I was still fairly new with the team, there was a little scene between Bill Quackenbush, who was an All-Star defenseman, and Jim Norris, the owner. Something was said, and Bill took his hankie out and said to Jim, with a little lisp, "Oh, DON'T say that," kidding around. And it took three guys to hold Jim off him. He was gonna tear Bill apart. So Quackenbush got traded that year. They got rid of him just for that, yet he was one of the best. If you ask "Was it etched in my mind that I might do something wrong, even if I didn't mean to, and I'd be gone?" Damn right, and that made me nervous, because hockey was my living.

Back in those days, it was an honor to play. Now, it's a livelihood, and you can make a great living. But then, it was more of an honor. You'd train four to six weeks, and there were so many guys trying to get jobs. There were only about 110 big league hockey jobs available in all six teams, split between Canada and the U.S. If you got hurt, you wouldn't even get a contract. It would all be over. And training camp was tough in those days. We'd play exhibitions all across Canada, and Jack Adams used to get all the money. His cash receipts used to be kept in a suitcase. He'd carry his damn suitcase with all the money in it. One time one of the players decided to move the case when Jack wasn't looking. When Jack realized it was gone, it was an ugly scene. All of us split laughing.

It's a lot easier to be friends with somebody than to get into a disagreement. My friendship with Ted diminished quite awhile ago. When we were in business, he did things that I didn't appreciate. He went behind my back to our partner, Frank Carlin and said he wanted Frank to get rid of me, that I wasn't professional enough. When I was younger, I thought Jack Adams was absolutely out of his mind when he said, "You can count your true friends on one hand, even though you'll have hundreds of acquaintances." And it ended up that he was right. What the old bugger said comes through, and it comes through more and more.

When I was a rookie with the Red Wings, I was too young even to drink. I started there at eighteen, and, quite frankly, had no interest in drinking. At most I'm a one or two beer man. Sid Abel was the one that made me drink. He said, "If you can't get relaxed, you're going to be in trouble." And he was right. God, I was tense when I was starting out. I would stay up all night long on the trains, thinking about the game. Clickety-clack, clickety-clack. I'd be rocking back and forth, thinking about hockey over and over. I would often be awake, practically the whole darn night. Sid also taught me to take a little beer and mix it with ginger ale. It was like a gingerbeer. It didn't taste too bad at all, and it made me sort of a happy warrior. I could have a sandwich and go to sleep.

The guys used to try to sneak their beer onto the train, under the nose of Jack Adams. Since I was the youngest, he'd never suspect me, and they had me put the beer in my suitcase and haul it on board. One time I had so much beer in the suitcase, I went to pick it up, and the handle broke off.

In the early days, it was always the four of us—Red, Ted, Marty and myself. I thought we were very close friends. We stayed together. And then Metro Prystai joined us a bit later, the five of us stayed at Ma Shaw's for quite a long while. She had a house near the Olympia Stadium.

Geez, it was fun. I used to get Metro in trouble. I don't think he knows to this day. He used to get phone calls from girls, and he had this sort of growl for a voice. And I could imitate him on the phone, and when girls would call they'd say real sweetly, "Metro?" and I'd say, pretending to be him, "Yeah, whatta ya want? Listen, you broads gotta stop calling me here." I'd really give the girls hell, then slam the phone down and start laughing. Then poor Metro would get these nasty letters. He couldn't figure out what was going on.

I didn't realize until later the full scope of some of the aspects of my relationship with Ted. We'd help entertain his business clients. We'd go to Carl's Chop House on Grand River and Ted would pay the tab, then we'd split the bill between us, he'd pay $20 and I'd pay $20. Then he'd keep the receipt and probably get the write-off. I didn't think anything of it at the time, but now that I know what he was doing, no wonder he said later I wasn't very businesslike. Also, Ted used to always give his clients my tickets to the Red Wings games, and get thanked for them. It wasn't until I started dating Colleen that I truly knew where my seats were located.

I spent less time on a team playing with Bill Gadsby, but we still became great friends. He was a real wildman! We had a lot in common, especially our choice of wives. The Sinclairs, Reg

Sinclair and his wife, Ronni, are also great people. In terms of hockey, we didn't spend a lot of time together. Reg joined our team in 1952, and for a while he played center on a line between Ted and me. We became great friends, then and even to this day, with the Sinclairs. We only see them once or twice a year, but we feel as close to them as anybody.

Murray Oliver, "Old Muzz," I really respected him. We named our son Murray after him. I felt so sorry when he got traded. A lot of people think athletes don't care, but they should have seen how upset he was that day. We told him to look on the bright side, he was at least tradeable. Better than some guys!

I don't think Alex Delvecchio ever got the total credit he deserved as a hockey player. You know, I played more hockey with him than I did anybody. Sid was a great centerman, but I played eighteen years with Alex. He would leave the impression that he was laid-back, sort of a no-sweat guy. Alex could have whistled while he was playing, but he would always get the job done.

I remember telling Mickey Redmond, when Mick was just getting going, "When Alex seems in trouble and everybody else stops, you just keep going. That's when you'll get the puck." Other teams would figure they had him, and Alex would have the puck on your stick in no time. It might be at his feet when, he'd be tied up in the corner, but he'd get it to you so quickly you just had to be ready.

Sid was my mentor. He taught me a lot of good things out there. Lindsay was so concerned about me, he used to tell me, "Spear that son of a bitch." He got me in more trouble. He'd be yapping like hell at their left winger, then the guy would nail me. And I'd say, "Oh, here we go again." Ted's mouth got me in more fights than any other factor. And Ted got his stick in everybody.

You live by the sword, you die by the sword. So guys would go at him, and he'd get that stick up in a hurry. He got the lumber up on me the first time we met after his trade. It was back in Detroit, and he was with Chicago. Right in front of our bench, Ted hit me on the head with his stick, so I punched him and he fell to the ice. I said, "What the hell are you doing? You want to play this way?" He said, "Friendship's not worth it." I said, "Then keep your so and so stick away from my face."

When I first heard the song, "Greatest Of Them All," about me, I was embarrassed. When they played it on the radio in Detroit I thought, "It's nice to have somebody think so much of you to write a song, but it makes you feel awkward." I did like the guitar part on it though.

I've always liked country western music. There's a new song out, called "Where Are You Now, Gordie Howe?" Just a while ago I was out driving around with Colleen, Winona and Bob Lambert, who wrote and sang the song. I'm coming down I-696 in Detroit, where they've added a new split to the road, now you have three freeways coming together at I-275. I think it's Highway 5 or something, and I got on it by mistake. So now I'm lost, and I'm thinking where the hell am I? And Bob pipes up singing, "Where Are You Now, Gordie Howe?"

Colleen is working with Bobby's agent, Jim Lewis, to arrange a video for the song and share the proceeds from it with the Howe Foundation. Bobby and his associates are good people. He just had an Ovation guitar made for me so I can learn to play my own song. I hope it lasts longer than the one Colleen bought me, which Marty and Mark used as a boat one day. Yuck.

It was funny. Eddie Shack and I were at a banquet one night, and people were performing and telling jokes, so we sang the "Gordie Howe Is The Greatest Of Them All" song. Then we sang "Clear the track, here comes Shack, he knocks 'em down, and gives 'em a whack, da-da-da-da..." Johnny Bower was there, and he sang his "Christmas Goose Song." It's comical and he sings it with his son, John. Then he said, "And now, there's a new hockey song out, called "The Bobby Hull Song," "To all the girls I've loved before..."

Back in the '60s I was having trouble with my eyes. They were burning and itching and I was having little 'floaters,' little spots run across my eyes. It was like a fly going by. You follow it with your eyes. We finally got Dr. Hesberg at Henry Ford Hospital to examine me. He was more than a little surprised and concerned about me, because he detected I had a partially detached retina, which had already started healing itself. He told me if it ever bled, or if I experienced increased flashes in my eye, I'd have to get to a doctor immediately. If not, it would lead to blindness. Although the chances in hockey of getting hit in the eye aren't as great, it still happens. We lost a great defenseman and teammate, Doug Barkley, when he was blinded by getting hit in the eye with a stick in the mid '60s.

Dr. Hesberg got me the phone numbers of eye specialists in each of the cities on our next road trips so I'd have immediate contacts both at home and at the hospitals around the league. I had to carry those numbers around with me for a whole year.

I'm not sure how I got the retina damage. It could have been any collision or hard hit that happened in a game. I know that one year, when I was playing with Parker MacDonald, we were being coached by Ned Harkness. It was near the end of my Detroit career. We were doing a drill, where we criss-crossed at the blue line, which was against everything I've ever been taught. In the drill I saw that Parker and I were going to collide, so I fell to the ice and Parker tried to jump over me. He's not much of a jumper and he accidentally kicked me right in the temple. Now I experienced a condition I never felt before. I knew where the bench was, but I lost sight of it. I couldn't focus on it. I headed for it, but missed the gate by about three feet, and banged into the boards. Lefty Wilson, our trainer, was standing at the gate and said, "Hey, down here, stupid." With that I figured I'd teach Lefty a lesson. I went down to the ice, as though I'd fainted. Actually, I felt like fainting. I was still light-headed and dizzy. Lefty ran over to me yelling, "Hey, what's the matter, big guy?" I told him exactly what was the matter. I said something bilingual, English and profanity. So he helped me back to the bench. The whole thing became almost as comical as the time I got hit in the mouth by Chuck Rayner and I caught my teeth before they hit the ice.

Although not an injury, the most painful thing I ever went through was the night I had a kidney stone attack. I was on the road and up all night with pain. In the morning I looked like a dead horse, but had to travel home. The pain was so severe it scared me. When I got home and showered, I went down stairs all doubled up. I said, "Colleen, get me some help." Oh, did it hurt! I had on a robe, and had my legs drawn up because I was in such pain. Our daughter, Cathy, heard me moaning and ran to see me. She started crying because she thought my legs were gone.

Colleen called Dr. Finley, and he told her if she could get me in the car, to bring me to the hospital. We managed that, and now I'm on my hands and knees in the front seat. It was rush hour, and traffic was backed up for miles. Colleen got off at an exit to reach the hospital by way of side streets. Finally, we get there. I went in to the emergency room all bent over and we run into Sonny Eliot, who's a humorous weatherman on Detroit TV. I said, "Not now, Sonny. Don't joke, it hurts too dang much." The attendants took me upstairs and injected me with something for the pain. I went to sleep and I passed the stone during the night. I was joking and said it was the size of a golfball. I guess it was pretty darn big.

The next morning, Colleen came into the hospital with my shaving kit and pajamas, thinking I was going to be there a couple of days. I said, "I won't need those, I'm playing tonight." She said, "What? Who said?." Here I was, practically near death a few hours ago. She was so worried. Now I tell her I'm going to play hockey. She said, "When you get out of the bed I'm getting in!" The irony was, I had a good night on the ice, scoring a goal and an assist. But I had to go off the ice in the third period because the pain and excitement finally caught up to me.

When I go to a doctor, I'm asked to list if I've ever had injuries to various parts of my body. I just put a streak from the top right to the lower left and write in "All the above." I've broken my wrist, had quite a few fingers broken, and fingers knocked out of joint. Let's see, I tore up my ribs. That was in Boston. Somebody left a gate open and it caught me directly in the ribs. I had a big lump where the cartilage holds my ribs together. That was a sore one! I took a shower, and the team doctor came in and said, "Mr. Howe, I can imagine the pain you're going through, and I promise to take A-1 care of you." He handed me a card, and the card simply had his name on it, the name of some person to see at the hospital in Boston and the address of the hospital. I had to get a cab and go alone to the hospital.

Two ushers went with me, to show me how to get in a cab with broken ribs. I couldn't bend over, so I had to drop to one knee and walk in. Fun! So I get to the hospital and into their x-ray department. Dr. Brown did a block on the area, freezing all the nerves. This numbed the pain and I said, "Well, I feel better.

Maybe I can fly home with the guys tonight." Then the whole world started to spin. So, I stayed overnight and left the next day. That block lasted for weeks.

Let's see, I tore up my collarbone. I was in an exhibition game in Sarnia, and I ran a guy right through the double gates of the boards behind the net. One gate flew open and he went out of the rink, but the other door did not come open and caught me right on the collarbone. It was diagnosed, at the time, as only a sprain. Then I had a similar accident AGAIN the next year. I got slammed into the glass at the penalty box gate. The doctor, Dr. Small, told me I had been playing an entire year with a broken collarbone, and now it was badly bruised. This upset me, because I was never told I had a break in that Sarnia accident.

I tore up my ribs another time, on the other side. I had a hernia operation when I was in Omaha. My first year in Detroit I tore up my knee cartilage and was operated on after the season. And then the next year, I hurt the other knee. And the following season they operated on that knee, and I missed about twenty games.

I have to figure I've taken about 500 stitches in my face. I had a bad cut on my cheekbone one time, and Dr. John Finley, tried something new. He didn't stitch it up with thread. He took a strand of wire, weaved it through my cheek, tightened it and cut it at both ends. And in two weeks, he popped out the wire and the wound was perfectly healed.

Then one year I hurt my knee and I couldn't flex it. I had a bursa sac on it. I had to have the knee scraped. Oh, was that painful. I broke my toe one time. Bobby Hull was taking a slapshot. I thought the net was ten feet to my left, but he wound up and the shot hit my skate. When he hit me, it was funny. He put his hand up to his mouth like he was sorry. I was skating

176

toward him at the time, and the puck didn't hit my toe directly. It hit the blade of my skate and broke it. My toe went right to the end of the skate and it broke. I went to the bench and said to the trainer, Joe Alcott, "Cut my skate off, please! My toe's broken." It was painful as hell. Joe responded, "It's a long way from your heart." As though nothing was serious unless it was your heart. I said to him, "My fist is a foot from your damn nose if you don't start cutting." They couldn't do much for a broken toe so I just suffered with it.

My left wrist bone created a painful problem near the end of my years with the Red Wings. I was operated on to alleviate the swelling and to help restore movement. Dr. Bailey, at Ann Arbor University Hospital, did the surgery and removed the end of my art bone, which connected to the wrist. It had been fractured at one point and had now become nearly disintegrated because of the loss of circulation. Although it was a painful recovery, it allowed me to continue to play hockey.

After retirement, I had very successful carpal tunnel surgery done by Dr. Clark in Traverse City, so I could get some feeling back in both of my hands.

I also broke my nose about fourteen times. I remember once Joe Garagiola, the TV commentator, asked me how many times I'd broken it. I said "None." He said "You never did?" I said "Nope, I had fourteen other guys do it for me."

And there was the time Teeder Kennedy's stick caught me under the right eye and scraped the eye. It also broke my nose and cheekbone. And that's when I went into the boards and had the serious concussion. Complications set in and I had trephine surgery to relieve fluid on the brain.

God, I remember being in that ambulance, going from Olympia to Harper Hospital. Every time we would turn a corner I felt like I was going to throw up. It was a horrible ride. I had the sensation I was falling, and I kept grabbing to hold on to something. I was so sick to my stomach and they kept saying, "You're okay." They took me right into the emergency room, and took x-rays. They kept me awake because it was a head injury. Then someone gave me a drink of water and I got violently sick again. It was then that they rushed me to surgery. I can remember they shaved my head, and that was like the same thing as losing teeth. You know, your vanity. And I said, "Oh, no, not my hair." I was given anesthesia and they started drilling into my skull. I was wide awake and I could feel the pressure. My head was tight against the operating table and I'm thinking, "Oh boy, I hope they know when to stop." I couldn't feel it other than the pressure and hearing the noise. That's a strange feeling. The doctors kept me awake for a long period of time after that, pricking my foot with a needle so I couldn't fall asleep.

When I finally did get to sleep, I think I slept for a whole day. When I finally woke up, I went into the bathroom and there was a big bandage across my right eye. I wondered if I had lost my sight, so I lifted the bandage up, saw my image in the mirror and said, "good" and went back to bed. Then Mum and my sister, Gladys, came in the room, and I watched them walk in. I was so surprised, because I didn't know they were there. Gosh, poor Mum, she was sicker than heck. She still hadn't recovered from her first airplane flight, and she was so worried about me. I said, "Oh hell, Mum. You take the bed." And I think my humor eased her mind.

It's funny what hockey players will do to play over injuries. Normie Ullman came to the rink for at least five weeks on crutches and went home on crutches, never missing a game. I had a special cast put on my wrist after surgery. I played, but I couldn't shoot the puck very well. My upper hand was still weak, and it is so important when I shoot. The wrist had initially been broken by a slash. You take so many of them, you don't know which one actually breaks it.

Bobby Hull had one of the heaviest shots. God, he could shoot that puck. There's an old joke about Bobby and his brother Dennis, who is one of the funniest people anywhere. He had a good shot, too, but not as accurate as Bobby's. The line was "Bobby can shoot the puck so hard and so fast, he can put it through the entire length of a car wash and not even get it wet." And the other guy says, "Yeah, well Dennis could do the same thing if he could hit the car wash."

Anyway, Bobby's slap shot hit me another time. It hit me on the shin pads. In a little while, I noticed my skate was sloppy. I thought sweat had gone into my boot. So I asked for a change of socks and to put the blower on the skate boot. I took the skate off and I had a half-inch of blood in there. The shot split the skin on my shin, right to the bone. They had to stitch it up on the inside and the outside to get it to stop bleeding.

I played at Houston one year with a broken foot until I got my 100th point. The instant I got it, I think I set up Mark on a goal and I said, "Thank you very much" and went right off the ice and had my foot put in a cast so I could be ready for the playoffs. Then, after the season was over, they came to me and said, "We made a mistake, you only have ninety-nine points." A reporter once asked me how many times I'd been hurt in a game. I told him I was hurt, somehow, in every game I played. It doesn't seem possible, but it's true.

It's pretty strange to think that Mum and Dad didn't ever see me play a game until the "Night" that was given for me at Olympia, in the thirteenth year of my career. I never got paid big

179

enough money to bring them into Detroit, and they couldn't afford it on their own. I used to talk to them about getting to Detroit some day, and Dad would joke, "I can't go anyway. Who's gonna feed the dog?"

When they drove an Oldsmobile out on the ice that night, they presented me with the new car, I was surprised enough at that. But when I saw Mum and Dad in there...well, that was as emotional as it could get. Even thinking about it now brings tears to my eyes.

COLLEEN: As I recall, that night was essentially created by Chuck Robertson, our dearest friend, and his committee which included Jim Pryor, John Curran, Jerry DeClercq, Bill Gadsby and Chuck O'Brien. We were just overwhelmed. Of course, having Gord's mom and dad there was a thrill. The Olds came out on the ice, and they announced we were given a vacation at a hotel in Florida. It was like a dream.

Later on, we found something was awry. We heard that the car hadn't been totally paid for, and I think Bruce Norris had to throw in some money to keep it from being repossessed. And then we couldn't find out anything about this hotel and the free vacation. We didn't know what to do, it was embarrassing. We were asking people, and nobody knew what the story was. Eventually, we found out where the hotel was in Florida, and we went there with the kids.

When Gordie Howe Night happened, I guess it was March of 1959, I stayed in the stands because I was pregnant with Cathy. She was born on the 24th. I remember the Bruins were there that night and they gave me a big teddy bear for the baby. The Wings flew Mom and Dad in, and it really was the first time they ever saw Gordie play. They never saw him play as a youngster or as a pro. There were so many children in his family, and his parents worked so hard. That was just the way they lived. But Gordie didn't think they loved him any less. In those days parents didn't get as involved with their kids activities, like so many do now, and kids got around without their parents driving them everywhere. Times were different.

Anyway, they had his parents in hiding at a hotel, and they were inside the car when it was driven on the ice. Gordie had no idea they were in there. Boy, was it hard to keep that secret. He was asked to take the ribbon off the car, and he looked inside, and from then on, it was so emotional. He was truly shocked. He just cried on his mother's shoulder. He almost collapsed. He just folded. Gordie holds his emotions in pretty well, except in some situations. It seems like every time he gets to center ice for a tribute, we all end up crying. It happened that night in Detroit and later in Detroit when he retired the first time, and again in Hartford when he retired the second time. But it was more emotional the night his parents got out of the car. People were crying in the stands. And then Gordie had to make a speech to the crowd, which was just going crazy. Plus, it was being shown on live TV in Detroit, and I thought, gosh, what can he possibly say after that? He was so busy wiping the tears away when they handed him the microphone. He just said, "It's a long way from Saskatoon." That's Gordie.

GORDIE: People always wanted to know if I was ever going to move back to Saskatoon, and there was a move to get Marty and Mark to play their junior hockey in Saskatoon. And I said "I'm not for that, because I worked my butt off to get where I am." That probably didn't sound like a very nice thing to say, but you have to think back to the days of the old National Hockey League. There were only six teams, and they were all out east— Detroit, Toronto, Montreal, Chicago, New York, Boston. That was my goal in life, my ambition, to be an NHLer. And I couldn't do that unless I got out of Saskatoon. I played for five teams and played twenty games in Saskatoon one year. You're not gonna learn very fast if you don't get the opportunity. As it was, I had to sit out my sixteenth year. I worked my buns off to get out of Saskatoon. I'm not knocking my home town or hockey in Saskatoon. I love going back there. I really wanted my kids playing fairly close to home, because I wanted to see them play. Thank God they played for the Detroit Junior Wings, and then the Toronto Marlboros, so I did get that chance.

MURRAY: There were things my father could do on the ice in terms of strength that no one else could do. I recall one game at Olympia, when a big fight broke out, and everybody's pairing off and my dad grabs one guy and he sort of pops him. Then another guy from the other team goes skating by and Dad grabs him and holds them both together. I don't know what possessed him to do it, because it's something I've never seen in hockey. And the crowd just went wild, watching these two guys who couldn't get away from Gordie. He just held them together. They couldn't move and they couldn't fight, because he had them totally tied up.

Another time I watched Dad in the WHA, he was playing against some big guy, a guy around six-feet, six-inches or so, and the guy was giving my father a hard time the whole game. He was taking runs at Dad, and really trying to make trouble. Finally, he ran at Dad, as Dad was trying to get off the ice for a line change. Dad just turned around and hit him once, and he knocked the guy out. I thought, that was great. It was like he was saying "You've given me enough. Now I'm going to give you something to remember me by." He had that incredible, incredible power, and that sense of domination in his game. You had to see him to know how different he was.

GORDIE: Probably the most famous run-in I had was with Louie Fontinato in New York, in 1959 I believe. He was out to get me, and he took advantage of a scuffle that broke out near their net to try and take a run at me. I saw Louie coming at me, thinking he was swinging at a dead target. He didn't know I saw him out of the corner of my eye. I slipped my hands out of my gloves, just holding onto them with my finger tips, and waited til he threw his right hand at my head. Then I moved, and he missed, thank God. Bill Gadsby was playing with Fontinato on the Rangers then. And he said "Had you not been aware that he was going to nail you, your career would have been over." That's how hard he had wound up to hit me, because he was skating up to me at full speed. He was gonna knock me out with one big punch. So he missed, and I dropped the gloves and was ready to go.

Whenever I got in a fight on the ice, I would grab the sweater of the guy I was fighting around the arm pit of his power arm. And that would tie him up, immobilize him. Wherever that arm would go then, I would just fend it off, and I could use my other arm. I'd reach in and do that first thing. With Louie, I got a lot of good licks in right away. I had his right arm tied up, so he finally switched hands and hit me just on the side of the head with his left hand. So I changed over, grabbed THAT hand, and swung with MY left. That's where he won a partial victory. I hit him so hard my finger came out of joint, and that was pretty much the end of the fight. That hurt. Did I feel sorry for him? No. We'd gone at one another for years. Emile Francis, the Ranger's general manager, said that whenever I hit the ice he knew that Louie irritated the hell out of me, so he'd try to get him out there against me, to get my mind off the game. I could never understand why Louie would get so excited.

Speaking of Louie, I learned a lesson about life from Colleen because of him. It was similar to a lesson I learned earlier about hockey, when I saw our defensemen, Jack Stewart, and Milt Schmidt of the Bruins, go against each other. They both felt that if they didn't draw blood that evening they hadn't had a good game. Those guys were mean towards each other. There was just a steady whacking all night. No fighting, just hitting. Miltie had a bad habit of coming down the right side while Jack was on the left. Jack wasn't that mobile. And Milt would go up in the air on one leg, like a dance move, to get by him. And he'd be out of control when he was in that position. So I studied what he was doing, and since I was the right winger on the outside, I went down and came up through the middle. And when he was up on that one leg, I hit him. Jack came into the locker room after the period ended, and he grabbed me and picked me right up off the seat, and said "Young man, that's between that man and me. You stay the hell out of it." And dropped me back on the bench. It was his fight, he didn't want me in it. Jack was something. He used to play with a very thick, really heavy stick. And I lifted it once, and said "Jack, how the hell do you shoot with a stick like this?" And he said "It's not for shooting. It's for breaking arms."

Years later, I was playing in a game after both of those guys had retired. And I heard a little commotion in the crowd. I looked over and saw Jack Stewart and Milt Schmidt in the stands. And they stood up, saw each other, and walked through the rows of seats to shake hands. And I thought, my God, what a tremendous picture for sportsmanlike conduct. And I told Colleen about it. I mentioned how the whole rink stood up and gave them a hand. It was really quite stirring. She said "You really feel that way?" And I said "yeah," and around her you gotta be careful what you say, because she picks up on things so dang fast. And this was one of those times.

We were planning to go out to Vancouver for a charity banquet in my honor. It was to raise money for handicapped athletes, and we needed to invite some of the speakers. Colleen said to me that if I was really sincere about what I saw between Jack and Milt, why didn't I call Louie Fontinato and ask him if he'd like to come out and join us in Vancouver. So I did, I called Lou. He and his wife came to Vancouver for a couple of days, and it was nice to see them. Lou's like a big puppy, he's a good guy. There are stories about how guys used to scrounge for money in the old days. In New York, when there were snow storms, he used to miss practice and shovel sidewalks for money. And I can understand why, too. In those days you could make more money doing that than playing hockey.

I remember the headlines in the summer back in Saskatoon after the season, "Hockey Bums Back Home." We were well thought of.

I enjoyed playing ball every summer in Saskatoon. We got paid to play, and it was damn near as much as I got for playing hockey. Roy Taylor was a scout for the New York Yankees. I went eight for eleven in a tournament in Indianwood, a small town near Regina, and I was hitting against an All-Star team from the Negro Leagues. They came up to Canada as a team. I was hitting very well, I hit for the cycle one game—homer, triple, double, single. I was a potential prospect of the New York Yankees, until they found out I played hockey.

I was playing in another tournament, up in Regina. And I got a telegram from Jack Adams, saying "Who's going to pay your bills if you get hurt? I suggest you quit playing." So I waited, because I wanted to play in Kamsack in a game. Then I sent a telegram back saying "Dear Jack Adams, are you serious?" I

185

figured it would take a while for him to find me. Well, he found me, right at that tournament. Because his next telegram said "I am serious." Though I think if Jack had seen me running to first base in that tournament, he would have torn up his telegram. I hit a line shot between the fielders, and the ground was muddy. It was raining, and I fell down three times on my way to first. I was thrown out at first, but I knocked in two runs, before I got thrown out on the play. I was really fast on my feet. I was laying in the mud, just roaring with laughter.

How Jack had originally heard about my playing ball was from an incident when I was playing third base. I fielded a double-play ball, stepped on the bag and fired over to first for the double play, and this guy nailed me. He spiked me, and I caught blood poisoning. Hell, I was about six feet off the bag. He was their first baseman. Not to say I'm vindictive, but I drag bunted three times after that, until I finally got him. He was in the baseline and I ran up his leg. And the guy acted surprised. He said "My God." He told me later "I figured I might as well stand there and let you hit me, because you were going to sometime." He was right!

Jack Adams, Fred Huber and I used to drive up to northern Michigan on a publicity tour at the end of each season. We did it as a promotion for the Stroh's Brewery. We'd go around the state for twenty-five dollars an event showing a highlight film of the Wings' season. Sometimes we'd have five showings a day.

One time we were driving north, and we had gotten around Flint, and Jack was driving. He came to a stop sign on a big highway that was about as big as a window, about a 12-foot sign, and he went right on through. I said, "Mr. Adams, did you know you ran the stop sign?" He said, "No, did I?" And I said, "Yes, sir." And he said, "Well, that just shows you how accidents are caused." So, he was a little tired. He gave me the keys, and that was the last he saw of them until the tour was over.

We'd go through the Upper Peninsula, and go to Marquette Prison. I talked to those guys and they were just like hockey players that got a penalty. Every one of them was innocent.

This was really a good way to add to my playoff money at the end of a season. Back in those days, if we won the first round of the playoffs, we would receive a thousand dollars per player. There were only four teams in the playoffs then, series A and series B. Actually, it was supposed to be a thousand per man, because it was $20,000 to the winning team, which would have roughly twenty players. But out of that money the coaches had to be paid, the trainers, even the scouts. So that thousand a man usually got cut down to about $700. And that's before taxes. Then, if you won the second round, that was supposed to be $2,000 per man, with $1,000 to the losers. So, if you won the Cup, after we had agreed to the shares going around, you'd make about $2,000 per man.

Now, traveling with Jack and getting paid mileage by Stroh's to show the highlight film, and making sometimes five stops a day, I got almost $1,250 just for the two weeks we toured the state. I could earn nearly as much at showing movies than I could by winning the Stanley Cup.

The weirdest event I attended was in a small town, where the local community gathered at a train roundhouse. I was supposed to show the film and answer questions about hockey. This was in the Upper Peninsula, and typical of a frontier town. Jack was doing his presentation at a nearby town, while I did mine in a town called "Bruce Crossing." (Wonder if that was named after Norris?) I had about eighty people in attendance. I just got started when sirens started blowing, whistles were going, and the sheriff ran in. He needed volunteers for an emergency. So a bunch of people got up and left, and I looked around and thought, well, I still have a bit of a crowd, I'll just go on. And I start again and there goes the siren. Somebody came running in and said there was a bad hit-and-run out on the highway, and people needed help. So away went just about everybody else. Honest to God, I was left there with three people and myself, talking about how we won the Stanley Cup. That was it. So I just sat down with this old couple and a young person and we just talked. But I did make three friends, at least.

Not only did I make money working the promotion for Stroh's, but it was a tremendous help in teaching me how to speak in public. I used to sweat blood about that, but Colleen told me all I had to do was be myself, talk hockey and answer questions. I liked it and got pretty good at it. Besides, it gave Colleen a chance to coordinate the program scheduling for me and to plan how to put the extra dollars to good use.

I had my superstitions as a player. I used to try to hit all the green lights driving to the Olympia. I thought it would be a good omen. When I liked my stick or if I scored a goal with one, I would remove one of the stripes from the shaft of it. We used Northland sticks, and they had three stripes wrapped around them, just above the blade. So I'd remove the middle one first. And I'd tell everybody in the dressing room if they were going to take one of my sticks, don't take my good one. If the wrapper is off, leave it alone. And I had certain undershorts. If I wore the shorts and we won the game, I'd put them away, and the day of the next game, I'd get them back on again. Finally, I thought maybe I'd better buy them all in one color. Then I wouldn't know which were the winning shorts.

Things really changed when Bobby Baun joined our club. We went to dinner up at Port Huron, where we were training in my last years with the Red Wings. This was long after Adams had left the team. Bobby and I were having a drink together and he called me a stupid SOB. And I said, "Okay, I'll go along with that. I've got my reasons, what are yours?" And he said, "I'm making twice as much money as you are." Bobby had just joined our team after having been with an expansion club. Well, that kind of woke me up. I said, "You're WHAT?" He said, "I'm making twice what you make." And I said, "Well, what do you think I get paid." And he told me exactly what I was making. And I said, "Then what do you make?" And he said "I'm making over $90,000." Boy, that hurt. And he said, "If that doesn't hurt you, Carl Brewer makes more on this club than I do." So there were *two* guys making a lot more than I was, and the club had always told me I was the highest paid player on the team.

I remember the funeral of Jack Adams. Everybody had said he was a pain in the rear to play for, and a mean old bugger. But one of the former players there said "Whatever thoughts he instilled in me about running a business, I do in mine and I'm doing a lot better now. I guess in the long run, he was teaching me." Another guy in our car said "Well, he was a miserable SOB and today he's a dead miserable SOB." That's the kind of mixed emotions you got about Jack.

He got on Ted and me one time in the papers about having a business outside of hockey which affected our performance. So Colleen and Pat Lindsay, to be funny, came to the arena dressed like millionaires, and were burning fake money with their friends. Then the media ran in and got a shot. It was all in fun, but Jack was not too happy about it. So we played a big game that night, real important, and our line played a hell of a game and we won. We're coming into the dressing room after the game, and Jack is shaking hands with all the players and slapping them on the back, and when Ted and I walked up, he turned his back on us. So Ted and I stopped and shook hands, and I said "Nice game, Ted, nice goal out there." Jack did so many things wrong, but he did a lot of right things too. I didn't hate him. I couldn't like him at all times, but I didn't hate him.

I've enjoyed much about playing hockey, but setting up a teammate for a goal—now that was the best. The two most memorable were the time when I assisted Mark when he got his first hat trick when we opened up the Summit in Houston, and the time I assisted Marty on his first goal for the Aeros. I loved both of those moments.

If I had advice for young hockey players I'd say what I said to Wayne Gretzky years ago, when he was just a kid. He said "What could you tell me that would really help me?" And I said "Well, I haven't seen you play yet, but if you want some good advice, I would say you have two eyes and one mouth. Keep two open and the other one shut, and you'll do just fine."

"Gordie's simply the greatest...and Howe. I feel proud to have been his linemate, coach and longtime friends of Colleen, Gordie and the Howe family."
—Sid Abel

CHAPTER EIGHT

POWER MAKER

COLLEEN: I've always had the feeling, and have always believed that Gordie felt the same way, that it's a privilege to work, and to earn a living honestly. I think if I couldn't get a job, I would create one for myself. Maybe that's because I was raised during the Depression, when jobs were so precious and few. People were hungry and had to find work to survive. Work to me means an opportunity to participate in the scheme of society, doing something that provides a service or product which others need.

Putting in hours, is fun if you like what you're doing or take pride in accomplishing a task. I know my capacity and I know how I feel. My mind is always going, a mile a minute, and I love life. Thank God I've always been healthy. I've only been in a hospital four times during my life. Four kids, four times. It's an asset that is partly due to my heredity, I'm sure. All I have to do is look at the health and ages of my grandmother and Aunt Elsie, both one hundred.

I'm a great believer in vitamins and minerals. I take them religiously every day, because I can tell the difference in my stamina. I figure if I'm going to ever be one hundred I'd better take care of myself. And today, I know that if I don't, I'll hear from Dr. Murray Howe! He cares about his mom and dad and offers good advice to us. Murray was always a philosopher by nature, and very wise for his age. People are drawn to him by virtue of his caring nature. They also respect what he says. It's also important to your life when you know someone loves you enough to guide you in the right direction, especially in health. He relentlessly works with programs which expose the tragic effects of tobacco on the public. He can speak both from his own findings and his personal experiences with patients. We're so proud of him.

I had a lot of jobs and businesses when I was growing up; they were all really exciting to me. I started out as an usherette when I was thirteen and, oh, I was so happy. It was at the old Riviera Theater in Detroit. This was my first real job! It wasn't like working at a nearby corner drug store behind the soda fountain counter or setting up a lemonade stand in front of my house to service a thirsty passerby, as I had previously done. This was a genuine job! I was only thirteen-years-old at the time and was I eager to make money. This job gave me the feeling of being out in the working world. However, I had to lie to get it. I thought of it as a white lie! A Mr. Kelly interviewed me and I could tell he liked me. I told him I was sixteen, the age requirement for working papers. He believed me, so I got the job with the contingency of bringing in my working credentials. No problem, right?

We had lockers where we could hang our clothes, and we put on our uniforms right in the theater locker room for employees. This was very formal. Movie theaters in those days were like legitimate theater is today. The ushers and usherettes escort you to your seats. We had to keep track of how many seats were empty, so if two people came out, we would usher another two people down and usher them into those seats. We even had our own little flashlights. I was so proud of carrying out my responsibility, perfectly. I could not do enough. Besides, I thought I looked very cute in my little usherette outfit. I loved the idea of working, of learning, of being responsible and having my own money. Especially the last.

I took a streetcar, you know the trolley type of transportation, to work right after school. This really separated me from all of my friends, but *I had a job*!

Then something unexpected happened. My first pay was stolen. All ushers received their money in cash in a pay envelope. It wasn't enough money to put into a check, so we'd get cash. I think my first pay was about three dollars in quarters. I was so proud of that money. I put it with my things. I couldn't wait to take it home and show my grandmother, who was staying with me while my folks vacationed. Now somebody had stolen it out of my locker!

I couldn't believe it! I would never steal from anyone! I cried all the way home on the streetcar. I never had anything stolen from me before. I was just broken-hearted. And when I got to the house, I cried and cried on my grandmother's shoulder. She said "Colleen, it's hard to imagine that people do things like this. It's a lesson that you have to be careful, and lock your locker." Then she insisted on giving me her own three dollars, even though it wasn't an easy thing for her to give. Three dollars was a lot of money to us in those days. It taught me a lesson in life that yes, some people do steal from others, and you have to be careful.

I went from usherette to running the candy counter at the theater. Now I was inventorying and responsible for handling money. Neat! I figured I'd own that theater in a few years, no doubt! I was the best manager they had ever hired.

Then the day of reckoning came. Mr. Kelly asked, as he had done many times before, when was I going to bring in my working permit. I couldn't lie anymore and I had to tell him I was thirteen and I couldn't get the papers. He was only mildly upset with me and felt bad that he had to let me go. It was the end of my job, my pay and my dream of, perhaps, having his job someday. I hated that day. Now it was back to trying to do something else and having to ask for money from my parents again. What a bummer!

In 1950, I was about a year younger than the kids in my graduating class in high school, because I had skipped a half grade during elementary school. This meant I graduated in January instead of June. Now I couldn't enroll in college until the Fall which meant I had to get a job. I found out at that time the Detroit Public Schools offered students an opportunity to apply for jobs through the Board of Education. I went there and filled out a form which disqualified me from most of the clerical opportunities. Oh, great! My four years of Spanish and all the other college preparatory subjects I carried didn't mean a hoot when it came to getting work. But I did have two electives that helped me that day. I took typing and was schooled in people skills during my cooperative retailing classes in high school. I loved the latter one, because I got a job after school which acquainted me with all phases of a department store and its functions. I also got paid and earned extra school credits as well. But after the class ended, I was back to square one, applying for a job.

I was informed that the Bethlehem Steel Company was looking for a file clerk. I applied for the job, and went for an interview at the General Motors Building in Detroit's New Center area. I was seventeen and I had never filed anything in my life; but how hard could it be? When I got there for my interview, I found out that there were many people trying to land this job, and they were all waiting to be interviewed.

I remember the interview, and meeting with a Bill Biddinger. He asked me up front, "Colleen, there's a whole bunch of people sitting out there that are qualified for this job. Why do you think I should hire you?" I hadn't prepared myself for a question like that, but something crazy came into my mind, a kind of "by the seat of my pants" thinking. I said, "Well, Mr. Biddinger, I know that anything to do with filing certainly involves knowing the alphabet." And he looked at me a little strangely, and responded, "Well yes, that's true." I went on, "I'm sure the other applicants know the alphabet, but I bet I'm the only one who knows it backwards. So I can file frontwards and backwards for you." He just sat there laughing. He said, "I'm not sure I heard right! You know the alphabet backwards?" I told him, "I sure do!" "All right then, go ahead, let's hear it." I rattled it off in about five seconds, "Z-Y-X-W-V-U-T-S-R-Q-P-O-N-M-L-K-J-I-H-G-F-E-D-C-B-A."

He nearly fell off his chair, and he said, "You've got spirit and are the kind of girl that would fit in here perfectly. You've got the job, you're hired." I guess he liked my humor as well, and so I got the job. It was interesting to me that something I had learned when I was a small child, when I spent a lot of time with my aunt, would get me a job. I remembered the day it happened, she was ironing and helping me learn my alphabet. I must have been only about three or four years old. I was so proud, because I could recite the alphabet for her, perfectly. "Okay, now that you really know it frontwards, let's learn it backwards." I thought that was neat, so I learned it that way, too. She showed me that there's a rhyming pattern to it backwards, as opposed to the sing-songy way of learning it frontwards. Z-W-X, W-V, U-T-S, R-Q-P and so on. Although I never really thought that seemingly little bit of knowledge would necessarily come in handy in my life, I still thought it was fun to know. Since that time, I'm always eager to learn bits of information I can gather from others. It's amazing how much it has helped me. I learned so much at that job. I offered to help anyone and everyone I could to learn what they were doing. They were eager to explain, because I could relieve them for a break occasionally. So I learned how to transpose pounds into tonnage on cardex equipment, how to work the switchboard, type better and meet and make friends with all the staff. I even met Mr. Charles S. Mott, president of the company. He was a very distinguished and pleasant millionaire. I never met one before. I dreamed of one day being a secretary or right hand gal to someone like this. His offices really impressed me, and I knew he was very philanthropic and respected him for it. Little did I know then that someday my son would train at Mott Children's Hospital in Ann Arbor. Ah, destiny!

When I left Bethlehem Steel it was when I was in charge of coordinating the schedules, messages and all of the needs of about twenty salesmen who traveled between the Lackawana and Bethlehem, Pennsylvania plants and the home office in Detroit. I had no difficulty handling this. It was a snap, and I enjoyed all of the salesmen, as well as all the staff. That job actually played a role in my meeting Gordie. I would take a bus to and from work, and I had scheduled my bus rides home so I could meet with my dad at the Lucky Strike bowling lanes at Grand River and West Grand Boulevard, where we would bowl and then go home together from there.

Now I heard about an even better situation, with a commercial art studio in the New Center Building. It was more money, in a smaller company, and I would be working as an office manager for the owner, Mr. Ferd Prucker. The studio and artists were very different, and more relaxed than a formal big business atmosphere, and I liked that. The only downside was that Saks Fifth Avenue was on the main floor of this building and I was getting a bigger pay check. The upside was I became friends with Carroll Tietz, the art director, and still receive holiday cards from him and his family. And sometimes the various artists would teach me something I could do for them, like opaquing. I loved it.

GORDIE: If Colleen Howe had been a hockey player, she would have played center. I can see her as a centerman, because you have the freedom to do what you want and go wherever you want to go. That would be my guess. She would be the one that everything centers around. Centermen also have the freedom to proceed on their own, and are generally the playmakers.

COLLEEN: What position would I play on a hockey team? Hmm. Not goalie. I wouldn't want anybody taking shots at me. I've had enough of that. I think I would like to have been a forward, because a forward is very much in control, has to carefully plan all moves, has more room to move in, can work with everybody else on the team, and when scoring a goal, gets all the credit.

When I first married Gordie, I never realized that hockey would last so long, that he would play so long, or that Mark and Marty would end up playing, also. I had no idea how stressful it would be just being Gordie's wife. And I came to realize that our business diversification would be so important to our future. We HAD to have lives outside of hockey. Nobody plays forever, not even Gordie, though he came close. He went thirty-two years and wanted to keep going. I knew we had to find other fulfilling income related activities in our lives that we mutually enjoyed and that would be financially rewarding. That's where we were headed when we went into our cattle investment. If we hadn't gone to Houston, if Gordie hadn't come out of retirement in 1973 to play with the boys, that's where we were headed in terms of a full-time business. In reflecting back, that wasn't meant to be. In three years after we were in Houston, the whole cattle industry hit all time lows and went under. We were hurt by it, but since we had our hockey earnings, we were saved from going under with it. It was unfortunate, because we loved the cattle business. It was the one thing I saw Gordie show as much love for as hockey. He couldn't wait to get out to the ranch; neither could the rest of us.

We had an offer coming in from Eatons of Canada back in the late '50s when Mark McCormack, founder of IMG, did me a big favor by choosing not to take on Gordie as a client. At the time we had talked to him, he just said he was busy building a mountain that everyone would want to climb. That mountain was Arnold Palmer. And, because he didn't know much about hockey, he thought it was not a good time to represent Gordie. Gordie felt rejected to some degree, but I like forthright people who tell you the truth. It's better than someone who tells you they'll do something, and then they don't. McCormack was the first to do this, so there were no other choices. I asked myself, who knew Gordie and his strengths, his appeal to the public, better than I did? In the beginning, I may not have operated on as large a scale as somebody like McCormack, but what I did was good. I was able to build long-term relationships with major corporations, who were eager to have Gordie Howe promote their products or be a spokesman for their company. Gordie knew I would do the best job possible.

You know what's most interesting? I learned that you don't have to know everything at first. You grow as you go. Dealing with people on a fair basis has merit. Literally, the most important factors in sports representation is to deliver quality and reliability. That's why there have been so many companies with whom we've had long-standing relationships. We've been happy with them over the years, and they've been happy with us having Gordie on their corporate team—Eaton's, Lincoln-Mercury, Emery Worldwide, Zeller's, and Rayovac. So we have been able to build a future with security, with long-term clients and good relationships. It certainly beats all those years in hockey, and only getting a monthly pension payment of about $1,400 in American dollars. It's pathetic to think that's what the man who played the game longer than anyone is paid. We needed to make corporate relationships work, to give us some freedom and to allow us to live a comfortable lifestyle, the kind Gordie deserves and all of our family deserves.

Often I'll hear people complain about having to pay bills and I'll tell them that's one of my favorite things to do. When they eye me with a stunned look, I explain that it's a matter of having the money to do it that brings pleasure. It's only bad when there's no money there. So that's why we diversify, and we don't depend on anyone else to control our revenue. We can live with our own performance, not that of others.

When Gordie was playing, hockey always had to come first. There was no question about it. Gordie was on the road the day Marty was born, and when he returned to Detroit the next day, his boss, Jack Adams, called Dr. Jim Matthews, my doctor, and tried to get him to find a reason I needed to stay in the hospital an extra day so Gordie wouldn't be 'distracted' by taking his new son home on the afternoon of a game. To me, that is just ridiculous.

One of my closest friends among the wives on the 1960 Red Wings team was Joannie McNeill, wife of player Billy McNeill. She was like a younger sister to me. At the time, Joannie was seven or eight months pregnant. After a Thursday game, Joannie got very ill. Billy called us from home saying that something was terribly wrong with her. He wanted the name of a doctor. Joannie had her polio vaccine, but she kept telling Bill she thought she had polio. When Dr. Jack Ronayne got there and examined her, they rushed her to Ford Hospital where she was put on a respirator. She did have polio and Billy was beside himself. They also had a very young little girl, Nancy. No one could go in to see Joannie, she was put in isolation. Her parents flew in from Vancouver and it was a waiting game. By Friday night, she was stabilized and beginning to breathe on her own. Jack Adams wanted Billy to play the Saturday game, so the doctors and everyone thought it was safe for him to go to Chicago to play the Blackhawks. Joannie died that night and he was not there.

Gordie was rooming with Bill on the trip, and when he was called, he had to tell Bill. It was the most horrible thing he ever had to do. It was also the most devastating situation I'd ever experienced. And to build in more shock, a few days after Joannie was buried, the Red Wings traded Red Kelly and Billy McNeill to New York. Billy and his in-laws packed up and took Nancy home to Vancouver while Red Kelly, newly married, held out of the trade unless it was to Toronto.

Not long after, Gordie and I asked to meet with some of the doctors at Ford Hospital, to explain to us what actually had happened to Joannie. I vividly remember driving home alone from the hospital, and thinking that if something ever happened to me, Gordie probably wouldn't even be able to come to my funeral. It was this overwhelming feeling that none of our lives mattered, that nobody's family mattered. Where were the values and the compassion? It was as though families and wives were not people. I will never forget the horrific feeling I had after Joannie died alone like that. It was as though there was no heart in this game and no regard for the personal lives of the players or their families. It frightened me. My fears then turned to realizing how much we'd miss the Kellys and the McNeills, and I cried.

It's hard to justify that hockey can effect your life to that degree; that a coach or general manager can tell your doctor when your children should come home from the hospital. They can lecture the players about when to have sex and tell them, like Jack Adams did, that every time they had sex it was like losing a pint of blood and to keep it in their pants.

It was more than just the fact that Gordie was away from me so much, it was how I was made to feel as a human being, how all the wives were made to feel. I came from a family that taught me self-esteem. I was proud of what I represented. In hockey, though, I was made to feel like my children and I were unwelcome baggage. And it goes on outside of hockey as well.

Last year, Gordie and I were invited to speak at the Crains Business Magazine Annual Luncheon in Detroit. This was a major event, and we were really looking forward to sharing our thoughts with everyone. Originally, we had been invited to promote the *and...HOWE!* book, but we had to tell Crains that a publisher we had rejected was doing an unauthorized biography of Gordie, causing us to delay our book until next year. They said they wanted us to appear anyway, with or without the book.

There was a full house at the event held in Southfield, Michigan. So many people greeted us, and we had a lot of old friends in the audience. There was a place card at each table telling about the program, and that Gordie and Colleen Howe were the featured speakers of the day. When it came time to introduce us after lunch, the master of ceremonies got up and began telling a bunch of old anecdotes about Gordie—the same old stuff you hear at every event from somebody who hasn't done their homework.

And this guy was the sports editor of one of Detroit's biggest radio stations. His introduction goes on and on and, not once, has he even mentioned me! A kind of funny feeling came over me, because I thought maybe I wasn't supposed to be speaking. We were seated at the front table, and I quietly asked somebody to pass me one of the program cards. I looked at it, to be sure and there it was: Gordie and Colleen, speakers! in huge letters. Now that I know I'm not losing it, I relaxed. Just then, this guy wraps up another old story about Gordie and says, "...and here he is, Gordie Howe. And his wife, Colleen." That was about it.

I almost didn't go up to the podium. What an insult! How tacky and very undisciplined. I went up on stage and I counted the two microphones and two podiums, which told me there was no way the MC didn't know I was going to speak. And, oh, I just remembered, he also raved about Gordie having gone to a hockey game there in Detroit to see his grandson play. "And to show you what kind of a guy Gordie is...I saw him at an early hour of the morning just to see his grandson play." Well, he was referring to Mark's youngest son, Nolan, and I was there as well. This doubly ticked me off.

As soon as I got on stage, I made a point to go directly to this person, extend my hand and say, "My name is Colleen Howe! How are you?" Then I said to the audience, "I just wanted to tell you that I, Nolan's grandmother, was also at that game, just to set the record straight." I'm sure he knew by then that I was not real happy about his lack of introduction. The station he was from also gave at least three interviews to the writer of the unauthorized book. How could he, after that, stand there before the crowd and say how much he thought of Gordie? I think it was unkind, and I felt a sense of injustice as far as being a woman is concerned. Some guys don't like women, or don't like me.

A lot of our talk that day was about the unauthorized book that came out on Gordie. If someone wants to buy a book like that, referred to in the industry as a "spoiler," meaning it's not very good and spoils it for the authorized story. This one was full of inaccuracies, and it was done with the full knowledge that our book would also be coming out. It wouldn't hurt the sales of our book, but it would confuse the public. We had even interviewed that publisher and writer to do *and...Howe!*, but decided not to work with them for good reason. They went ahead anyway! Nice, huh? It's our story, and you would think someone might respect our right to tell it, and not try to make a quick buck by getting their book in the stores at the same time as ours. Cute! However, we surprised them and delayed our book to the following year.

It's no fun dealing with these things. You end up involved with negative issues, instead of concentrating on positive things you want to share with people. But you can get eaten alive if you don't fight back. As an aside, when we were recently at the American Book Sellers Show in Chicago, our attorney, Wayne Logan, was over at the booth of the publisher who did the unauthorized Howe book. He was looking to see if they were promoting the book. One of the heads of the firm approached him and started up a conversation. Wayne asked if they were still carrying the book and why they didn't do it with the Howes. The guy told him that the Howe's wanted to work with them (a lie), but that their 'a__hole lawyer' screwed up the deal. Wayne asked what the lawyers name was, and the response was, he didn't know. Wayne then showed him his name badge and politely left. GULP!

Aside from books, there was a move about fifteen years or so ago, when we were in Hartford, to make a movie about the life of the Howes. These Hollywood people approached us, and naturally, we had an interest. Certainly the concept of a guy playing hockey alongside his two sons, and being a grandfather and playing so well at the age of fifty, ought to make for a pretty interesting screenplay. It was going to be a television movie-of-the-week.

The first thing this producer wanted to do was to get a writer out to Hartford, to interview different members of the family before he started on the script. He also wanted to include an interview with the women in the Howe family—that would be Mary Howe, Marty's wife, and Ginger, Mark's wife and myself. Mind you, this writer was highly recommended by the network as one of the top script writers available. We were impressed.

When the writer got to Hartford, I was out of town on business, and I had yet to meet him. Gordie picked me up at the airport when I returned, and I asked him about the writer and his impression of him. Gordie told me that he wasn't certain about him, that he was different! The writer had followed the players around for the last couple of days, and he seemed like a nice guy, but unusual. Creative people often have their offbeat personalities.

Usually when we work with people on projects, they become like friends or family to us. They get into our lives, and I like to deal with people that I can have a personal relationship with, along with the professional one. I want to be able to relax around the people I work with, and have a mutual trust with one another. That's why most of the people we do business with remain our friends long after the business association is gone.

Gordie told me the guy needed to meet with me because he wanted to begin interviewing the Howe women; to get what they think down on tape. That sounded great to me, since I was eager to go forward on the project.

That first night I was back from a hectic trip, the writer went to the game with Gordie to do locker room taping, while I stayed home catching up on phone calls and mail. Both of them came to our house right after the game. We had made arrangements for the writer to stay at our house that night, because of my interview time and because we had to get up for an early morning practice the next day. Because this guy had such outstanding Hollywood credentials, I was eager to meet him. As soon as he and Gordie got to the house, there was an introduction. I got right to the point, asking the writer what he wanted to do about the taping tonight. He said that he wanted us to do whatever we would naturally do when we got home after a game. He'd like to see us in our normal setting, going about our normal habits and he would join us! I told him we usually would get ready for bed when we got home, have a cup of coffee or tea and maybe watch the late news. We liked to relax after the excitement of the game.

He thought that sounded great, because it gave him the chance to experience what our daily lives were like. And, since we were casual, he'd relax, too. So he went in his room and got his pajamas and robe on, and came out to join us for coffee. That was no big deal to us. We like being very relaxed with people, and since he was spending the night at our home, we didn't want him to feel uncomfortable.

We met in the kitchen, and proceeded with our tea to our favorite spot in our home, the loft, located up a series of stairs and overlooking our living room. We started talking about that night's game and some information he needed from Gordie and the two of us together. By now, Gordie's very tired from playing the game and he excuses himself to go to bed. He said, "You guys haven't talked yet, so you don't need me. You two can catch up and I'll see you in the morning." With that, Gordie heads for some sleep. Mind you, the writer is taping all of this conversation.

Now, this normal taping session turns into the craziest, and least expected, situation I've ever encountered. I'm glad now I can't remember this guy's name.

While we were having our tea, I told him I was certainly prepared to spend as much time as he needed with me tonight, because I wasn't going to be available again soon. There's no furniture in the loft expect for a large, round coffee table and a built-in seating area with big pillows on it for lounging. We are seated on the floor area and he puts the tape recorder on again and begins to ask me questions. After a while, he said he was getting tired of sitting on the floor and asks that we sit up on the built-in bench. I thought, no problem, it's more comfortable. He moves the tape recorder and we go on with the interview.

As I am talking, I notice he kept moving, all the time. He was a real antsy little guy, a nervous type. I figured he was probably just really interested in what I was saying. (Only kidding!) He's talking to me very earnestly, asking questions. Now, I'm talking away, and as I turn back to face him, I suddenly notice he's got his legs pulled up with his hands on his knees and his robe has parted. He had on no underwear and everything was exposed. And naive me, I think he doesn't know this, I looked away and I'm trying to keep talking and stay on the subject, and I'm thinking, what the hell did I just see? This poor guy. He doesn't know that it's sticking out, so to speak. I feel embarrassed for him. I'm thinking, God, he's going to be so shocked when he finds out what's happened. And during this thought process I'm talking away, giving him all this information about hockey and our lives and the kids, and at the same time in my mind I'm going, oh...oh...oh, why me?

Then I think that if I could just get him to move, we could get out of this situation because, apparently, he still hadn't noticed what I saw. So I told him I'm not comfortable up here, and let's go back down on the floor again, on the cushy carpet. I figured, of course, by moving the problem would go away.

Well, we got down on the floor, and now it's worse. Now I don't know what to do. I'm starting to get frightened of him. By this time I know this is not an error. Instead of his legs being pulled up, he's got them wide open. Now, I'm really afraid of him. He's a wacko. I just met this guy, he's a big Hollywood writer, and he's a flasher!

My mind is running wild. 'Oh my God, maybe he's even a killer.' All kinds of emotions go through me. I'm embarrassed. I'm nervous. I'm fearful. And, I'm angry. What does this guy think he's doing?

I recalled the producer we had worked with before, "Oh, you'll love this guy. Great guy, great writer." And here he is, exposing himself to me in my own house. Hello, Hollywood, in Hartford.

(FLASHBACK: I remember when I was a kid, I had an even more traumatic incident when a man with a knife tried to drag me in an alley with him. I managed to escape. I handled all that, so I could sure handle this.)

I assess the situation. 'Okay, I'm in this. I don't think he's got a knife. Should I be afraid of this guy, or is he a mental case?' And I knew that all I had to do was go down four stairs, go down the hallway, up some stairs, and wake up Gordie, who would break his freaking neck for him. I also remember thinking, "Thank God he's interviewing me first, what if he had done this to Mary or Ginger?"

Then I had this thought: This project's over, write this one off. So much for this movie. And this guy suddenly says, out of the blue, "Do you like having your feet rubbed?" Oh my God. Now I know he's sick! And I'm not going to let him see that I'm panicking. I'm going to still act like I'm not wise to him, because I figure he'd get his kicks out of scaring me. These guys probably get excited by everything from soup to nuts, excuse the pun.

I'm trying to think, how can I get out of the room? He was between me and the doorway to the stairs. Would he grab me? Would Gordie hear me if I yelled? Fear was really setting in, everything was going through my mind. How am I going to get out of this? Finally, I decided to stand up, and I just said "I don't know about you, but I'm really tired and I think I'll just go to bed." And I was out of that room in a flash. I didn't wait around for him to react. I moved so fast. And I ran up the stairs and into our bedroom, and I almost jumped inside of Gordie's body, asleep in bed.

I didn't dare wake Gordie and tell him. I figured I was safe then, and I'd get rid of this creep in the morning. For one thing, Gordie would have gone down there and beat the tar out of him that night. I didn't want that kind of a scene. I mean, he would have bounced this guy like a basketball. Worse yet, Gordie would call Marty who lived next door to us, and then the guy would be history.

I thought, I've got to call California in the morning and get this sicko off the job and out of town. I knew he was supposed to leave for the early practice with Gordie, and I'd take care of it after he left the house. I never went to sleep that night, I was clinging to Gordie's back and thinking, "What if that guy comes up here to our bedroom?" Our home was very contemporary and the master bedroom had no door on it after you reached the top of the winding staircase that led to it. We've got a maniac in the house! My brain was going a thousand miles an hour.

In the morning I quietly asked Gordie to be sure he took the writer with him and didn't say another thing. When I heard

Gordie leave with this guy the next morning, I put in a call to California. Unfortunately, I had to wait for the time change to reach the producer: When I did, I asked him, "Are you sitting down?" Then I told him what had happened, and said, "You send a guy like that to my house? Do you know what a sick man he is?" And he's saying "Why, he's one of the most esteemed blah blah blah..." Yeah, right! Get him out of town, IMMEDIATELY. And the Hollywood people are full of apologies. They couldn't believe it! They're so sorry and all that. I said, "I don't want apologies. Just get him out of town." And I said, "Look, if I tell Gordie, he'll kill him. And if Marty finds out, Marty will kill him if Gordie doesn't. I can't guarantee what will happen if this guy sticks around. I am really angry right now." I wasn't afraid by now, I was mad! The more I thought about it, the angrier I became.

By this time, I was thinking the heck with Gordie or Marty, I'LL knock this guy into a wall if he comes near me. He was small anyway! I was ticked off, too, that we had spent a lot of time setting up this movie project, and this threw everything out the window. It doesn't make for a good working relationship when your writer is Mr. Flasher. The people in Los Angeles told me they'd send another writer, but I was in no mood for doing anything with any of them again.

Now get this. We think the guy has left town, but he hadn't! I went to the Whalers game the next night, and I'm sitting with Peter Kelly, our attorney. I had told him the whole story because he had been involved in negotiating the movie arrangements. Peter said something like, "Well, thank goodness that guy is gone." When the buzzer ends the period, I excused myself to get a coffee at the concession stands, and there HE is! He was standing at the top of the stairs, waiting for me, against a wall. Now he's looking and acting like a different person, he seems panicked himself. He says, "I've got to talk to you. I can't leave town until we have spoken." I told him, "I do not want to talk to you. I want you to leave." He said, "I've got to explain." I said, "Well I'm not going anywhere with you to hear an explanation." (Once was enough!)

He said, "Oh no, I understand. I apologize. I'm a very sick person. I've been seeing a psychiatrist for some time, but my family doesn't know about my problem and I don't want them to find out." And I said, "Well you are sick, all right, and hopefully you'll continue to seek help, because you need it." I wasn't afraid of him now, he just seemed totally pathetic. Now, I'm almost becoming a counselor to him. He has tears running down his face and he's all emotional. I said if he had pulled a trick like that on one of my daughters-in-law he wouldn't believe what might have happened to him. And that basically was it. I told him to get help. I just said "You're talking to the wrong person here. You have to go back and face the people you work for and your family. You're no longer involved with us."

He left town, and I never heard of him since. I don't know what happened and I don't want to know. Maybe I was too sympathetic to him at the game, but he seemed so pathetic.

How do you figure you'll get an exhibitionist to write your movie-of-the-week? I told Gordie the whole story a couple of days later, after I was sure the guy was gone. He had asked, "What happened to our writer? "He took off," I replied—End of movie! The network had hand-picked this guy. They sent us a flasher, and we, unknowingly, invited him in to our home. What were the chances of that happening?

COLLEEN: I know I must be blessed in surviving some of

the most life threatening experiences. I've survived two small plane crashes in my life. In one of them, I was coming back from skiing with some friends in northern Michigan. We had to land on the I-75 freeway, right in the middle of traffic, and the plane went up in flames right after we got our luggage out of it. People came running up and started yelling at us for blocking traffic. We said "What did you want us to do?" I don't know if my life is charmed, but it sure is different.

One time I innocently went out to Colorado to see my Great Aunt Elsie. And I decided to take advantage of being out there by driving to Colorado Springs and visiting Colorado College in that town. Murray was trying to decide what college to attend, and he knew Colorado College had a good hockey program. It wasn't a scholarship deal, but he wanted me to assess the campus and hockey facilities and staff.

I called the college, and a fellow who worked for the athletic department said sure, come on out, and that he'd take me for a tour of the facility and give me information on their program.

I was very excited about seeing this campus, because everything is so beautiful there. I flew into town the night before and rented a car to get to the hotel where this man would meet me in the morning. We met in the lobby. He introduced himself and was very pleasant. He couldn't be more helpful. He said "Well, come on, Mrs. Howe, I've got my car outside, let's take a tour of the campus." So far, things couldn't have been better.

Now, as we approached his car, I notice that there's somebody sitting in the front seat, on the passenger side. I didn't think much about it. Maybe it's another representative of the school or someone else is taking the tour also. He opens the back door for me, and I get in, behind the third person. Immediately, I begin to wonder what the heck is going on because the person in the front seat is a woman in her pajamas. She has a robe on, and her hair up in curlers. She doesn't say a word, just sits there staring straight ahead. I'm thinking, "What is this?"

Naturally, I said "Good morning, how are you?" And she says, real bitterly, "I'm not good." I said "Oh." And the guy gets in. You can immediately sense the tension between these two. Oh, Oh! So I politely say, "Maybe this isn't a good time for you to take me on this tour. We could do it some other time. That would be fine." And he said, "Oh no, now is fine. No problem."

So off we go in the car, and he's pointing out various places of interest around the school. "There's the library...there's one of our dorms." Then, out of the blue, she turns around and says "If you're wondering why I'm here, I just caught my so and so husband with one of the female students of this school. And I'm not leaving this car!"

Oh. Okay. Now, the guy never turns around. He keeps driving, and says over his shoulder, "Ah, forget her. She doesn't know what the hell she's talking about." I said, "Look, why don't we go back to the hotel." "No, no," he says, "forget her. I want to show you the campus, and that's what we're going to do."

Naturally I'm going crazy in the back seat. How could I get caught in the middle of a domestic fight like this? And I couldn't believe he was subjecting ME to it also. He just keeps driving around, giving me the tour, while she's sitting there next to him, just fuming. This goes on for awhile, sometimes in dead silence.

We stop at the athletic center, and we get out of the car to look around. She stays in the front seat, sitting there in her pajamas, this angry look on her face. I'm trying to get the whole thing over with, rapidly. He says, "Come on, let's go in the building," and I can barely understand what he's saying, because

I'm thinking "Am I dreaming? Is this really happening to me?" I want to go back to my hotel and get out of town.

This tour lasted two hours. After awhile, she starts screaming at him, while we're driving, and he's saying "Aw, shut your mouth!" And they're going on and on. I can't imagine subjecting anybody to this kind of nonsense. And she's trying to get me to side with her, "Yeah, I caught the SOB red-handed. This probably isn't the first time, either." And I'm just sitting there with this bewildered nervous look on my face.

We pull up at another place on campus and he says, "Okay, here's our next stop." Real cheerful. Then he says to her, "Just stay in the car and shut up!" And that's the way it went, for the entire two hours. They wouldn't stop fighting, she wouldn't leave, and he wouldn't stop the tour. I was going to see that campus come hell or high water, or maybe over someone's dead body!

Needless to say, Murray never went to Colorado College. The University of Michigan had much more to offer.

It seems I was forever getting involved in some major assignment or project, probably because I either volunteered for it, they knew I couldn't say no, or because they felt if they came to the busiest person they knew, I could take on one more job. I've never thought of myself as a "Sports Barbie Doll," who sits around looking important. Aside from that, I've become much more interested in BIG projects than in little ones, and I feel nothing easy is necessarily worth doing. I'm also a person who is always ready to fight injustice. I guess that's why I'm drawn so much to Bonnie Lindros. She will go to the end of the earth to right a wrong. Yeah, Bonnie, even the media is praising you now. Time is the only element that tells the really lasting image of someone.

Well, I don't plan on ever retiring, especially from doing whatever is possible. I love being involved in challenging opportunities. One of those came to me when we were living in Connecticut. It was at a meeting where I first met Barbara Tucker; a long time friend of mine since then. The get together was to ask whether or not I would consider running for Congress in the first district of Connecticut. A campaign was beginning as a special election to fill the seat of an incumbent, Bill Cotter, who had just passed away. This was in 1981 and the office had to be filled immediately because it was months before the November election.

The Republican Party had already named a former mayor of Hartford, Ann Ucello, as their candidate, but the Barbara Tucker group felt that someone more formidable would have a better chance of winning. Hence, they were meeting with me. Wow, I was a bit surprised. I guess I had never thought of entering a public office, even though I supported various people in campaigns and loved the thought of how proud I would be to carry out, and fight for changes that would make a difference in people's lives. I also was a fighter for justice, and someone who would go the full distance to bring about change. Actually, not unlike a Ross Perot, I wouldn't always see things getting accomplished in the bureaucracy found in present day government. I'm not even certain that our Constitution is defined as to what our forefathers meant it to be. First of all, all men are not created equal and never will be. And had I gotten to Congress, I would have been in favor of removing the rights of a voter if that voter does not exercise or appreciate that right. Then they would have to do something to earn the right to vote. There is too much taken for granted in our society today.

Perhaps my fighting and caring was the reason why this meeting was being held. I don't know, but it got my attention.

April 15, 1953—Wedding.

Florida Honeymoon.

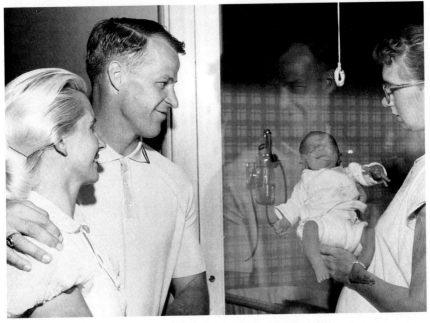

No, little Murray, Jack Adams won't say when <u>you'll</u> go home.

Marty meets dad at the train depot in the early morning hours.

Having Christmas without the hockey dads. Left to right. Claire Arbour, Joannie McNeill, Colleen, Teresa Delvecchio, Joanne Arbour, Corinne Delvecchio, Mark and Marty, Kenny Delvecchio, 1956.

Our first home on Stawell in northwest Detroit—1953.

Reg Sinclair came to Detroit from New York in 1951, and was centerman for Lindsay and Howe.

Gordie, Red Kelly, Metro Prystai, Marty Pavelich, and Ma Shaw at rooming house.

Sid Abel trying to talk Cathy into being the first female hockey player.

Cathy loved horses at an early age—1966.

Cathy, a track star in Houston.

Cathy teaching herself to play the organ.

Jaime, age 15, on Brandy.

Jade, age 8, on Casey.

At the ranch with friends Becky, Jeremy, and Josh Tarleton.

Wade and Cathy Roskam.

Grand opening of the Howe Arena, Traverse City, Michigan.

Mark A. Hicks

Steve Yzerman and Wayne Gretzky helped the Howe Foundation during fund raising on 65-city tour.

Last visit to Olympia.
Trumbull, Gordie, Skov, Delvecchio, Pronovost, Peters, Dea, and Wilson.

The Old Red Barn, where all the memories go on forever.

*Only time wearing a leather helmet was
after skull surgery.*

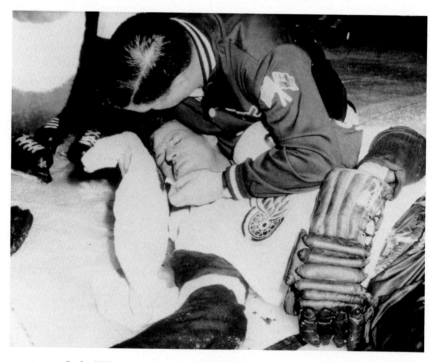

*Lefty Wilson, trainer, attending Gordie in Toronto after the
impact of Eddie Shack's stick.*

1959—Our second home on Sunset Boulevard in Lathrup Village, Michigan.

Friends helping us move; Frank Carlin, Al Kaline, Pete Goegan, and Red Kelly.

Off to the races with Carol and Frank Carlin.

Marty, Bryan Watson, Gordie, Murray Howe, and Mark at Gordie Howe Hockeyland School—1967.

*Gordie having fun with youngster at signing session,
July, 1970—Vancouver, British Columbia.*

*Our first skate at Gordie Howe Hockeyland,
St. Clair Shores, Michigan.*

Colleen, the Power Maker, in 1981
Congressional run, Hartford, Connecticut.

Beattie Martin and Colleen,
Waskesiu, Saskatchewan.

Mark and Ginger help with my campaign funding at
Gordie's Place Restaurant in Glastonbury, Connecticut.

The ABA show in Chicago to launch Power Play Publications, Inc. with attorney Wayne Logan and Raina Kangas of Logan & Company.

My assistant, Dawn, with husband Brian, daughter Taeler, and Bonzo Aspenleiter.

A little PR for Zellers through Mike Bermingham
of their men's wear department.

Zellers' Heroes of Hockey Team featuring Perrault, Shutt, Gordie, Sittler,
Bossy, Laperriere, Giacomin, and Savard.

*A new career in modeling
for Zellers.*

Mark and Marty posing for a Zellers ad.

*Diane Gordon, director of public
relations for Zellers, at signing for
Heroes of Hockey.*

*Gerry Pace, photographer, and
Isabelle Ethier with Gordie at photo
session in Montreal.*

Bill and Mary Burley,
Burley's Ice Supply Company.

Jeff Lake, Optimum
Public Relations.

Meeting with Del Reddy to promote books throughout the U.S.

Mind you, this was at a time when I had full responsibility for our company, Howe Enterprises, which has now changed to Power Play International, Inc. My big concern was how could I run for political office and continue to fulfill my necessary roles in the management of our company, which provided us with our supplemental income. I told the group I'd give them an answer in two days, after I conferred with my family, and other people I would want to talk with plus the people who worked for me.

One of these people was Barbara Kennelly, Secretary of State in Connecticut. Barbara said to go for it. She would look forward to campaigning against me if I were to win the nomination from Ann. Barbara was then planning to run for the seat on the Democratic ticket. It would have been fun to have had the chance to do that. Another reason for running.

Everyone encouraged me to run and before I knew it, I was a full fledged candidate with a staff, headquarters and everything that a campaign is all about. Once I announced, several other politicians came on board, which was another thing that I wanted to accomplish in my efforts. This made it an even more exciting race for the public, for the candidates, and for me. Every day I would study issues, raise money, speak to every conceivable group old enough to vote, raise money, knock on doors, raise money, stay up half the night to talk to and answer the questions of the people called delegates, who sometimes acted like they were in control of my life and not just my vote. But they are a part of the ridiculous process that brings a candidate to the ballot for the people to vote on. Some of these people were in these decision-making positions because they knew someone or they knew what they were doing and sensed their responsibility to all of the candidates and the voters. One fellow told Gordie that he sought to be a delegate so he could offset his wife's Democratic vote. He even placed a challenge before her that he'd get the position. And this was who I had to convince that I should be the Republican choice?

I ended up nearly taking the convention vote away from Ann Ucello through most of my opponents throwing their votes over to me. But since that didn't happen, I had to exercise my option to go to a primary, which was a real risk for me, because so many Republicans register as Independents since Hartford is largely a Democratically-motivated district. This way those people are not seen as Republicans by anyone. And in a primary, only voters who are registered as a Democrat or Republican can vote. Duh! It was not a good night for me at the polls, and I was defeated. Ann went on to a no contest campaign against Barbara Kennelly. Barbara remains a Congressperson even today. And Gordie got back his wife.

The experience of that election taught me a lot about the electoral system and about the cost of a campaign. It is virtually impossible for anyone who is from mid-income America to assume the cost of a campaign. And how does that guarantee the public to have the best representation possible?

During our sixty-five city charity fundraising tour, I met up with Beattie Martin, an experienced politician and long-time friend of Gordie and myself. He told me it struck him as very unusual for a POWER MAKER to run for any public office and that he was surprised when he heard I was in a race for a government office. I had not heard that term before, so I asked him to explain. He said that a POWER MAKER was an individual who spends all their time making other people powerful. He thought that was what I had done most of my life for Gordie, and others that I had promoted, for the sheer belief in their success. I guess, in a way, I thought he was right for the most part, but I had never heard the term before. Perhaps all of our lives we look for the POWER MAKER type of person to be around.

When I think of what I do for our corporations, I think I could use a half dozen POWER MAKERS to assist me with the responsibilities involved between Power Play International, Power Play Publications and the Howe Foundation. I counted the number of functions I perform for each of these entities. It is no less than thirty-four that I personally coordinate, manage and create. Whew, it wore me out just looking at the list! But it would be much like having thirty-four children. They generally come one at a time, so you adjust with each one and soon you don't realize how many hours they require and how much of yourself is consumed by them. Boy, I'm sure glad that we don't have children to raise at this point, and I wonder how I ever filled both roles years ago. Guess everything was on a smaller scale then. Sure!

I'm really happy to have my assistant, Dawn Blamer, plus her brother Dan, as our CPA. Terry Perrelli has provided us with bookkeeping for years, and is vital to our business. Wayne Logan and Doug Bishop do our legal work, putting contracts and intellectual properties together for me. Greg Wolff continues to do our insurance. Our daughter, Cathy, is heading up activities for the Howe Foundation, starting with the sixty-five city fund raising tour we took in 1993. Except for the donation the Red Wings and the L.A. Kings gave the foundation, all the rest of the nearly one million dollars stayed in the communities in which it was raised. Cathy is currently working night and day to hold a "Riding with the Stars Celebrity Rodeo" in Winston/Salem, North Carolina in August of 1995. We'll be there!

One of my most favorite things in all that we do is the fan mail. Gordie and I have several little pen pals, besides our grandchildren. One that comes to mind is Cory Walton of Tulsa, Oklahoma. Cory is nine-years-old and we'd advise all you scouts reading this to keep an eye on him. What we like most about letters from kids like Cory is that they remind us every day that all is right with the world. That's why I keep so many photos of our family everywhere I work, because they make us feel so good about life.

Another one of the most motivating things about what I do each day is found in each of the functions I perform. PEOPLE. I love people! And, working with them gives me great joy. If they don't, I don't work with them anymore. Some told me I don't build business, I build relationships! Come to think of it, that's probably true. I just never thought about it in that context. Perhaps that's why we have continued to have such long-standing agreements with so many companies. We've had ten years or more with all the hockey clubs Gordie played or served in other capacities. Then there was Lincoln Mercury and Eatons from years ago. We are now going into our ninth and tenth year with Rayovac of Canada and the U.S., putting them into the category of one of the longest standing companies with whom we've dealt. John Moran, former president, brought us to the company. It was then that we got to know Tom and Judy Pyle, the owners. We've enjoyed our liaison to the company, John Daggett, and are having the opportunity to work in correlation with various other members of the marketing and public relations groups. All the staff at Rayovac are like family to us, and we enjoy having the opportunity to work closely with them in benefit of the Rayovac goals. A special function we attend at Rayovac each year is the Andy North Golf Invitational, traditional in support of Special

Olympics.

Companies we have been involved with for five years or more are Bank of Nova Scotia, Neilsons Chocolate Company and Emery Worldwide. Mr. Emery did something for Gordie that surprised him. He gave Gordie some shares in the company at an employee reception. Gordie had never even received stock from any of the hockey clubs he worked for over the course of thirty-two years. It touched Gordie, and we appreciated what Mr. Emery said about him. John Emery had a bad experience with an athlete that the company had engaged and thought he would never want to deal with another one, until he met Gordie He felt Gordie exemplified what dedication was really all about. He was the first one there and the last one to leave. It's always nice to hear it from THE BOSS. By the way, that's what Muhammad Ali nicknamed me.

We work with many companies now, that we have a special relationship with in business and hold in high regard, starting with the Christian Stick Co., who also own Northland Stick; Burley Ice Supply Company and Ice Specialties with Bill and Mary Burley; Kosch Food Services Company in Gordie Howe's Tavern and Eatery in Traverse City; Quaker State Oil; Parkhurst Card Company with Brian Price; and that special corporation in Canada called Zellers. We've had the pleasure of working with Diane Gordon and Mike Bermingham as our liaisons to the company. They guide us through the various departments of service that Gordie renders for the company, be it appearances, books, tours, photo shoots, travel, additional items for endorsement plus all the men's wear products approvals or Club Z advertising. We are especially grateful to Zellers for their commitment to the Howes and our company, Power Play Publications, as well as this book. It is certainly an unprecedented relationship between a corporation and an athlete like Gordie who, by the way, is also a member of Zellers Masters of Hockey Team this year.

Thanks to all of the past and present companies who believe in us and make our lives productive and meaningful. We don't ever want to retire! It's too much fun working with you.

GORDIE: I want to publicly say that I honestly believe Colleen deserves a place in the National Hockey League Hall of Fame, Builder's Award category, for the things she has contributed to the game. She put her home up for collateral to help build the first private hockey rink in Detroit. That started the many thousands of other rinks to be developed, which opened up the facilities for American players. She was the founder, developer and manager of the most successful, and first Junior program Detroit Junior Red Wings, a team that competed in a Canadian League and won several championships. She was relentless. She helped make the World Hockey Association a success, with her behind-the-scenes moves, mainly meant to remove the under-age draft ruling, but turned out as a way to increase salaries throughout all pro hockey. It was her suggestion that opened up drafting kids under twenty, and that's how Marty, Mark, and I ended up playing together. I think she was the first woman to negotiate contracts with any hockey team. She has been an executive who has promoted the game around the country. She produced seven award winning instructional hockey videos. She has fought for the rights of former players, and was instrumental in bringing about evidence for the Koski Minsky firm during the pension law case to recover pensioners' money, that was removed from the pension fund.

She has planted seeds, and they have grown. There are guys in the Hall, owners and executives, who have done a hell of a lot less for the game than she has done. And everything she ever did was a struggle, because she was a woman and not a multi-millionaire. She also won't like it that I'm making this a public statement. When people have accomplished what she has, I'm sure she thinks people don't need to be reminded.

COLLEEN: Gordie Howe Hockeyland in St. Clair Shores, just northeast of Detroit, was one of the most exciting ventures we ever tried. Back in the '50s and early '60s, a lot of U.S. kids wanted to play indoor hockey, but there just wasn't ice. I crossed the border into Windsor at three and four in the morning just to get an hour of ice at the old Windsor Arena, or any facility east on Highway 401 leading to Toronto. The only facility in the whole Detroit metropolitan area, besides the old Detroit Skating Club used for figure skaters, was a drafty old place at the State Fair Grounds, which was used to keep farm animals during the Michigan State Fair. It was only open four months a year. Water leaked through the ceiling and onto the ice, causing major holes. There were spaces between the ice and the boards where a skate could wedge. When they cleaned the ice, it was with sort of a forerunner of the Zamboni. I don't know what it was but the maintenance man didn't really know how to drive it, and sometimes he ran into the boards. And was it frigid in there. We may as well have been outside.

We'd take Marty and Mark there for games, held at five in the morning, when they were real small, and you could never get practice time. Marty started skating at five, and Mark was four-years-old. They skated at a small outdoor rink called Winter Wonderland on Schaffer Road, I believe. The owner was Grace and she was a marvelous person, always so sweet to all the kids. The O'Neill family were involved, too. Grace was their aunt. They had two boys who played on the team with Marty and Mark.

Those were the days when I began driving them everywhere to find ice for games, singing old songs in the car and trying to make our way through snow storms. Thank God for station wagons. And the sons of other Red Wing players were on some of those teams. Kenny Delvecchio and Jerry Sawchuk come to mind. But so did Billy Cirualo with CCM and Bob Goodenow, President of the NHL Players Association now. And I never met a boy that got in trouble who was playing hockey during those years. Who had time? Besides that, we enjoyed each and every one of them.

Our first sponsor was Teamsters 299, Jimmy Hoffa's local. I thought, hmm, those guys might like some good PR, and I know they like kids, so let's try it. They didn't bat an eyelash. They agreed. Jimmy always liked to watch Gordie play; he was a big fan. And we knew his nephew, Chuckie O'Brien. He had helped organize "Gordie Howe Night" at Olympia in 1959. Jimmy Hoffa and Jack Adams always called Gordie "Power." So, we have "Power" and "The Power Maker." Anyway, the union gave us money for the kids, and we were able to do things like set up tournaments and travel to Canada to play.

Our next sponsor was the Roostertail Restaurant in downtown Detroit. Millie and Joe Schoeneth led the league in sponsoring for our team most of the early years. They took a personal interest in all the kids, as did many of the big sponsors who followed like Mike and Marian Ilitch, Mike Adray, Chuck and Jean Robertson, Myr Metal and all the many generous companies throughout Michigan. They not only built players, they built men.

Driving the kids all over to play hockey, and not having any real ice in our own town, an NHL city, didn't make much sense to me. Finally, we got the idea in the early '60s to get together with some other couples, good friends of ours. The

Larivees, McCarthys, Currans, Taubes, and McGonigals to discuss putting up an indoor facility.

The biggest problem was getting the financing, because there was no track record for the banks to see. But an equitable deal was struck with St. Clair Shores. We got our first mortgage from a bank and the second through ABC vending who took over our concessions, and Gordie Howe Hockeyland on Harper Avenue became a reality. Believe it or not, we signed away our homes to do it (not too bright). But we never gave it a second thought, because we were so convinced that this would really go and we really believed in it. It's funny the things that you'll do that maybe doesn't make good financial sense, but need, belief and hard work makes them work.

We would only take money out when it was hockey school time in the late spring and early summer. But otherwise the dollars were left in there. It was very exciting to feel we had broken ground for the future. And we eventually ran Hockeyland twelve months a year, and twenty-four hours a day. Kids came from all over Michigan and Canada to play hockey there.

GORDIE: It all started with Colleen's boldness and belief. I was hesitant, but she said, "Okay, we'll put our home up for collateral. It will succeed!" We were in a $40-50,000 home, and as a conservative Canadian, I'm thinking "Oh, God." But that Hockeyland place opened up the floodgates for all the arenas that eventually got built all over Michigan and the U.S.

TOM: One of the great pleasures of my youth was playing warm-weather organized hockey in 1962-65 at that Hockeyland. After having frozen our keesters off outdoors for so many years, there was something indescribably satisfying about playing an exhilarating game there in June, and strolling out into the warm sunshine of a St. Clair Shores afternoon immediately afterwards. It seemed almost surreal.

By 1961, all of us were now half-taping our sticks, with white tape at that, in imitation of Gordie. We used to stare at his picture on the wall of the Hockeyland with that same old awe, even though we were now cool-guy teenagers and seemingly beyond childish hero worship. Colleen correctly recalls that somebody stole the "R" off the sign outside—this is the east side of Detroit, after all—so it read "Go die Howe Hockeyland." It was our understanding that whoever absconded with the "R"—and I figured it was somebody named Ron, Ralph, or Richie—was not sending a message of "Go die." Instead, we all assumed the future felon was giving Gordie the kind of ultimate accolade you would often hear accorded him in hockey-mad Detroit—"he's God, Gordie is God." In 1995, when an exuberant fan said that of Gordie at an autograph session—"I'm tellin' ya, this guy's God"— Gordie recalled that "they used to say that about me back in Saskatoon in the summers. They'd say 'God, are you back home again?'"

COLLEEN: One day I went into the women's lavatory at the rink and there were two girls trying to pull the sink off the wall. The big one was standing on it, jumping up and down trying to dislodge it, while her friend was trying to pull it out from the wall. Now, sometimes when I run into something like that, I lose my regard for my personal safety. I said, "What in the heck do you think you're doing?" One of them said, "What business is it of yours?" I said, "I own part of this place and you're going to get your fat butt off that sink right now and come with me to the office." "Oh yeah?" "Yeah," and I grabbed hold of her and the other one, and marched them right out. Afterwards, after I settled down, I was thinking that if they'd wanted to, they could have flushed me down the toilet. They were pretty big girls. So that was the end of freedom in the bathroom for women. We then had to get a key from the office and sign in to use it after that, except for open skating. That kind of situation was definitely not what most of the kids who went in there were like. I never scratched my name on somebody's property or defaced anything in my life so I really have a problem with vandalism.

When we'd go over to the Hockeyland, Gordie would always want to go check back in the mechanical area to see how things were running. When John Curran had a generator installed, it helped tremendously with the cost of electricity. It took a certain time before the generator paid for itself, and then our financial picture looked good.

I don't recall that any of us made a huge sum of money, because it was split between several investors. But we made money when it was eventually sold. The important thing was that we proved to the financial institutions that we could make money with indoor ice rinks, and that it wouldn't be a losing proposition. Gordie was awfully worried about putting our house on the line, and he was right to be concerned. But, we were just convinced that it was going to work, and that we would make it work, and we did. After we left for Houston, the place was sold, around 1974 or '75. So it did well for about twelve or thirteen years, I think. And now there are indoor arenas all over town. The Hockeyland helped everybody to be able to skate and play hockey closer to home, and gave many little kids a chance to start learning the game.

GORDIE: One of the new owners of the Motor City Mustangs, the RHI team Marty's coaching, told us that he was in our hockey school there one year, when he was real little, about five or so. And he said he had long hair, and as he was skating he couldn't see where he was going because his hair kept getting in his eyes. I didn't remember this, but he said I took him over to the bench, got a pair of scissors, and gave him a haircut on the spot. I bet his mother wanted to zap me.

COLLEEN: Gordie and I don't desire to ever be extremely wealthy. The more money, the more pressure. We just want to be comfortable. We like having nice things, we like being able to go on vacation and not having to worry about how much it costs. I think people should examine what really makes them happy, so they know what it is they want and can think about where they're going. There are people who have $15 billion and are looking for ways to make $15 billion more. Why do people do that? I don't understand that kind of pursuit at all, unless you gave away the first 15 billion.

I've always wanted us to have what I would consider a good life, where if we want to do something for somebody, we don't have to count every penny or worry if we'll have enough for ourselves next week. We have our home here on the Bay, and I love being able to look out on the water. It's something that's a part of my life. I'm so thrilled to be fortunate to live on the beautiful West Bay.

When I was a little girl, my grandmother had a place in Empire, Michigan, about a half hour west of where we live now in Traverse City. We used to drive up there from Detroit, and it was really a long trip. Today it's four hours or so with the I-75 freeway, but back then with the old roads and old cars it was really an all-day trip. I would come up with my Aunt Elsie and Uncle Hughie. They had an old coupe, and I would set up on this tiny area in the back of it, and lay down and go to sleep during the trip when I wanted to. But every time we'd get to Traverse City, every time we'd pass through and I'd see the beautiful bay, I'd say to my aunt and uncle "I'm going to live here some day."

And when we moved here, my great-aunt remembered my quote. She said "I know why you moved to Traverse City. You always said you would get a house there." So, again: Is it by chance or destiny that my life has worked out this way?

GORDIE: That's Colleen. She's like a gardener. She plants a seed, and it grows.

"What I am is God's gift to me; but what I do with my life is my gift to him."—Colleen Howe

"We are proud of our long association with Gordie and Colleen Howe. Gordie's tremendous athletic accomplishments are only matched by his generosity and kindness."
—Tom and Judy Pyle, Owners Rayovac Corporation

CHAPTER NINE

THE HOWE HUMOR

GORDIE: Story 1. I used to take the kids down to the stadium with me whenever they wanted to go. I can remember one time I took Marty, when he was little, into contract negotiations with Jack Adams. I sat him on my knee, patted him on the back, and was rocking him while I talked contract. I was hoping to melt the old bugger's heart, maybe. But Marty fell asleep, so I remember I had to lean over the top of him to sign the contract.

The funny one was when I took Mark into the dressing room with me, when he was only about five. Jack came in, hollering and screaming at us, throwing orange pieces around. We'd had a few bad games, and he was really hot at us. When he stopped for a second, you could hear a pin drop in the place. Then Mark piped up, "Hey Dad, who's that big fat guy?" Ooh, my career flashed before my eyes while we were all trying not to laugh.

Jack didn't say anything. But a full week later, out of the blue, Jack walked in and told us from now on there'll be no more kids in the dressing room on the day of the game. That was what we called the new Mark Howe Rule.

COLLEEN: Story 1. Some of our famous "Aunt Elsie" stories are about her adventures with her birds. Although they're sad on one hand, being there made them quite humorous, too.

My Great Aunt Elsie turned 100 this June, 1995, and she's just a wonderful person. She's been one of the dearest people in my life, and our whole family just loves her. Elsie has always loved having animals. She was raised on a farm and has been around animals and various pets all her life. I had a little dachshund once when I was young, and when we moved my mother didn't want it to go with us so it ended up at Elsie's. She kept little Fritzy until it died in later years.

It's difficult for an older person to care for a pet that needs a lot of attention. That's why a bird is ideal as a companion for someone up in years. Our friends, Kelly and Jerry, raised cockatiels and hand-fed them after they were born, which draws them to human touch and closer to human beings. I bought one of them for Elsie. These birds sit on your shoulder. Of course, they'll do other things on your shoulder as well so you had to be watchful. We'd always have to clean Elsie's shirt after we gave her "Tweety". Occasionally I'd have to tell Elsie that there was something on her shoulder. She'd say, "Oh, that bird has been there, oh dear"— but she was never real concerned with that sort of thing. She was just crazy about that bird.

These are somewhat expensive birds. I wanted to pay for it, but Kelly and Jerry knew my Aunt and loved her like everyone else, and they said they'd take care of it if it was for Elsie. They loved Aunt Elsie and wanted to give the cockatiel as their gift to her. At that time we owned a condo right across the west bay from where we are now in Traverse City, and our daughter, Cathy, and Elsie were staying there until they found a place to live. They could walk right out the back door and be on a little beach. It was convenient for short walks. One day when I was there on the phone, I turned around to see that Elsie was outside, and she had the bird on her shoulder. We kept the bird's wings clipped because we didn't want it to fly away. I could see that Elsie was talking to the bird, and the bird started talking back to her. Elsie would make a sound, and then the bird would make a sound back to her. I thought it was such fun for Elsie. Then I remembered to look and see if the wind was too brisk for the bird. The next thing I know, Elsie comes waddling back to the condo, just screaming and throwing her hands up in the air. The bird was no longer on her shoulder.

Apparently a seagull had swooped down and scared the bird so badly that it took off out over the bay. The poor thing could only go about 15 feet because it's wings had been clipped. So it flew out and went right into the drink. There was just enough wave motion that there was no way it could have survived. Oh, Elsie was so upset over her "Birdie". I rushed out in the freezing water with my clothes on trying to find the bird, but it was no use. It was gone. Now we have no bird and she is feeling depressed, because she blamed herself. I told her it just couldn't have been helped.

This was when Elsie was about 85, just a young chicken or, should I say, a young bird. And she was feeling as though she'd never get another bird. I told her that I'd call Jerry and Kelly and I bet her anything she can get another bird. So sure enough, they sent another cockatiel.

Now Elsie has this new bird and we tell her not to go outside with the bird, at all, please. The rest of this story is a humorous tragedy. Now, Elsie, being an older person, walks a little stiff-legged at times. When she rests she's usually in a reclining chair, where she spends a lot of time watching her television shows. Now the new bird would always sit there with her, usually on her shoulder, and she just talked to that bird by the hour. I can't remember what she named it, but it was great company for her. If the bird wasn't right there on her shoulder, she would call it and it would come to her right away.

Elsie also didn't use a remote TV changer. She would merely get up and shuffle toward the television set with that stiff-legged walk. She would change the channel, but she would never turn around to return to her favorite chair. Instead, she would always walk backwards to the chair, plopping down to sit in her big chair. The bird apparently went onto the chair when Elsie got up to change the channel. Then when she went back to the chair, not seeing the bird, she sat on it! For some reason she didn't realize what she had done. Meanwhile, she continued to scold the bird for not coming to her when she beckoned. She just couldn't figure out where it had gone.

For the bird, it was tragic! After Elsie changed the channel, she watched a program. After a while, she noticed that the bird was missing. She began to look around the room and say, "Okay, you bad bird, where are you? Don't think you can hide from me." You can imagine this scene. "You come here. Where are you, you naughty bird?" Other times when I had been there and the bird wouldn't come to her, she'd say, "You're going to get it, you bad bird you. You'll be sorry."

Elsie continued to sit there and watch the entire program. I'm sure the poor bird was dead instantly, the second she sat down, mainly because of the hard way Elsie falls back in her chair. When she lands she really plops down hard. She called again, "Okay Birdie, where are you?" She stops watching TV and is really calling loudly for the bird. "You know you're being a bad bird! You're not coming to me when I call you." With that she got up and looked everywhere for her fine feathered friend. She looked in the bedroom, in the bathroom and throughout her apartment calling, "Where are you, you bad bird? You're not coming to me!" Then she turned around and saw it there in the chair, dead and flat. She phoned me and was feeling terrible, while she told me the story.

She said, "I sat there and I called that bird for two hours and I didn't know I was sitting on it the whole time." Now I'm trying not to laugh on the phone, but I'm hysterical inside. I could see this whole situation taking place. Then she says, "I don't know what to do with the poor little thing." So I said, "Elsie I'll be right over." So I went to her place, and of course, there it is, kind of flat looking, eyes bulging out. Believe me, that bird never knew what hit it. It died instantly. Elsie is not large or fat, she is small, but you can tell she likes to eat.

It was terrible. We called her "Elsie, the bird killer", and then she'd get mad at us. She wasn't really angry, but she'd shake her finger at us and say, "Now you know I didn't mean to ever hurt that bird. I wouldn't hurt that bird in a million years."

After this happened, Cathy found a cartoon that showed this huge person, who was on the telephone saying, "I just cannot find that puppy." And you see the back end of this dog, hanging out of the crack of the dress of this gigantic person. I thought we should have made that a little bird in the cartoon, and put Elsie's name on it.

The Elsie stories are so humorous. As she got older and got harder of hearing, she would speak louder in public. When we went to church and she couldn't hear everything that was being said, Elsie would say, "WHY DON'T THEY TALK LOUDER? I CAN'T HEAR A THING THEY'RE SAYING". This was in Glastonbury, Connecticut, where we lived. On certain Sundays we had an older minister she just didn't enjoy. When he spoke, she'd blare out "I DON'T LIKE HIM. I DON'T GET ANYTHING OUT OF WHAT HE SAYS." It was kind of humorous, because the minister knew it was her and took it in good spirits. One time we took her to a service and sitting there in the pew waiting for the service to begin. It was then Elsie found out that Reverend Schultz, the pastor she liked, wasn't going to be there. It was just one of those things, he had some emergency, and so the senior minister was about to give the sermon. So Elsie yells, "OH NO, WHAT IS HE DOING HERE? I DIDN'T COME TO HEAR HIM!" Now this Minister is laughing, and everyone's laughing. Meanwhile he's saying, "Elsie, it's okay, I'll be very brief."

Elsie's been a central figure in my life. She helped raise my mother, and she cared for me until I was twelve. She turned 100 this year, and right now she could still tell you everybody's birthday in the family, plus the day they were married, and the day they died. She can go back into all those dates for her parents and all of her brothers and sisters. I think there were 13 of them. It's just amazing. Of course, I always kid her by saying, "You know, Elsie, no one doubts anything you say. We take whatever you say as Gospel because how are we going to ever prove it isn't right?" How she remembers so much I'll never know. Her memory reminds me of Gordie's after he got the number of the player who hit him some games ago.

COLLEEN: Story 2. When he was a bit younger, Mark and Ginger's son, Travis, who's our first grandchild, became a collector of all these cards and special things from all the athletes and the hockey players. He had so many trading cards that he became an expert at collecting. One time he and I went to a card collector store in Traverse City.

I think this was when he was eleven years old. I had a lot of fun listening to his wisdom about cards. In fact we bought a card together. Actually, I financed the card and told him that when he sold it, I'd take half of the profit. As I recall, it wasn't a Gordie card, but it was some card that Travis saw and he said, "Woo-oh, I haven't seen one of those in a long time."

We were talking about collecting in the car on the way home. I just was in this crazy mood. People don't perceive me sometimes as being humorous because I always have the serious side of things to do. I'm very different from that, actually. I do have my humorous side. It's an impetuous kind of humor, and at that moment I felt it coming on. I said, "Gee whiz, Travis, we're heading in the wrong direction here. If we really want to get rich in the collection business, we should start collecting all the hairs that fall from your grandpa's head. He's always talking about his hair falling out in the sink." I continued, "All we have to do is go up to the sink and get some of them. We'll put them in little vials and just put them away for a long time and someday they'll be worth a lot of money. They probably are worth a lot of money right now. What would somebody pay for a fingerprint or a hair from the head of Gordie Howe?"

Travis was saying "Yeah. Great idea!" I was tickling his imagination because kids are very open to ways to make money. You can tell how industrious they are because their minds get churning. Now he was getting into this. He said "Yeah, Honey, that would be a GREAT idea." I really had him going, when I said, "And just imagine what they'd pay for hairs from other parts of his body."

He looked at me with this strange look, and he said, "Honey, you're really funny." Then he thought for a little bit and said, "You know, they probably would pay more for those, wouldn't they?" We both laughed all the way home and even told Gordie about the idea. He laughed and told us his secret of what stops his hair from falling...the floor!

COLLEEN: Story 3. We were involved in hockey schools for many years and over that time a lot of players, Gordie's teammates and our friends, have helped out instructing the kids. Bryan (Bugsy) Watson was a favorite of ours, and the youngsters really enjoyed him. One of the things Gordie used to stress at camp was the use of peripheral vision, seeing action out of the corners of your eyes, so you can anticipate a play or react to what's coming at you.

One day Gordie got over to the rink at Gordie Howe Hockeyland and there's Bryan, and he has all the kids lined up. Bugsy says, "Here comes Gordie. Okay, now guys, get ready! Gordie, come over here. Now, guys I want you to show Gordie how you've been practicing your peripheral vision." So the kids all stand there looking straight ahead, and Bugsy says, "Okay, go to the right!" And all the kids' eyes shoot to the right. "Now, go to the left!" And all the kids shoot their eyes to the left. "Look to the right! Look to the left! Look to the right!" The kids were all looking like those little owl clocks you've seen, or like they were watching a tennis match. What a humorous sight!

There was always a lot of fun that would go on at our hockey schools and it was something we encouraged. Once in a while there would be a parent, however, who would be standing there with a stop watch making sure their child got, exactly to the minute, the amount of ice time they were expecting. Of course, people would always want to ask Gordie about what's the right kind of skate, stick, padding, gloves or helmet. There was even advice regarding how to make kids grow faster. They saw Marty was quite big for his age, so that qualified us on how to raise giants. If we had known Bonnie and Carl Lindros then, we could have sent those questions on to them. This one mother said to Gordie, "Oh, I wish I could get my son to grow. Boy, Marty is big for his age. How do you get a boy to grow?" And Gordie said, "Well, there's no secret to that. You just put some manure in his shoes." Gordie always kept his country humor. Gordie's just being funny, obviously, but wouldn't you know, she actually took him literally. Days later she must have been thinking about it, because she came back into the session and said "Gordie, is there a certain kind of manure that you put in the kids shoes?" I've often told Gordie he had to be careful what he told people, because they take him literally.

GORDIE: Obviously I was kidding the lady. But by the way, the answer is "horse manure."

COLLEEN: Story 4. Bless her soul, there was a woman reporter in Houston by the name of Anita Martini, who has passed away now. Fun name, Anita Martini. How about a beer, you know, Anita Beer? Anyway she was quite a popular, activist kind of gal, and very respectful with the players and extremely knowledgeable about sports.

She was making a big case for going in the dressing room and being admitted into there the same time as the male reporters. It was all over the papers. So when Gordie and a bunch of the players were at a luncheon, the question of women in the locker room was a hot topic. Someone asked Gordie what he thought about Anita going in there after the games. Gordie said, ""Well, you know, when you're a person in a position like I am, there's very few secrets that you have from the public. I have only one and I'm going to make sure I keep it." The crowd just roared. Anita was there and she laughed, too. She always enjoyed Gordie for his humor. I think he has that kind of personality where he can take something that is dramatic, too serious or controversial and make it humorous for everyone. He's so quick on his feet. Like

236

the time some reporter called him to ask how he felt about John Ziegler and Gil Stein, both attorneys and former NHL presidents, getting so much more pension money than the players. Gordie responded, "What I think is ... I should have been an attorney!"

GORDIE: Story 2. I used to laugh on the ice quite a bit, because of different situations. One time I got into it with Noel Picard, a big defenseman with Montreal, at the Olympia. I can't remember how it started, but we squared off and I went to swing at him, and I stepped on my stick and went on my prat so fast it was unbeliveable. Some people thought he hit me, but it was an accident. I was laughing because I felt so ridiculous.

Weird things happen and even bad things seem funny on the ice. Cummy Burton used to play for us. He always skated with his tongue out, like a whipped dog. I used to tell him if he got hit in the head he'd lose his tongue. One time he was circling behind our net with his stick out in front of him, and it got stuck in the mesh. The other end caught him between the legs and he went—BOINNNNG!—almost into a full cartwheel. It was the funniest fall I ever saw. Everyone on the bench was just roaring.

Another time I was killing a penalty with Bugsy Watson. I went into the corner with a player from Toronto. I took him out, and now I've got the puck. Bugsy's all by himself about 20 feet in front of their net. I put it right out to him, and he settled it down and got ready to shoot. Then he teed it up a little more, then he had to get it away in a hurry because the opportunity was almost gone by now. When he shot it, he damn near hit me with it, in the corner! How can you be 20 feet from the net and miss it by 25? I looked at Bugsy, he looked at me, and we both started to laugh and by the time we got back to the bench we couldn't stop. Sid Abel looked at us and said "It's not THAT funny." I told him, "You had to be there."

GORDIE: Story 3. Once in a while some things weren't very funny and that's what I felt like when someone called me "BLINKY." I used to blink repeatedly for a couple reasons and a combination of causes. A doctor once told me my blinking was caused from the red dye in my gloves coming off when I rubbed the sweat from my eyes during a game. I was apparently allergic to the dye. My hands even blistered from that dye, too. Whatever treatment they used to dye the old plain leather gloves really got to me. Marty was also allergic to those dyes, too. He had to wear white gloves underneath because his hands used to blister very badly. It didn't bother me that people in cities we'd play would call me "Blinky." The only time it did was when somebody asked me to sign an autograph "Mr. Blinky" and "Mr. Elbows." I can't say this in a book, but I leaned very close to this guy's ear and said "_____ you." You should have seen the look on his face. It was beautiful.

Much later in my career my blinking became so intense I went to see Dr. Hessberg at Ford Hospital in Detroit to examine me. He told me it was a virus of the eye, gave me medication and the intense blinking ended.

There's a hilarious story connected with my blinking. We were playing New York one night, and Gordie Stratton came out for the faceoff. He looked at me and started blinking like hell. I thought, so you think it's cute to mock me! When the linesman dropped the puck and I speared him and down he went. Bill Gadsby, a New York Ranger then, skated up and said, "Gordie, what the hell did you do that for?" I said, "He was mocking me." Bill said, "For cripe sakes...he blinks worse than you do!" Geez! I said, to Bill, "Well, tell him I owe him a beer, I'm sorry. I didn't know. Poor guy."

Occassionally, though, the blinking actually helped me when I was single. When I'd be blinking while at the speaker's table during a banquet, I'd suddenly see girls all winking back at me. It was a good way to get their attention.

GORDIE: Story 4. Tiny Tim came to Detroit when he was really famous in the late 1960's, as I recall. I was surprised to find out that he was a big fan of mine. In fact, he signed a picture and they sent it over to the Olympia for me. It said "Dear Mr. Howe, Keep Puckering Those Nets." The reporters asked me my response, and I just said "Well, it just shows that you can't always pick your fans."

I remember once when Mark was sick around that same time, and I was sitting up late with him. We were watching the old "Tonight Show" with Johnny Carson, and Tiny Tim was on with a group of stars. The question came up, if you were ever hospitalized for 24 hours, and could only pick one person you'd choose to be with, who would that be? One of other the guests, I recall, said Richard Burton. Carson asked him why, and the guy said "Well because sooner or later, Elizabeth Taylor would have to show up." That got a laugh. Then somebody else said something. Then Carson asked the same question of Tiny Tim, and he replied "Oh, Mr. Gordie Howe." I yelled, "Oh, God, No!" And Mark burst out laughing so hard, it broke his fever! Here was this young kid, sicker than hell, laughing his buns off. Imagine, cured by Tiny Tim.

GORDIE: Story 5. My mum loved a good joke, but, basically I get my outgoing sense of humor from my dad. My dad's was very funny. I don't know if this is appropriate for a book, but someone once asked him how his sex life was . He said "It's great...I make love ALMOST every day. I ALMOST did it Monday, I ALMOST did it Tuesday, I ALMOST did it Wednesday." It always got a laugh.

I remember one time when Dad and I were at a banquet in Edmonton, and a newspaper guy was the master of ceremonies. He was quite humorous. Dad and I sat at the head table, and this emcee is going on and on about having important people at this table. Then he says to me, "Gordie, relax. I'm not talking about you. It's the fella next to you. The heck with your goals and games and everything. If it wasn't for that guy sitting there with you, you wouldn't even be here." My dad really got a kick out of that, and the crowd did, too.

The emcee then says to my father, "Mr. Howe, how old are you?" My dad said he was 80. "That's fantastic," the host says. "Now let me ask you a question I've always wanted to ask someone like you. At what age...does a man lose his sex desires?"

Oh geez, I just put my head in my hands. My dad was capable of saying almost anything, so I didn't know what he was going to say. I'm covering my face, just in case.

Then my dad winks at the crowd, and pats me on the back. He looks at the guy and says "Young man, you'll have to ask somebody much older than I." Boy, what a fantastic answer. And was I relieved...!

GORDIE: Story 6. We were in Edmonton, on the ice before the game warming up back in 1979. And the time-keeper called me over to his bench. He had a big smile, and he said, "Congratulations, Gramps." Mark's son Travis, our first grandchild, had been born. The call had just came from Colleen to the press box that both Ginger and the little guy were doing great.

So I went over and said "Mark, they want to talk to you." I didn't tell him what it was about, I wanted to watch his reaction. He got the word, and immediately went off the ice into the dressing room and I followed him in. He's looking around, I didn't know what the hell he was doing. Then he took his stick and went "Yaaaa-hooo!" and laid into the stick rack, and parted it with one shot, and 40 sticks just exploded all over the frigging room. Somebody said "What the hell are YOU mad at?" He said "I'm not mad, I'm a father! Yeeaah!"

So I'm sitting there, just enjoying Mark's reaction. The little bugger went bonkers. I'm thinking,"Well, I gotta do something special to celebrate. I'm gonna go out and score the fastest goal ever scored by a grandfather in this world. Wouldn't you know, I got one on the first shift. I thought, hah, I got one for the little guy. Fastest goal by a grandfather. Maybe the FIRST goal ever by a grandfather, too, come to think of it...! And Mark got an assist!

COLLEEN: Story 5. While Mark is busy concentrating on winning a game in Edmonton, I'm sitting in the father's waiting room pretending I'm a dad. It didn't take me long to look that way. I had never played this role before. Every time the nurse came out to talk to one of the dads I'd jump up and ask about Ginger. The response was always one of a calming voice telling me to relax and they'll be out to tell me when anything was going to happen. It seemed like hours and then a nurse came in to tell me it would be anytime now, that the baby was almost delivered into the world. Now, that was good news since I couldn't stand this anxiety any longer. Now, I'm watching every minute go by on the clock — for 2 MORE HOURS. I was terrified that something had gone wrong and no one was telling me. I started to knock on the double doors where the nurses came and went. Finally, after a time, the nurse came through them to tell me I was a grandmother of my first grandchild! She explained that there had been a complication but that Ginger and the baby were fine and I could see them very soon. They'd come back. I immediately ran to phone the Edmonton Arena to get word to Mark about his first son. I never mentioned what *I* had gone through for hours. I don't ever envy fathers in waiting rooms. I saw Ginger and beautiful Travis. I remember the first words Ginger said to me, "Nobody ever told me it would be like this." I guess she really had a hard time. I left the hospital so thankful that we're all blessed that night for Ginger, Mark, Travis and the goal scoring grandfather, Gordie.

GORDIE: Story 7. I've had interesting experiences at golf tournaments. George Blanda, the old football quarterback for Chicago and Oakland, played with me in a tournament—I won't say where in case we could still get caught. We played against the assistant pro at this course and Bob Cousy, the Celtic basketball star. And we had a great time. George and Bob and I had just done a commercial set up by Colleen with Etonic Shoe Company.

George and I tied through 18 holes, so we had a playoff, and they beat us. It wasn't a big deal on the bet, just for laughs, maybe for five dollars or something. It was just for bragging rights basically. And when it was over, and the time came to pay them, George said to me, "Well, we were really competitors, we showed them." And he offered me congratulations. And I said "Well yeah, that's fine, but they collected." And Blanda said "Oh no, we come out of this as winners." And I'm thinking that maybe they didn't wear helmets back in Blanda's day! I said "George, what are you talking about? I just paid them because we LOST."

He said "Gordie, I know it sounds funny right now, but the

next time you go out to play another game, by the time you're done with the first hole, I think you'll agree with me. You'll see things in a different light, and I think you'll realize what I mean. You'll see that you were a winner today." I couldn't figure out what the heck he was talking about, and put it out of my mind.

So, I was out playing golf, maybe a couple weeks later, with Mark. Sure enough, at the end of the first hole, I got up to the green, and reached in my bag for my putter. Whoa, there's two putters in there! One of them wrapped in cellophane, brand new! Then I knew what he meant. My guess is that George lifted a putter out of the pro shop and put the dang thing in my bag. It's a Zebra putter, in case somebody's missing one.

So I got rid of that thing quickly—immediately, as a matter of fact. And there's a young man named Mark who appreciated the whole incident, because HE got a new putter. He had no idea where it came from, or why his Dad was so generous. It was really humorous. That dang George, I haven't seen him since. I wonder why?

GORDIE: Story 8. Glenn Johnson was one of Michigan's finest young amateur golfers, who won the Michigan amateur championship many times. He's also in the Michigan Sports Hall of Fame. He's a good all-around athlete, as well, and a good guy. One time he wanted to come down to the Olympia, and put on the blades to skate and horse around with the Red Wings.

So, since he was also friends with some of the guys on the team, we fixed it up so he could skate with us on one of those optional practice days we used to have once in a blue moon. Well, he was coming up the left side during the workout, and I was coming down the right side, just fooling around. Then I made a run at him, just for fun. Most players know when you're alongside the boards you usually get away from them when somebody's coming at you. And I thought he'd do that. But, no! He moved into the boards at the same instant I did, we collided, and down he went. At first I thought he was hurt but he convinced me he was okay and went home.

Man, he was cursing, saying, "There goes my golf." I felt awful, since I knew it was right at the start of the golf season. He called me in the middle of the night. He was really sore by then, it was taking effect. He had gone to the hospital and had cracked a rib or two. Poor guy! All I could say was "Sorry, I didn't mean to do it." He said he was calling this late because if he couldn't sleep, he wasn't going to let me sleep either. Glenn never asked me to take him skating again. Golf, anyone?

GORDIE: Story 9. Once, about six or seven of the Red Wings went down to see curling at The Detroit Curling Club. It was the only curling place in town. Down around Forest and Second Avenue? It was an old building.

We were down there at a function. It was the first time I ever saw the size of the rock they throw, or "stone," whatever they call it. It was 30- or 40-some pounds. The building had a low ceiling, and a strip of rippled ice. I was looking at it, and they invited me to throw a stone. I said to myself "Now, I'm not gonna be a wimp here. I am NOT gonna throw this thing short of the end zone." So I threw it...I threw it with everything I had. I really rifled it. I stuck my foot in that back support and came flying off of there a little too strong, and threw it like I was bowling.

Suddenly everybody's yelling "Look out!" That stone went rocketing at about 20 miles an hour, quickly shooting right by the two guys with brooms, right through the rack area, and took off, hitting the back wall. They had a little scoreboard hanging there with numbers on it, and it blew the numbers right off the board I hit it so hard. By now people were turning around and saying "Who did that?" but I left quickly. I was hiding in the back of the building. They should have told me that stone gets down there in a hurry.

GORDIE: Story 10. Sid Abel was our coach, and we were playing in Chicago, probably around the mid-sixties when Phil Esposito was just starting to come into his own. Phil was having a great night. He was dipsy-doodling all over the ice, and Sid said "Somebody run into that guy and remind him that there is some opposition out there." Sid was getting a little mad, Esposito was making fools out of some of our guys.

I took it upon myself. So I lined him up. And as soon as he came across the blue line, I went off my wing, and I nailed him. And...there was a little misunderstanding, the sticks came up, and there was yapping back and forth. The linesmen parted us, and we were headed for the penalty box when Phil said something to me. I turned around and said "WHAT did you say?" And he said "And to think...you used to be my favorite!" Geez, what could I do? I almost burst out laughing right there.

GORDIE: Story 11. I used to have fun. When Jack Adams would send me out on the ice to argue a penalty or ask a question of the referee. I'd go over to the guy, maybe Red Storey, who was really a good guy and a great referee, and he'd say "What does the old bugger want now?"

I'd say, "Well, he just told me to tell you that you are the dumbest SOB in the game. You're lucky if you can find the whistle with your mouth. The BB's from your whistle are rolling around in your head. He says you're a dumb-a__ jerk." And I used to really go on and on, as if Jack had really told me to tell him off. I was just making it all up. So the ref would get mad and say, "Why that big fat so and so!" Then I'd skate back and tell Jack what the referee was saying about him, only I'd expand on that, too, making up more insults. He'd say "Tell me exactly what he said." So I'd say "He says you're big and fat and don't know anything about hockey, and you never have." Then Jack would explode. I'd get those guys arguing like crazy. What fun!

I was just lucky they never got together and talked it over. Actually, Jack eventually stopped asking me to go out and ask what was going on. Maybe he suspected what I was up to.

That's the difference in the referees today. I think now they're told not to associate or fraternize with the players. You could go up to the refs of old and talk to them. They'd say, if you griped about a penalty for something you did, "Hey, I let you get away with three already, so stop complaining. One out of four isn't bad." It was a little game within the game.

One time, Red called a penalty on one of our guys, and I said "Red, not him. He wasn't even on the ice when it happened." And Red said "Well give me credit. At least I got the right team." And the player went in the box.

A big fight would break out, and Red would skate in and say "Gentlemen...I have to catch a train at such and such an hour. That doesn't give me much time for a beer and a sandwich. I would appreciate it if you would show a little respect and concern for the old referee, and part company." You had to listen to him. He was quite a guy, and a compliment to the game. Referees, back then, were much more a part of the game.

COLLEEN: Story 6. I'm not exactly sure about this story, you'll have to check with Murray, but our family has always been

246

very sensitive to the needs of animals. We couldn't see an animal in trouble without trying to help. Cats, dogs, you name it. Mark and the rest of our family once picked up a cat that had been injured along Highway M-72 near Bear Lake Road. Once they got the cat in the car, it went crazy and started tearing up the car, and it ended up with Mark's family outside the car and the cat the only thing inside it.

Murray was the one, though, that set a family record for helping a deer that had been hit by a car. He was driving and saw it by the side of the road. He pulled over to see if he could help. Now, this seems like the most impossible story, but he actually gave this deer mouth-to-mouth resuscitation. The deer revived, and ran off into the woods. To me, it's so wonderful that he would think to go to that extreme, but that's Murray.

MURRAY: Story 1. Let me say this: My dad's a great hockey player. And he's very proud of my accomplishments. But as I got older, and he got older, the accomplishments become larger. This deer story has become some kind of family legend. What happened was, I was driving down a road between Northville and Ann Arbor, where I used to live, and I saw a deer lying in the road. So I stopped. I figured somebody had hit it and it was dead. There was blood coming out of its mouth, and he was in the middle of the road, so I just dragged him off so another car wouldn't hit him.

When I got him to the side, I noticed he was still breathing. So I thought, Gosh, I'm a second year medical student. What do you do for a deer? I stayed there with him, and just petted him and kept him calm. All of a sudden, he started waking up a bit more and I pushed him, I helped him get up on his feet, and in a flash he just bolted off. I deduced what happened was that he had run out and been hit by a car, got knocked unconscious, and came to after I got him off the highway. I figure I still saved him because he would have gotten picked off by the next car for sure.

So, Dad can be proud of that. But once and for all, no, I did not give mouth-to-mouth resuscitation to a deer. I don't think I could have gone that far.

GORDIE: Story 12. Bill Gadsby coached us for a couple of years, and he was fired for allegedly not being "sophisticated." Then along came Ned Harkness, who had been a college coach, and he used THE four-letter word at a pace that would set a world's record.

He would get excited, and just swear like a trooper. And in between periods of one of the games, I sat there and counted the exact number of times he used the big "F". The next time we had a meeting, I was telling the guys how many I had counted, it seems like it was about 80-something.

So we have this meeting, and Ned's chirping away, and I look around the room and see the fingers popping. Everybody's counting, keeping track...one-two-three-four-five. It was so funny. Alex Delvecchio and I started laughing and we couldn't stop, it was like in school. "What's so funny over there?" "Nothing, coach." It was hard to talk our way out of it.

Frank Mahovlich joined us in Detroit for my last three years with the Red Wings, when our coaches were Bill Gadsby and Ned. Frank is a great guy, a very interesting guy. An unusual guy and a deep thinker. If you know him you really appreciate him, but he's one of a kind. He's the kind of guy who worries about other people, he thinks about their situations a lot. I remember once he made me call home three times to see how Mark was doing when he was sick. In fact, Frank said to me,

"Gordie, what are you doing at practice when Mark's sick?" I said "Well, that's what doctors are for." And he said "If my kid gets sick I don't go to practice." And I said, "Frank, you haven't been in Detroit too long."

We were playing on the road one time, I think we were in Los Angeles, and Ned turns to Frank between periods and says— "Mahovlich...get the lead out!" That was all, just "Get the lead out." Now it had to be at least a week later, maybe even longer. But Frank was sitting next to me in the locker room, he's got his head down, and is staring at the floor. I could tell something was eating at him. I said "Frank, you doing okay?" He said "Yeah." I said "Looks like you've got something on your mind." He said, "Yeah, I do." I said "It's nothing with the family, is it?" He said "No." So I said "Well what's bothering you?" Frank looks at me and says "What did Ned mean when he said 'Get the lead out?' That was Frank.

I'll tell you, when they fired Bill Gadsby, they took the heart out of Frank Mahovlich. Frank loved Bill, loved him as a coach and as a man. When they got rid of Bill, it just bothered him so much. Again, that's Frank's nature. Sometimes you'd hear criticism of Mahovlich, "Aw, he's sleeping out there." Frank wasn't sleeping. He was thinking and caring about a good friend.

GORDIE: Story 13. There are always lessons to be learned in hockey. As a defenseman, there are two places to put your stick when somebody's winding up for a shot. One is to flatten it out in front of your toes, that helps stop the shot AND helps your toes. A lot. I know because I got mine broken by not putting my stick out there. Or, you put that stick as far out of the way as you can, because when it's there in front of you, you can get some strange deflections.

Now, Doug Barkley had an awful habit. He was right handed, and he would put his stick out with his left hand almost straight in front of his left foot. One night Bobby Hull came down on him, and let a shot go that caught the heel of Doug's stick, and came up and hit him square under his cup. Right in the filberts.

Doug went down in a heap, and is rolling around and moaning and groaning on the ice. You can only imagine how it felt, the way Bobby could shoot. So Bill Gadsby comes skating up to me and says, "Is it THERE?" And I said "Yeah, right!" Good guess. Poor Doug's laying there moaning, and Bill leans over him. He says "Doug... Doug." And he gets a response, "Uhhhhhh...what?" from Doug, who could barely talk. Bill says "Quick, open your mouth." So Doug does anything anyone tells him to at this point, and he opens his mouth. Bill looks in and says "Yup...there they are." Geez. Even Doug had to laugh. Bill says, "Aw, he's okay." And Doug said "No, no way, I'm not." He really got hit. I think it changed his voice. It went up a few octaves.

COLLEEN: Story 7. Gordie's father had quite a sense of humor. And the day that Gordie retired from the Red Wings, in 1972, he was in rare form. This was the year after Gordie's mother died, and Gordie broke down when he mentioned her during the ceremony. We were all on the ice at Olympia—the children and I were out there with Gordie. Bobby Hull said a few words, along with the Mayor of Detroit and the Governor of Michigan were present. And Spiro Agnew, the Vice President, was there and read a letter from President Nixon. Now Gordie's dad, at some point in the ceremony as they were retiring Gordie's Number Nine jersey, reached over and goosed the Vice President. I have no idea why he did it.

I don't know if anyone saw it, but it was done in front of

about 15,000 people and the TV cameras. I don't know how the story got back to Gordie, but he asked his father why he would do something like that, and he just said, "I've always wanted to do that to a Vice President." Dad just reached out, pinched him and let him have it right there on the ice.

In addition to all the Howe family, many of my family were at the event also, like my mother, my great-aunt and my grandmother. Grandma was having a fit when I bumped into her in the room where they were serving food. And she said to me, "I wish you would do something or speak to Mr. Howe, please." And I said, "What's the matter, Grandma?" And she said, "Well, I was in the food line, and that Ab Howe kept coming up into the line and then kissing me." So I told her, "Well, Grandma, that's not bad," And she said, "I know, but he's French kissing me." Leave it to Ab Howe to give every party a real lift!

GORDIE: Story 14. I used to take Marty and Mark on fishing trips as often as I could during the summer. As Murray started to get a little older, maybe around eight or ten, I decided that I'd take him fishing, too. There'd be just the two of us, for a little bonding period with him.

We went up to Sault Ste. Marie, Ontario, and we really had fun. I put him in the back of the boat and let him run the motor. I think it was the first time out for him and he was really having a ball. He didn't care if we caught fish at all, he just drove us around flying through weeds and everything, and singing this damn song, all day long. He never stopped. Finally, I said "What's the name of that song, Murray?" He said, "I don't know. I'm making it up."

The funniest thing was when we came through Canadian Customs at Sault Saint Marie. The border guard stopped our car and said, "What's your reason for coming into Canada?" And we said we were going fishing. He says, "Where were you born?" So I said "Canada, and my little boy was born in the States." He says, "What's your name, sir?" I said Gordie Howe. He said, "What do you do for a living?" I said I played hockey. Then he said, "You play professionally?" I said, "Yes," and the guy said, "What did you say your name was again?" Well, little Murray's sitting there listening to all this, and he's impatient to get going. All of a sudden he pipes up, "Boy! You have got to be the dumbest Canadian in the world if you don't know who my dad is!"

Oh, God. I thought, This is it! I'm going to jail. Luckily the guy didn't get mad. He laughed, and he looked into the car at Murray, and said "I might be, son."

"Gordie Howe is the greatest Hockey Player of all times. He is the reason I became a hockey fan. The Kaline Family is proud to be great friends of the Howe family."
—Al Kaline, former Detroit Tiger & Baseball Hall of Famer

" The Howes: Gord, the consummate player, who has brought class and prestige to the world of hockey over 6 decades. Gord & Colleen - good parents, concerned, caring humans, and to many, treasured friends."
—Reg Sinclair

CHAPTER TEN

SITUATIONS

COLLEEN: I always felt that if Gordie wanted to leave the game, at any time in his career, we had the courage, the spirit, whatever it takes, to survive such a change in our lives. We're survivors. It's the same as when Gordie almost lost his life on the ice. He just wasn't meant to die, and he could come back from it. We are always ready to cope with any change that might alter life for us as a couple.

There are times when you have to look at the rest of your life. You finally see that there *is* life after hockey. Not many people want to think about that when they're in the game. They get so involved and the time goes by each year. But you *have* to think ahead to the future sometimes and really look at where you're going! And that's what we did during Gordie's first retirement. He had been playing all his adult life, starting at age 16 in Galt, and put in 25 seasons in Detroit. By 1971, the Red Wings were doing badly, the management situation at Olympia was disorganized, and Gordie was playing in pain with severe wrist problems. It was time to re-evaluate where our lives were going. It seemed we were unhappy, going separate ways and on the road to nowhere.

Let me tell you about a game we used to play with our kids around the kitchen table called "Situations." It was usually in the summer when all of us got the chance to sit down at a dinner table together. When we'd play this game, where everyone gets their turn to pose dilemmas to the others at the table. Then everyone would take turns telling what they would do in the situation. It was serious, but sometimes it would end up being funny. I once posed the question to everybody: If the house were to catch fire, and you could only take one thing with you on your way out, what would that be? I think one of the kids said, of course, they'd take our dog, Skippy. I think those kids would have saved Skippy before they rescued their parents. And the joke was that everybody agreed I'd go running out with my calendar. Now you have to appreciate that my calendar has every schedule known to man. It was my diary, my salvation. My whole life's work, income, bills, birthdays, and all our schedules were in my calendar. So they were right, I'd grab it first. Only kidding. The whole point of the game was that it was thought provoking, and would get us thinking about what matters in life and how you would go about accomplishing something. By 1970 and '71 Gordie and I were playing real life "Situations" and re-evaluating our lives for the first time since we'd been married. Only this was not a game.

This point in time was when, I'd say, our relationship was in danger of going on the rocks. With all the stress and pressures Gordie and I were under, things didn't feel right. It felt like we were getting apart from each other, rather than closer. We had to make a decision about what we were going to do to resolve this for our marriage, the children and us. A part of it was that Gordie wasn't happy at what he was doing. The Red Wing organization had taken a lot of the fun out of the game for him. He was 43, and it made it harder on him to be playing on a team that wasn't going anywhere. The question was, should we be away from hockey completely, in some other field of endeavor. And for the first time we were contemplating—if Gordie didn't play hockey, what would replace what we both love so much? I was married to the game as much as Gordie was after all those years. I really believed in the sport. I developed and was working with the Junior Wings. Marty and Mark were on that team, and it had made history as far as a U.S. development team playing in a Canadian league. I, too, believed in the sport, which didn't always mean I believed in everybody in it.

We decided our needs were taking a back seat to the sport. We had to think about pursuing other areas in life, as a couple and as individuals. We knew it could be challenging to find financial security if Gordie left hockey. That was why we started to invest in the cattle industry. There had been no talk from the Red Wings of any opportunities if Gordie retired. In a sense, we were a part of what could be called a mid-life crisis. In the backs of our minds we thought that we'd have to say good-bye to everything that we'd built in Detroit. Gordie was so loved there. It would be a shame not to enjoy the benefits of all the things he had sacrificed for the team. I was a Detroiter, and most of my activities as well as personal friends and family were there. But, maybe we'd have to say good-bye to all of that.

Then, in the middle of this, tragedy struck and Gordie's mother died accidentally. She had fallen down the stairs in our cottage at Bear Lake. We had left her there with the kids and Dad when Gordie and I were away in Toronto at the first event put on by the NHL Players Association. It was just inconceivable and devastating that this could happen. I just loved his mother, Kate, so much. She was a mother like no other. She was kind, soft spoken, generous, warm and loved by everyone who met her. And she had meant everything to Gordie. We never dreamed of losing her like this, so suddenly, and at the place we loved so much. I should have listened more to the premonitions I had about leaving her, Dad and the kids there alone.

When we all arrived at Bear Lake during their visit with us, I had real concerns because we had added a deck onto the cottage and there was about a 40 foot drop from the deck to the hill down below. It wouldn't be of concern, normally, but the carpenter didn't have the railing on yet. I wasn't satisfied until he got over there to complete a temporary one, so I could enjoy peace of mind while we're in Toronto. When the quick fix railing was on, I was feeling that, now, no one would be hurt there in a fall. How could we have predicted that it was the wrong place?

Then Mum said two things the day before I left to join Gordie in Toronto after he drove Mark to Detroit for his baseball game. Firstly, she cried when Gordie drove away and she and I sat down while I tried to comfort her. It was so unlike her, especially when she knew he'd be back there in two days. When she stopped crying she said, "It's just that when a person is my age, and a child of mine says good-bye, I sometimes get the feeling I may never see them again." How that struck home after her death! Then, when I took her all along the shore of the lake in a Sunfish sailboat she was totally enjoying herself and, as she gazed out over the lovely water, sky and trees, she said, "I wish I never had to leave here!" It was then that I thought seriously about having them come to live near us. Gordie and I discussed it and he said, "Dad will never leave Saskatoon," and I told him "It never hurts to ask." We never got that chance.

When Gordie finally decided he would retire, and they had the ceremony for him on the ice at Olympia, he talked about one member of the family not being there, his mother, and he couldn't go on. All of us on the ice broke up. And the entire stadium was in tears. They remembered the moment that Mum got out of the car and hugged Gordie at center ice in 1959.

That's the kind of strain we were under at the time of Gordie's first retirement. There was just such turmoil. We had decided to get away from hockey, but Bruce Norris, the Red Wings owner/president, became very upset that Gordie was leaving. He tried to act like a counselor to us. Even a marriage counselor. This was strange coming from a guy who couldn't hold a series of his own marriages together.

GORDIE: It's interesting that shortly before I retired in 1971, I had been tracked down and called one time in Vancouver by Clarence Campbell, the president of the NHL. At that time he promised that the league would have plans for me after I left the game. He said, "Don't do anything until you hear from us if you retire." Well, I retired and I never heard from the league. I did end up going to work for the Red Wings, but that was a mistake. The way they operated was far from my thinking and I knew it was only a matter of time until I left there. The opportunity to play with Marty and Mark in Houston was the answer to my prayers. It was a dream becoming a reality, and it was also the perfect reason to leave the Red Winds and get paid handsomely for my services. When I placed a courtesy call to Bruce Norris, just before the press announcement, to tell him I was going to Houston to play with Mark and Marty he said, "Well, somebody just let something slip through the cracks there with the league when you quit two years ago. I just want to tell you that if you stay with the Red Wing organization we'll pay you $50,000 a year and the NHL said they'll pay you $50,000 to work representing the league. You'll be making $100,000 a year." And then he adds, "But of course that means you'll have to do a lot more than you've been doing!" Geez. That did it for me! He just couldn't understand that money wasn't the priority. I said "Bruce, you don't get it. This is going to be the thrill of my life." In all the years I played for the Red Wings, I could never understand Bruce.

COLLEEN: Being around Bruce Norris was sort of like being in Oz. Everything was unpredictable—our futures, his behavior, and the attitudes of the people who were around him. There was always this huge entourage around Bruce, the people who were his pals. If he was drinking, Bruce was capable of all kinds of strange behavior. I was scared to death of him but tried to never let him know it.

He appeared to be an absentee owner, he spent most of his time in all kinds of places. We visited him twice in Fort Lauderdale. The first time, we went to tell him that Gordie was leaving the Wings. Bruce was so different that day. First of all, he was not drinking and he was alone, which was unusual. He slumped down in his chair when Gordie said that he was going to leave. We weren't there to threaten him or demand something better. This was a courtesy visit. But he kept saying, "What can we do?" Gordie said, "Bruce, we're not here to talk about staying, we just didn't want to leave until we talked to you face to face." Gordie never felt that he had much control over anything that was going on with the Red Wings. Sure, he was involved with Bruce's insurance companies, Norin, Inc. and the Olympia Agencies— where even Mike Ilitch was a client. But where Gordie really should have been was with the hockey club. Instead, the club always found something else that Gordie should be doing, which really told us that the people who were running the hockey club really didn't want him there. It indicated to us that, possibly, Gordie stood as a threat to those people who ran the hockey club.

Maybe 25 years is just too long. There are times when I thought we should have made a new start sooner, left the Wings before we did. So now we told Bruce, "We just want to go, do our thing together and get away from this environment." I was busy at the time. I was very dedicated to the Junior Wings, looking after our family, a home and all the myriad of responsibilities that filled my days, yet things just didn't feel right. I didn't see Gordie happy in his career. He really didn't have much to be excited about, and I thought that he needed, and deserved, to have more in his life. We needed a lift. We needed to get a fresh start. It is time to step away once it gets to that stage. Imagine, Bruce thought that the whole situation was about money.

Bruce seemed very awkward with certain people. He often spoke in an awkward manner. Perhaps that's why he enjoyed drinking, because he needed some courage or reassurance. He always had an entourage of people surrounding him all the time. They were always walking down the hallway with him at the Olympia. That was why this one time was so unique when we saw him alone, perhaps because to our knowledge, no one knew we were going to see him.

GORDIE: I don't know why Bruce treated us the way he did. When his half-brother, young Jim Norris was in Detroit, he wasn't different and we liked him. Their dad, James Norris Sr., was great! I used to feel sorry for him. All that money, ownership of teams, and his love for the game of hockey—yet he couldn't even get to watch the games. He'd come into the dressing room and come over to shake hands. Sometimes he'd sit down and talk to us before a game. And then he'd have to leave before the game started because his heart was too weak to take the excitement.

Once I ended up watching shuffleboard in Libertyville, Illinois with the Norris group. There was Sid Abel and Bruce Norris against young Jim and someone else—I was watching. Anyway, Bruce got half snockered, took the disc and threw it down the court. It bounced off the back rail, hit a couple of things and landed on the board, and Bruce says, "We win!" Then, Jim

Norris got mad and said, "That's enough of this crap! Come on, we're going home." He grabbed his wife and they left. Meanwhile Bruce is yelling after him, "awww, bad loser, bad loser." They acted like spoiled brat kids, and I worked for these people?

Bruce had a buddy, a doctor, who always hung around. He used to bring him to our games. One day this doctor started talking to me like he's an expert on hockey, and saying what's wrong with our team. I just couldn't take it. I said, "Doctor, don't tell me how to play the game of hockey, and I won't tell you how to shove your finger up somebody's butt." Bruce had a lot of different people who hung around with him. I remember there was a guy in the front office who played up to Bruce all the time. He was at some function in Detroit, and apparently Bruce got bored and said, "I'm going down to Florida, come along with me." The guy turned to his wife and told her to go home. He was going to Florida with Bruce. Not too many guys could get away with that. I know I couldn't and wouldn't want to.

COLLEEN: Bruce owned a motel complex down in Homasassa Springs, Florida. It had an animal compound where they would put on a lion show featuring "Clarence the Cross-eyed Lion." We vacationed there a few times when Gordie was still playing. Usually we'd be joined by Bill and Edna Gadsby, our dear friends. We always paid our own way. There were no freebies from Bruce. You knew Bruce was about to arrive on the scene when the help would start sprucing up the place, and when they got his big cigarette boat out and ready to go. I remember the day when Bruce showed up with a girlfriend. They got in the boat and he announced he wanted to take everybody for a ride. Gordie and Bill were already on the dock so Edna and I told them we'd just check on the kids and grab a hat or scarf. Bruce told Bill and Gordie to hop in the craft and when Edna and I were only about 100 yards from the boat, Bruce guns the boat and takes off. He hollers, "There's no more room in the boat," and goes roaring away. Oh, I was angry. Edna and I both were dismayed, but not surprised.

I wondered what was this game Bruce was playing? Why did he feel he had to do something like that? I was also very upset with Gordie for letting it happen. When the guys got back, I asked Gordie why he didn't insist on getting out of the boat. Gordie and Bill both said, "We were as surprised as you. What were we going to do, jump overboard?" I said, "Yes, I would have!" I was essentially sick of the whole spoiled Bruce thing. Every time we ever saw him, except for the one time I mentioned, it was always as though he was playing a game with you, particularly if you were a woman. I was seething over the boat incident, and Edna, who never gets too upset, was angry, too.

Soon after all four of us went to dinner, we all calmed down. Everything was fine. Now we don't have Bruce on our minds and we're having dinner in the restaurant Bruce owns. Well, wouldn't you know it, in comes Bruce and his girlfriend. They don't come over to say hello. He ignores us, and they sit at another table. Occasionally he turns toward us. And after a while, he starts yelling things over to our booth. I can't remember exactly what he said, but it was annoying. You couldn't really make any sense out of it. It was something about refrigerators or what makes Colleen happy. Obviously he was feeling no pain. This was Gordie's boss, the guy who signs the paychecks, and he's acting like a total fool. We are sitting in our booth with Edna next to me, on my right. Every time Bruce yells something, I can feel Edna grabbing my leg, as if to say, don't say anything. She knew what I was thinking.

Finally, Bruce comes over to our table with his girlfriend and a half-empty tray of leftover hors d'oeuvres they didn't eat. He sets it down on our table and says, "Here, we're finished with this if you'd like it." Then he left. I'll tell you, he came very close to getting a tray of leftover hors d'oeuvres right in his face. It's what you feel like doing, but then you think, this guy is the big boss. What was all this about? Now I'm really angry. Here's somebody that says he reveres Gordie so much. So does he hate me? Or doesn't he know how to deal with women and that's the problem? He's Gordie's boss, he controls our future! I never, ever could figure it out. It wasn't just me or us, Bruce was just as rude to Bill and Edna and anyone else he felt like embarrassing or insulting. But it seemed like he used to give me real attention, and I never knew why.

After Bruce left, the next thing you know his right-hand man comes trooping in, over to our table, and announces, "Bruce wants to take care of your dinner, he apologizes." That was Bruce, insult people and then send an employee to fix things up. I said, "Well, you can tell Mr. Norris that we wouldn't think of allowing him to pay for our dinner if he was the last person on the face of the earth." He said, "I can't do that." And I said, "You better do it, and *you're* not paying for our dinner, either. *We* are going to pay for *our* dinner. We *do not* want him to pay for it. We do not want him to pay for *anything* for us." That's how I felt. Edna said, "Yeah, I don't want him to pay for *our* dinner, either." But the guys are saying, "Naw, let him pay for it, to keep peace." That's the guys. Talk about two different attitudes. As far as I'm concerned, if you're mean, cruel or angry with me, I don't want anything from you, except to have you go away. Besides, Bruce was never really sorry about anything because he went right on

262

acting the same way.

Bruce was very daring, he loved to drive fast and ride boats. We went to a big party out at one of his homes on stilts out there in the coral flats in Florida, where it's very shallow. The waterways are all marked where to go and where not to go, and what areas are dangerous. Because it was only accessible by water, someone took us out in a boat. We weren't real comfortable there. Gordie and I don't really go to cocktail parties very much, we've never been cocktail-type people. It's not our favorite pastime. You meet people, they shake your hand, and get dragged around. "Oh, this is Gordie Howe's wife." People rarely know my first name, so I have to make sure to say, "Excuse me, my name is Colleen." At this typical party at Bruce's stilt house, everybody was drinking a lot. People were getting pretty polluted. Gordie and I thought it was time to leave, but there we were out on the water. How do we get home? We asked someone about getting a ride back to the mainland, and they said "Oh, Bruce is going to take you back." Oh, fun! How did we get so lucky? Everybody is drinking and Bruce is the leader of the band. We believe drinking and operating a boat is dangerous, particularly in that kind of shallow water. But what could we do? We couldn't leave by ourselves and Bruce obviously had put the word out that we were *his*! So we waited for Bruce to decide he's had enough of the party, and we finally got in the boat with him. This was one of his cigarette boats, a giant, long racing craft. It was made just for speed. We started out and it was pitch dark on the water. Bruce immediately put the craft at maximum speed, opening it up to give us a thrill ride. I'm thinking that I have four children at home, a house, a life and so forth. And I really don't want to lose any of those things just because somebody's showing off. Now I'm hoping and praying we just get back, real soon. I was saying Hail

Mary's, and I'm not even Catholic. To make it even worse, Bruce decides to start cutting across these marked areas of shallows, where the signs say 'DO NOT CROSS, SHALLOW WATER'. Now, Gordie and I don't know these waters at all. Bruce is trying to terrify the hell out of us and he knows it. He turns to me as we're roaring along and says, "Am I scaring you?"

I wouldn't give him the satisfaction of saying 'Yes!' even if it was probably written all over my face. That's just what he wanted. So I casually said, "No, not at all," as calmly as I could. I wasn't going to let him know that he was scaring me. But I'll tell you what, I was relieved to finally get back to that dock. It was such a bizarre situation to be in because here he is, the boss, and your husband is an employee; in fact, the longest standing employee in all the Norris holdings. It was as though Bruce wouldn't do things to Gordie, and would never abuse Gordie. But, lucky me, I got to be the target. Again, it was me that night in the boat. Maybe he knew those dangerous areas like the back of his hand, but how could I be sure? He had been drinking, it was pitch black, and at that speed we could have been killed if we'd struck the bottom.

GORDIE: We had to get our backs up against something to hold onto, just in case there was an accident. I think he was clipping along about a foot above the coral reef. I thought he'd rip a hole in the bottom of the boat, at least. He liked to scare people. He thought it was thrilling.

COLLEEN: Once he invited me into a car with a cheetah. He owned this animal sideshow right near Homassasa, and was involved with Ivan Torrs' Studio where they made a lot of animal films. He had a lion called Clarence, the Cross-Eyed Lion, that our kids used to love petting. He had other wild animals and reptiles, too. He invited Gordie and me for a ride in his car over to the show at Homassasa Springs where he kept alligators. Bruce would tease them by hanging meat down on a rope and try to make them jump for it. He'd tease the alligators for a long time, sort of like his employees and their wives.

So Bruce invites us to get in his car. He opens the door and gestures me into the back seat. Well, I took one look and saw this cheetah sitting there on the seat. It scared the hell out of me. Another test? I thought, "he is not going to see me flinch." This cheetah was a big animal, but apparently it was tame. He used to walk it around on a leash. Still, it made me very nervous. And he's watching for my reaction. So I get in and I'm thinking that if this thing was riding in the car with him before, then it must be okay. I figured that he couldn't possibly let something really disastrous happen to me. Sure! All of this was running through my mind, and I knew he was testing me. He didn't know I had already survived being abducted at knife point when I was a child, a fire in a plane, a crash in a plane and a hotel fire. I guessed at this point that my entire past was preparation for today. I always felt like Bruce was trying somehow to continuously test me. I was too proud to show that I was scared, so I just got in the car. I wouldn't do that now, but I did it then. I thought, I hope this ride doesn't last forever. I'm looking over at this cheetah and it's looking back at me. I'm thinking, oh my God, I'm in the back seat alone with this cheetah. Gordie was in the front, naturally, and Bruce was driving and turning around to look at me. I'm sure he found this very humorous. He was watching my reactions.

I said to Gordie after, "Why didn't you say something? Why didn't you get in the back seat with that damn thing?" I guess I did such a good job of convincing Bruce I wasn't nervous that Gordie believed it too. It was a beautiful animal actually. It was gorgeous. But it was also another one of Bruce's games, and I was to be the endangered species.

When the Red Wings would have a wind up party at the end of the season, we always felt uncomfortable. The team never won a Stanley Cup after 1955, so the end of the season would always come on a sour note, like a loss in the playoffs or a bad regular season. So you would have players, wives and front office people drinking a lot, and usually feeling dejected about how the season had ended. It's just such a terrible letdown if you lose, and everybody just wants to go home. But, you also want to say good-bye to people, especially to those who would leave town right after the season.

There was one season-ending party in particular that was just a disaster. I can't remember if this was in '61, 63, '64 or '66, because we got to the finals and lost all four years. That was frustrating to everybody, and Bruce was especially upset that night. And, he had been drinking heavily. The party was being held at the Olympia room after the game, and we waited as long as we could before going in to join everybody. Gordie said, "Let's just go in for a short while, and then we'll go home. We'll say hello around the room and say goodnight to Bruce and leave." Well, good old Bruce was in a bad mood. He was in a mood where he was going to nail everybody and anything that bothered him. I was sitting by myself while Gordie was off talking to some players and getting us something to drink. Bruce sits down with me and starts tearing into me, yelling at me and swearing. I'd hardly been in the room ten minutes when he started in on me. He caught me alone. I could smell the alcohol on his breath, and he was really on the attack. I was so flabbergasted when he started talking, I was just stunned, and started blinking my eyes. He said, "Don't bat your eyes at me!" I can't remember everything he said because I was so shocked! He told me I wasn't good enough for Gordie and I didn't deserve a guy like him, and that he knew what I was doing when I was going skiing.

It came to me that I used to organize the Red Wing wives to go on ski trips. It was a lot of fun because we all got a chance to get away, just the girls. I made all the reservations and I went and rented the skis. We'd go up to Cadillac, Michigan in a couple of cars to relax and have fun. But there was some grumbling about that, as though I was supposedly leading the wives astray.

When things like this happen, I start to cry; it hurts me, it demolishes me. But, I didn't want to cry in front of him, so I turned away from him and saw Gordie looking over at me. Gordie knows where I am in a room all the time. It's a funny kind of a thing between us, like radar. If he doesn't see me, then he wants to know where I am and then he'll start looking for me. Gordie could see I looked upset, so he came over and said, "What's the matter?"

Well, I was ready to cry my head off, I felt stupid. It just shocks you to have somebody come up and attack you out of the blue, especially when, if I rebutted I didn't know what he'd do next. You don't know how to react. I was devastated because he was so cruel, so angry. Gordie got our coats and we were out of there. I didn't tell him until later what Norris had done, until we drove home. Who knows what would have happened if Gordie had gotten involved! I was really tired of all this abuse and cried all the way home.

GORDIE: As if that wasn't bad enough, after we left, Bruce really lost it.

We got calls the next day about what happened. I was playing on a line that year with a guy named Parker MacDonald. Parker had a good year playing on the first line, but didn't do so well in the playoffs. For some reason, Bruce never liked Parker and I guess he blamed him for us losing in the playoffs, which was crazy. Parker had gone through a very bad personal time just before the playoffs, and he was having a tough time. Bruce knew about it, and it just seemed to make him madder at Parker.

Parker had broken up with his wife, and he was at the point where he couldn't sleep nights. And we were trying to bring him around. Alex and I told Sid Abel what the problem was, and we were trying to help the guy. Then, after we lost one of the playoff games, Bruce came in and said to me, "Where's your damn friend Parker?" I said, "I want to tell you, what's happened to Parker shouldn't happen to a dog." I wanted understanding and fairness for Parker. He was having a family crisis, and I wanted him to keep his job. I told Norris the problems Parker was going through, and Bruce looked at me and said, "What does that have to do with hockey." Bruce was all heart!

After we had left the party, Gadsby tells me he and the boys were sitting around having some beers. Parker was on the far side of the room, behind a small bar, and Bruce goes over to him. He extended his arm to Parker, like he wanted to shake hands. Parker put his hand out, and Bruce grabbed it, pulled Parker towards him causing the bar edge to drill him right in the upper chest. It caught him right around the heart, and it dropped him. Bruce was a big man, a lot bigger than Parker. Then, Bruce ran around and grabbed him by the throat, and started choking him. Nobody could believe what they were seeing. He was choking Parker like he wanted to kill him, and Parker was totally helpless. I was told Parker was turning colors, before Bill Gadsby ran up behind Bruce, and finally grabbed him by the hands, and bent his thumbs back to get them off of Parker's throat.

They said he was like a wild man. He was so big, and very

strong. Naturally, Bruce's pals hustled him out of the room as soon as they got him up. The story was that they put him on a plane to somewhere that night, and he woke up the next day with a hangover and both thumbs hurting. Supposedly he was asking people how he had hurt his thumbs and how he got where he was. Some of the people who saw it said he could've killed Parker if Gadsby hadn't pried his hands off his neck. If Bill hadn't been there, who knows!

A few years later, Bill was coaching the Wings and we were doing pretty well. It was just two games into the season and Bruce fired him and never told him why. The only reason the front office gave was that Bill wasn't "sophisticated" enough. Some people thought that Norris finally found out that it was Bill who hurt his thumbs that night. Anything was possible!

COLLEEN: Bruce wasn't important in our lives. I think you give someone like that too much attention, because he had such power and control over our lives. He came up to me once at the Michigan Sports Hall of Fame banquet in Detroit and says, "You don't like me, do you?" What the hell do you say to something like that? I could have said, I don't dislike you, Bruce, I dislike the things you do. I never did one bad thing to him. So I merely said to him, "Bruce, I can't afford not to like you." I didn't know what else to say. I was afraid of him. I'm not a psychoanalyst, but he must have realized that Gordie and I had something good going, something he never had. Perhaps he felt that I had too much influence over Gordie, who was the team's prize possession, and that threatened him.

At another one of the season-ending parties, I was dancing with a doctor friend of Bruce's. This was the same doctor that Gordie gave some medical advice. He whispered in my ear, "You know Bruce loves you." And I was shocked and said, "Oh, really?" And he said, "He really does, but he doesn't want you to know." And I said, "Well, he's doing a very good job of it."

When Bruce died, Gordie and I sat and reflected, not so much on the stories or the things that had happened between us, but how sad it was that a man with so much power and money, who could have really helped people, chose not to give real meaning to his life. I know that Bruce did help some people. He did some things behind the scenes to help friends of his who were in trouble. He'd get them jobs or help them financially. But he could have made a bigger difference in a lot of people's lives, including ours. Instead, he seemed to ignore so many of those opportunities. And he lost millions and millions of dollars before he finally sold the team. It all ended very sadly.

I reflected on that one day we flew down to Florida to tell him Gordie was leaving the team, and I saw Bruce in such a different light. He was alone, and he was sober. I remember we were on a couch, and he was in a chair across from us. And he said, "I really envy what you two feel for each other, because I've never known what it is to have somebody love me." It shocked me. I had never felt sorry for Bruce, but he seemed so lonely, so different that day. I believed what he said. Gordie and I had never seen him like that. He was this very sad and concerned person, not this seemingly crazy, scary guy. The way he lived he seemed he never placed a lot of importance on life. He had a "so what if I die, who really cares?" attitude. A person can begin to think that way if they don't feel loved by anyone. And, even though he did the things he did to me, I still felt compassion for him.

CHAPTER ELEVEN

HOUSTON

GORDIE: During the years I was retired and working in the Red Wings front office, I honestly think they didn't know how to utilize me, or were trying to find a way to make me leave. This was during the days when I had a contract to represent Lincoln-Mercury on their sports panel. Colleen did a good job developing and managing that agreement. It was a good deal with a great company. They provided us the use of two cars. Most everyone in the program became good friends. It was something I enjoyed and wanted to continue. Can you imagine, while I was under contract with Lincoln-Mercury, the Wings' front office sent me to an event that was, unknown to me, the unveiling of the new Chevrolet car line. I was upset and in a terrible position. The Wings insisted I go up to the microphone and say something. So I went up and said, "It is quite an honor to be here at Chevrolet's big occasion, especially that you would invite a man from the Lincoln-Mercury sports panel to speak." Actually, it was a good thing I said it that way, because one of the reps from Lincoln-Mercury happened to be there. He said to me, "you gave us a little stamp of approval, and I'm glad that you did because Iacocca was also in the crowd." He was with the Ford Motor Company then, Lincoln-Mercury's parent company. Lucky for me, I was thinking fast, otherwise it was a lose, lose situation for me. If I left, the Wings would have been furious and if I played along with a promotion for Chevrolet, then Lincoln-Mercury would have every right to

271

remove me from the panel. Colleen felt that the Wings just didn't care about what supplemental income producing agreements we had or if they jeopardized them.

At times I thought the Wing's front office did their best to embarass me. Once, I went out to Telegraph and Grand River to a banquet for them, and when I walked in, the place was jammed. I had been told I'd meet the people from the hockey club there at the Red Wing table. Well, I show up, and there's no one else there. I waited around for a while. It was uncomfortable being the only guy at this big table. Finally, I said "B.S." and turned around to walk out. Some fellow stopped me and said, "Gordie, I think I know what's going through your mind." He had eight people come over and sit down with me. Later as I was driving home I'm thinking, "I hate those lunkheads!" It's a good thing I stayed because, although no one had told me, this group had an award that was to be presented to me at this function. They honored two restaurant owners in Detroit, Joe Muer and Chuck Joseph, then called me up to honor me with a plaque. The whole situation was typical of the kind of lack of consideration there was from the Wings from time to time. It was the opposite of how I was informed when I went somewhere that Colleen arranged. There have never been any surprises and she makes certain I look like a genius with all the information she provides me.

I was flying out of town right after that banquet, and called Colleen from the airport. I was so mad about this whole ordeal. I asked her to call the team and let them know I was upset that they had stranded me at this banquet. Colleen did so and conveyed my message. Once again, she was pegged a "troublemaker." I told them when I got back, "Hey, that wasn't her idea, it was me who told her to call!" We constantly went through that type of situation.

However, the turning point in our lives came when the Red Wings learned that Marty and Mark were drafted from the Marlboro Juniors by the Houston Aeros in the WHA.

COLLEEN: How did Marty and Mark get drafted by the WHA? It began because I'm a curious person, and I think about a lot of things that could be changed for the better. One night when I was at a Junior Red Wings game, I was in the stands talking to a pal of ours, Weldy Olsen, and I said, "Doesn't this just kill you seeing all this talent and knowing that they can't get in the big leagues til they're 21?" This was because the NHL had a long-standing arrangement with the U.S. and Canadian Amateur Hockey Associations, not to draft players until they were 20 years old. Weldy said, "Yeah, especially with kids being bigger and better these days." I said, "It's really crazy. Isn't it too bad the WHA doesn't go their own way and change the rule." And Weldy said he wasn't sure where they stand on that issue. With that, a light bulb went off in my head. I didn't know either! But I was sure going to find out! What if?, I thought.

The next day I had our secretary, Dorothy Ringler, make a call to Gary Davidson's office, the president of the WHA. I didn't want to tip my hand, so Dorothy Ringler just said that she was the mother of an amateur hockey player, and she wanted to know: Did the WHA have the same agreement as the NHL not to draft underage junior players? He surprisingly responded that he didn't really know but he'd check on it. Now, this was during the WHA's first year of play, 1972-73. Gary called back, and said that the WHA did not have any such agreement. Cowabunga! Now I knew, and was certain that no one else in the WHA or the NHL realized this factor and how it would impact both leagues and the history of hockey. Amazingly, Davidson never told anyone in the WHA after Dorothy's inquiry. Maybe he didn't realize what this really meant, but I could see this was something that could turn hockey upside down.

Because it seemed so simple, I couldn't believe it. This couldn't be true. That WHA was under no age restriction on drafting young players. And nobody knows about it? Nobody had checked on this? I guessed everybody assumed the WHA was abiding by the same underage draft rule as the NHL. I learned a long time ago in my career that to get hockey people to do something you've thought of, it is best to merely plant the seed of information with them so they believe they thought of it themselves. Then let them take the credit. If I told them something, especially being a woman, or worse, a wife, they probably wouldn't listen—not everyone, but a large majority.

Now I'm like a kid in a candy store. I'm excited because I've got this information which apparently no one else has except Dorothy and Gary Davidson. I'm going around thinking, oh my God, oh my God, because there was a bidding war starting to break out between the two leagues, and this would be a major coup for the WHA. The Toronto Marlboros, Marty and Mark's team, won its Memorial Cup junior championship in a fabulous final game. It was probably the greatest game Mark had ever played in his life, he was voted the Most Valuable Player in the playoffs. He had just dominated the final game. Marty had played magnificent defense, and Gordie and I were just so excited about how well both boys and the team had done. After the game everybody was celebrating, and Gordie went into the locker room to see the boys. Now Bill Dineen and Doug Harvey, the staff of the Houston Aeros in the WHA, were outside the dressing room. I went over to Billy, who we had known from when he played with Gordie on the last Red Wing Stanley Cup team. He congratulated me about the boys, and he said "Boy, Mark was just fantastic out there. How many more years does he have in juniors?" Mark was only 17 at the time, so I said he had two or three more years left. And Marty was 18, so he, too, had to wait before he could be drafted. And I said to Bill, "It's a shame the WHA has the same underage draft agreement with the CAHA and USAHA as the NHL, isn't it?"

Billy is one of those guys who's not very vocal, but his brain is always working. He looked at me so funny, and he said, "Well, we probably do. I assume we do." I could see that the wheels were turning. It was like an arrow just went through his brain. "I guess we'd better check to make sure." He and Doug went off and talked, and I figured the seed was about to take root.

They went back to their hotel and Billy calls Davidson the next day and asked him about the WHA/Amateur status. Davidson told him it was interesting that this was the second time he'd been asked about this subject and tells Dineen that the WHA has no such agreement, and guessed that WHA could draft anybody of any age. Billy, I'm sure, went into orbit. Now Houston has this information first, so they've got a clear shot at Mark unless Davidson tells everyone else in the WHA. Believe it or not, Davidson never told any of the other teams. I don't know if he realized how important this could be to the success of this league. Can you believe it?

I just wish I could have been there for the WHA draft in Winnipeg. It must have been exciting. Like an atom bomb going off. Houston's turn came. The Aeros announce their choice: Mark Howe, of the Toronto Marlboros. Now the other teams start screaming and pounding their tables. "Are you nuts? You can't draft him, he's underage. You just wasted your first-round choice. It's against the rules!" So Billy calmly says, "Oh yes I can." Now they're all screaming at Gary Davidson to tell Bill he's crazy. And

Davidson told them Bill was right. He could draft Mark. The WHA were not under any agreement. Wow! Now, all the WHA teams might as well rip up their draft lists. It's a whole new ball game. I would think the other teams must have been furious at Davidson. I mean, he's the league president. Why didn't he tell them? But, nobody asked except Dineen.

Now Houston drafts Marty Howe. That was when Bobby Hull, who was with Winnipeg, and had been the big fish the WHA landed to get them off the ground that first year, told the Winnipeg guys, "Cripes, you know what's going to happen here? They're getting the Howe kids, and they're going to get Gordie to come out of retirement! I can feel it, you watch. They're going to end up with all three Howes in Houston. Draft Gordie, and at least then they'll have to trade us for his rights." And they told him, that was ridiculous. The funny thing was, Bobby was right and the Jets wouldn't listen. At that point WE didn't even know it. It wasn't in our minds yet. But Bobby figured it out before anybody. It was, after all, a natural!

Next, Clarence Campbell, president of the NHL, called me and Gordie at home. He told us that their board had convened and they wanted us to tell our boys that if they went to the other league they would ruin all of junior hockey. They'd be playing in an inferior league. The whole thing would be tragic. Oh, right! Gordie and I told him that we would not tell our boys what to do. This was their decision. Now, he was trying to pull my strings, based on my dedication to working so long at developing the Detroit Junior Red Wings. He was saying this was a threat to all junior hockey. He said this would keep kids from going to college. Also, since Gordie was still working for the Wings front office, he was appealing to Gordie's loyalty to the old league. As if they had been loyal to him. And we just reiterated that this decision really had to rest with the boys, and we weren't going to tell them what they should or shouldn't do. If they didn't go, it would be because *they* decided not to go, not us. And if players really wanted to go to college, they'd find a way to go to college. They'd do it in the summer or whenever they could. The fact was, a lot of these kids were ready to turn pro, and they could have made a good living at it. The salaries were finally going up with the war between the two leagues and many of these players needed that career money.

GORDIE: When we talked to Campbell again the next day, Colleen offered him an idea for the NHL. She explained that all they had to do was match the money that the amateur players would make if they jumped to the WHA, and put it in a trust for them so they could receive it when they got drafted in the future.

COLLEEN: I thought it was a great idea. Clarence could never say we didn't give them an answer on how to stop juniors from going to the WHA. The NHL board refused to go for it. The result was that the salary war continued, which was great for the players, the WHA got new credibility, and it provided opportunities to a lot of young players who wouldn't have had a career until much later. The whole situation had a ripple effect that is still felt today. And has junior hockey been hurt? They're still the major source for draft choices. You can't say that the WHA had a bad effect on the futures of young hockey players. The WHA merely gave an alternative to a lot of players, young and old, and it opened up opportunities for more players. The WHA and young players needed each other.

GORDIE: I got all the publicity, but I was the add-on in this deal. When we were talking about what kind of offers the boys could expect to receive from Houston, I just kiddingly said, "I wonder what they'd offer for three Howes?"

Talk about seeds being planted! My dream of playing hockey with the boys came about because of a game Colleen put on in one of her charitable efforts in Detroit. It was the March of Dimes, and it had the Junior Wings playing the parent club. We had an All-Howe lineup that night. I was lent to the Junior team, so I was playing up front with Mark and Marty, my brother Vern was on defense, and even the little guy, Murray, played with us. It was really a fun game. They sold out Olympia with about 11 or 12,000 people there. We got such a great ovation from the fans. I think we played until it was tied, like about 10-10, and then we arranged with the goalie that young Murray would score with five seconds to go on the clock. The crowd went ape. This was in my last year with the Wings, and the team had been doing poorly. I told Colleen after the game, "That was the happiest I've seen the fans in this building in years."

I was really proud of Colleen for what she had done in setting up this great event, and raising all this money for charity. It was a great concept. And I remembered looking around the ice, seeing Mark and Marty out there with me, and thinking, boy, wouldn't it be great if this was real. The boys were about 15 and 16 at the time. Little did I know, that a few years later Colleen would be talking to Bill and Doug, planting seeds.

GORDIE: It was just such a thrill to play with two of my sons. The only regret I had came in Hartford where it all ended. We had been with the Whalers for two years and had done very well. Then the Whalers were going into the NHL in 1979-80. That was a big deal for all of us. Then Jack Kelley, for some unknown reason, sent Marty to the minors. Oh, that hurt. Part of me went with him. And he felt so shocked. That's one of the few times in my life that I've really reacted. I really lost my cool. I told Jack, "I'm not complaining, but God, for all that I've done,

Cathy's holiday fun on "Home Ice" in Lathrup Village, Michigan, 1968.

Stanley Cup time with Jack and Helen Adams—1955.

Celebrating birthday's of Grandma Ovens,
Great Aunt Elsie MacDougall and Uncle Jay.

Gordie Howe's Tavern and Eatery celebrates
Aunt Elsie's birthday June 4, 1995.

"Hockey...Here's Howe!" school stars Gordie, Ron Grahame and Marty.

*"Hockey...Here's Howe!" school in New Jersey with
Travis, Marty, Mark and Gordie.*

Brad and Ellen Boyes supporting "Hockey...Here's Howe!" school in Abbotsford, British Columbia.

Eric "MVP Award" Lindros, guest instructor, with pals at "Hockey...Here's Howe!" school in New Jersey.

Gordie promoting instructional book "Hockey...Here's Howe!" in hard cover.

Grandpa Howe with first grandchild, Travis,
in Hartford, Connecticut.

Five generations, mother, grandmother, Colleen, Mark, Ginger and Travis.

Murray, age seven.
The prelude to later saving a deer's life.

*Upper Deck Commemorative uncut card sheet for Howe's 1993
65-city charitable fund raising tour.*

*Paul Sackman, formerly of Upper Deck Card Company
and Brian Price of Parkhurst Cards.*

Jim Pryor, Jerry DeClercq, John Curran, and Bill Gadsby listening to
Chuck Robertson, Chairman of Gordie Howe Tribute night.

Spiro Agnew, Vice President of the United States, pays tribute to
Gordie at the Olympia, March, 1972.

Murray, "If the house is on fire, I'll take Skippy!"—1969.

Famous Studio, Montreal, Quebec

NHL President, Clarence Campbell hands Gordie a book, not a job.

*Mum and Dad Howe join us on
our Hondas at Bear Lake, Michigan.*

*Mum resting with Skippy
at Bear Lake, September, 1971.*

*Colleen and Gordie go for a stroll
on Bear Lake Beach, 1979.*

*A familiar site, number "9"
sailing on Bear Lake.*

Randy "Coach" and Sue Omer, the leaders of the family of friends at Bear Lake, 1995.

Murray at Homosassa with "Clarence, the Cross Eyed Lion".

The Gadsbys and Howes enjoying Homasossa, prior to the Norris arrival.

Red Wing, Bill Gadsby, before he was suddenly released by Norris.
Big Frank Mahovlich is on the right.

Colleen at Junior Wing awards dinner, just prior to the Aeros drafting of Mark and Marty, 1973.

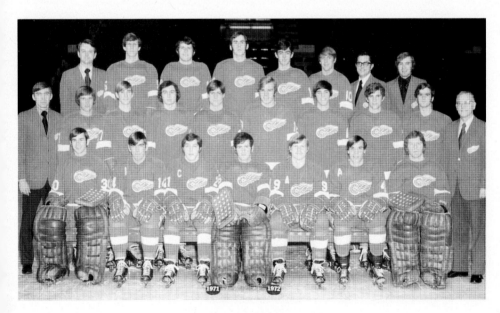

Detroit Junior Red Wings, 1971.

Gordie wondered why he was put into the Norris
insurance business and not on the ice.

Bruce was always looking over our shoulder
and keeping us uncertain, 1965.

Colleen skiing at Boyne
Mountain, 1961.

*Norris with Dr. Hubert, who tried to tell Gordie
what was wrong with the Wings, 1962.*

*Skiing with Louise Kaline, Teresa Delvecchio and Shirley Lunde
at Boyne Mountain, January, 1961.*

Norris, Gordie, Colleen and Delvecchio at first retirement, 1971.

We thought polled Herefords were our future.

couldn't you have given us the chance to play one game together in the NHL? If something happens to Marty, or Mark or myself, and we don't get a chance to play together in the NHL, I can't promise what I'll do." I was so uptight, I even knocked a few things off his desk. I could have nailed him right there.

Well, Marty did get back up with our club to play, but they made it awfully difficult for him. I give Marty and Mark all the credit for what they did in those seven years. People don't realize it, but that was a lot of pressure to put on those two young men. I got all the attention and publicity when they were the ones who deserved it. These were two teenage kids playing darn good hockey. They had to hold their own, and they had people saying things to them like, "You're not as good as your father" or "Your old man stinks and so do you." They were so professional, they never let things get to them. I was really proud to play on the same team with them.

COLLEEN: Once Gordie got drafted by the Aeros, everybody forgot about how young Marty and Mark were, how good they were, how fantastic it was for them to be going to the same pro team. Suddenly, the story is "Gordie's Comeback". It was as if Marty and Mark were tagging along with Gordie instead of Gordie tagging along with them, which is what really happened. It really was a miracle, the way everything fell into place. No one really planned all this. It happened in stages, then it became obvious what the possibilities were. And the key thing that made it happen was that these two kids, as young as they were, could be as good as they were at that age to play in the pros, and play well. Again, they were the ones that made it happen. Gordie was the icing on the cake. But because he's not just a sports hero but sort of a folk hero, his name and his return overshadowed them and their accomplishments. American kids turning pro in those days was rare. For two brothers to win together in Toronto and then move to the big leagues was unheard of. I just don't think they ever got the real recognition they deserved. Certainly they were really glad to have Gordie along, but the fact that Mark was the youngest player ever on the U.S. Olympic hockey team at 16, when he won a silver medal, or the great story of these two American brothers playing together in the pros got overshadowed by the attention on Gordie. That's the effect of his fame. But I never heard either of the boys complain, or say anything about it. I was so proud of them, especially the maturity and class they showed.

MARTY: It was really exciting, getting to play with Gordie. He had been off the skates for a couple of years. And when we first got started at practice, he was turning different shades of purple. I think Mark and I were a little worried about him at first, after all, he was 45. But I'll tell you, after about five or six days, he just became a different person on the ice. He snapped out of it, and just began to control the puck and the play. We were happy to have him on our team as a player, because he was the best guy out there.

GORDIE: We went down to Houston early and skated. The reasons were twofold. I wanted the boys to be introduced to most of the guys on the club by the time training camp started, so they wouldn't be known as Howe's kids, they'd be Marty and Mark. That worked out perfectly, because they made friends before the team even officially started. I figured I'd get in shape early, and I was having a tough time of it. I didn't know, but the boys were calling Colleen at home. They were concerned, they said I was pale and struggling. Then, Billy Dineen announced, early on, that they were going to hold two practices a day. And that's the only time I really questioned my decision to play. I confided in Colleen and told her this might be the biggest mistake of my life. That these two practices a day are either going to cure me or kill me. Suddenly, at the next practice, I felt like I'd been skating all year. I felt really good. It was like I broke through some wall, and I was on my way. I knew then I was okay.

Mark came over to me that day, and said "Geez Dad, you're feeling better, aren't you? I said "Yeah, does it show?" He said "Number one, you're not running all over the ice for your passes. Number two, your color's back in your face. And number three, I see both of your cheeks are back on the seat." That was funny! Anyone reading this who has hemorroids knows what Mark was talking about. The whole training experience was like something out of the "Rocky" movie. I was overweight, and Colleen posted my weight on the refrigerator in bold numerals, 223, as a reminder. I was running near our home, trying to lose weight and get my wind back. I ran, rode bikes and lifted weights. You talk about getting hurt playing the game, this was REAL punishment. My runs got longer and longer. I would take 100 strides running, then I'd walk, and then run again. Then it was 200, then 300, and then I got to the point where I could run the whole thing without walking, and the last 50 yards would be dead uphill. I am not a great runner. It was the first time I'd ever really tried running as training. We have great runners in our family, my Dad was a great runner, and Marty and Cathy were excellent, Colleen did a 10k once and Murray has been a marathon runner. But me, no way. Mark and I are the non-runners in the Howe family. When Harry Neale was our coach at Hartford, he wanted me to run. The first day I did pretty good. I ran close to two miles, and did it in about 14 minutes. The second day I did it in 18. The third day it took me 20. The fourth day it rained, and I said "There really is a God." Harry said "Maybe you shouldn't run," and I agreed with him wholeheartedly.

If we ever had second thoughts about leaving Detroit, Bruce Norris helped us get rid of them real quickly. First, he thought I'd give up the whole idea of going to Houston if he just offered me more money. I said "Bruce, you don't seem to understand. This is going to be the thrill of my life, one thing I've wanted ever since we played the March of Dimes game. It's been part of my thoughts, part of a dream, that it could become real. And now it's come. I'm going to be playing with the boys." And I also said "I'll never, ever set foot in the Olympia office as an employee again." I felt good after that, I went off to play golf. I had told him about it before I talked to the press, I figured I owed him that as my employrer. After I played golf that day, we went public with the announcement. We were on our way.

COLLEEN: When we went down to Olympia to say goodbye to our friends in the building and collect Gordie's last paycheck, they had deducted travel expenses we had recently incurred from booking with the Norris's travel agency. We had been using Olympia Travel for years, and we always paid our bills right on time. But because we had the nerve to leave the organization to start a new life with our family, they took it upon themselves to take that money out of Gordie's last paycheck. Is that just unbelievable? What, were we not going to pay our bills, and leave town like thieves in the night? Gordie showed me the check—it was some small amount after that deduction. It was supposed to be for much more. That was when we knew we had made the right decision, and we were glad to be getting out of Detroit. What a petty and insulting thing to do. Pat Lannon, the comptroller, felt so bad about having to hand this to Gordie.

By comparison, when we got to Houston it was such a contrast. The first hockey contracts I ever got to do were in

Houston. They had no problems dealing with a woman. That would have been unheard of in Detroit. In fact, the Aeros President, Jim Smith, welcomed me. He listened. We did a deal very quickly with the great assistance of Gerry Patterson who was my mentor at that time. The Aeros were so gracious to us and the kids that we thought we had died and gone to heaven.

Then when we flew to Houston for orientation on the team and to hold a press conference, they picked us up in a limo, and took us to a hotel where we all had our names on the doors. Irv Kaplan, the new owner, could not have been nicer. Molly Ann, his wife, brought Cathy and me dinner one night when we were trying to unpack things in our new house. They put a sign up on a skyscraper downtown that said, "Welcome to Howeston" for the opening game. It was just so totally unlike the treatment we'd had in hockey all those years in Detroit. It really wouldn't have taken very much to have made us feel wanted and happy.

GORDIE: We spent a great deal of time promoting the World Hockey Association. In fact, Marty, Mark and I went on an entire promotional tour prior to our season.

One of the television shows we did was "What's My Line" in New York. And I recall that Soupy Sales was one of the celebrity panelists, and of course I knew him from the old days in Detroit. The three of us signed in, and the panel had masks on so they couldn't identify us. A couple of general questions were asked, and I gave a couple of, say, leading answers so that Soupy was able to guess our identities after only a few questions.

It was funny, because Mark was pretty upset with me, he wanted to fool them. He said to me, "What did you tell him for?" So I explained my thinking to him. I said "We're here for publicity, and we're alloted five minutes on the show. Now, if we spend all that time fooling them, and they keep on asking questions, it eats up our time to promote the league and the team. If they get it in one minute, well, that gives us four minutes to talk things up, and that way we get the message across."

The next program we went on was also in New York. I was trying to save the kids from being nervous on TV, so I was lengthening my answers. And, after that show Marty said to me, "Why do you talk so long giving your answers?" I said, "Well, maybe I'm being a little too protective of you guys, but I didn't know if you wanted to talk or not." And Marty said "Yeah, we'd like to talk."

I remember the next program we went on was "The Mike Douglas Show," and I went over to Mike and said "Listen, I've got a little problem here. I guess I've been talking too much on this tour, and the boys haven't had enough time to speak for themselves." Mike Douglas said "Who told you that?" And I said "the big guy there, Marty." Douglas said "Well okay, we'll take care of that."

So when we went on camera, he said to the boys "Marty, you sit here next to me. Mark you're next. And we'll put the old guy down at the end there and we'll see if we have any time to get to him." And the two of them talked like jaybirds, I don't think I got a darn question in. He did it as a favor. It worked out okay.

I thought I was in pretty good shape by the time we opened the season in Houston. Our friend, Bobby Kincaid, our equipment guy, kept me laughing so much in the dressing room that I never thought about my back. I don't know how Janet, his wife, can take it. But, wouldn't you know, I had back spasms the night before the opening game. So I was put in traction. Boy, it was sore. Maybe it was the excitement of the game coming up, but they put me in traction all night. For the game, our trainer Bobby

Brown, attached a little black box to my back whenever I came off the ice and it had a wire that sent a pulse to my back. It kept me in the whole game. And if that wasn't bad enough for our opener, they spelled my name wrong on my sweater, "GORIDE Howe." It was funny. Marty spotted it first, because he walked out on the ice right behind me and he says, "Hey, Goride!" We went out there in that first game and got beat, and when we were coming off, the crowd was cheering us. And Mark, who's a particularly hard loser said, "What are they nuts down here? We lost." I said, "Mark, they appreciated the effort." That's how nice the fans were there. And the nice thing about that club was we did everything together. If there was a party or get-together after a game, everybody was invited.

In Detroit, when none of us were making much money, we used to get together and everybody would throw five dollars on the table. And we'd sit down. If you were only a two-beer man, maybe two or three, like I was, you couldn't be called cheap for not buying another round when you were finished drinking. This way, everybody tossed in. And if Delvecchio said "We need more money in the pot, put in or get out," you could say, "See ya later" and get going. And Houston was like those early days in Detroit. The gang was constantly together. In Hartford, one of our problems was we were never together. There were at least five little cliques.

Those first couple of years in Houston were the most fun I ever had in hockey. God, it was fun. We had a great trainer, Bobby Brown. I remember calling Colleen after I saw him work, and I said, "Half of your worries are over, the trainer is fantastic."

Lefty Wilson had been our trainer in Detroit for many years. Lefty was really a great guy. But, with all due respect, he was really brought to the club as a spare goaltender and had no

285

real trainer experience. He didn't know how to put a band-aid on. But he learned. We had a guy in Omaha who broke his arm on our first road trip. And Lefty wrapped it in black stick tape. And I thought, oh God, are we in trouble or what? I remember going in there once and I said, "Lefty, I put these pants on, and they've got no charley horse pads, no thigh pads. The pads are gone." And Lefty yells, "They're in the red trunk, go help yourself." So I went to put them in, and they fell through to the floor. And I said, "Lefty, the pockets are ripped in the pants." And he yells, "The needle and thread are in the blue one." So we did everything ourselves. He'd say that he was no 'G. D. trainer'.

Lefty had been our backup goalie in Omaha when I was there in 1945-46, and he was a good one, too. He filled in a few times when he was with the Red Wings. He played for us or for the other team if their goaltender got knocked out. I hit him right in the throat one time when he filled in for Toronto. I said, "I got you in the thinnest part of your body." Lefty was a hell of a goaltender. A great goaltender. It was just that we had such great goalies back then that it was hard for Lefty to crack the lineup of Lumley, Sawchuk, then Glenn Hall. Sawchuk was the best I ever saw. I studied him, and God he was quick. Glenn Hall played some outstanding games for us, too. When you play in front of somebody for so many years, like we did with Ukey (Terry's nickname), you appreciate the saves he made.

Bobby Brown, God rest his soul, was our trainer in Houston. He was the best. The greatest trainer I ever had in my career! I remember we had a game out west, and Wayne Rutledge was our goaltender, but he hadn't played in a while. Well, he started hyperventilating after the game. He was in the shower, and he fell to the floor and hit his head. Bobby had seen guys die on football fields from things like that when he was the Houston

Oiler's trainer. So we jumped in there to help Wayne, and he finally got him breathing right. Wayne was yelling, "My leg, my leg." He was cramping up. So Bobby yells, "Rub his legs." All of us started to do this, and Rutledge had eight hands on him rubbing him down. Just when Bobby would say "Okay, he's all right now", Wayne would start yelling "Oh, it's cramping again!", and we'd start rubbing again. We all got a hell of a workout, and Wayne was all right. Bobby always knew exactly what to do.

We finished practice in Edmonton one time and a kid went down and started to swallow his tongue. Bobby saved his life. If I had a bad back and wanted to play, he'd say "No." I'd tell him that I'm good enough to play, and he'd respond, "No, you're not. Until I turn you back over to the Coach Bill Dineen, you're mine. I'm the boss." So Bobby probably saved us from a lot of injuries, and embarrassment, too.

COLLEEN: Once we were in Houston, we got really involved in promoting hockey. This wasn't, after all, a traditional hockey town, except for a minor league team that used to play there. It was really quite a job to get recognized, and we were willing to do anything to sell the game. The Houston management was very receptive to my promotional ideas. That was a shock, after being ignored all those years in Detroit. The Howes even got personalized license plates, which was very unlike Gordie to go around advertising something like "Aeros 9." But it was worth it to support the franchise in any way we could. The previous year, Bill Dineen even reluctantly volunteered to go for a ride on an elephant in the Shrine Circus parade. He was riding into downtown Houston, waving to the crowd, when something happened that surprised Bill. The elephant in front of Bill's relieved himself on the street. Bill's elephant came strolling up,

287

put his trunk into the liquid, sucked it up, and proceeded to blow it up in the air in a huge spray that splashed all over Bill. Now, you have to love hockey to make a sacrifice like that. All joking aside, Bill singlehandedly built the perfect club and we'll never forget what he did for the Howes.

We did things to promote the game that were incredible, even to the point of being crime-busters. Well, I can't say that was on our minds at the time, we were doing what comes naturally, but again, it helped to promote us and the Aeros team.

GORDIE: We had just dropped Mark off at a shopping center in Houston, the Galleria, to drive Colleen's car home. She had met me there earlier in the day. And as Colleen and I were pulling away, I thought, "That's kind of stupid. I should check to make sure Mark doesn't have any trouble with the car." So I turned around and went back. There was a guy at the door there when I got out who said, "Mr. Howe, Mark got the car and everything's fine." So I said, "Thank you," and I just happened to look over to see two couples walking along, and I see this kid standing up on a potted tree. All of a sudden, he leaps off that pot and grabs the purse right off this lady's shoulder. I looked at Colleen in the car, who had seen it too, and I remember the exact words she said, "If you want him, let's get him."

So I jumped in, slammed the car door, and we're heading towards Neiman Marcus store where there's a crossroads. There's also a divider and we bounced over that, just like in the movies. Then the thief ran in the other direction, and I said to Colleen, "Keep your eye on him," and I turned and went after him. He went across a road, so we jumped another median. I went down this street where he's running, and he jumped up over the curb. We flew up over the curb in our car. This was really getting exciting. Now, I'm closing in on this guy. My adrenalin is pumping. He's running across this flat plot of land, headed up a knoll to a freeway. We've got to get him now! Naturally we're catching up with him. He's got the purse swinging from his hand the whole time. He was fast, I'll give him that. I chase him west across this flat land, and now I'm trying to figure out how to stop him by hitting him or clipping him without hurting him. I didn't want to break his leg or kill him, but I wanted to stop him somehow. So I'm thinking of pulling to a stop, and trying to catch him on foot. I wasn't crazy about the idea, but it made sense at that point. Just as I'm getting ready to get out and try to catch him, he throws the purse back in my direction. I slammed on the brakes, I jumped out and started going after him. The purse was safe now, but I still wanted *him*. I figure the S.O.B. has got to be tired by now. Up to this point, Jesse Owens looked like a second place compared to this guy. I figured he had to get tired soon, so when I go to take off after him, Colleen jumps out of the car and yells, "Where are you going?" I said "He's got to be tired, I'm gonna get him." And she said, "What if he has a gun? S...T...O...P...!"

OOH! I stuck my heels in the ground and came on back. I always said she's smarter than I am. So we were going to go pick up the purse and head back to the shopping center when the husband of the woman who lost the purse ran up, and he was panting like hell. He said "Did you get him?" I said "No, he's going over the freeway. But he dropped the purse." So we went up and got it, and he said "Good, he didn't have time to get into it and take anything." He told us "I really can't thank you enough. I own a bar, and I'd like to treat you to a meal and everything, because we're so grateful." I said "That's fine, but if you really want to thank us, my name is Howe and I play hockey for the Aeros, and it would be great if you'd come to a game. That would be thanks enough." And he said "That we will do."

Well, we got a lot of publicity about our adventure, having told the PR department about our escapade. The strange thing was, one reporter wrote that I ran the guy down and caught him and wrestled him to the ground. Then I remembered we were in Texas and the tales are bigger and better there.

And what was really funny was, a couple of days later I'm driving in my car, and I get a call on the CB. A guy says, "Breaker for Aero 9. Is that *the* nine?" I said, "You got him." And the voice says, "This is "Evel Knievel" (an off-duty motorcycle cop with an imaginative CB name), what do you say we pull off at the next exit, I want to buy you a beer." So I pull off and go have a beer with Evel Knievel. And old Evel says, "I've got to ask you a question, Howe. Are you out of your G.D. mind?" I said, "Why is that?" He said, "You're famous, and that guy you chased could decide to come back and get you. Things could get pretty damn hostile." I said, "Naw, the newspaper screwed the story up so much the guy won't even recognize it was me."

How good was the WHA? Well, I know the NHL was better overall, the players were bigger and smarter and faster. But we had one hell of a team there in Houston. Our defense was NHL caliber. We had guys like Mark and John Tonelli who went on to become standouts in the NHL, All-Star players. Marty would have been much better if he had received some decent coaching and a pat on the back once in a while. The year after he led the best plus/minus stat on the team, Larry Pleau told him not to be concerned about training camp because Marty was too old and they were going for youth. Like father, like son!

Ronnie Graham was a very good goaltender. Our team at

Houston would have been in the top six or eight teams in the NHL in the mid 1970s. And the chemistry was tremendous. We were a unit! Everybody was pulling for one another. That means so much to a team. And that was the major reason we won two championships. Around that time, the Houston management challenged the Red Wings to play some exhibition games by having us come into Detroit, but they said no. That might have been interesting.

(GORDIE WON THE LEAGUE'S MOST VALUABLE PLAYER AWARD IN THE WHA IN HIS FIRST SEASON, '73-74. IN HIS FOUR SEASONS AT HOUSTON HE SCORED 100, 99, 102, AND 68 POINTS, THE LAST WHILE MISSING 18 GAMES TO AN INJURY. HE REBOUNDED WITH 96 POINTS AT THE AGE OF 50 THE FOLLOWING SEASON AT NEW ENGLAND. HE LEFT THE TEAM WITH FIVE GAMES TO PLAY IN '74-75 TO HAVE A CAST PUT ON A BROKEN FOOT, THINKING HE HAD NOTCHED 100 POINTS, ONLY TO HAVE A POST-SEASON RECOUNT DROP HIM TO 99.)

Somebody asked me one time, "Compare the dream of playing with your sons to the reality of it. Did it live up to your expectations? And I simply replied, "In my dreams I never got cramps." There was only one drawback to playing with Mark and Marty. I couldn't watch them when I was playing with them. It would have been fun just to sit in the stands and watch the kids play. I did get to watch Mark and Davey Keon kill penalties for us, and that was a real pleasure. Geez, how those two could skate. They are two of the best skaters that ever played the game. They could go out and kill penalties for the whole two minutes, skating circles around everybody. Mark was such a great left winger, they literally shortened my career in Hartford when they sent him back on defense. Because I could read him and he could read me, we were really a good combination on a forward line. And Marty came on strong with that team, he did everything asked of him on defense. I really believe they never got enough credit for what they did, they both accomplished a great deal. We won four straight division titles and two WHA championships, the Avco Cup. That's pretty darn good.

I can't say it enough. Marty and Mark had the talents. I was just a bonus in the whole deal.

COLLEEN: Everything with the WHA was so different, it was just incredible. They didn't have any hangups in dealing with me, they were so open to everything. Maybe that's what happens when you get some competition into the arena. Suddenly there was a threat to the old established NHL, which really controlled everything about the game. This could only be good for the players, who had been held down too long. In those early days of the WHA it was the easiest thing in the world to get a contract done, and we weren't looking to soak anybody, to bleed them for money. It was a good two-way street and we were treated well for the first time in our hockey careers.

1974: A PERSONAL ACCOUNT WRITTEN BY COLLEEN HOWE AFTER THE FIRST YEAR IN HOUSTON: It was not until New Year's Eve that the total realization hit us. The Howes truly were living in Texas and working with the Houston Aeros of the World Hockey Association. So much had happened since we first learned of Marty and Mark being pro draft choices and there had been little time to think of all the many changes and adjustments which would affect our lives.

Last August, after much emotional strain and planning, we

chiseled the Red Wing emblem off our hearts and headed for Houston wearing the blue and white insignia of the Aeros. What anxieties, fears and questions prevailed as to what the future would bring for all of us! We prayed for good health and with God's help we would find the strength and wisdom to meet any challenge and obstacle we encountered.

My thoughts as a wife were filled mainly with concern for Gordie's physical abilities. After all, he was 45, retired for two seasons. Would it be too much strain and drain on him? I knew he would never settle for a limited ice time situation which was initially proposed. But after much deliberation, conversation and a major medical examination, I felt relieved and knew that it was important for Gordie to participate with his sons on a team. An opportunity such as that would come to few, if any, in a lifetime and he needed this experience to fulfill a dream which began so many years ago. Now, a hundred points, a first All-Star, and potential MVP ago, Gordie has completed one of the most successful hockey seasons of his illustrious career.

The four Howe offspring occupied my maternal thoughts. It is not an easy decision to uproot a 14-year-old daughter from the only community and friends she has ever known, but Cathy, like the rest of us, soon found that Houston had much to offer her as long as she was willing to open her heart and mind. The adjustments and changes have all served to contribute to and strengthen her emotions and maturity. Now, many friends and activities later, Cathy truly enjoys Houston, her experiences and future dreams.

Murray, our youngest, gave us most cause for concern with his decision to remain in Detroit to continue in his minor hockey program. So many times we almost reversed our agreement to let him stay behind, but we felt he deserved the same opportunity to

293

pursue his hockey endeavors that both Marty and Mark received. With Houston's programs offering very little compared to the Detroit system we decided to make guardianship arrangements with the Robertsons for Murray's welfare and security in our absence. This whole situation made me realize how important it was for me to lend whatever assistance I could to the Houston Hockey Association in order that other families moving here from the North and East would not have to separate because of the needs of the program. Now, with an extremely successful hockey and school year behind him, Murray has followed the Howe tradition of doing "his thing" in the best possible manner. He has even become the only Karate expert in the family. With hockey five nights a week and Karate the other two, his year has passed quickly.

Marty, who was picked in the late stages of the minor drafts by the Aeros, proved to his coach and the league what he was capable of, earning himself a regular position on the squad. Although opportunities seem to come late to him, following in the footsteps of both his dad's and his younger brother's greatness, he has learned to appreciate his defensive role in hockey. After he had successfully paved his way into the junior ranks alone, there was no doubt in our minds how Marty would meet the challenges presented him in a new pro career. Now a plus average ago, Marty promises to be one of the outstanding, hard-nosed defensemen in the league.

Mark, having so many expectations of him this season, was under unrelenting pressures. He was a slated superstar, following in Dad's skates, and the youngest player in the league. Now, having completed an outstanding year in the beginning of his pro career, he sits on the brink of a Rookie of the Year award as well as a confirmed second All Star berth. If desire, talent and hard work are the combination to be a superstar, then, as predicted by many, Mark will be there.

As for the WHA, we were pleasantly surprised that, in its infancy, it held the competitiveness, appeal and continuing efforts to improve during its rapid growth. Now, over 100 games later, we have learned the major advantages and tremendous need for this league. It has opened, and will continue to open, greater job and salary opportunities to hockey people. One of Gordie's philosophies, is that whatever a player sows, the future generations of players will reap. Now *he* has sown the seeds of his hockey knowledge and talents in both the NHL and the WHA in order to serve to further this great sport.

The team was another mystery to the Howes that was solved immediately upon our arrival in Houston. There was no resentment toward all the attention which surrounded the arrival of the Howes. Instead we found a special group of players and their families who blended themselves into a championship unit with each person contributing their maximum toward a successful year. An AVCO World Cup later we know now that this team was a winning combination of personalities unlike any other we have known. They had what it took, on and off the ice, and gave more.

Much of the success of the team was reflected in Irvin Kaplan and his wife, Molly Ann, the majority owners. We felt concern over the owners only until we had met them. It has been a most refreshing experience to have the outstanding guidance, leadership and friendship offered this team by the Kaplans. They have made playing hockey a pleasure. This was a universal feeling throughout the team.

To uproot established business relationships and possible future job opportunities were other questions which weighed heavily on our minds earlier but we realized that Houston had more to offer in investments and future growth than one could ever imagine. And, let's face it, the whole difference is being with the job environment which is conducive to happiness. Now Gordie has found this in the faith extended to him by the Aeros, as well as having faith in what he could contribute to hockey once again. As in the past my primary business role, as manager of our investments and enterprises, is to control and coordinate all of the past, present and future business ventures in order that Gordie, Marty and Mark could concentrate on their responsibilities to the club. I questioned my capacity many times early in our move but some very successful negotiations later, with qualified guidance and advice, I feel I have met the challenge and most of the goals I intended to achieve.

For me, my only regrets are being separated from dear friends, but those relationships are never lost regardless of how much time passes. My role as wife, mother, friend and business manager leave me little time for loneliness, and I find myself quite proud and thankful to be part of the Howes of Houston.

To play or not to play, that is the question for Gordie for this coming season and the Howes will stick together with his decision. There is the opportunity to play in the Russia-Canada team series, which presents a brand new challenge. Now we ask ourselves, can Gordie Howe play with his grandsons, not just his sons?

This was a perfect year and one which will always live in the minds of the Howes as our most memorable.

Chapter Twelve

It's Been Better Than A Dream

MARK: The first time I hurt my back was when we were playing in Houston. I was out by the blue line, and a guy flicked the puck up in the air to get it over the line, and I jumped up into the air for it. I didn't get it, and I came down and something just popped in my back. I stayed late after the game, then left to drive home. I had a townhouse, which was next door to Mom and Dad's place. We bought three of them in a row to get a better buy. I had a little 280Z Datsun at the time. I got to my place and I couldn't get out of the car. So, I drove over in front of their place and started honking the horn. Dad had to come out and pull on me. I couldn't move. He finally got me out of the car.

I had a lot of pain associated with it. I ended up going to Connecticut the next year, when I signed with Hartford. Then I had a lot of problems for about a year and a half to two years. The condition was getting way out of hand. The team doctors couldn't seem to do anything to help me. They just said I had bad posture, and that was why I had all this nerve pain down my leg. So, I found a doctor who gave me a book to read. He said "See if these symptoms seem the same as yours." It described back pain when you go to the movie theater or if you're in your car and you can't sit in one position for more than two minutes so you're constantly moving. A lot of it made sense, so they gave me some epidural steroid injections, which go right into a little sac around your spinal column. He said it works on 50 percent of the people and if it works on you, it'll take away all your inflammation and pain. At that point I think I had been playing six to eight weeks where I couldn't even touch my knees when I'd bend over. And I was only about twenty-four. So, if I'd been thirty-four, I wouldn't have been able to play at all, but because I was twenty-four I could get by. After the injection, I got up. I could stand there and touch my toes. It was like a miracle. I went back and started playing again the next day. So, I've had a separated shoulder plus busted ribs in my career, even the really serious injury with the net. But there's nothing as bad as having a bad back when you're trying to play hockey.

I remember one time we were playing in Colorado, before I found the new doctor. I was getting so depressed over my back complications because there was pressure from the team to play better. I'm trying as hard as I can and I'm playing well, but not as well as I think I'm capable of playing. So, there's pressure from myself and pressure from the team. Meanwhile the pain is something that I'm enduring every day. So, one night I went out and I had too many drinks. Ginger was down in Florida visiting her mother. I called her and said, "I've had enough, I want to quit." So, she kept saying, "You don't want to quit." I said, "I'm tired. I don't want to live the rest of my life with this pain. It's just awful." She said "Well, when you wake up tomorrow morning and you still want to quit, fine. I'll meet you back home. Just sober up a little and give me a call tomorrow." I called her the next day and said, "I guess I don't want to quit. But I have to do something." And when we got back from our road trip I told the team manager I was going to find my own doctor. I had to do something. He said, "No, you can't do that." I said, "Then I quit."

I said I'd had enough. Then Howard Baldwin, the Whalers owner, called me. He said, "Look, just do what you have to do.

Find somebody to get yourself better." I said "I don't care if you pay me or not." He said "No, we're going to pay you." I told him "I want to play hockey but I can't play the way I am. It's just too much." So, after this new doctor helped me, I got so much better. Periodically I would still have problems with my back but never to the extent that I had back then. It was so bad for a long time.

When I was with Philadelphia, I had a couple bouts with my back where I missed three or four weeks over a six or seven year period. But then, we were lifting weights out in L.A. as a team one day and something snapped in the right side of my back. I'd never had anything on the right before. We played two days later in Vancouver, and I couldn't reach my skates. You don't mind playing through that, but I got into the second period and it was awful. I told the trainer, look, I just can't go anymore. He came back and said "They want you to finish the game." I said, well, all right. That's the way I am, I said fine, and went back out. There were maybe three shifts to go in the game. I went behind the net and just turned. I didn't want anybody near me. I went down, I just collapsed. And that put me out for almost a year and a half.

What happened was that I had herniated my disc and it was pressing on my nerve. The whole top of my foot was numb. It took a year and a half before they found what was causing it. It was amazing. I had four series of MRI's. Had a myelogram. It didn't show up on that. It showed up on one CT scan. One little picture. So, then I had major surgery. The surgery really relieved my pain but I couldn't play golf for three years. I couldn't do any twisting or turning at all.

There were certain side-effects that I had from the surgery that I just had to learn to live with. For the most part, though, I'm pain-free ninety-eight to ninety-nine percent of the time now. After I had my surgery I had one point where my body just locked up. I didn't have pain but I had no mobility. I met a doctor from Philadelphia who began working on me. I've had him here in Detroit three times this year. When my back goes out he comes in and within two days I feel great again. I believe so much in what he does. The one thing that's nice for me is that I know when I'm done playing — and I'm pretty sure that I'm already retiring and that I think my back is going to be at least 99% healthy. That is the one thing that I am concerned about. I know Dad has asked me about retiring a couple of times. I've said, no, I'm going to be okay. Then I watch him having trouble going up and down stairs, and I look at his swollen wrists, and I wonder if I'm doing the right thing by continuing to play.

It's hard to see my Dad in pain, especially knowing how tough he is. I remember, in Houston, when I first moved from home to an apartment. I went back home to have my game meal with him one afternoon. He was cooking some hamburgers and he had them on the broiler. He used to just reach in and pull everything out with his bare hand. But this time he went to retrieve one of the burgers and as he reached in the oven, the top of his hand touched the burner. He pulled his hand out and he just said, "Oh, darn it, that hurts." He had really burned his hand. We had a game that night and he just put a little Vaseline and a bandage on it, and shoved it in his glove. The back of his hand looked like raw meat. I looked at it and thought, Oh my God, I could never play a game with my hand like that. So, I know how tough he is and that's why it bothers me to see him having trouble going up and down the stairs. The other day, here at my house, he started up the stairs and he couldn't make it. So, he stepped back and got some momentum to get going again.

When Dad has problems, you really notice because we take for granted he will never change. I've always joked around about him being so tough. I've said his nerve endings just don't make it to the top.

I separated my shoulder earlier this year, where my collar bone meets the sternum and the top couple of ribs. The ligaments there just gave way. It was painful and, at about 2 a.m. when I was trying to go to sleep, the pain really started to become intense. If I sat up straight or stood up, I was okay. Then as soon as my head went back about 1/2 inch off balance and I had to support it with my chest muscles—I couldn't do it. I spent the first three nights going down to the lower family room, propping up a couple pillows on the couch and going to sleep sitting up. You can't lie down or be comfortable when you have a bad shoulder injury.

I got hit real hard when I sustained the injury. I don't even know who hit me. It was in a Sunday afternoon game against St. Louis. It was a big guy, but I really didn't see who it was because he came in from the blind side. I remember when I first started in hockey, although I was somewhat smaller in stature, I skated so well that when I got hit they never got a big piece of me. Now, I'm a touch slower, but that's all the opposition needs to make a check more effective. I remember when I used to go to Dad's Red Wing camps and the average size of the guys on the team was 180 pounds. Now, I'm 185 and I think the average player is nearly 197.

In Houston I started out as a left wing, and played on a forward line with Dad. The last year that I played there was '76-77 and Billy Dineen was coaching and we had a lot of injuries. I had just come back from sustaining a separated shoulder after

301

being out of the line up for four weeks or more. The team only had probably twenty-five or twenty-six guys under contract because of the budget. Then a couple of our defensemen got hurt, so Billy played me back on defense and it worked out great. The next year we signed with Hartford, and I went back to playing forward again. I did that for a couple years and then the leagues merged. I remember we were playing a game in Buffalo. We had a light morning skate and I played left wing. Then when I went to the game, I saw my name written down to play defense, so I erased it and put it back on my line. Our coach came in and said, "Who's screwing around with the blackboard?" I asked, "Why am I playing defense?" It would have been nice to have at least practiced a defense position, maybe working on some three on two rushes or something. But that was that. I'll never forget my first shift. I stepped on the ice. My partner pinched in and the puck bounced over his stick and Gilbert Perreault came flying down the ice. Now it was a one on one against me. The only thought going through my head was oh, Lord, please help me. I'm saying to myself—if you've ever performed a miracle in your life, do it now. Gil was stick handling all over the ice, and the puck bounced over his stick and went in the corner. I went and laid on it, got a whistle and a line change. I was out of breath, and so nervous.

In Hartford we were very thin on defensemen. I had to play my position thirty to thirty-five minutes a game. When I analyze it, I had a lot of quickness, could pass really well, get the puck out quickly, and put the puck on my teammates' sticks rather than just throwing it and giving it to the other team. I think these were the reasons why they put me back on defense. From then on, I spent ten years playing thirty to thirty-five minutes a game.

That may have actually extended my career, but it might have hurt me financially, because you don't score as many goals.

However, that's never been my priority. I've always considered myself a team player. Whatever I could do to help the team win is what I did. It's always worked out. It's strange now because when I'm with some of the Red Wings and I see myself on an old hockey card, I'll say "Oh, there I was in my old left wing days." They'll say, "You played left wing?" "Oh yeah, until I was twenty-four."

It's an odd feeling, being the oldest guy in the league. Both my Dad and I have been the oldest players in the NHL. Longevity obviously runs in the family. I was twenty my third year in Houston—they signed John Tonelli, who was younger. Until that time, I was always the youngest player on every team I'd ever played on. Now it's twenty years later and I'm at the other end of the spectrum. It's hard to imagine how my dad must have felt being in a dressing room and playing with guys who weren't even born when he first started playing. I guess it's a matter of genes, attitudes and the love for the game. It's still so incredible that between Dad, Marty and me we have a total of sixty-six years of play.

It was through a lot of ironic twists that I ended up on the 1972 U.S. Olympic team. In the playoffs with the Junior Wings the year before, I hurt my knee quite badly. They thought I was going to be fine but then it turned out that by September I had knee surgery. I was 16 at the time. Marty had gone to Toronto to play with the Marlies and I probably would have gone if I was healthy. But since I needed knee surgery, I was going to be out for about two to three months. I decided to remain with the Junior Red Wing team. In my first game back in the lineup, sometime just before Christmas, we played a fund-raiser exhibition game against the American National Team, which was the Olympic team. In that game, one of their left wingers got hurt. Their management had seen me play and invited me to go to their camp in Minnesota and try out for the left wing position. Mom and Dad told me, they were trying to have the Olympic team guarantee me a spot on the squad because they didn't want me missing all that school just for a tryout. The team said they couldn't do that, but it was the chance of a lifetime, so I took it. I recall there were three of us that tried out for the spot and I was thrilled being chosen.

So, there I was at sixteen, headed for Sapporo and the Winter Olympics. Three players from Boston were on the team, and they said that I could live with them while we trained in Minnesota. I thought that would be great. I got there and found out they hadn't paid their phone bill in I don't know how long, so we didn't have a phone. When I wanted to call home, I had to go down the street to a pay phone. It was nearly twenty below zero half the nights I was there so when I put the phone up to my ear, it almost froze there.

These guys were great. Stu Irving had been over in Vietnam. He got called back from the war. Dick McGlynn was the outgoing one and a crazy, funny guy. Robbie Ftorek, who I think was engaged at the time, was a real down to earth kind of person. They were all terrific guys. I remember the first day there and the coaches are trying to figure out how much money I need for living expenses. I told them these guys weren't going to charge me rent because we were only going to be there a month. Living at home and being sixteen, I told them I could get by on $50 a month. They said, "Well, we'll give you $150 a month just in case." I said, "Wow, I don't need that much." They insisted I take it, so I got $150. I thought I was in heaven.

The first day of practice we left the rink and we're heading down this freeway and McGlynn was driving. He gets off at an exit and is halfway down a ramp when he realized we're on the wrong exit. So, he stops and backs right up the ramp. I'm in the back seat watching all this. This is my first extended stay away from home and I'm thinking, "Wow, this is nuts. This is nuts and this is great!"

Everything worked out really well, and I had the experience of a lifetime. I was a five-minute man on the team. My job was to get out there and create havoc. So, I'd run around and do just that. The one thing that I was always able to do best was skate fast, so I'd just skate fast and bump players. I took quick shifts in thirty to forty seconds and get the heck off the ice. We had a good team, with guys like Timmy Sheehy, Henry Boucha. Our goaltending was stellar. For me, a sixteen-year-old on a two-month vacation from school, who could ask for more?

It would come down to the last game to determine our outcome. Even if we won our final game we still could finish fourth. But, the Soviets beat the Czechs in their last game, which guaranteed us third place. We had a tied record with them but we had beaten them head-to-head. And Sweden had an excellent team but somehow they lost to Finland. So, that put us into second place for the silver medal. It was incredible.

My high school teachers at Southfield Lathrup did a lot for me to see that I didn't get behind in my schoolwork. I went in to get all my homework and they said "Look, just go to Sapporo and do your best. We'll work things out when you get back." I had a couple courses that they wanted me to read on the trip. They said, "We're going to be covering 120 pages, and we want you to just try and keep up on that." When I got back, a couple of teachers let me study the work I missed and take a short exam on it. I also did an audiovisual report of my Olympic experiences for the class. Everyone was excited for me.

We were at camp in Minnesota for three weeks. Then we went to Colorado to get used to the higher altitude for about a week to ten days. We flew to Tokyo and spent a week there before going up to Sapporo for the two weeks for the Olympics. So, there I was, my first time in Japan. At the Olympics you live in dorms, and you have cafeteria food every day. I think I got $1700 for meal money and expense money. Back then you got 330 yen to a dollar. Now it's closer to 87. I bought suitcases and presents for everybody back home. We were wearing what I thought were really gaudy looking clothes. We had to wear the national team uniforms. They had big leather, blue-brimmed hats with a U.S.A. logo. Half of the stuff I brought home I'd just barter for. They wanted the hats big time, so I'd show them what I wanted in return. Something might cost 27,000 yen and I'd say, "I can't afford that." Then I'd find out that was only about $100 in our money. I bought everyone at home a present.

It was a great learning experience for me. I might have been too young to realize what a great accomplishment it was, and how lucky I was to have the opportunity to play on that team and win a silver medal. I remember when I came home. The first Canada Cup was that year, and I told my Dad "I think Russia is going to win the series, but only at around five games to three." Then I remember sitting out on our deck when they were playing the first game and Canada was ahead two to zero in the first two minutes and Dad's saying, yeah right, great scout you are. The Soviets ended up winning, seven to three. And I said "I told you they're not too bad." I wanted Canada to win but I was glad the Soviets won that game, just to prove that I wasn't wrong. The

Swedish players, the Russians, and the Czechs—players comprised some great, great hockey talent over there that I never knew existed.

It was an unforgettable opportunity just being in Japan for three weeks. I remember Ftorek and I were rooming together and we were sitting in the room. I was watching TV, "Bonanza" dubbed in Japanese, while Robbie was writing a letter back to his fiancee. All of a sudden, the lamp, the TV and everything shakes. It was an earth tremor. I'm looking out the window, asking myself what the hell is happening? It was a lot for anybody to go through, especially for me being away from home for the first time. My parents could not join me. I think they felt Dad might detract from my achievement and that it would be a greater experience for me on my own. They were right, and when I returned home, I told my Mom that the first time I felt the true meaning of being in the Olympics was when I was at the opening ceremonies, when the torchlight parade took place. There was this tremendous feeling of pride and patriotism that overtakes you, and you feel like crying. It was then that I put the other reasons I was glad to be there, behind me. I still think of that trip every time I see my silver medal hanging in my home.

You always associate good times with winning. I do, anyway. I know playing in Houston was really great. We had a team that ended up in first place for four straight years. We won the Avco Cup championship twice. Those were great times. The year before that, Marty and I were together in Toronto. We won the Memorial Cup and I won the MVP of the tournament. As an individual, that's probably the highest award I've ever achieved. One of the years of the Avco Cup, I was runner-up for the MVP.

Our goaltender, Ronnie Grahame, won it. He kept saying I should have won it. He was so stellar, he deserved it hands down.

The down time was probably the few years we were in Hartford. But when I got traded to Philadelphia, everything changed. It was a world class organization. Everybody said I felt that way because I got out of my Dad's shadow. I don't think that was it at all. I went from a small market where nobody even recognized certain players to a big market where you got more attention. I had a couple years in Hartford where I played a lot better than I did for a number of years in Philly but I didn't get the recognition.

In Philly, it was a far more team, and leadership, oriented game and it was a team that was used to winning. It was simple. You do *your* job, everybody does *their* job, and you win the game. Hartford wasn't that way. We had to do a lot of guy's jobs. Probably the best thing about Philadelphia for me was the owner, Ed Snider. He really cared for his players and you knew it. It was a nice feeling. He lived and died with that hockey club. I think that team started to fall apart when he left to live in California. But he's back in Philly now and I think that's one of the main reasons that club is winning again.

I was under a lot of pressure when we went to Houston. I remember the first couple of practices we had where I'd have such a bad migraine headache, I'd have to leave the ice or be throwing up all over. I had done that a lot as a youngster. It was just from so much pressure I was putting on myself. Billy Dineen grabbed me one day and said, "Look, you've made this hockey club. Just relax and play." I said, "Oh, okay." He was a great coach, and he had great empathy for people, so guys liked playing for him.

In my mind, I wanted to prove to everybody that the reason

I was there was not because I was Gordie Howe's son. The reason I was there was because I was a good hockey player and I was going to prove it. I remember when we signed to go to Houston. I told Dad that Marty said he wanted to sign right away. The fact that Dad was going, too, changed my mind from thinking I need one more year of Junior. I signed a contract for $500,000 at $125,000 a year. Dad, in all the years he played, never made that much. At the time I wasn't sure I was ready. Dad told me the way you improve is the way you've always done it. "You play against people better than you. You make mistakes, you analyze what you did wrong, and if you can correct those mistakes, you don't make them again and you're a better hockey player. Plus, you're getting paid a lot of money to do it." It took me a while, however, until around January that first season to get to the point where I knew I was where I belonged. At first I felt like a rookie and, I guess I was a rookie.

The Aeros were a great group of guys. This helped me out so much to play on a line with Dad. In the first two years of the league, it was such a thrill to play with him after having gone to almost every single Red Wing game. It was a player's dream to be in my skates. I saw so much that Dad did in those games, but I didn't see nearly as much as what went on with him every day in practice. I could never have imagined what it would be like to be on the same line with him and doing so many champion things together on the ice. It was a real thrill to watch him that first year. Imagine, he was 45 and 46 years old those first two seasons, but yet he was the best player in the league. It was amazing for a guy 45, who retired for two years, to do some of the things he was doing. Also, he was still a pretty vicious hockey player, too. I know there were the critics who said, well, it's the WHA and it wasn't as good as the NHL, and there was no doubt about that.

But it was very good hockey and it got better as the years went by.

I don't know if it was because he was more aware of me or whether he even thought about it consciously, but when he'd go to pass me the puck, he'd throw it slower than he did to the other players. Perhaps it was so it would be easier for me to handle. But, by the time the puck got there, because it came so slow, it gave the other team enough time to adjust to it. So, when the puck did get there, so did one of the opposition and I got clobbered. I waited maybe a week and then finally said, "Dad, you've got to throw the puck harder. I'm getting creamed." He made the adjustment.

Back then, I could skate better than just about anybody in the league. Dad hated to dump the puck in the opponent's zone, but sometimes we had to dump it in, so my job was to be the first guy in there after it. So, I'd go in the corner and I'd get there first and I'd get hit by the opposition. And then, I'd really get crunched. And every time, what was happening was that Dad was coming in and hitting the guy who hit me.

It was about two weeks later that I finally said "Dad, you've got to quit hitting a guy when he's hitting on me. You might be hurting him, but you're killing me." So, from then on, he just said "Well, you get in there and do your thing and then get the hell out of there. And then I want you in front of the net."

Gordie was so big and strong, even at his age, he could fight off two guys and he'd just put the puck on my stick. My job was to be there and shoot it. A lot of times I had to yell at Dad for the puck. I always called him Gordie. I'd say "Gordie, Gordie, I'm open!" I think I told my mom once that he was always Gordie on the ice unless he got hurt, and then he was my Dad. But that was very rare. Most of the time, he did the hurting.

I've never met anybody even close to the way he was on

the ice. How tough he was. And it wasn't just the opposing team that he gave it to, sometimes it was his own teammates in practice. I'll never forget one New Year's Day. Marty was one of the few guys who was sober and it was a New Year's Day practice. We'd had a couple days off, that was why we practiced that day. There had been a big team party for New Year's Eve the night before, and some of the guys were still going strong. A couple of guys came in the dressing room. One guy had a beer in his hand. Things were normally pretty loose back then but not that loose. I was with those guys and I left my beer outside. I sat down next to Dad and he said, "You're with those guys?" I said, "Yeah." He said, "Thank God you're smart enough to leave your beer outside this room." I said, "Well, I think you raised me better than that."

So just about everybody on the ice was working on their hangover or just starting one. Marty had left the party about 3 a.m. So he probably only had about four or five hours of sleep. I remember going down to the ice and one of the guys who had the beer in his hand raced over and took a vicious swing with his stick at Marty and cut him severely over the eye. I remember Dad going over and just jamming his fist right in his mouth. I remember a couple guys yelling at my Dad about it, asking why'd he do that. I remember him saying, "If anybody wants to screw with me or my kids, here I am."

I don't know if Dad remembers that. I'm sure Marty remembers, although most of what happened was after they had gotten Marty off the ice. It was a pretty good cut that he took, probably 6 stitches worth.

I remember the last three years that Dad played with Detroit, especially the last year, when things had deteriorated with the hockey club. It got real bad. He tells me now how I used to drive him nuts because I asked him questions all the way to the rink and then after the game all the way home. I remember being an inquisitive kid. One time we were driving to a game against Chicago and he said, "Keep an eye on that Keith Magnuson." He said, "I'm going to get him. I owe him one for hitting me with a cheap shot from behind." So, now I'm a little more fired up for this game. I remember sitting there and watching and waiting for something to happen.

GORDIE: Oh, Keith Magnuson, yeah. What a funny guy. He played defense for Chicago near the end of my time with the Wings. I'd yap at him from the bench, "You won't last ten minutes!" He looked like a nervous wreck out there. Every now and then he'd take a run at me, and he'd leave his face wide open. Bobby Baun would do the same thing. They're honest, they come straight at you and, boom, you have to walk over the top of them. Keith used to complain, about "Howe...and his wipe!" because I used to wipe my glove across his face every chance I got. I could irritate the heck out of him. He'd get a lot of penalties, whacking at me. I wasn't mad at him. As a matter of fact, I used to rent boats from Keith out in Saskatchewan. Hell, I felt sorry for him, the way he was going he wasn't gonna live! He was wired all the time, jumping like hell. High on life, I guess.

MARK: The face-off was in the Chicago end and Magnuson was right behind it. Dad was on the inside of the circle, towards the front of the net. Chicago won the draw straight back. Magnuson grabbed it. He went behind the net and Dad just came in from the other side, and rifled an elbow right in his head. He's starting to go down but then Dad grabs him by the back of the head and just slams his head down. I don't know if he hit his knee or not but it was close to it. He was down and just out cold. Dad just skated into the penalty box. After the game, he was smiling.

312

He said, "I got him." That was the only time he told me when he was going to get somebody.

I remember in the first year of the WHA, Dad was coming down the ice and he made a defenseman from the other team cut into the middle. The guy never saw me, so I came from the other side and I just nailed him. As it turned out, I separated his shoulder. After the game, Dad said, "way to go." He said, "I've been trying to get that guy for years."

But look at how he is off the ice. The people who know my Dad never ever talk about Gordie Howe in terms of what a great hockey player he was. Everybody who knows Gordie Howe says what a great person he is. Since I've been back in Detroit, people always come up and say, "Oh I know your Dad and we used to do this together and we did that. And, boy, he's such a great player." As soon as they say that, I know immediately that they aren't very good friends with Dad.

GORDIE: Mark always speaks up. When we were first training in Houston, somebody tripped me in practice and I banged into the boards head-first and I lost consciousness. They took x-rays, and I was okay, but it was a good bump. I told the boys not to tell Colleen, so she wouldn't worry. First thing I know, Mark tells her, "Hey Mom, Dad hurt his head."

Once when he was little, I came home from practice and he told me that he and his mother had bought a Christmas present for me. I said, "What is it?" and Mark said it was a secret, he couldn't tell. So I said, "I'll give you five bucks if you tell me" and he blurted it out.

One night in Houston, a call went against us, and Mark skated by the referee, Bill Friday, and called him a "blankety-blank homer." And Bill blew the whistle and said, "That's ten

313

minutes for the kid," a misconduct penalty. So I skated over to him and said, "Bill, how do you know he was the one who said it?" He said, "Because he says the same thing every time...in a squeaky voice. Tell that kid either to change his line, or his voice."

So he goes over and tells the scorer the penalty. And as he skates back past me, he says, "You tell the kid a homer I may be. But a blankety-blank...I'm not. "

MARK: I remember Dad only spanked me one time. He whacked me in the rear end. I don't know if he even remembers that. I think I got caught stealing or something. I'm sure I more than deserved it.

I think I'm more like my mom. In the way that I think. I guess a lot of it connects to how she taught me to be analytical about things. And that helped me a lot when I made my move here to Detroit. I loved it in Philadelphia. It meant so much to me to be there. But, I put down on paper the good things about staying in Philly and the good things about coming to Detroit. She taught me how to make lists. When I examined the lists, they didn't even compare. Even though my heart was telling me to do one thing, stay in Philly, I looked at the lists, and I said I have to go with what I need, which was Detroit. So, it wasn't even close.

I think my wife Ginger has changed me a lot. Ginger's taught me how to be more independent and speak my mind. Now, if I don't want to do something, I just say—hey, I'm not doing it. She's helped me a lot that way. I think the way I used to interact with people is more like my Dad's way. I think that's probably because I spent so much time with him when he would be signing autographs at games or doing his tours or going to golf tournaments. I learned by watching him, how to just sit down and relax and talk about things. I'm more easygoing like he is in that way. So I'm a mixture of my parents, but actually I think I'm more like Mom, the list maker, doer, and unafraid to try anything I want to do. I love being a home engineer, at times, and tackle some huge project for our home with Ginger. We design entire rooms together. We're both good at it.

One of the best things about my childhood, was that as a kid I knew that we were always going to have a stable home. There are so many divorces now, but the question was never raised at our home. They had their differences like all other parents do, but we never ever saw them hurt each other. I always knew that they had such a commitment to each other and to us, there was nothing in their lives that mattered more than their children. Nothing. That was always the most evident. They sacrificed so much of their own lives together for their family. All those years that Dad traveled during the summers working, and Marty and I would join him for the last ten days or two weeks on the west coast of the Canadian tour. The reason he was doing that was, well, I think he was making probably $20-30,000 a year as a hockey player. He'd make $20,000 for doing a one month tour. But that $20,000 enabled them to buy a summer cottage, to buy a sailboat, ski boat, motorcycles. So, every dime they made went into providing us with the luxuries that they never even dreamed of having as kids. God knows how many miles my Mom put on the car. I think one year my Mom told me she drove me nearly 30,000 miles to all the games we used to play here, there and everywhere, mainly all over Michigan and Ontario. Marty and I played together every year except for two, with one of the years being when he played up in Toronto.

When he turned sixteen, my folks bought Marty a car. Then they bought me a car the next year. They had never had a lot of money to do all that. When Murray went to school, they bought him a home near campus at the University of Michigan. They financed his whole education. When my sister got married, they said look, we'll pay for the down payment on your house or pay for a big wedding. Of course, they paid for both. When her first marriage ended, they did so much to support her. And they give so much now to all the grandkids. For Christmas one year, they bought life insurance policies for all their grandchildren and they pay for it every year. Meanwhile, I know they still have their home in Connecticut that they can't sell. We keep telling Mom to quit buying all these things for her family.

I remember once Mom talked to me about being executor of their wills. I said, sure, I'll do it. She said we're going to leave twenty-five percent to each one of you. At the time I was doing a lot better than everybody else financially, so I said you don't have to leave me twenty-five percent. You don't have to leave me anything. You've done so much for me. I think that's probably what's kept our family closer than anything is that they've done everything for their children. I have kids now, and I know how so much of your life as a married couple is quickly gone. A lot of that comes from devoting everything to your children. In that regard, Mom obviously had by far the biggest load. She did so much for all of us. She's the main reason we have a close family.

Marty and I used to beat the heck out of each other until the year he went away to Toronto to play hockey. Then we started to miss each other. We've been really close ever since. We see each other quite often. We don't see Cathy and Murray as much. I think having a four year gap between us makes a difference. I've seen Murray probably five or six times since we've been back in Detroit. It's fun to see him and see his family grow. I saw Cathy quite a bit for a while but now that she's down in North Carolina we don't get a chance to see each other, but we talk quite a bit.

I was telling Mike Krushelnyski from our team yesterday that the question I get so often is, "What's it like to be the son of Gordie Howe?" I said, "Heck, he's the only father I've known." I don't look at him as a hockey player. I look at him and think of how well he's treated me. My Dad was always there. He did everything for me. I look up to my father. I would expect that if I'd been born into another family, I would still look up to my father the same way. But I know I've been lucky to have Gordie as my dad.

When you get into playing hockey, that's when it's been different. You see Dad get paid all this attention. If we were at a restaurant, he'd sign a couple things, he's always nice to people. But, his primary focus was to be with Mom and all of his children.

When we played hockey, at least ninety-five percent of our time was spent with my Mom, going places and doing things, because Dad was playing in the NHL. And our team used to play twenty-five to thirty games here in Michigan, and then we'd play the rest of a ninety-game schedule all over Ontario. We'd go there and sometimes we'd get abused by the fans. Just verbally, and I think some of that was because we were American kids playing Canadian teams. They really gave it to us because we were Americans. But then Marty and I got a little extra because we were also Gordie's kids. You know, your old man stinks, or, you're no good—those kind of comments.

I remember my Mom told me one time, and it helped me a lot, she said, "Don't compare yourself with your father." She always felt that I was very analytical about my own performance and she thinks I'm real intelligent about the game. She said, "You know how to assess your capabilities. If you go out and play at 100 percent of those capabilities, that's what will make you happy."

I still use that thinking to avoid all the comparisons. And I don't read the sports sections. I don't read what's written about me. I used to read them when we were playing in Hartford. I had a lot of good press. A lot of good things were said. I remember in Hartford once, though, that some guy wrote an article and said something negative about Marty. I canceled the paper, and Ginger said, "Where the heck is the paper?" I said, "I canceled it." So, she reordered it. We went back and forth like that five times. She loves to do the crossword and I said, "I don't want the paper around." They wrote an article and cut down Marty unfairly. Then, they called my Mom the "Queen Bee," for some sarcastic reason. I said, "What does my mother have to do with the Hartford Whalers playing hockey?"

I went in one day and a guy from that paper tried to do an interview with me, trying to write something nice about me. I just blew up at him, screaming and hollering to stick his paper where the sun doesn't shine. Then we traveled somewhere the next day and I went up to the guy and apologized. I said, "I was very unprofessional. If you have any questions, just ask me, but don't ever try to be my friend."

I think a lot of people have misconceptions about Mom, but I don't know if there's any about my Dad. No, I think most people know my Dad from meeting him. He has a certain charisma and I've only met a couple people in my life who have that. I remember we'd be practicing, and there would be kids in wheelchairs sitting on the other side of the glass, in the rink. Dad would come by and take snow and even though the kids were paralyzed and couldn't move, he'd put the snow over the glass with his stick and dump it on their heads. They couldn't move and they're freezing, and now they've got ice melting all over them.

And they sit there smiling and laughing. If somebody else came along and did the same thing, they'd get a dirty look or tears. You tell me what's the difference? There's a natural charisma there.

And Dad's always giving his time. If he's doing a two hour autograph signing, and there's 400 people still there when it's time to go, he'll try to stay until they're done. That's the way he's always been. And I think when people meet him, they take to him just like that. That's something, in my opinion, that you can't teach. That's a God-given thing.

I think my Mom's received a lot of undeserved criticism from people around the NHL because of things that happened years ago. I heard a lot of things from Mom and Dad about situations they had to cope with, and it was unpopular to take on Gordie so they blamed her for a lot of things. When Dad wanted more money and Bruce Norris said, "Well, I hope that makes Colleen happy." Insults like that. In so far as being a negotiator, Dad's good nature told him to put his trust in people and he would merely say, "Just treat me fair, that's all I ask." I've done that in my life too. It's called mutual respect. But often people didn't keep their word, and that's where Mom came in. Some people get offended having to deal with her because they have trouble dealing with women.

I think when Dad found out later how badly he got cheated by certain people he trusted, it really hurt him. For me, to wear a Red Wing uniform is great. But, to play for the owner in Philly, Ed Snider, was really nice because I knew how much the guy really cared about everyone, and that meant a lot to me. I don't think Dad ever had that in his whole career and I don't think most players have ever had that experience. And it doesn't have to be just about money. I had always heard what good owners Mike and Marian Ilitch were before I came to Detroit. The guy comes and talks to you and asks about your kids. And it's a genuine thing. It's not a phony thing. So I've been fortunate.

My mom goes by the turtle philosophy—hard on the outside, soft on the inside and willing to stick out your neck to get ahead. A lot of this has been because she has been hurt, disappointed and burned so many times. So I don't blame her for being cautious and working wisely. I know why she does it. It's for the family, her business, her husband, and her self-respect. That's what she's done her whole life. There's no doubt in my mind.

I have an ongoing two year contract with the Red Wings, to work in some future capacity. I'm going to wait until this coming season to let them know if I'm playing anymore. A guy asked me in Vancouver the other day if I thought I could last as long as my father played. He had to be kidding.

I just turned 40, and I finished my 22nd year. Dad played til he was 52, and for 32 seasons with two years off in between. I asked the guy "Do you think I can play for another 12 years?" A lot of the things Dad accomplished no one will ever be able to do. I said that if my back was good, I think I could play another three or four years. But not with my back as it is now.

I remember my life's dream once was to play ten years in the NHL and make 20 grand a year. And then I figured I'd have the world right where I wanted it. Now I look back and I never dreamed I'd play 22 years. Never dreamed I'd make the All Star Teams. Never dreamed I'd win championships with my brother and my dad. When Marty and I were growing up, there were few, if any, American kids playing big league hockey. And we both made it in the pros. So it's been better than a dream.

GORDIE: There's a great picture we have that makes me feel good. It was taken after the game the second championship we won in the WHA, the Avco Cup. And it's a picture from behind of Mark resting his head on my shoulder. I remember we were both exhausted. It was in Quebec City, and it was our second championship, and Mark skated up to me at that point, put his arms around me, and said, "Nice career, Dad." I said, "Hey, you little bugger, I'm not through yet." It means a lot.

COLLEEN: Mark and Ginger are the ultimate planners and budgeters. Mark called me one night. He was so proud to tell me about the fact that when he's through with hockey, he probably won't ever have to work again, that all the children's education were all solid. They have done what they should, and prepared, and been prudent about their money and their family priorities. I think that's very admirable, but that's always how Mark has been, even as a child. He knew exactly what he was doing and where he was going. When he'd do his homework and when he'd play, he calculated everything.

That's wonderful, and I'm so happy that he wanted to call and tell me how proud he was of achieving his goals. His tone was, "Mom, I just wanted you to know." Because he knows how good it makes me feel for him and his family.

CHAPTER THIRTEEN

SETTING THE RECORD STRAIGHT

AS A CHILD, GORDIE WAS OFTEN HIT BY HIS FATHER.

COLLEEN: There was an unauthorized book out that claimed that Gordie's dad used to hit him in the head. That's absolutely false, and it made us both very angry.

GORDIE: My dad never touched me, other than the couple of times he kicked me in the butt. He'd threaten us, but he didn't hit us, much the same way I treat my own kids.

GORDIE ONLY DRINKS AN OCCASIONAL BEER, AND DOES NOT DRINK IN FRONT OF CHILDREN.

GORDIE: Yes, I'm a one or, at most, a two-beer man and I rarely drink any alcoholic beverages today.

I try never to have a beer in front of kids. It's my thinking that I don't want any kid ever taking a drink because they saw Gordie Howe doing it.

I've had times when I've been at signing shows and someone would offer me a beer. I'd tell them I didn't believe in drinking around youngsters. And they'd tell me they'd put it in a cup for me. And I would ask them, "Since when don't kids have a sense of smell?"

GORDIE HAD SUCH A RIVALRY WITH ROCKET RICHARD THAT HE ONCE ILLEGALLY JUMPED ON THE ICE TO STOP A RICHARD BREAKAWAY.

GORDIE: Yes, I did it. It was up in Montreal, he came out of their end on a breakaway, so I went out and stopped him. I got a two minute penalty, for too many men on he ice, but he didn't score. He didn't score on the power play either.

GORDIE LOST A GOAL POINT WHEN HE SHOT A PUCK THROUGH THE BACK OF THE NET DURING HIS PURSUIT OF RICHARD'S FAMOUS 1953, 50 GOAL SCORING SEASON RECORD. THAT LEFT GORDIE WITH ONLY 49 GOALS, ONE SHY OF 50.

GORDIE: That was a myth. I don't know where the tale got started. It was probably from some fan wishing I had gotten it. There *was* one goal that I didn't get that year, though, and that's been talked about. What happened was Red Kelly was going for a record, of twenty goals. We were playing in Boston. Red shot the puck and I deflected it. I remember very well, that after I touched it, it hit Hal Laycoe of the Bruins, and then went in the net.

I said I had gotten the goal, and Laycoe said, "He didn't score it, it went in off me." So, I figured then it would be a tainted goal if I argued for it, and I didn't want to take it away from Red that way, so I let it go as Red's goal. I knew I had touched it, because I remember getting the puck right away. I recall it would have been my 200th goal. So, I actually scored my 200th goal twice. And, yeah, the other one would have been my 50th.

Another myth is that we lost in the playoffs that year, '53, because I was so tired out from trying to get my 50th at the end of the season. That didn't bother me so much. It really didn't make that much of a difference to me. The pressure wasn't anything compared to going for 545, surpassing the Rocket's record in 1963. That was the toughest grind.

*BECAUSE OF THE EXERTION AND THE HIGH TOTAL
MINUTES HE USED TO PLAY IN EACH GAME, GORDIE
WOULD LOSE AT LEAST FIVE POUNDS.*

GORDIE: Yes, when I was younger, playing for the Red Wings, I used to average losing between five or six pounds a night. There were some really hot nights when I think I lost ten or eleven pounds in a game. But that's just fluid which you can replenish. I do know that, in the playoffs I would really get weak from all the fluid loss. If you look at some of those old pictures, you can see how thin I got.

*AS A BOY ON THE PRAIRIES OF SASKATCHEWAN, GORDIE
USED FROZEN ROAD APPLES FOR HOCKEY PUCKS.*

GORDIE: Another old myth, that was more of a joke. If we didn't have pucks, we used tennis balls. Shooting cow manure around could have its drawbacks. Can you imagine being the goaltender in the spring?

*BECAUSE OF PROBLEMS WITH READING AND SPELLING,
GORDIE FLUNKED THE THIRD GRADE TWICE.*

GORDIE: No, that's ridiculous. I don't know where this story got started. The truth is that I did fail a grade, once, and they sent me to summer school. I went, then returned to my scheduled grade.

*AS A HANDSOME YOUNG HOCKEY STAR, GORDIE
ATTRACTED THE NOTICE OF TEENAGE GIRLS, WHO
WAITED FOR HIM OUTSIDE DRESSING ROOM DOORS. HE
WAS SO SHY THAT, TO AVOID THEM, HE WOULD CRAWL
OUT REAR WINDOWS TO ESCAPE.*

GORDIE: Yeah, I did go out a window in Omaha when I

was seventeen. Because of this one young lady who was chasing me. I lived about six blocks from the arena, and I'd walk home from the games. This girl used to always approach me, but I was kind of shy. Then she finally confronted me and said "Don't you like girls?" And I said "yes." She said, "Well, don't you like me?" So I just said "Well, I like girls with gray hair." It was just a joke, of course. I just didn't have a lot of experience talking with girls, or being around them. I was trying to avoid her.

After the next game, I happened to look out the front door of the locker room when it swung open. She's standing there. And she has dyed her hair gray. It was then I said "I better get the hell out of here" and I went out the back window. I think I ran home, too. All the guys were laughing at me. Tommy Ivan, our coach, laughs about that yet.

PLAYING IN THE ERA WHEN THE SLAP SHOT WAS POPULARIZED BY BERNIE GEOFFRION, THEN EMPLOYED WITH GREAT SUCCESS BY BOBBY HULL, GORDIE NEVER TOOK MORE THAN A HALF-SLAPSHOT IN HIS ENTIRE CAREER.

GORDIE: It's true, I never took a conventional slap shot. I never took a real high back swing. I just went about half way. I used to use a semi-slapshot when playing the point on power plays. Using a shorter back swing, rather than raising the stick up to the moon, gave me a chance to allow a player I could pass to, to get into position. I always felt you're really committed when you went way up with a full backswing. With a half backswing, I had the opportunity to shoot, pull it back, pass it, do whatever I wanted to do. It gave me more control.

GORDIE, BECAUSE OF HIS SERIOUS INJURY IN THE 1950

*PLAYOFFS WHEN HE REQUIRED SKULL SURGERY, HAS A
METAL PLATE IN HIS HEAD.*

COLLEEN: This is untrue and I think that misinformation started after Gordie had to have a procedure called trephine performed after he suffered a serious head injury in 1950. Complications followed his initial accident and fluid began to form on the brain. The doctors needed to drill into his skull to relieve the pressure on the brain caused by the fluid. I think people thought a plate was put in his head due to this injury.

*ONE OF THE LONGEST-STANDING CONTROVERSIES IN
HOCKEY STILL INVOLVES GORDIE'S 1950 INJURY, WHICH
NEARLY COST HIM HIS LIFE. ALL SIDES CONCEDE THAT
GORDIE, AT HIGH SPEED IN A PLAYOFF GAME AGAINST
THE MAPLE LEAFS, WENT TO CHECK TEETER KENNEDY,
MISSED HIM, AND CRASHED HEAD-FIRST INTO THE
OLYMPIA SIDE BOARDS. THERE WERE VARYING REPORTS
CLAIMING THAT KENNEDY'S STICK DID, OR DID NOT,
STRIKE GORDIE IN THE EYE BEFORE HE TUMBLED INTO
THE BOARDS. RED WING FANS SWORE IT DID.*

GORDIE: Kennedy hit me all right. He was coming down the left side, which is my area because I'm the right-winger. I came down to back check, and was trying to anticipate where Kennedy was going to go if he passes the puck. When I got close to him, I took a look over and I saw Sid Smith of the Leafs going down the middle. Now when Kennedy made the pass, he came around with his stick, putting it up into the bumper position to help himself, extending it out to ward me off if I was going to hit him.

But meanwhile, I knew where Smitty was, and what I did was lean forward to put my stick in position to intercept the pass to him. So I left my face rather low to the ice, and when Kennedy came around with his stick, he spiked me with it. The only thing I recall was trying to close my eyes, but it didn't work. His stick hit me in the eye and nose, and I ended up going into the boards.

Some people said Teeder did it on purpose, but I don't think so. He was going to get hit, and I was the guy that was going to hit him. He was coming around with his stick for protection. Then he moved the pass on the back hand, and anytime you pass on the back hand, you follow head high with your stick. Things like that happen.

A LONG-STANDING DETROIT LEGEND SAYS THAT GORDIE ONCE PUT ON A TIGER UNIFORM AND, TAKING BATTING PRACTICE WITH THE TEAM, HIT BALLS INTO THE UPPER DECK OF TIGER—THEN BRIGGS—STADIUM.

GORDIE: Yeah, I hit a couple up into what they used to call Greenberg Gardens, the upper deck in left field. Don Lund was throwing batting practice, and he was just laying them up there, so I was fortunate to hit a few out there.

Actually, I'll never forget suiting up with the Tigers. I remember some of the players, like Harvey Kuenn. Some of the guys on their pitching staff said that day, "Hold on. Stop what you're doing, and watch this kid in right field. He's going to be the best thing you ever saw." And they were hitting fungoes out there, and this kid, this long, lean kid is running out there with the grace of an antelope. And the arm he had, this beautiful throwing motion, where he'd one-hop it perfectly to the catcher each time. He was beautiful to watch, and they said, "Remember this guy." I met him that day, and it was Al Kaline. It's funny, I remember I was nervous around him, because I was so impressed with his ability. He was younger than I was, but I felt funny. That's how good he was. And as I got to know him I knew he was a great person, too.

*IT HAS BEEN REPORTED THAT RED WING GENERAL
MANAGER JACK ADAMS USED TO PRESENT GORDIE WITH
A BLANK CONTRACT EACH YEAR, WHICH GORDIE WOULD
FILL IN BY WRITING A THOUSAND DOLLAR RAISE FOR
HIMSELF.*

GORDIE: I was the only one in the room with Mr. Adams, and the stories that he'd give me a blank contract each year and I'd write in a thousand dollar increase are not true. When I went up to his office, I'd just look at him and say, "If I'm supposed to be one of the best, pay me accordingly and I'll sign it tomorrow." The next day I went back and he said "We're giving you a thousand dollar raise," and I signed. In those days a thousand was like ten thousand or more. I was a big believer in bonus incentives. If I succeeded, the team succeeded. It also affected how the team ended up, how I did in scoring and our success in the playoffs. I remember one year I doubled all my earnings by winning the Most Valuable Player award, being named to the All-Star team, winning the scoring title and the Stanley Cup (1952). I made nearly an additional $9,000, which I believe was a little more than I got for the whole season's pay.

I talked to Jack the next year and I said, "Why don't you give me half of that in my contract as a raise, and forget the bonuses?" And he did, and that was a good raise. Another year, I went to see him and he threw a contract on the table, and said "Here you are young man, sign this." And I told him, that agreement was less than I made last year. He told me, "Naw, naw, naw." While I said, "Yes, yes, yes." It was about six or seven thousand less than the year before. He looked at it, and said, "Oh, wrong one." He threw it in a drawer and slapped another one on the table which was considerably more.

What Jack actually told me, was that I would be the best paid player on the Wings and __PROBABLY__ the best paid player in the whole league. Supposedly what other teams were paying their players was a secret. Contractually, we were legally bound not to talk about our salaries with other players, even our own teammates. And no one did back in those days.

AS THE STAR OF FOUR STANLEY CUP WINNING RED WING TEAMS, GORDIE IS THE PROUD OWNER OF FOUR WORLD CHAMPIONSHIP RINGS.

GORDIE: No, we never received rings. I think the best I ever got after winning the Cup was a silver tea service. There's not much you can do with that, unless you really like tea.

But a few years ago, a very nice thing happened to me. Tommy Ivan, my first coach, arranged to have a Stanley Cup ring with a diamond made for me. It's a handsome ring. I wear it every now and then, or take it out of the box just to admire it. When I saw that ring when he sent it to me, I said to Colleen "My God, look at this. Do you think I have a friend?" And she said "Tommy's not just your friend, he loves you." It really meant a lot to me, and it's one of the most thoughtful things anybody's ever done for me. Tommy's a guy whom I've always respected, and somebody I've regarded as a really good friend. He was the only NHL person who called us to wish us well when we were in Houston. That takes a big person.

IT IS SAID THAT GORDIE, EVEN AFTER HIS FINEST YEARS, WOULD BE WORRIED ABOUT MAKING THE RED WINGS THE NEXT SUMMER AT TRAINING CAMP.

GORDIE: It wasn't a matter of being worried or nervous.

What it was, though, was that I was unemployed. There were no long-term contracts in those days, you played one year at a time. You'd sign your contract after training camp. I was concerned that if I didn't perform good and play well in camp and the pre-season, or if I got hurt, it would cost me my entire income.

It was a damn healthy thing for me to be concerned. I never relaxed, at least not for several years. We had no assurances, no guarantees, nothing. If you made a mistake and called somebody a name, or angered your bosses somehow, you could be out of a job, out of the league. If you got hurt enough to be out of the lineup, or had some kind of career-ending injury, that was it. You were unemployed, period. It could all end in a split second. There was good reason to be as concerned and conscientious as possible.

WHEN WAYNE GRETZKY SCORED HIS CELEBRATED 802nd GOAL IN 1994, HE ECLIPSED GORDIE'S CAREER GOAL-SCORING RECORD.

GORDIE: It became a sort of pop-history fact that Wayne moved ahead of my career scoring total with that goal. The fact is, that it passed only my all-time NHL regular season record of 801. My career goal record is 975 in regular season play. Wayne, is approaching my mark of 975. He's a super player and has worked very hard to reach this plateau in scoring. No matter what era we play in, 975 is a lot of goals. My playoff and regular season total is 1071.

GORDIE BRIEFLY CONSIDERED MAKING AN NHL COMEBACK TO PLAY ALONGSIDE WAYNE GRETZKY...AT THE AGE OF SIXTY-ONE.

COLLEEN: Yes, we were out in L.A. in 1989, when we

were following Wayne's mission to break Gordie's NHL points record. I told Wayne to hurry up, because I had a commitment for Grandparent's Day and had to leave soon. Bruce McNall, Wayne's boss and the owner of the Kings, had flown us out to Palm Springs for the games and a golf outing. There was some joking going on, among all of us, about if Gordie was still in good enough shape to come back and play a game in 1990, and about putting him in the record books for his sixth decade of play.

It was one of those things that, the more people talked about it, the more it seemed possible. Bruce McNall was off the wall, running around saying to people, "Just think, we might get Gordie out here to play with Wayne." This got overheard, and the next day, I don't know how many media calls we had concerning this possibility. The Kings had to help us handle them.

Actually, I think the idea caught Gordie's fancy. We got the impression they were serious about it, but we were naive as to how sincere they really were. I know Wayne was excited, he kept saying "Gordie could play in his next decade." I remember John Candy, the actor, was there with us and he was excited about the idea too.

I really look at Gordie very realistically. He is almost superhuman. If HE had wanted to play an entire YEAR that year, I believe he could have done it. He has never embarrassed himself, and if he could have fun doing something, why shouldn't he do it, doesn't he deserve it? Gordie was under contract to the Hartford Whalers at the time, and they said basically, "Hey, if Gordie Howe is going to play for anybody, he'll play for us." So, things fell apart after that, and McNall backed off the idea and it never was seriously discussed again. But, yes, it was seriously discussed and considered for a while.

GORDIE: Did I think I could have held my own on the ice

at that time? No doubt. It wouldn't have been a problem.

GORDIE ONCE KNOCKED STAN MIKITA UNCONSCIOUS WHILE A GOAL WAS BEING SCORED AT THE OTHER END OF OLYMPIA STADIUM.

GORDIE: Stan was a great hockey player, but Ted Lindsay had him running around high sticking players when he was new to the league. He got me in the lip and the guys on his bench said, "You shouldn't have done that, Stan." And he said, "Aw, I'm not afraid of that old guy."

Anyway he watched me the rest of the game. He told me later, "I wasn't a dummy. I kept my eye out for you, and nothing happened." We played another game, nothing. Another game, nothing. One more game, no problem. Then Chicago came into Detroit for a game, and as Stan said, "All of a sudden I woke up on the bench."

What happened was this—I set up Alex Delvecchio going in on the Chicago net all alone. Stan and I were alone at the other end of the ice, so I pulled my hand out of my glove real fast and hit him right between the eyes. It knocked him right out. They picked him up and put him on the bench, and gave him smelling salts. He said the first thing that came in focus was a teammate, I think it was Dennis DeJordy, their backup goaltender. Stan said, "What happened?" And Dennis said, "Number Nine." Stan laughs about it now.

Not only didn't I get a penalty on that one, I got an assist too. All the eyes were on the breakaway at the other end. I always said I played hockey religiously. I believed it was better to give than to receive.

AS A KID, GORDIE PRACTICED HIS AUTOGRAPH AT HOME

BECAUSE HE DREAMED HE WOULD BE A FAMOUS
HOCKEY STAR SOME DAY.

GORDIE: I began practicing writing my name as a boy. One night I sat down in the kitchen and started working on my autograph. I was bugging my sister-in-law Amelia, Vern's wife, and my mother. I yanked at my mom's skirt, and she said, "What do you want?" I showed her the autographs I was working on, and I asked her which one she liked. And she picked the one that I use to this day.

COLLEEN HOWE WAS A PROFESSIONAL FIGURE SKATER.

COLLEEN: I think because so many players married figure skaters, such as Andrea Kelly, Joanne Hull, and Marlene Geoffrion for example, and because Barbara Ann Scott was mentioned to be linked to Gordie one time in a news article that this got confused with me. There was no validity to it, however, I do skate but never did professionally.

GORDIE AND TED LINDSAY ARE FRIENDS.

GORDIE: Ted and I, have over a time period, had some major differences which have definitely caused me to consider what used to be a friendship nothing more than the fact he is a guy I used to play on a line with, but nothing more.

COLLEEN HOWE RAN FOR UNITED STATES CONGRESS.

COLLEEN: I ran for congress in 1981 for the First District of Connecticut. I took my Democratic opponent to a primary where I was defeated. It was an exciting race and I felt I did accomplish going as far as I could go in light of the fact I was new to politics.

JACK ADAMS WAS HATED BY GORDIE

GORDIE: Sometimes I did not agree with and hated what Jack did in regards to controlling peoples lives, and his apparent lack of sensitivity when he was angry, but he did have another side to his nature, especially when he was away from the arena. He was like an overly strict parent to me and an unpredictable boss. He did instill some of the disciplines I have in my personality today. Many helped me immensely, especially establishing good work ethics. In a nutshell, I hated some of the things he did, but not him as a person.

COLLEEN AND GORDIE ARE OPPOSED TO UNAUTHORIZED BIOGRAPHIES

GORDIE: We were opposed to the recent unauthorized book because it had so much erroneous information in it and because it was developed knowing full well the Howes were underway with their own book. We rejected the writer because we felt he wasn't right for the book.

At a recent American Bookseller's Show the publisher was questioned by the Howe's attorney, Wayne Logan, regarding why they couldn't get the Howes to do a book with them. The publishers response was that the Howe's wanted to do a book with them but their "a__hole" lawyer wouldn't let them do it. He didn't know he was talking to the guy to whom he was referring. Wayne gently advised him by showing the fellow his name badge.

We are not opposed to unauthorized biographies. Stan Fischler has done one on me. No problem. But when a writer and a publisher know that you are about to do your own book and deliberately create a "spoiler", we're opposed.

JACK ADAMS TURNED GORDIE AGAINST OTHER PLAYERS

GORDIE: Jack only once talked to me about a player, Ted Lindsay. It was after Ted was trying to act as my agent while attempting to offer Jack a package deal for the two of us. Jack told me not to ever let Ted do that because it would always benefit him more than me. Jack told Ted to get lost when he suggested the idea.

THE 1993 65-CITY GOODWILL TOUR DID ONLY FAIR BECAUSE SO MANY NHL CLUBS PASSED ON PARTICIPATING.

COLLEEN: Our goodwill tour was never meant to be dependent on the NHL Clubs. They were approached first as a courtesy. It was a once in a lifetime event where Gordie, in commemoration of his 65th birthday, could personally thank the many fans in those cities for all their past support. It also helped each respective club by raising money in each city to benefit a worthwhile local charity. The cities that did participate were pleased and, collectively, were a part of raising nearly a million dollars. I was disappointed in some of the negative attitudes that our daughter, Cathy, ran into while she volunteered to help us launch, what turned out to be, the most unprecedented charity tour ever accomplished by a sports family. But I've learned that in doing something so monumental, there is always some adversity. It's part of life that teaches us many things.

THERE'S A FILM SCRIPT OUT THERE SUPPOSEDLY DEPICTING SOME HOCKEY WIVES, INCLUDING COLLEEN, WHO ARE SELLING ITEMS OUT OF THEIR CAR TRUNKS IN ORDER TO PAY FOR THEIR HUSBAND'S UNIFORMS AND SKATES.

COLLEEN: This is the most ridiculous fantasy I've ever read. It reminds me of the time I overheard two lady fans, who sat behind me at a game, talking about how they thought the team wives washed all of the fellows uniforms. There is no validity to this story.

GORDIE, RED KELLY AND OTHERS LISTENED TO JACK ADAMS AND NORRIS AND VOTED DOWN ESTABLISHING A PLAYERS UNION TO BE HEADED UP BY TED LINDSAY.

GORDIE: The vote was not whether the players wanted a union but, rather, it was to vote on whether or not to strike. The Red Wings voted not to strike.

THE ROCKET AND GORDIE HAVE NEVER BEEN FRIENDS SINCE GORDIE BROKE THE ROCKET'S GOAL RECORD OF 544.

GORDIE: Things have changed but, at the time, I hated the old (bleep). Of course, he hated me too. There were a few guys he hated worse than me, like Lindsay and Stan Mikita. But that was then. Now, Rocket and I are pretty good friends. We do a few things together, and he and his now deceased wife, Lucille, were our first choices to be included in a book Colleen produced a few years ago about former players and their families, entitled "After The Applause." So I think that shows our respect for him.

Rocket said in the paper once that "Gordie might have more goals, but my goals were more important." I told somebody "I don't want to fight with Rocket, but I'd like to say that his goals meant bugger-all to me." Essentially he's such a proud man. He was a goal scorer, I was a goal scorer. I had to take him out, he had to take me out. That was our job from the blue line in, Rocket was such a powerful man. He had one habit I perceived, however, he would come down and cut across the blue line because he liked to get to the center of the ice and shoot. Everything was quick wrist shots. So one time, as he came across the blue line, I really nailed him. We ended up in a fight.

There was a flurry of people around. Somebody pushed me from behind and I went down to one knee. And for some reason, Rocket was under my left knee. I waited, and when he looked up, I popped him. I whacked him a pretty good one. Then all hell broke loose, and when they got us apart we were yapping like jaybirds at one another. Then Sid Abel poked his nose in, and said to the Rocket, "Aw, you big frog, you finally got what you were asking for." And Rocket goes—BAM!—and breaks Sid's nose. Then I started to laugh, it looked so darn funny. Then Sid went in and did a job on the Rocket, again.

Rocket was talking about that episode a little while ago. He said "I took on your whole damn team, no wonder I lost." Even in a loss, he could be proud. The guy is unbelievable.

COLLEEN: Rocket is so interesting. In New York one year, they held a great induction ceremony for the Madison Square Garden Walk of Fame, which consists partially of viewing all these magnificent plaques that have been established throughout MSG in honor of these various athletes. As you walk along, and you see them at various levels, they appear to be made of bronze. Some are embedded into the floor and others are on the base of pillars.

We were at this ceremony with Rocket and other renowned athletes like Wilt Chamberlain, and Bob Cousy. Even Muhammad Ali was there who always calls me "The Boss," which now has become my business nickname. After a reception, they asked all the guys to go and stand at their plaques. Gordie and I stood by his plaque, which was on the base of this huge pillar. Most of the media people were around Ali. And as we chatted I looked over, and saw no one was standing with Rocket. I told Gordie I thought I'd go over to talk to him. As I approached him I looked at his plaque on the floor and said "Your plaque is so beautiful, you must really be happy and proud." And he said, "Same thing, always. My plaque is on the floor, and Gordie's is up on the wall." We laughed.

CHAPTER FOURTEEN

LOSE ONE DREAM, FIND ANOTHER

TOM: By the end of their fourth season in Houston, with a new owner on hand, relationships had waned between the Howes and the Aeros. Although the team had won its fourth straight division title—and led the entire World Hockey Association in points for the fourth straight season—in 1976-77, it was the Quebec Nordiques that took the Avco Cup. Between them, Gordie and Mark had missed 41 games due to injuries during that year, while Marty played every game. Gordie had appeared in only 62 games, and though he notched 68 points in them, it guaranteed his first non-100 point WHA season. Actually, it was his first NEAR 100 point campaign. He previously had registered 100, 99, and 102 point years. He took himself out of the final five games of the '74-75 season after registering what scorers told him was his 100th point with an assist on a goal by Mark. It was then that he revealed he had been playing with a broken foot in order to reach the 100 point plateau. After the season, it was said that a mistake in arithmetic had been made, and his total was only 99. (What a familiar number!)

Before the '76-77 season had begun, the WHA and the NHL had agreed to a 21-game inter-league exhibition series. The WHA surprised most hockey analysts by winning thirteen, losing six and tying two of the matchups.

What had been an ideal arrangement for the family in Houston began to unravel with the acquisition of the Aeros by a new owner best described as "difficult." George Bolin's personal manner and the financial difficulties that now plagued the team made it certain that Gordie, Colleen, Marty and Mark would be moving on at season's end.

In December of 1976, as the turmoil was festering, Gordie and Colleen received a letter from John Ziegler, attorney to Red Wing owner Bruce Norris, and later President of the NHL, that sent a jolt through the Howes and would ultimately ignite speculation throughout the hockey world that the Howe family might return to Detroit, the NHL, and the troubled Red Wing franchise. The team was in terrific trouble on and off the ice—a league-worst finish in '76-77 and many empty seats in the once perennially sold-out Olympia. The timing seemed ideal for the acquisition of the Howes, and the return of Number Nine as the once and future king. What resulted was a nightmarish series of flip-flops by the Detroit hockey club, and a public relations battle in which Colleen Howe was vilified in the Detroit media as having vetoed the dreams of local fans who yearned to see the Howes back in Red Wing red and white. The process involved bizarre actions by the Wings, and ultimately an expert media smear job done on the family by a new General Manager who obviously did NOT want the Howes anywhere within one hundred miles of Olympia Stadium—old friend Ted Lindsay.

The letter that began it all, and thrilled Colleen and Gordie when it was received at their Houston home:

December 8, 1976
Dear Gordie and Colleen:
  Since seeing you at Olympia, some thoughts have returned which I have played with from time to time. Perhaps they are best described as daydreaming; nevertheless, I felt that I should

communicate them to you. I guess as I was writing both of you to thank you for coming to Detroit (NOTE: for a charity appearance), I decided I might as well impart these thoughts to you. At worst, you could say—not interested.

I think I can say that since we have made the changes at the hockey club level, a new spirit and re-establishment of credibility has been obtained. I think all of us know and have learned from the many mistakes that were made during that unfortunate time. There is no question, however, that the hockey club is still suffering, to some extent, from some of those mistakes. Nevertheless, there is a job to do and those of us who think of hockey and Detroit as being almost synonymous must keep on working to try to restore or regenerate the kind of spirit in the community that makes the game and the business fun.

One of the best ways I can think of to achieve this is to reunite the Detroit Red Wings and the Howes. I know I don't have to belabor the point that the respect and adulation for the Howes among the fans in Detroit is unequaled in sports, and with good reason.

As you may have heard, either by rumor or in the newspapers, we are in very serious consideration of proposals for the building of a brand new arena. This will either be a downtown site or in the suburbs. The latter, confidentially, has a greater appeal to us providing we can obtain the necessary financing.

With the movement into a new arena, and the slow but steady improvement of the hockey club, I believe we are on the threshold of a new and exciting era for the Red Wings and the total operations that go on at Olympia. There will, of course, be much work to be done both internally and externally with the public, fans, media, etc. With a new building, we must also look towards new concepts, new ideas and blend them with our old policies.

One of the more pleasant and exciting daydreams pictures our Detroit operations entering into a contract with a Howe Corporation. The Howe Corporation, in return for financial and other considerations, agrees to supply various services that might range from management, public relations, customer relations, marketing and professional hockey playing.

If any of my daydreaming sparks an interest, there would be certain steps to be taken before any serious discussions took place. For example, I am enclosing a copy of the NHL By-Laws dealing with the rights as to defected players. If the Howes' present contracts expire prior to July 1, 1977, then probably any club in the NHL is free now to negotiate subject to its obligation to make equalization.

This letter is my own undertaking. However, I know from various personal conversations with Bruce that he would welcome "reconciliation," and I am certain that he would be very amenable to establishing a substantial relationship in the total operations in Detroit with the Howes.

I appreciate that the scars may still be deep, but I hope not too deep to mend. I just have to believe that the best combination in Detroit is Howe-Norris and that such a combination would be for the good of Detroit hockey, Detroit, the Howes, and the Norris family. If my daydreaming is totally out of line, please ignore it. I would understand and still wish you all the best in whatever route you chose. Kind regards.
Sincerely, (signed) John
John A. Ziegler, Jr.

COLLEEN: When we started our fourth year in Houston and the ownership changed, we had to deal with someone whose personality conflicted with ours in every way and it was then we

342

Dorothy Ringler and the Power Maker holding on to their secret about the WHA. Dorothy, you were the greatest in Detroit and Houston.

George Gellatly

The game that started it all...the March of Dimes charity game between Red Wings and Colleen's Olympia Agencies Junior Hockey Team, February 17, 1971 (her birthday).

The Howes in business huddle in Houston, Texas, 1975.

John Wood

Conferring with Tom Hazell of Sun Life Insurance and Gerry Patterson regarding the Aeros' contracts.

Our Grand Champion polled Hereford heifer at the Michigan State Fair.
Our cattle, not the Wings, were winners, 1972.

Aeros' trainer, Bobby Brown, the Greatest!

This was the perfect team on and off the ice with Bill Dineen, coach and general manager, Jim Smith, president, Irv Kaplan, owner, Bobby Kincaid, equipment manager and Bobby Brown as trainer.

Danny Connolly

The first and only, playing president of a hockey club, November, 1975.

*Mark's 200th point, March 27, 1975. Aeros clinch first place in league.
Grahame set WHA record for shutouts.*

Mark, Gordie and Marty, WHA All-Stars the first season.

The Howes and Bill Dineen at the WHA awards,
viewing the league's Gordie Howe MVP Award.

"Boy Dad, that was a long playoff!"—Mark Howe.

Javette

We often went dancing in Houston at the
Kaplan's ESP Night Club.

Howe sweet it is! Marty and Mark watch Cathy get a big hug
during center ice birthday celebration for Gordie, 1974.

*The Howes enjoy the humor of Dick Cavett at his show
taped in Hartford, Connecticut.*

*1988—The Howe Clan, with the first six grandchildren gather on the bow
of Mark and Ginger's yacht in New Jersey.*

Mark making moves at the early age of six.

Detroit Pee Wee All-Stars, including Bob Goodenow (now NHLPA president), front left, Jim Chapman, coach, far right, Mark Howe, second row center, and Don Fardig, assistant coach, far left.

"Will you lace my skates dad? I'm too tired." —Mark.

Mark as Junior Wing, 1972, age sixteen.

Mark in Sapporo Japan with Billy Harris at Olympics, age sixteen.
Olympic Silver Medal winners.

Starter featured three generations of Howes in jackets.

Mark at NHL All-Star game in St. Louis, February, 1986.

Philadelphia Flyers' Mark Howe wins the 1986-87 NHL Emery Edge Award for the best overall plus/minus stats with a plus 86.

Mark, as Red Wing in Detroit, where he began his hockey development.

The Mark Howe Family, Travis, Ginger, Azia, Nolan and Mark. The Detroit Red Wings and Stroh's sponsored the first of the 65-City Birthday Tour, 1993.

Our friends, Jim and Sharon Janz. We had to cancel speaking for them because Mark was seriously injured on the net.

Azia, age thirteen.

Nolan, age nine, visiting Honey and Pee Paw in Traverse City.

Travis, age sixteen.

Nolan, age eight.

A full house, what a team! Three number "9's" and two number "4's".
Hull, Beliveau, Orr, Howe, and Richard at a Montreal fund raiser.

Madison Square Garden Walk of Fame plaque for Gordie.

1978—Howard Baldwin honoring Colleen by inviting her to drop the puck at center ice for a Whalers vs. Aeros game.

Our home in Glastonbury, Connecticut.

realized that all we had worked for would no longer last. We sat down together to assess our options, desires and needs. We did so and, collectively, decided that I should seek a contract with another city and team. With the okay of Mark and Marty I had already started dialogue with Boston through Harry Sinden. It was about that time that we received the surprise letter from John Ziegler. He really wanted us back in Detroit. It was a very compelling letter. It pulled on our heart strings tremendously. After everything that had happened, and how we had been treated, to get word like that was not something to dismiss. Needless to say, we were very excited and could not resist contacting John. Gordie and I got very emotional after reading that letter and what it meant, that we could go back home and be welcomed back in Detroit. It also meant rejoining our friends there, and most of all that we could play a vital role to help the club recover.

We thought we'd all be able to put the past behind us. And this could work. Really work! Deep down, we waited a long time for this letter. However, it turned out to be my worst nightmare come true.

We figured we had done everything we could do for Houston and it's team. What had been such a great situation for so long was quickly going from bad to worse with the new ownership. It started with a meeting where this new owner told the players that the team was hurting a little bit for money, and they wanted everyone to defer their next paycheck. Gordie and the boys were there and they said no, for good reason. Our income already was deferred and had been throughout the four year term. The difference between our situation and the other players was that we were already on a deferred compensation arrangement. For those who don't understand what that means, it's that you work and perform a service for which you get paid later on. In addition, our compensation was paid out over twelve months, not within the length of the season, so we always were in arrears with receiving the dollars we had already earned. We didn't do this for tax reasons. Our reason for doing it, all along, was to help the club, in all four years. The deferment gave them a chance to spread out their payments to us until they developed more revenue through their season ticket holders and other revenue. This arrangement is especially helpful to the cash flow of a new club which, of course, Houston was when we signed with them. Any time a club can make this arrangement with a player, it's beneficial to the cash flow of the franchise. A lot of players won't do this, because they want or need the money in their hands so they can earn the interest on it, instead of the club having the use of it. So, as far as the Howes were concerned, the Aeros were already holding money that was due to us, and which we had already earned. We assumed all the other players were paid to date, but we weren't. Certainly we wanted to help the team, but not by letting them use more of our money. Besides, deferring anything with this club was risky, as everybody finally found out.

In the end, none of the players who deferred their salaries that day, to our knowledge, ever got paid. We did not trust this new owner, and he ended up reneging on the remainder of our deferred money, as well as our playoff money for that year. So much for sacrificing. We think the team got their playoff money from the league. It was their obligation, then, to disperse it among the players. That year, the Houston Aeros spent it, and never gave any to the players, to our knowledge.

The management in Houston leaked the story to the media that all the players were deferring their salaries for the good of the team, except the Howes. The papers printed this half truth story. Later we told our side, but the initial damage had been done. Our relationship with George Bolin, and the new management, was a disaster. He was trying to throw the blame in our direction, while in fact, he was watching the franchise go right down the tubes. And the pettiness that took place was revolting.

Gordie owned a Leroy Neiman painting, which was presented to him at a Summit Stadium center ice ceremony. He hung it in his office at the Aeros headquarters. Gordie, at that time, had been serving as president of the team. By the way, he was the only playing president in hockey history. Not long after when George Bolin became the new team president, he went in and took the painting. He said anything hanging in the team offices belonged to the club and that because Gordie was working for the club at the time the painting was presented to him it belonged to the club. How tacky can it get?

Years later, when we were in Houston, we ran into Bolin at the Houston Club, and he greeted us like long-lost pals. He confided to us that he treated us the way he did because he knew the club was going down the tubes and he figured that would motivate us to go to another club. Spare me!

Was this also the reason George sent Bill Dineen over to my travel office to tell us he had traded Marty, Mark and Gordie to some unknown team?

It was interesting for Bill to learn, which apparently everyone at the Aeros overlooked, that all three Howe contracts contained no trade clauses so trading of the Howes was not possible. The only thing that was accomplished by this was to destroy any good relationship we had left with the Aeros organization. I even sent a letter to the owners, inviting them to hear our side of what George and the papers were saying. But they didn't bother. That was it! It was all over!

At the time, after we received the letter from Ziegler, I

figured Bolin had done us the greatest favor in the world. We could now leave Houston with no regrets. Ziegler had pulled on our heart strings. Actually, both Gordie and I cried when we read that letter. I got so emotional because it was the first time they admitted that they had made a mistake by letting Gordie leave Detroit. And now they recognized that all of us could assist them in helping the Wings to recover.

It all seemed too good to be true. Not only were they interested in having the Howes back in Detroit, John's letter talked of an overall role for us as a family, working within the organization. He brought up the mention of a Howe Corporation, dealing with aspects of management, publicity, promotion, hockey playing and marketing. Even some involvement in the new arena. Wow! How did all this happen? Could these people have really changed?

LETTER, JANUARY 14, 1977, JOHN A ZIEGLER JR. TO COLLEEN:

Dear Colleen:

Thank you for your note of January 12. I have discussed the subject with Sam Pollock and he and I have agreed to chat some more. I have not raised the matter with Harry Sinden because I know he would be violently opposed....

It was good to see you again. Hopefully I will have some affirmative answers in the near future so we can discuss the total concept more specifically. Best regards to all.

Sincerely, John.

COLLEEN: So I set forth contacting the necessary people in order to make it possible that Marty, Mark and Gordie could continue to play together and we, as a family, would be in either

Boston or Detroit. One of the problems was that the boy's rights were held by two different NHL teams—Marty's by Montreal, and Mark's by the Boston Bruins.

The first thing I did was talk with Sammy Pollock on the phone, with Marty present. Then they talked. Sammy was wonderful on the phone. He said he believed that if the Howes wanted to go to Detroit or anywhere, he would do everything he could to make that possible. He wished Marty well and said he thought this was a good thing. What a class guy! He quietly did what he told us he'd do. He sold Marty's rights to Detroit. That was the first thing that happened. So, mission accomplished there.

HOUSTON POST, February 26, 1977: "Wings Get Rights to Marty; Eye Mark, Gordie. The Detroit Red Wings made a bid to revive their flagging fortunes Friday by acquiring the rights to Houston Aeros defenseman Marty Howe from the Montreal Canadiens in an apparent step to reunite the Howe family in the city where their father grew to a quarter century of greatness.

I am proceeding immediately to explore the return of the Howe family to Detroit and the Detroit organization, said Alex Delvecchio, general manager of the Wings who centered Gordie Howe through most of his twenty-five years as the mainstay of the franchise. We will also discuss the future employment with the Wings of Gordie, Colleen, and Marty, and I will endeavor to acquire the NHL rights to Mark from the Boston Bruins."

DETROIT NEWS: "Wings Take Step to Regain Howes. Delvecchio said, I've talked to Colleen and they sound very receptive to the idea of coming back home. I think Gordie found out a year after he left here that he would rather be here. Everything is in our favor.

Boston general manager, Harry Sinden, said yesterday that there was no chance he'd trade the rights to Mark. 'Would the Pope leave the Vatican?' Sinden said."

COLLEEN: The next move was to talk with Boston because they had Mark's rights, but Boston wanted Mark, as well as Marty and Gordie. I had been dealing with Harry Sinden all during this time, in a very honorable sense, while still giving us an option of Detroit or Boston. I knew Harry had dreamed of having Mark on his team. It was always his dream, and he was wonderful. He met and talked with me on numerous occasions away from Houston. We knew we were leaving Houston and most everyone knew we were leaving, but Marty, Mark and Gordie were still playing so it was awkward for them to be present. I explained to Harry essentially what was happening. I told him that since he had Mark, and if he wanted Marty, we could work out some reciprocal arrangement whereby he could talk to Marty if he would let Detroit talk to Mark. So, at that point Marty and Mark would be going together either to Boston or to Detroit. It was very simple.

As simple as it was, however, new players kept coming on the business side of things. Enter Ray Rozanski, a super business organizer, who was brought on board to work with me by the Boston owners, the Jacobs. Ray's job with us was to begin to handle the Howe deal outside of the club's hierarchy of Sinden and Paul Mooney, the Bruin's president. Mainly this happened because Ray was revamping many of the non-hockey business changes for the Jacobs brothers, including seeding Gordie with one of their companies, called Ramco Steel Co. This would be in lieu of Gordie playing for the Boston team. Interesting! Ray was my kind of guy and we hit it off right away. He was straight forward and knew his stuff, a real no-nonsense, cut through all the bull kind of guy. He worked with us to position all the pieces of what each of the Howe's, Marty, Mark and Gordie would specifically be doing, in hockey or in public relations, for his bosses. Ray was forthright, conceptually oriented and trustworthy. A breath of fresh air.

Oops! Here comes another party out of the blue. Howard Baldwin, a charming guy who was president, and one of the owners of the New England Whalers in the WHA. He called about having us consider going to Hartford. I was very open with Howard. I said, "Howard, to be really honest with you, we're probably going to Boston or we're going to Detroit, and I don't know how that's all going to turn out, but we're not in a bidding war." I was not even talking about dollars to anyone as yet. So, he said, "Well, I just wanted you to know that if anything changes we're here and we'll be there for you."

So, now we have three possibilities, two very active ones, with Hartford in the wings. Things were moving forward very nicely. We were so excited about the possibility of Detroit working out, that's where our hearts were, but Boston had put a very appealing offer before us....a five year contract guaranteed! The guarantee was the first thing I discussed with them; mainly to ensure the certainty of the dollars we would negotiate. Many things were starting to bubble by the middle of March.

When John Ziegler was talking to me, he said the organization wanted Gordie and me to put together a proposal for what Gordie, specifically, would be doing for the club. He was...what?...49 years old that March, and he wasn't sure if he should continue to play or for how long, if he did. Our major concern was establishing a long-term involvement with the Red Wings, and coming up with the right position and duties for

Gordie, to avoid what had happened in Detroit when he first retired in '71.

Then, the day that I was supposed to meet with John and Bruce Norris in Detroit to discuss any and all possibilities regarding our involvement with the Wings, the club held a sudden press conference and announced-surprise! Delvecchio is fired and Ted Lindsay has been named the new General Manager. I was shocked! What a turncoat way to deal with us and Alex! My feelings had nothing to do with whether or not Ted Lindsay should or should not be GM. What irritated me was that they hadn't even met with me to see the proposals Gordie had me put on paper for our meeting that very day. They didn't have any idea what I was going to propose to them. They had stressed that all avenues were wide open and possible. So, the questions are, if we were truly being considered as a major part of the Red Wings future and if we were to be involved in so many levels of the team's operations, wouldn't it seem proper for them to have notified us ahead of time that Ted was being appointed GM? It was also stated in their announcement that Ted was being given total control of the operation.

Throw into the mix that Ted had been publicly critical of the WHA and Gordie's comeback—something about it being a lousy league if a forty-six-year-old year old guy is their best player. And, that I knew Ted was uncomfortable with me representing the Howes. At the onset this did not seem like a promising situation.

I had always wondered when Ziegler and I talked why Alex Delvecchio wasn't there. I even mentioned it. We were working on agreements with our attorneys in downtown Detroit, and John said that Alex was busy. It was shortly thereafter that he got canned. All this was bringing back flashes of the past!

When I first found out about the Lindsay situation, I was in Toronto. Murray was playing junior hockey. He was there on the same team with Wayne Gretzky. I missed him and went there to see how he was doing before I went on to Detroit. I had dinner with Murray and the Badalis at their home where Murray lived at the time. After a delightful evening, they took me to my hotel near the airport. I got in the door just as a media guy, who had seen me at Murray's game and knew where I was staying, called and asked me, "Why are you going into Detroit tomorrow?" Because I wasn't sure why he was asking, I said, "Oh, just to check on the Howe Travel Agency!" Which was also true. He said, "I know why you're really going into Detroit. You're going in for the Red Wing press conference naming Lindsay as general manager." Oh. "Well, that's very interesting," I said, "they're starting to bring back the old stars to help rebuild the team." What was I going to say? What could I say? I really had no idea what was going on.

When I went into Detroit and my office the next day, I called Ziegler. I just said to him that there was really no reason for us to meet. Obviously they had withheld from me information on big changes within the organization that could easily affect our proposal. And, they hadn't even bothered to look at what it was that Gordie was proposing. Now, let me be clear about one thing—Gordie was not looking to be a General Manager. In fact, Alex had the job. People may think that's what Gordie wanted to do and he was ticked off because Teddy got the job. To clarify, that wasn't true at all. But somehow that's the word that went, or was spread, around by somebody. I think the team had already started a PR campaign to get themselves off the hook on this deal, and we didn't even know it yet. I suspect that Ted didn't want us there at all—he even had the nerve to say that Mark wasn't worth

351

trading a first-round draft pick to Boston. Gordie thought that was a joke! Any hockey person could back that up. Just check the history of Lindsay's first-round picks, and you'll see none of them had a career even one-fifth as good as Mark's.

What confused me, and still does, is why did Ziegler send the letter and talk to us all the way up to Lindsay hiring as though the Wings really wanted us back so badly? Then the team turns around and hires somebody they knew would not mix well with us? And keep it from us? Was it Norris? Did he change his mind at some point? Or, did he just throw the whole organization over to Ted one night? Maybe Ziegler got caught in the middle, I don't know. But things ended that very day, the day we were supposed to discuss our plans for the Howes' future with the Red Wings. At THEIR request. It was just unbelievable! If we had referred to history, however, we should have never believed that anything would change with that group. With all their promises, nothing had changed at all. It was disappointing, but a lesson learned. Now we knew we would never be back in Detroit again. For the first time since all of this began, I cried.

In reflecting back, I don't believe for one minute that Ted wanted the Howes in Detroit. All you have to do is look at his public statements from then on, his criticism of us in Houston, his refusal to fairly trade for Mark, his shots at me in the press for having the nerve to try to "run" my own family. This was a guy who wanted the Howes back in town? This was a guy who was going to negotiate with us? I don't think he ever wanted us involved in any way, but he had to play it that way with the press, and he needed a fall guy to blame it on when the Howes didn't return. Of course, that guy was me. Ted wouldn't even talk to me on the phone when he called person-to-person to talk to Gordie! The operator said it was long distance for Gordie from Mr. Ted

Lindsay. I said that Gordie wasn't home, but that I was Mrs. Howe and would speak to Mr. Lindsay. He would refuse the offer to the operator and hang up! How's that for being an open-minded negotiator? Yet, all this time, he was giving the impression in Detroit that he's doing his best to try to get the Howes back. I don't know, but it's possible that Ted did not want to become boss in Detroit and still have to be in Gordie's shadow. As big as the news story was that Lindsay was back as GM, it certainly would not have approached nearly the same excitement as if Gordie and the boys returned to the team. And if that's the case, that could well be why he wanted to queer the deal.

So back on March 17th, when I told Ziegler that it all looked useless, he put Bruce Norris on the phone. And Norris said, "Oh, come on now, Colleen. We can straighten all this out." I said, "No, Bruce, we can't straighten it out. Because virtually from the first letter that we received, I thought everything had changed there. Obviously it hasn't and I'm not here to play games. Mark and Marty want to find a place to play and we need to find a place to live and a future for Gordie and me."

From there on, Lindsay continued to refuse to deal with me, and he nailed us in the papers every chance he got. And, the participation of Ziegler and Norris ended. We never heard from them again so the whole thing had become one big nightmare and waste of time on the part of Sam Pollock, Harry Sinden, Alex Delvecchio, John Ziegler and us.

DETROIT NEWS AND DETROIT FREE PRESS. QUOTES FROM TED LINDSAY, MARCH AND APRIL 1977:

Asked about negotiating with Colleen—"I'd rather talk to Gordie about what his feelings are."

On bringing back the Howes—"I have no objections if we

can get a good deal, if they recognize what I want. One thing that does concern me, when they got that paycheck in Houston and they took the money and they didn't share it with their teammates, that bothers me quite a bit....this indicates, and this is another reason I want to talk to Gordie, that they were only interested in themselves and not in hockey."

"I believe Colleen is instrumental in all of this. I really do. Gordie has just gone along with it to keep family harmony....as I say, it shows you're only interested in that aspect of the check, not the game. I really believe that Colleen runs that family.

There's no room on this club for one strong man and one strong woman.

Colleen and I have always been good friends. If it came to that, and Colleen is their negotiator I could sit down with Colleen. No problem there at all. I might sound as though Colleen and I are enemies and don't get along, but that's not the case. We've never had a cross word in our association.

THE WINDSOR STAR:

"I hope soon to be able to sit down and talk with Gordie, he claimed. There was heavy emphasis on the GORDIE."

About the two boys, Mark and Marty—"I've been reading things that they don't want to play in Detroit because it's a bad town. I don't think it's a bad town and I don't like them saying that. Maybe they were misquoted, so we'll have to have a talk about it.

I'd be interested in a package as long as Colleen didn't try to run my hockey club. I'd want Gordie off the ice, though. I want people here to remember him as he was."

CHRONICLE NEWS SERVICES:

"Ted Lindsay, new general manager for the NHL Red Wings says the price for Mark Howe, 21, is too high. I'm not going to give up a first round draft choice because that's why our organization is in trouble. If Boston wants a first-round draft choice, then we're just going to go our separate ways.
(Boston's GM Sinden)....has been talking to Mark Howe and suddenly he's talking to a family. And you know, he's not interested in a family. Colleen is the one who's selling that, you see. She's the one that initiated that."

DETROIT NEWS:

"Sinden also reaffirmed his position on Mark saying, the Bruins would only trade him as a last resort. Sinden said, Mark could mean as much to the Boston franchise as Bobby Orr did. He has charisma and is a great player."

CYNDI MEAGHER, DETROIT NEWS:

"It is an interesting question why Norris suddenly decided to give Lindsay the full control he's demanded....it's anybody's guess, since neither Norris nor Ziegler showed up at the press conference. Mine is that this is another desperation move.

I would like to say Norris analyzed the situation carefully for weeks and concluded Lindsay was the man for the job. I do not believe that's what happened....things were done in such a slapdash—or maybe just an unfeeling—manner that Alex Delvecchio, after nearly 30 years with the club, had to be flown to New York Tuesday to be fired."

DETROIT FREE PRESS: "Howes Still Want Wings.
Colleen Howe said Thursday that despite receiving 'offers

that would knock your eyes out' from the Boston Bruins, just about the only thing that stands in the way of the Howes' return to the Detroit Red Wings is a phone call.

The Howes, she said, have agreed on the first draft of a contract with two other clubs but have been holding them off—with increasing difficulty—in hopes of signing with Detroit. But no one from the Red Wings made them an offer or talked with them about their return since Ted Lindsay took over as GM.

We're sitting around waiting for Detroit to make up its mind, she said while in town for business. Gordie says, Have you heard anything? And I say, No. We're not going to wait around until August, I can tell you that..."

DETROIT NEWS: "Nothing New On Howes.

...Lindsay said there aren't likely to be any new developments in the return of the Gordie Howe family to the Red Wings.

I don't see what's going to happen to change things, Lindsay said. Boston knows we're not going to give up the No. 1 draft choice for the rights to Mark Howe, and Boston won't settle for anything less.

I will call Gordie again, but it's not going to change anything. It'll just be to reaffirm my position. We go back a long way and I'll talk to him as a friend. I've already told him I'm not going to give up the No. 1 choice, and he's probably passed that on to Colleen.

I've made my position clear. Colleen made the statement that the Howes weren't coming here. Then she said she's waiting for a call from the Red Wings, indicating that we were holding things up. I don't know what she's trying to do. Well, I don't want to get involved in controversy with anyone and I'm not going to.

Lindsay made it abundantly clear he has more pressing problems at the moment."

COLLEEN: We finally resigned ourselves that we had to give up any idea of going back to Detroit. You could say that's part of decision-making, only it wasn't our decision and yet it was still happening to us. All those games they were playing. I was very honest and wasn't playing games. I gave a phone interview to a reporter after a couple of weeks had gone by and they still hadn't talked to us. I let Lindsay have it with both barrels. I'd had it. I mean, we'd been taking insult after insult in the media from Lindsay for two weeks, and had never said a thing. It was obvious now that he wasn't going to deal with us at all, and that was so incredible after what we'd been led to believe was going to happen. I was disappointed, and I finally said so. If Lindsay wouldn't talk to me on the phone, what were we going to do? Gordie didn't want to negotiate, he was still playing for Houston at the time and wanted me to handle it. He told Ted that, and Ted knew the situation. But he kept playing these games in the press. And we had had our hearts and souls in the hopes of returning to Detroit. The paper reported my conversation as a "long and rambling" one. The reporter, who didn't tell me he was illegally taping the call, sent the tape around and it was played on a morning radio show in Detroit. Now I'm angry about how the whole issue is being portrayed as a feud between Ted and me. It was insane and cruel and definitely did everything but help the situation.

So Ted got his team, and he got his way. I think he only lasted three years, and the Wings ended up in last place again during the two seasons before he left. And his Number One draft choices either played very little or were gone soon after he got fired. And I think he ended up having to sue Norris, for unpaid deferred money of all things.

Maybe it was a blessing in disguise that we didn't go back. The turmoil there just got worse and worse, the team kept having all kinds of trouble and the fans stayed angry. Sometimes I have to wonder how having the Howes there would have changed all this, on and off the ice. The Detroit fans got deprived of having Gordie in his final years, of having him retire in the city that he really grew up in, and having Marty and Mark in their prime. But it just wasn't to be, and it was totally out of our hands. It had seemed like our dream come true, but it turned out to be a lose-lose situation. Everybody lost with the way they handled things. It was just amazing how a great organization like the Red Wings could just go downhill like that. The only way it ever turned around was when Norris finally sold the franchise to Mike Ilitch.

LETTER, COLLEEN HOWE TO JOHN ZIEGLER, APRIL 12, 1977.

Dear John:

To clarify matters—following your letter of December 8th, 1976 and our subsequent telephone conversation, a personal meeting between us was arranged on January 3rd at your home. Based on a warm relationship and conversation we agreed to pursue an agreement between the Detroit Hockey Club and the Howe family.

After the acquisition of Marty's rights from Sam Pollock through both of our endeavors, a further meeting was arranged by me with our counsel present. At this meeting you and I agreed that I should prepare a presentation for you which would outline how Gordie, Colleen, Marty and Mark would best serve entering into an agreement with the Detroit Hockey Club. It was understood that all negotiations with the Detroit Hockey Club would be limited solely to you and, further, Bruce Norris.

Following that meeting and your verbal, mutual consent agreement regarding Marty and Mark's rights, I proceeded to ensure Boston's consent as well. After this was almost immediately accomplished, which took a special effort on my part, I took the independent step, not having heard further from you, to contact you to set up an appointment at your next available time, and during the conversation I clearly indicated Gordie and I had developed ideas to present to you. These concepts, John, took considerable time, effort and dollars to put together.

Then, twenty-four hours before our meeting scheduled for March 17th, the Detroit Hockey Club announced a five-year, all-control contract with the new General Manager. (Note: Ted Lindsay.) There was never so much as a courtesy of notification of this to Gordie or to me. In our previous discussions you had led me to believe that everyone in the organization was expendable, and there were no obligations with anyone which could not be taken care of. From this, it was my understanding that a carte blanche concept of ideas could be projected to you outlining how the Howes could assist the Detroit Hockey Club in improving its overall product image and marketing potential.

We even thought further towards the arena operating corporation situation in which you also expressed an interest in the Howes' considerations. I verbalized this to you and we met briefly on March 18th when it was agreed that Gordie and I would discuss things further with Bruce. Since Bruce found it necessary to immediately realign his organization through Ted Lindsay's leadership and ideas, Gordie and I did meet with Bruce on March 23rd to advise him that we would now await a proposal to us. Since that time we have heard nothing from either you or him and assume from this that there is no longer any interest in consummating any arrangements with the Howes. This is regretful and certainly disappointing to us, however we cannot continue to hold in abeyance the other organizations who, in good faith, have continued to hold open their offers while I attempted to personally see what Detroit had in mind. They, as well as you and the Howes, have many obligations and arrangements to be met concurrent with decision-making.

This being the case, would you be so kind to advise Boston as to what arrangements can be made for Marty's rights which you acquired from Montreal, and subsequently sublet to Boston through the mutual consent arrangement. It would be equally appreciated that you advise Ted Lindsay that our agreement of contract communications take place solely between you and/or Bruce Norris with Gordie and me. We have never been advised to the contrary, therefore until such time as you advise, we will continue to keep our negotiations at the presidential and legal level of the club.

John, I thought we had a positive thing going which I believed both parties wanted to have happen, and Gordie and I are truly disappointed. We have acted in good faith and sincerity and wish you and the Club all the best....since Ted does not regard Mark as having the value of a first-round draft choice, I hope he gets a good one.

We also regret after our sincere conversations and your heartfelt letter expressing that bygones be bygones and a positive approach to having the Howes consider and work out an arrangement with the Club, that a new General Manager would be hired who would refuse to discuss contract with me, and in addition take public pot shots at all of the Howes. This was hardly a way to expect us to continue our otherwise constructive talks.

As I expressed from the beginning, Gordie and I plan to be living in Detroit in the future and we'll look forward to seeing you at the Red Wing games regardless of the outcome of any contractual endeavors. Certainly at any time you wish to call upon us, Gordie and I are willing to listen and assist you.
Sincerely, Colleen Howe.

Once we had given up on ever hearing anything from the Red Wings, we were free to deal with Boston solely. We had a very lucrative deal with the Bruins, involving both Marty and Mark and a deal for Gordie that he would work as an executive for a company owned by the Bruins' parent company. He was to be vice-president of sales. For some reason, Boston wasn't interested in having Gordie play for them, even though he was playing terrifically. He was playing full-time, and had been a top ten scorer each season. I'm sure some of that was the whole stigma about the WHA being inferior. Heck, we saw some of the best hockey we ever saw in the WHA. But this was a premier opportunity for Gordie from a business perspective and a great deal for the boys, and we intended to go ahead with it. It was a five-year agreement for everybody, worth almost $2.5 million GUARANTEED! The contracts were all drawn up, and they were to be signed in Detroit, of all places, in late April, I believe.

It was ironic that the guy who helped negotiate the contracts, Ray Rozanski, with whom we had become friends, had warned me that if the Bruins' general manager, Paul Mooney, ever got into the talks, he'd screw it up. My thinking at the time was, no way! But I still remember the concern with which Ray said it.

Now, Gordie and I are at the Pontchartrain Hotel in Detroit in order to sign the Boston contracts with Marty and Mark the next day, when I get a late night call. And it's Paul Mooney. And he said, "I know you're going to sign those agreements tomorrow morning, but we just have one little problem." I said, "like what?" A middle of the night problem? So he said, "We just can't do the guarantees on the contracts. The Bruins Board of Governors just won't do it." I said, "What??? Paul, that was discussed and decided and agreed upon before we ever talked money or developed contracts. That made the difference in the entire agreements we have developed. That made the difference in the number of years to which the players were committing. Now you say you can't guarantee?" He said, "Well, yeah, but you know, you don't have to worry about it. We'll cover it." I said, "No, just a minute, it does make a difference." I said, "I really have a very difficult decision to make right now. Unless I'm given further notice by Mark, Marty or Gordie, we don't have a deal now, and we won't be at the signing tomorrow." I really felt like they were playing hard ball in thinking that they had us in such a position where *we* had to sign. The contracts were drawn, Detroit was no longer an issue and they believed they had us over a barrel.

I called Ray Rozanski and I told him what had happened. And he said, "I told you, Colleen. I told you that guy would mess this up. Please, don't do anything right now. Just sit there, give me a few minutes and I will call and find out if it can be resolved. Maybe I can salvage this."

As I waited for his call I thought to myself, here we had been talking with them for all of six months, and this comes flying in at us, literally at the last minute. A lot of effort and dedication had gone into these agreements. Gordie was ticked off. He said, "Screw 'em," when Ray called back (quote-unquote). And Ray said, "I'll tell you what, Colleen, as far as I'm concerned, no matter what you decide to do I still want to talk to you about Gordie working with Ramco Steel." Just call me back when you decide." I called Marty and Mark immediately and said the Bruins are pulling a power play and we have decisions to make. They also had to decide to go ahead with this or not. I never made those kind of decisions for them. And they both said, "No way." The feeling was, if that's what Boston's doing now, what will it be like for five years. So, I called Mooney back and I said, "We don't have a deal. We won't be there." That was the end of it....in a half hour's time.

I sat on the edge of the bed, trying to understand all this. I mean, what a bizarre six months this had been and now we're thinking of options. I suddenly remembered my promise to call Howard Baldwin if we needed him. I thought "Could he have known this was going to happen?" Howard had been waiting in the background so patiently through all this rigmarole with Detroit, and now Boston. Anyway, I picked up the phone right then in the middle of the night and did what Howard said. "Well, Howard, Detroit is out of the picture and Boston just reneged on our agreement. We're ready to talk to you. Howard didn't hesitate a second. He said "What time is it there now? And how early can you get up tomorrow and talk to us? I will be on a plane and be there the first thing in the morning and we're gonna lay a ten-year solid contract on the table."

And the next morning, sure as heck, Howard and his comptroller, Dave Andrews, were there with a ten-year agreement, guaranteed. Howard said, "I'm glad they screwed up, Colleen. This is a great opportunity for the Whalers." And this was a more stable arrangement for us, because we'd remain in the WHA and there were substantial owners in Hartford. They were the guarantors of our contracts to full term. That's like standing up and making things right. Plus, the Whalers even absorbed paying the deferred money and the playoff money the Aeros reneged on.

They even encouraged me, and provided office space for Howe Enterprises, to be in their office complex. We were very excited about the Hartford deal. Howard was ecstatic in that Gordie would still play for as long as he desired, and the boys were still together. The deal helped secure Hartford's franchise future. If ever there were a WHA-NHL merger, it could secure them a spot in the NHL.

We had some great years in Hartford, off and on the ice. Gordie's deal was that he could play to whatever point he wanted to, and then work in the front office. It turned out that we stayed there for 15 years. It's a great city, with some really wonderful people, although hockey is a harder sell there being in between New York and Boston.

So, we were off to Hartford. Good-bye Houston, good-bye Detroit, hello Hartford. The good Lord always looked after us! Lose one dream, find another!

"When I was nine years old, I attended The Gordie Howe Hockey School in my home town--I was in awe then. At 36, I've become good friends with Gordie and his wonderful wife, Colleen--and I'm still in awe."
—Dave Coulier, Flying Saucer, Inc.

CHAPTER FIFTEEN

THE PRICE WE PAY TO PLAY

GORDIE: I still get on the ice occasionally for charity events with the Celebrity All Stars and for other special fund raising events. Sometimes I even fill in a game with some of the senior players in Traverse City. I don't miss the grind of the pros anymore. I ache too much afterward. When I was asked how many times I got hurt in playing hockey I said, "I was hurt in every game I played and so are most players. It's either major or minor but it happens. That's the nature of the game."

I loved practice when I was young. I could skate all day. I dreaded practice when I was going through my final years, when I developed so much arthritic pain. Players practice more than they play, naturally, so when they start to dislike practice, they realize they've lost some of their enjoyment of the game. That's why before I retired in 1980 I told Jack Kelley, the G.M. in Hartford, I was ready to play another season and also serve as an assistant coach with the team. I would assist in practices and get behind the bench if I was sitting out any games. And out of the blue, he said, "No thanks, we're going to youth." It really dumbfounded me. I thought if I acted as an assistant coach, it would be a perk to the Whalers. I would have filled two roles, one as a coach and two as a player. And it would have been an introduction into the coaching field for me. I think they had my retirement all planned before I went to meet Jack. I got so ticked off that I said, on the spot, "Well, then you can shove it, I quit" and I walked out. When

I got home and told Colleen she was upset with me, and rightfully so because I faithfully promised her she would be the first person to know if I ever wanted to retire for the last time. She said "I wish you had told me before you made a decision. We should have talked it over." The situation robbed me of retiring the way I wanted to go out, and it was my becoming upset that helped them to retire me. Colleen felt that I, not anyone else, should announce my last and final moment. Instead, the Whalers did it for me. They immediately set up a press conference for the next day. That was why when I spoke at that event the next day, I said "I can damn well still play the game." The public didn't understand and the press didn't know what had happened, but I was upset, and had screwed up royally. It was a bummer.

COLLEEN: I was infuriated at Gordie and the whole situation. Gordie and I had a pact made long ago, one that allowed him to think through any final decision to retire from hockey, when that time came. It was that he would tell me before anybody else. I told him, "I think I deserve that, as your partner in life. I shouldn't hear it from someone else or after the fact." He readily agreed at the time. But because he got upset and reacted too quickly, he really fell into a trap of no return. By the time he got home and told me the Whaler's had already called a news conference, Gordie felt there was no way to rescind what he had said. So he robbed himself of controlling one of the most monumental moments of his life, that of truly assessing his decisions on his own terms. It also robbed him of the opportunity to play one more year if he wished to do so. He had played 32 years, longer than anybody, and had done all the things he had done for the game. Why shouldn't he be the person who decides when, and how he's going to retire? It shouldn't have been induced by someone else. And even if it was, it should have been dealt with in other ways. I always felt personally robbed of feeling good about the last time Gordie would put on a pair of skates. The fans were robbed too, of knowing when he would play his last game. I didn't want to make Gordie's decision. I wanted Gordie to make it, but only after some discussions with regard to his future. I wanted to add support to enable him to do what he wanted to do, and in the way he wanted to do it. He'll always regret what happened, because he did not want to quit that year. I guess I just can't let him out of the house!

GORDIE: I played in all eighty games the previous year, in fact 84, counting the playoffs. Starting the season, I think I had eight goals in the first fifteen games or so. (NHL RECORDS INDICATE GORDIE AT THE AGE OF FIFTY-ONE HAD ELEVEN GOALS BY THE FIRST WEEK OF DECEMBER, 1979. HE LED THE WHALERS IN SCORING IN '77-78 WITH 96 POINTS, AND HAD 43 POINTS IN '78-79 WHILE MISSING TWENTY-TWO GAMES DUE TO INJURY.) I was joking with some of my teammates, "I'd better slow down, or they'll want more goals for next year." But then Don Blackburn took Mark off my line, and started me playing with a mish mash of other lines, I think you'd call that the mud system. Throw it against the wall and see if it sticks. One of the guys, Nicky Fotiu, would run into you if you were on a two-man breakaway. He was dangerous. Then Blackburn started cutting back on my playing time, and I just accepted that I'd live with it. I was seeing less and less ice time. When I was playing my last game at Olympia against Detroit, he said "Do you want a rest?" I said "Rest? I thought you had retired me at the halfway mark." The only good thing about sitting on the bench is that you can't get hurt . Oops, I take that back. I did get hurt on the bench once. I leaned over to see what was going on, and Brad Selwood's shot hit me right in

367

the eye. It didn't cut me, because it hit me flat and pushed my eye inward. I knew I'd get a swollen eye from it, and Brad was very concerned. He came over, and said "God, I'm sorry Gordie." I said "Don't be sorry. Just be thankful you shot it. If somebody else shot it, I would have been hurt."

Retiring from something you've lived with your entire life is a real emotional thing. The Whalers had merged with the NHL that last season and I played, and I was glad to have the opportunity to say I played in that league with Mark and Marty. It was a better league all around and I could still hold my own. It was a better league than the WHA because of three essential differences—overall the players were faster, stronger, and smarter. I knew that. I'd been there. I remember when Ted Lindsay made his comeback in 1964, he'd been out for four years and he called me and said "Do you think that am I doing the right thing?" I said "Sure, Ted, you could help the Wings tremendously." I gave him all the reasons why I felt that way, and suggested that he not set his performance target too high. To shoot for 15 goals or so, he'd be a plus-hockey player, provide leadership, and help out the team in various ways. He did just that. I wish he had been as nice to me when I made my comeback with Houston. He said it was stupid. I sat down and talked to Guy Lafleur about his comeback after he had retired in the '80s. I told him the one thing he had to think of was: "Don't die with the music in you. Period!" If you know you're through, fine! If you're not sure you'll find out! You'll know! It will only take a month. I would have known if I felt I was through playing in Hartford but there was no doubt in my mind I could still play. I really wasn't through yet! You know when you are!

Regretably, and unfortunately, I never knew that when I played my last game in my last season, it was REALLY my last pro game. It was in the playoffs against Montreal. Blackburn didn't play me for, geez, nearly all of the last couple of periods. I had scored a goal in the game before, which turned out to be my last ever, on an assist from Mark. Then Blackie sat me out in the next game. It hurts because, now I know, it was my last game!

COLLEEN: I had never heard Gordie say during his last season that he didn't want to play, or felt like he couldn't. He wasn't feeling bad, he felt the same as he did the year before. Since I did all those contracts I would have suggested to him that he ask that they trade him if he seriously wanted to play. That last year should have been an option to Gordie that no one should have denied him. I don't see why someone else should have been leaving Gordie with no option to play. Gordie had just gone down to the office to pick up some mail. He dropped into Jack's office to discuss this idea he had while he was there. Then suddenly his career is over! It wasn't Jack's fault. He said what he believed! He wanted Gordie to retire. We often wondered if the team doctor had anything to do with Jacks's decision.

GORDIE: The Whaler's had asked me, prior to the previous season, "You'll turn fifty-two this season, how much do you want to play?" I said "I want to play so much I don't want to miss a shift," which was how I felt. And Jack Kelley said "Well, I was talking to the doctor and he thinks you shouldn't play." And I asked "why?" because I felt great. Basically, the reason the team doctor didn't want me to play, was because if I was hurt he didn't want to be responsible for my care. He wanted me to sign a waiver saying I couldn't sue him if I had a medical problem from playing. He had run tests on me and he said he thought I should call it quits. I asked him "Why, is there something wrong with me?" He said that my tests were great, but he thought I should hang them up just in case. I asked "In case of what?" And he told me, in case I die, that I could get hurt or die at my age. I guess he was afraid of me dying of a heart attack in a game. I thought that would be my concern and responsibility, not theirs. And I wasn't concerned. I never heard of a team physician, without valid reason, telling a player he shouldn't play.

COLLEEN: When we converted our WHA agreements over to the NHL format our attorney, Peter Kelly, got a letter from that same physician, stating that he wanted something signed for him that would state that all three of the Howe players would never sue him for any care that he gave to the Howe's in the past, present, or future. When we had this doctor ask for a release like that, we really wondered what he was afraid of. When Peter called me to get my response I told him it would be exactly what he was thinking. So he told the doctor to "stick it" gracefully. The doctor never pursued it further, but it indicated to us he should not have been selected as a team physician if he wasn't prepared to accept all the players, unconditionally, under his care.

MARK: My impalement on the net began with an innocent kind of play. It was in the 1980-81 season. It happened when I was skating fast towards our net. It was a three on two play and I was back on defense. I got back rapidly and turned to take away the passing lane on the far side of the net. John Tonelli (Tonto) was coming up the middle and hit me from behind, sending me flying into the net on my back. I put my feet up and bent my knees so I could absorb the shock of going into the net. Just as I did that, the net lifted up slightly and the sharp metal center flange on the ice, in the back of the net, also lifted up and stabbed right into me through my pants and underwear. The net never came off the posts. I remember lying on the ice and my thoughts were...I was dying.

GORDIE: The old nets, from post to post, used to be like a figure three at the base, where the frame sets on the ice. That center piece, the middle of that three, came to an extremely sharp point. And it was ground down, so that any puck that came in there and hit it, around that point, would fly up into the mesh of the net rather than shoot back out.

In Hartford something they did with the nets added to making the point even more dangerous. When the nets were brought onto the ice from where they were stored, there was about a six-inch drop down to the ice level. So when maintenance were pulling the nets onto the ice and dropping them down, they were bending the narrowest part of the center piece causing it to bend an inch or two upward. It did not lay flat on the ice. I guess nobody really ever noticed it or paid any attention.

In hockey language, Mark was backing up on the play, and as a defenseman you have to check to see that the right winger is covering the left winger of the opposition. That allows you to slide over to pick up the other two on a three man rush. You can go nose to nose with the other two. Well, Mark slid over and looked, and his right winger had stopped and let his guy, his check, go. Now, what Mark had to do was to go like crazy towards the right post to head off the play.

As he did that, he took a check across the back from John Tonelli, and with Mark's speed and that extra shove from behind, he was going head first into the net really fast. So he spun around just in time as he hit the net to lift up his feet into the meshing to cushion the blow. But he was going so fast, his knees collapsed, the net raised from the impact, and that five inches of metal in the center piece stuck right into his buttocks area, penetrating almost all the way to his hip. Fortunately it missed his sphincter muscle, and just missed his spinal cord by a tiny fraction.

I was up in the press box, watching the game, and I started on down right away. You could see a little blood on the ice at first, and I said "Oh, God." When I saw him wiggling I said "Well thank God he's moving, he's not paralyzed." Then I saw more blood, and when it's your son lying there, your heart is in your throat. It's a horrible experience. And I knew he was hurting badly, when I saw him bite his hand. That really petrified me. I had no idea at first, how gravely injured he was.

I don't want to add negative aspects to a story that's already bad enough, but as I'm hurrying to get downstairs, a guy, who obviously wasn't watching the game, stops me for an autograph. It was so stupid. A fan next to the guy yanked him back into his seat, and said "That's his son down there, you idiot."

I get down to the locker room, and the doctor said to me "Here, have a look." I don't want to be gruesome, but I could have stuck my hand in the laceration. It was that big. I almost got sick, and it scared the heck out of Mark when he saw my face. He had a certain numb sensation in the wound by this time, and he was frightened. Thank God I was at the game to stay with him. I almost didn't go to the game that night because Colleen and I were speaking at a huge event in Vancouver the next day for our friends in Amway, Jim and Sharon Janz. Colleen said she could do the laundry and packing and in general get us ready to go so I should go to the game. I'm happy for her now that she didn't see what I experienced, but she always has regretted she wasn't there for Mark at that moment. They have always had their special something together that has bonded them and she's great in a crisis. She makes things happen. The thing that got me upset the most was that there was a phone call made from the Whalers doctor to his associate, Dr. DeMaio, to go and meet Mark at the hospital, but he wasn't told it was an emergency! We found out later that he was just told, that Mark Howe got a laceration on his behind so when he got a chance, to drop by the hospital to stitch him up. So Dr. DeMaio completed what he was doing, and came over to the hospital about an hour later, after he felt Mark was registered in emergency. Actually, Mark and I had been waiting there for him for quite awhile, and we were awfully upset. When Dr. DeMaio did get there and saw how serious it really was, he was furious. He apologized to us, said it was inexcusable. He told Mark he was very sorry, but he was going to have to take him up to the operating room immediately to clean out and make certain of what's inside the wound." They had to put Mark's legs in these stirrups to probe that huge laceration and to determine just how much damage may have been done inside.

COLLEEN: I was at home finishing what I needed to do to get us on a plane the next day. When suddenly the phone rang and it was Mary, Marty's wife. She said "Have you been listening to the radio?" I said, "No," and she said "Well, Mark is hurt and we think quite badly." I said "Oh, my God, what happened?" And Mary replied "We're not getting any information, so we don't know for sure." I'm wondering what to do? Do I jump in the car, drive to the arena, wait for a phone call, or what? I knew Gordie was at the game, but he hadn't called. A million fears and thoughts raced through my head all at once. I think it's a natural reaction to fear the worst when you can't get any information and you're not there. I kept trying to stay in control and to think to myself...maybe it's not too bad.

I thought about the first time I ever saw Mark hurt. He was just a little guy, about six-years-old. His team was playing in Ontario, and he got cut on his upper lip. It was a small rink so it didn't take me long to run down to the first aid room under the stands. I opened the door and I saw him lying there on the table.

373

He said to me "I've got a bad cut, Mom." So I'm talking to him trying to calm his fears. Then the doctor came in with something to numb Mark's lip. Then he starts stitching up the wound, pulling slightly on it to tighten the stitches, I guess I must have gotten pale because Mark looked at me and said "Mom, I think you better leave the room, cause I think this is hurting you more than it's hurting me." He was right.

I was also wondering if what happened back then was the prelude for what we'd be in for later on when it came to hockey injuries. Well, I found out in Hartford, unfortunately. It's so strange. Mark, as easily as not, could have died or been paralyzed, from the injury he had that night in Hartford. I hated hockey that night, I hated everything about it. At that moment I wish we had never gotten involved in it. It was the only moment I ever regretted taking my sons to a rink.

Then Gordie finally did call, after he had talked to the team doctor who was making light of it as just a bad cut, but nothing serious. That's the doctor who told Dr. DeMaio not to hurry, it wasn't an emergency situation. Just a laceration of the buttocks. Actually the flange on that net had penetrated him almost to the hip, right along the spine, but we didn't know that yet. The doctor even asked to speak to Colleen and told her it wasn't something to be concerned about. Sure! Then Gordie got back on the phone and said an ambulance was going to take Mark to the hospital to stitch him up. I said to call me when he got there. I waited, and waited, and no call. I was really getting frantic then. I suspected it was worse than they had told me.

MARK: I thought I had punctured my intestines. I was lying there on the ice, and I kicked myself off the metal point with my legs. The trainer came rushing out and he's yelling "Are you all right?" I'm yelling back "Just cut off my pants!" "Cut my pants off!" I remember looking up at some of the other players, and their eyes were huge. I was bleeding a lot, I lost three and a half pints of blood that night. When they carried me into the dressing room, I remember I kept asking "Am I going to be all right, am I going to be all right?" I was screaming, and they were stuffing towels into the wound to stop the bleeding, and they were playing with my toes to see if I was paralyzed.

Dad came in, and he grabbed hold of my hand. And he said "I want to see what's happened to him," and the doctor said, "No." Dad said "He's my kid, and I want to see it." Then when he looked at it he just about broke my hand. I thought, oh shit, this is really bad! Everyone kept saying "You're going to be all right, you'll be fine." And they finally took me to the hospital with Dad following. Dad and I sat there for probably an hour or so, waiting for some kind of care. By that time, I was more relaxed, I believe I was going into a state of shock, because I couldn't feel any pain. I was numb.

Then Dr. DeMaio shows up, and he takes the towels away, and says "Oh my God." That really scared me! He said he had gotten a call at home that somebody needed a few stitches and to come down to the hospital. He said "I don't mean to scare you, but we have to get you into surgery right away. This is pretty serious."

GORDIE: After Dr. DeMaio did the exploratory surgery, he told Mark he was a very lucky man and that the good news was that the Good Lord used a surgeon's knife to put that big spear into him that cleanly while managing to barely miss so many vital parts. He thought it was a miracle there wasn't any permanent damage.

Well, I was very grateful to Dr. DeMaio. They packed the wound. Later, it abscessed on Mark and they had to make another hole in him to take care of the infection.

MARK: I was out for a day. I'd finally wakened, and the nurses said it was important to get me out of bed. I was so weak, that Dad picked me up and I couldn't stand or anything. I kept saying "I'm going to get sick." Dad said "Well, go ahead," and he just stood there and held me and I got sick all over him. They had to put me back in bed. A lot of it is hazy to me, but I remember my one hip was so swollen it was about twice the size of the other one.

By the second or third day, I was out of the severe pain. I was in. The doctor came in and told me he was in Vietnam, and had seen so many things but I was one of the luckiest people he'd ever known. I kept asking if I could play hockey again, and he said, "Yeah, but it's going to take a while."

But then the wound got infected. They had stitched up about two-thirds of the cut from the outside, and they left the rest open so hopefully it would heal from the inside out. Naturally, it didn't, it healed from the outside in and this little pocket in there abscessed. I was running fevers of 102 and 103 every day. He finally took a knife and stuck it in me, and opened me up from the other direction to get to the abscess. He cut all the way through to it, and I could feel all this warm stuff running out of me. As awful as it sounds, that's what worked. It felt like that was what really helped me. This was about three weeks after the accident, and when I left the hospital after that procedure, I was finally hungry for the first time in all those weeks. Ginger was driving me home, and I said, "Oh God, I've got to eat." I couldn't wait. We stopped at a Burger King and I think I had two or three Whoppers. It was incredible how much better I felt.

Poor Ginger. She had to deal with all this. I remember that game when I got hurt was one of the few that had been televised at home that year, so she was at home watching the game with our son, Travis. I had asked Dad at the hospital to call Ginger and ask her to stay home, because there wasn't anything she could do, and I didn't want to worry her. But she had seen the big pool of blood on the ice on TV. And my son Travis, who was two or three at the time, had a stick and was playing ball hockey with it while watching the game. Then he was lying on the ground and rolling back and forth, and throwing his arms around, saying "Oh look Mom, I'm Daddy...I'm hurt!" After I came home I had to take a bath about four or five times a day, and I couldn't take care of myself at all. Ginger got sick looking at the wound, and it was a couple of weeks before even I could look at it. I think the whole thing was harder on her than it was on me.

GORDIE: Mark's injury also created a situation where I got myself in a little trouble. I was working in the team's front office after retirement, and when I went to the Whaler's office for our next executive meeting, I brought up the subject of communication between the team doctors and other physicians. I used Detroit as an example. Dr. John Finley is the team doctor there, and has been for many years. If there's a problem with an injury, where he knows it's out of his field, he takes care of the condition to the best of his ability and then refers it on to a specialist in a professional way. He communicates and follows through. He also utilizes a team approach, and cares about the players and their families.

In Hartford we only had one doctor, and often he was the only doctor on staff at the games. So at this meeting the executives asked me, "Well, what do you suggest?" I said, "It would only cost us a few tickets for a couple of extra doctors to be at the games." There wasn't even a doctor who went to the hospital with Mark.

I told them that Dr. Finley, in Detroit, is the type of doctor who would treat you and follow up on his treatment. Let's say you suffered a head injury in a game, and he'd give you some medication, he'd always ask, "Now, when are you going to bed tonight?" And if you said "one o'clock," he'd be giving you a call at home at five minutes to one. He'd want to know how you were reacting to the medicine? How's your heartbeat? Any dizziness, sweating? You'd tell him, and he'd say "Fine, now what time are you getting up?" If you said, "Well, when the kids do, I'll probably be getting up around 7:30 in the morning." Sure enough, you'd get a call at 7:35 and it would be him. And if there was any kind of problem the next day he'd say, "I want to see you down at the hospital."

So I told the Hartford people "THAT'S the kind of treatment I'm talking about." In Hartford we were letting guys go home at the end of the season without instructions on how to take care of their injuries during the off-season. And certainly what happened with Mark, the delay and the original miscommunication, pointed out the shortcomings we were having in Hartford. Mark had an injury that really could have been permanent, even life-threatening without proper treatment.

I related all this to the Whalers, along with the aspect that, when somebody's injured, get a doctor to see him at the hospital immediately. I knew I was talking to the wall when the general manager, Jack Kelley, said "We have all the trust in the world in our medical men." I thought that was an unusual thing for someone to say at that point when you've just had an injury that, easily, could have cost a player his career or his life.

Right after that, we had to go up to Boston for a tournament, and Jack said "Do you mind if we leave a couple of hours early?" And I said "No problem, is it something important?" And he said "Yeah, I have to see a dentist in Boston." I thought, Whoa...time out, and said, "We have a team dentist right here." And he said "I don't trust him." So I figured that was a double standard, and Jack said "Well, I shouldn't put it that way. I've gone to this guy in Boston for a long time." I couldn't believe he had said that.

MARK: It was a long-lasting recovery. I played about six weeks later. The night I got hurt I weighed 191 pounds. When I played six weeks later I was 170 or 171. Our team was fighting for the playoffs and I just wanted to get back and help out. I felt terrible. And the following year was the worst of my career. I didn't have the strength for anything. If I had been with a different organization I might have recovered sooner. Because nobody in Hartford did any conditioning work. I had done a little on my own, but I didn't know really what to do. It took me to the end of the next year before I started feeling better again.

I ended up suing the manufacturers of the net and the Hartford Civic Center for not maintaining the nets. I didn't do it for money, I wanted them to change the way the nets were made, because the league had promised Dad and me that they would do it and they never did. The nets were still the same, long after I recovered. I got traded to Philadelphia about a year and a half after the injury. I had a real good season there. The Flyers knew about my lawsuit, and they said they were supporting me 100 percent, which was nice. They were a great organization. It didn't get out in the press. It wasn't political. It worked out, and I got the nets changed. My opinion was one injury like that was one too many. My kid was beginning to play in those rinks, too. I busted my ribs four times playing hockey, and three of those were from running into the goalposts before they changed the way they anchored the nets. So anything I could do to protect pro and amateur players, I thought, was a wise move.

By the way, I want to clarify that Tonelli never checked me in the back viciously, nor did he ever intend my injury to be that bad. In fact he said he called the Whaler's and left several messages for me to say he felt so bad about it. But much later, when he hadn't heard back from me, he thought I believed he did it on purpose, but his messages never got through to me. I told "Tonto" that there was no problem whatsoever. When we played together on the Aeros we were good buddies and I knew he would never try to deliberately hurt someone like that.

COLLEEN: What I remember most is that the doctor told Mark how the metal went in there on an angle, and that it somehow managed to just miss his spine, his sphincter muscle, and everything that would have caused him to never walk again.

I'll say this, if I had been at the hospital that night, we would have gotten some quick service for Mark. That's the difference between Gordie and me. He loves his son as much as I do. But if people don't react right away, I take action. I would have had doctors in there so fast their heads would spin. I don't know how many times they had to change the sheets while Mark was waiting for the doctor because he was bleeding so much. Gordie was really mad. But I would have been more than mad. And there is still a lot of things that concern me about this injury, and the way it was handled. The story went out that the team doctor was there to take Mark to the hospital, rode in the ambulance, and carried him in his arms into emergency. That's a bunch of garbage. And the videotape of the injury has somehow managed to disappear. We couldn't get a copy of it anywhere. Somebody at a television station Gordie called, said they thought it had been erased.

MARK: Yeah, everything disappeared. I had a policeman

friend who lived in Avon, Connecticut, who brought a tape of the accident to our house about six months later. He asked me if I wanted to see it, and I said I would. I watched it once. I was sitting on the end of a bed watching, and when it showed me going into the net, boy, I stood up in a hurry. I said "I've seen enough" and gave the tape back. I couldn't watch the video any longer, it was so gruesome. Even now, he can no longer find the video tape.

GORDIE: Even though it ended the way it did, my last year with Hartford provided me with two of the greatest experiences I ever had in the game, or in my life for that matter.

Scotty Bowman invited me to Detroit for the 1980 All-Star game, my twenty-third all-star appearance (an NHL record). It was a very generous offer on his part, and he took a lot of guff for it. He named me to the Wales Conference team, and the game was played at what was the new Joe Louis Arena in Detroit. The ovation I got from the fans there was just unbelievable. When I skated out I got very sentimental, the crowd was really cheering and chanting my name. What helped me out was Lefty Wilson, our old Red Wing trainer, was over at the bench. I felt like I wanted to crawl into a hole, so I went over there and said "Lefty, help me." You should have heard what he said, only about every fourth word would be printable. That made me laugh, and I was able to skate back into line with the other guys. Reed Larson of the Red Wings jabbed me in the chin, and that helped break the tension too. I don't care how long you've been around, or how many games you've played. To get that kind of fan response, you just feel very, very fortunate. I think I've always had a love affair with the Detroit fans. It's never changed. They've just treated me so great. It's a very comfortable feeling, to have all those friends there in the seats. If the players treat the fans nicely, then they're

381

going to get it right back.

COLLEEN: What a wonderful moment that All-Star game was. We learned from Scotty that he had to fight to have Gordie on the team. Apparently he told the league, "You can't have this game without Gordie Howe. If he's on the ice it will thrill those people to death." It's amazing to me that anybody would have been against Gordie playing, especially there. That empathy indicated a lot to me about what kind of person Scotty is. He's willing to take heat to stand by his convictions. That was also the game where I didn't have a ticket for a seat anywhere. While the game is on I'm running all over the stadium looking for somebody I know who has an extra seat. I went to the ticket window and there was no ticket for me. They said it was probably an oversight! What else is new? Finally, I bumped into an NHL executive who apologized, and politely let me sit in his seat.

When they announced Gordie that night, it was one of the most incredible ovations I've ever heard in my life. It meant so much for Gordie and the fans to share that moment together. The same kind of thing happened at the Olympia, when Gordie and the boys played in Detroit for the last time. They chanted "Gor-die, Gor-die" for twenty minutes. It totally overshadowed the game, the home team, the Red Wings, everything. It was amazing. The fans stayed after the game, standing and cheering, what seemed like forever. I hoped he'd come back on the ice and I was surprised that he didn't and knew something was wrong. Actually, Gordie was trapped in the locker room. The media and others had him pushed against the wall while the fans were pressed against the door to the room. It was gridlock. I was up in the stands, thinking "Come out, Gordie, just take one last bow." He couldn't get out to take a curtain call. It was an unbelievable scene.

GORDIE: The fans in Detroit never forget when they like

THE PRICE WE PAY TO PLAY

you. And our coach, Don Blackburn, did one of the nicest things for us. He surprised me and started Mark, Marty and me as a line. Boy, that was a thrill. Especially being in Joe Louis for my first NHL game. All I said to the kids before the faceoff was, "Make it short and fast and get off the ice before they score on us. Don't let them score." Geez, wouldn't that have been something? After all that cheering. Oh, God forbid!

MARTY: Yes, it was fun. Don Blackburn didn't have to do it, but he was a classy enough guy to start the three of us, and he put me on the wing. There's a nice picture somewhere of the three of us out there waiting for the faceoff. I always laugh when I see it, because if you look at that picture, you can see a view looking towards our bench. And there's a guy standing up at our bench. Because after the face-off, I was supposed to get off and let a forward on. I'm a defenseman, I'm not supposed to be a scorer! Right? So, we win the draw, and I was damned if I was going off the ice. It was like full speed ahead, let's go for the gold. We had a good shift, and we kept it down in their end. Besides, I got to run around the whole ice surface for a change.

GORDIE: Very few people realized that Bobby Hull and I retired from the same club in the very same year. I think the oldest line in history played in Maple Leaf Gardens one night. It was Davey Keon, Bobby Hull and me. We did it to drive Harold Ballard, the Leafs owner up a tree. Davey had been a big star for Toronto, and he was probably the youngest of us, being maybe in his early forties then. We had all joined the WHA, and here we were back in the NHL. We got a couple of goals. I think. I got one and Davey got one or two, and we beat Toronto that night. Boy that was fun.

COLLEEN: I remember when Gordie first retired in 1971.

He said it only takes one day for you not to feel part of the team. You go in the dressing room, and you know you shouldn't even be there, and you don't understand the inside jokes that everybody's laughing about. When you retire, you're just no longer a part of that room.

I recalled when Gordie's father retired from his job with the city in Saskatoon, it was also quite a similar feeling. It was really hard for him. He would go back down to where he worked and hang around, because he was lonesome and still felt he was a part of those people's lives. But he was not a part of the scene anymore and he felt awkward and in the way. The guys were almost too busy to say hello. Players suffer the same thing. Suddenly you're not a hockey player anymore and not part of the team's inner sanctum. Retiring seems much harder on men than on women who work. And it was especially hard for Gordie's father, particularly after Gordie's mother died. He never thought that Gordie's mom might die before he did. It was very lonely for him in that house.

GORDIE: It seems like both times I retired, someone was missing. In 1971, it was my mother. Then, when I left Hartford, my Dad died.

COLLEEN: Gordie went out to visit his dad sometime around that last season with Hartford. I think it was just before Dad found out he had the throat cancer that ultimately brought his death. When Dad heard Gordie was coming to see him, he said "You're not going to stay in a hotel, are you? I want you to come and stay with me. I've become a good cook, and a good housekeeper. Wait until you see."

He was just as lonesome as all get-out. And Gordie said "Sure I will." When he got there, Dad had moved out of the bedroom where the furniture was that Colleen and I had bought

384

him and Mum. He moved into the other bedroom so Gordie could have the bigger bed. And he had the house all nice and clean. He was telling Gordie how great he was getting along, how well he was doing. Of course, the more he talked about it, the more Gordie realized how wonderful he really wasn't doing. He fixed Gordie a meal."See, isn't this good? I told you I've turned into a cook." It was obvious Dad was thrilled to have Gordie there.

They talked for a long while, and when Gordie went to bed that first night, he was just about getting to sleep when he heard some noise. Gordie thought, geez, what's that? It was dark in the room, and he thought he had heard something. So he opened his eyes and looked over, and there was his dad standing in the doorway to his room. He was just standing there, looking at Gordie lying in bed. This tough old guy, this pioneer, just watching Gordon. He always called him Gordon. Gordie didn't say anything, he stayed real quiet. He was wondering if his dad was walking in his sleep. Or was something wrong? Should he say something? But his dad just walked over real quietly, leaned over, and covered Gordie up with a blanket, and then left the room. Tears began to soak his pillow.

CHAPTER SIXTEEN

I Do Not Like You, Love, Murray

Mark seemed to always be the one who would try to do things with me, give me things. Mark gave me his motorcycle. He had this customized van and he let me use it for four years in high school. Out of the blue, he just said he was married, he didn't need it any more, here you can use this. He's a very, very unselfish person. Marty's a great guy, but very quiet, very tough to talk to. Marty and I, our relationship has improved drastically in the last four years. Because now I'm a grownup and I used to drive Marty wild 'cause I was just a hyper little guy. He's such a quiet guy and so I used to get under his skin. Now I know more, I know Marty better, so I know how to be so that I'm not irritating to him and I respect the things that he likes to do. But he's a tough guy to know. You really have to work your way in slowly with Marty. But he's a great guy and he'd do anything for you. Cathy is such a sweet person, again she would do anything for you, just a very caring person, like my mom. But Cathy was sort of the renegade when we were growing up, she was the one, I think, who maybe was starved for attention. It was hard on her that my brothers were always in the newspaper and my dad was always in the newspaper and she was never in the newspaper. I remember one time she said to me, "They didn't say anything about you and me in that article." I said, "Cathy, we didn't do anything. If we did something, we'd be in the article." It just never bothered me, probably because at least they always included me in saying, "The youngest son, Murray, is still working on his hockey career," something like that. They wouldn't say Cathy's name at all, and I think that bothered her. And it was too bad because she had so many talents that were far beyond most of her peers. She was stronger and faster than all of her classmates, including the boys, pretty much through high school. I mean she was an incredible athlete. She ran track, but then she just quit. I guess she quit because she never received recognition in the newspaper. She was looking for the same sort of attention as my brothers and that just wasn't going to happen in a girl's sport. It was as though even if you're the best girl athlete in the world, who cares? You know, I always felt bad for her because of that, she always wanted more. Cathy and I got along real well together. When our brothers would go off to some function for sports or whatever, we'd end up being buddies because there was nobody else around to play with. Now we get along very well, talk a lot on the phone and share family stories about whose kids are doing what.

It's funny, quite often people react when they hear my name is Howe. Usually what happens is they ask, "Oh, any relation to Gordie Howe?" And then they laugh and they don't even wait for the response, because when they see me, they don't think it's even remotely possible. They don't even hear me usually. But when they do, then it's sort of disbelief. You know, then they say, "Oh no you aren't." I say, "Well, then fine, I'm not." And they say, "You mean you really are?" I say, "Yeah I am." "No, you're not,"—and we go back and forth like this. You see this little guy, he's a doctor, he lives in Toledo, Ohio, how could this be Gordie Howe's son?

But now it's even more fun because with our son being Gordie, we get, "Oh, isn't that cute, they named him after that hockey player, Gordie Howe." Or they say, "You must be big hockey fans." "Well, yes we are." And we knew it was going to be a double-edged sword for our son. In fact, it was like putting a bulls-eye on his back in certain respects. But in others, we thought it would open doors for him. But most of all, it was a tribute to my Dad, not for his hockey skills, but for his greatness as a person. And since no one else had done it in the family, we figured if we didn't do it, it wasn't going to happen, and we thought it'd be fun. Whenever little Gordie hears anything in the paper about Gordie Howe or he hears a song about him, little Gordie'll say, "Hey, that's my name." He gets a big kick out of that.

My father truly is one of the few real heroes around today, and he is because he is exactly what his image portrays. He is the nicest, most down-to-earth person that you'll ever meet and he'll do anything for anybody. He is completely humble about his abilities. To this day, he doesn't think that anything he did on the ice was all that remarkable. He really feels that he just played a game that he really loved and he did it to the best of this ability. He doesn't think that it is as remarkable as people think. He's the only one who seems to think that way, of course, but that's what makes him great. He's humble and unassuming.

People say, gee, it's too bad your dad didn't grow up in this era of the big bucks. But I think that was a gift to my dad, really, because that's a big part of what's kept him humble. He had to keep diversifying. He had to have summer jobs. He always lived in a modest, middle-class neighborhood because that's what he could afford. I think that kept him down-to-earth with the people around him. Money doesn't help you if you don't have time to enjoy it, and he still had a lot of time to himself in the earlier years of his career. He was able to enjoy his family and enjoy his life away from the ice, whereas the star athletes now sometimes can't.

Our parents have helped us to realize that we are so

fortunate in our lives, which has enabled us to do all the things that we've done. We've also been able to stick together as a family, so we really feel blessed.

COLLEEN: Murray was always so quiet, and enjoyed being by himself. He loved people, but he loved having his quiet time. When he was about five he was still sucking his thumb, and Gordie, who rarely ever said anything even a little harsh, said to Murray something like "If you don't stop sucking that thumb, it'll fall off." Apparently that hurt Murray, and got him mad.

One day, right after that, he came upstairs from the basement and said "Mom, do you know Dad's address at the Olympia?" And I said, "Sure," figuring that he had friends that wanted to write for an autograph or something. I wrote the address down for him. But, instead Murray wrote a letter to Gordie, venting his anger over the thumb issue. A few days later, Gordie came home with his fan mail from the stadium. He told me there was a letter from Murray in his mail, and that it was the funniest thing he'd ever read.

We read it and almost died laughing. It merely said, "Dear Dad, I do not like you. Love, Murray."

MURRAY: I mailed this letter out and I forgot about it. Then I came home from school one day, and my Dad's sitting at the kitchen table. And Mom says, "Oh Murray, your father has something he wants to ask you about," and hands me this letter. I'm standing there, and now I'm in fear. I had totally forgotten about writing it and I truly did fear my Dad. He never, never hit us, not any of the kids, even once, but just the thought of what would happen if he ever DID, scared me. I mean, if he even remotely raised his voice, it was like putting a hammer on your head. If I ever thought I was doing something he didn't like, I'd just stop, right then. A lot of this was also because of respect for him, but there was fear there, too.

So I looked at this note, and my heart sank. I thought for a second, and said, "Oh, don't you get it, Dad? It says I don't like you...I LOVE you!" I still remember that as clear as day because I remember seeing the "love" at the bottom and thinking, I'm glad I wrote "love", because this is the only way to get out of it. My dad didn't make a big deal of it. He just looked at me for a second and said, "That's good, I'm glad you love me." He must have been trying not to laugh. I just remembered after that I would never, ever write a bad note to anybody.

I guess I was striking back one other time. I made my parents think I had gotten lost after a game at the Olympia. I hid out in the stadium and they left without me. I think my dad had corrected me about something. I had done something he didn't want me to do. So, I thought, well I'll fix them, after the game I'll just sort of hide out for a little while and let 'em sweat it out, which was really just a horrible thing, you know, from a parent's perspective.

I knew the Olympia like the back of my hand, so I knew I would be safe at the time, but they didn't know that. My friends and I would run around through all these little corridors in the back, and I'd talk with the security guards and we'd just have a lot of fun. So when they found I was missing and came back to get me, boy, that was one of the few times my Dad got mad, although he didn't raise his voice at me, he just gave me a really disappointed look. He was angry at me for making my Mom upset because, although she wasn't hysterical, she was close to it. I felt awful.

They don't know that this was a deliberate act on my part. I lied and told them I had been reading a book and lost track of time. Actually there *were* many times that I would be sitting in the stands reading. During the Junior Wings games I used to do that a lot. And everyone would joke about me getting lost in a book, but this time I was sabotaging them. I guess they'll find out now. Oops!

GORDIE: Sid Abel had trouble with an aneurysm. This was when Murray was going to medical school at the University of Michigan, and he was making the rounds there at the hospital. Well, he heard Sid was a patient. So Murray walked in to his room, and Sid was lying in bed. He'd been opened up from the shoulder blade almost to the hip. He would have been in trouble if they hadn't been able to find the problem. They operated, and took care of him. Obviously, he was experiencing pain. Murray went in his room and asked, "Mr. Abel, how are you doing?" Sid said, "I'm fine, doctor, thank you." And Murray said, "You might not remember me, but you know my Dad." And Sid said, "Who might that be?" And Murray said, "Well, he played on the right side of your line for many years." Sid looked at him and said, "Gordie's your father?" And Murray said, "Yes, sir." Sid, then, stuck out his hand, and said "DON'T touch me!" When I heard that, I laughed for a month.

MURRAY: About five years ago, for Father's Day, this was probably one of the most memorable experiences of my life, I took my dad white water rafting and it was just him and me. We camped out overnight and I arranged the whole shebang. He liked that I had everything arranged so that he knew we were going to stop for dinner and to set up camp. But , he had no idea where this location was since it was a surprise for him.

It was rafting in southern Pennsylvania on the Ohio Pile. We got in a raft with this couple and the guy was just sort of, wimpy, and his girlfriend was a real strong gal. We were the four people in the raft, and we're going down these rapids which are pretty challenging. But I'd done some white water rafting before and I thought this was actually a little too tame. So instead of steering clear of some of the big rocks, I tried cutting 'em a little closer. This guy is in a panic and he's sitting on the bottom of the raft half the time because he can't hold on, while his girlfriend is loving every minute of it. My dad and I are just having a blast. Dad was trying to fight it a little bit, because he was still a bit apprehensive This was the first time he had done this. I kept, literally, steering us into as many rocks as I could, so we'd fly up on them and go down off them. Meanwhile, Dad's saying, "Murray, cut it out!" And the whiny guy could never figure out what was going on, he couldn't figure out why we were hitting every possible rock. And his girlfriend wasn't even paddling any more, she was just having a blast. When we got out, Dad was laughing about this guy, how scared he looked.

GORDIE: We hit every rock. Every rock. We didn't miss anything. The guy who was with us got so scared he dropped his oar. We were even caught in this whirlpool, turning round and round. Then we went into this four-foot dip after we hit a huge rock. I could hear Murray roaring, he was laughing so hard. I looked back, and I see that he's steering us into every damn rock. So I started whacking him with my oar. "You bugger, I wondered why we were hitting everything!" He said later, "Ah, it's no fun if you don't hit a few things."

Another time I had a water adventure with him was out on Traverse Bay, only it wasn't so funny. It was a very windy day, and Murray wanted to go out on our two sailboats, small Sunfish boats. I was a little concerned because I hadn't tested the ropes on those things for a while. I don't think we'd had the boats out for a year.

MURRAY: The bay gets real rough, and the wind kicks up

when you least expect it. You can have forty-mile-an-hour wind out of nowhere. I said, "Dad, come on let's got out and we'll have this little race." We do everything competitively, just for fun. He said, "Oh, I don't know, it looks sort of rough out there." I said "Aw, come on, come on," and I finally dragged him out there.

GORDIE: We got Murray's boat rigged, and he sailed away. Then I pulled my boat into the water. And oh God, the water was cold. It was only about fifty degrees. It was also very rough. It was so windy, our boats were flying. I could only see the center board of Murray's boat in the water. When you're only riding about six inches over the water in those things, and you hit a wave, the water would hit you, and you'd yell...it was so cold it would take your breath away. All of a sudden, my sheet line breaks. And I'm in the water and the boats blowing away.

MURRAY: We're racing along, and then Dad's Sunfish flips. And that water was ice cold. He got the rope all wrapped around him and he's trying to get the boat back over, but he's having a tough time. I tried to turn around and get back to help him. The wind was so strong and blowing right at me so I couldn't get back quickly. Every time I tried to go in his direction, I'd have to turn or go in irons and have to try to get counter to the wind to get going again. I was yelling, "Dad, I can't help you!" I was scared.

GORDIE: When I hit the water, it was so cold my throat seized up on me. When I went to breathe, I just couldn't. And I came up under the sail, so I had to swim out a little bit from underneath it. I can understand now when somebody falls in the water and drowns that there's no water in their lungs when they're retrieved. Fear just takes you over and you're almost paralyzed. You can't inhale. I tried to suck in some water to drink, to get my throat open, but nothing happened.

I made a quick assessment of my situation. I figured if I went down, I'd go to the bottom, and the bay is very deep. I'd heard the air goes out of you and you sink. I didn't want them to have to search for my body if I did drown. Then I tied the sheet line to my wrist, that way I'd stay with the boat. It's funny what goes through your mind. I could see Murray trying to get back to me, trying to jibe turn, but he couldn't get through the heavy wind.

Just when this had gone on long enough to really scare the hell out of me, all of a sudden my throat went "pop!" and opened right up. I sort of gasped and my big honker opened up, and I could breathe. I said, "Oh thank you, God." And I said to myself, now relax. I slid up on top of the boat, which was still upside down. I'm sitting there, and the wind is still blowing like hell. I said I'm going to sit on this boat until I hit the sand. A neighbor went by in a boat and I waved, and I couldn't say "help." I couldn't say a word. I still couldn't talk. So I waved, and he waved back and kept right on going. He was a doctor, too.

MURRAY: I didn't know how desperate he was. I figured he was okay. There was no way I was going to dive into that water, because it was freezing. Now had I seen him go under, I would have gotten over there real quick and jumped in, but Dad was hanging on. I could see he had hold of the boat, so I thought he was all right. But he was real cold and oh, he was really peeved at me for that. I mean he didn't raise his voice, but I knew he was upset. I said, "Geez Dad, I saw you go over, but I couldn't get the thing turned around."

GORDIE: I said, "Son, you were a great help." It was a frightening experience I asked for, since Colleen had warned me that the bay was too rough for the "now and then" sailor in a small sailboat.

MURRAY: Dad always has good ideas, he's a quick

thinker and reacts well in emergencies. That's typical of him to think to tie the line to his wrist even though he had on a floatation device. I don't know that I would have thought of something like that.

COLLEEN: Neither one of these two ever realized the panic I was in seeing Gordie in the water. There were no neighbors on the beach who had boats and the key for our boat was up at our house. I headed there as fast as I could go. It's a ways to the house, but I got the key and ran back down to the beach. I knew Gordie couldn't survive in that water very long. I kept watching the boat and now could see he was on top of it. I had to hand crank the shore lift to get the boat in the water, then get it started. By the time I got out there, Gordie had managed to upright his Sunfish and was headed home. Boy, I gave him hell, and then I hugged him because I was so scared.

MURRAY: Since I was five years old, I've been writing letters and poems to my parents, mostly my mother. I don't do it very frequently now, probably it's just a once-a-year type of thing. But I just like to be creative, I like to write poetry. As I've gotten older and my own kids are taking more and more of my time, and my career just is seeming to escalate, I have to really, really concentrate and make the time to do it.

My mom did so much for us when I was growing up, I always want her to know how great it was and how much I appreciate it. I know there are a lot of people who have moms that just never gave a crap, you know, or did the bare minimum. But she always did whatever she could to make things great for us. So whenever I get the inspiration, I let her know how I feel, because no matter how many times you tell somebody it still sounds good to hear it again.

2/17/86—POEM TO COLLEEN ON HER BIRTHDAY
FROM MURRAY:

"Now that I'm a doctor, and you now are a friend
You continue to give of yourself, without end
And it's not all the gifts, or the money that you spend
But the way that you love us, Happy Birthday my friend."

Love, Murray.

TOLEDO BLADE-OCTOBER 27, 1994
"Sylvania Joins War on Tobacco"
By Rose Russell Stewart

You've heard of "Star Wars." Now there's "Tar Wars," and it has nothing to do with the movies.

Tar Wars describes the war declared on tobacco products, and the battle is raging in the Toledo area.

Dr. Murray Howe learned about the tobacco education program developed by Colorado physicians who wanted to modernize tobacco education, two years ago. The curriculum targets fifth graders, and since its inception, more than 80,000 fifth graders in thirty states have been exposed.

Responsible for bringing Tar Wars to Ohio, Dr. Howe said the program provided him the impetus for approaching government in an attempt to decrease the access of cigarettes and tobacco products to minors.

"Tar Wars educated me to the problem of tobacco control," said the radiologist, who practices at Toledo and Flower hospitals.

His campaign has resulted in a Sylvania city ordinance to

reduce the accessibility of those products to children and teens under eighteen.

The measure also prevents manufacturers, products, wholesalers, or retailers of cigarettes of tobacco products from giving, selling, or distributing them to anyone under eighteen. Anyone who violates the measure can be charged with a fourth degree misdemeanor.

"Our community's philosophy concerning kids and alcohol abuse and drug abuse is that you are accountable for what you do based on the law and the rules," Mayor James Seney said.

"The law is that if you are under 18, you are not to have tobacco products in your possession," he said "[The ordinance] was passed as an effort to strengthen that situation."

Dr. Howe began his campaign in Sylvania because he lives there, but other communities will also be targeted. Meanwhile, statewide coalitions are working to increase excise taxes on cigarettes, making them expensive to deter teen access.

"These are different fronts that people are working on from the state and local levels," he said.

Locally, the Glass City DOC, a nonprofit program coordinates tobacco control efforts. About thirty physicians are involved in the preventive health care, he said. Nationwide, about 10,000 doctors are in DOC.

Through Tar Wars, fifth graders get an education in tobacco advertising.

"We talk to the kids on their level and really give them the tools to look objectively at tobacco and make fun at the ads and see the humor behind them, the dishonesty behind them, and the gimmicks they use to trying to sell the products," he said.

To raise community awareness, a Tar Wars poster contest is under way.

"Tobacco is not the 'in thing' anymore," he said, "It's a life-long way of slowly ruining your life."

"The majority of all new smokers are children," Dr. Howe said, "with thirteen being the age of initiation. Those who continue smoking are addicted by the time they reach high school. Statistics also show that three-fourths of those who begin smoking as children do so the rest of their lives."

"That type of knowledge made me realize I had to do what I could to reverse this process," he said.

Research also shows that nationwide, seventy to ninety-five percent of children are successful at purchasing tobacco products. Fully 100 percent can obtain the products from vending machines.

"So that's part of the problem. Even though it's against the law to sell to minors, it's not enforced. That's why I'm going to local government."

CHAPTER SEVENTEEN

WE'VE ONLY JUST BEGUN

GORDIE: Colleen and I love to walk from our home on Peninsula Drive about four miles to downtown Traverse City. On the way we often treat ourselves to a soft ice cream if we're in the mood. We'll walk all the way downtown. It's beautiful along the bay, and good exercise for us.

A little while back, someone went by in a car, and they must have recognized us, because the guy slowed down and did kind of a double take. That sometimes happens. We get a lot of vacationers up here from Detroit and Chicago. I meet a lot of hockey fans on the streets. Anyway, this guy turned around at the next corner, and came back around again, to double check, I guess. As he went past us the second time, he was looking at us all the way. He didn't realize he was approaching an intersection, and that the guy in front of him had stopped. "Bang." At that point, a very wise lady said to me "Quick, turn down this street and keep walking. I think we should pretend we didn't see that!"

GORDIE: We don't have that multimillion dollar income. We work like anyone else for what we get. When we do something we get paid. It is our company and we enjoy what we have because of the opportunity to do what we want. I still work to support us, and whatever I do I get paid for, and that's my work, my appearances and endorsements.

I get asked sometimes, "How do you feel about charging for your autograph?" I just tell them that when I fly to these appearances, the people who put on the show have to pay the air fare. They also have to pay for a hotel room, plus they've got to make a profit on their show. They also rent a hall and pay for the items I sign. It's a business—there's a charge and there's a profit. I've heard that my autograph isn't as valuable on the collector's market because I've signed so many over the years. Well that's okay with me, because at these shows I can sit and meet 1,200- 1,500 people in an afternoon, and most often there's not a single one who doesn't say "thank you, thanks for coming." These are people that otherwise I'd never meet or talk to. Now, they can say, "Yeah, I met Gordie Howe" and if that's important to them I think it's great. A lot of people I've met at some shows walk off without asking for an autograph, they couldn't care less. They just want to say hello and, perhaps, shake my hand.

I feel I've worked hard for the privilege of signing these autographs and meeting these people. I worked too hard at being Gordie Howe to not enjoy it.

Sometimes it gets awkward in public. If you're at a restaurant, people often come over. Generally, they will wait until we're done eating or wrapping things up, but every now and then somebody will actually come up, pull out a chair, and sit down. And I just have to explain nicely that I'm spending some private time with my wife or family, and ask them to understand.

When Mark's son, Travis, was a little younger, we were at the All-Star game in Pittsburgh, and Mario Lemieux was sitting not too far from us. I said, "Travis, you've got Lemieux's picture, haven't you?" He said, "Yeah." I said, "He's right over there, go get him." And Travis said, "Yeah, but he's gonna eat." I said, "He's not eating right now. And you're right, if he's got food in front of him that's the wrong time. But he hasn't been served yet, so just go over and say 'Mr. Lemieux, I play hockey too.' Hockey

400

players like kids, just go ask him." So, Travis gets up and starts over but as soon as he does, the waiter puts the food down in front of Mario, and Travis makes an immediate u-turn and comes back. But Mario saw him and called him over. Travis went back, and Mario very politely signed about seventeen pictures.

COLLEEN: In many ways, Gordie is more in demand these days than when he played. People want to see him and meet him, and have him show up at their events. After all, he really is a living legend. You can't go touch Babe Ruth. We always laugh and say the stories about Gordie make him sound like Paul Bunyan. But most of the stories people tell about him are true. It's hard to expand on the reputation of Gordie, because he really is all those things people say and think. He's a symbol, a symbol of hockey and a real hero to a lot of people. I've saved nearly every fan letter Gordie has received since we married in 1953, I've stored thousands of pieces of mail, and it's amazing what people write to him for and the kinds of feelings they express.

I'm the eternal collector and pack rat. My collecting started years ago when I kept everything from camp, school, church, vacations, you name it. I've also tried to preserve everything that was vital to Gordie's career. Often he would come home with some program or souvenir and I'd add it to the collection. A few of the items are in Gordie Howe's Tavern and Eatery here in town. But the priceless items are the original skates, sticks and jerseys that were Gordie's, Mark's, and Marty's. I have several hundred pictures, videos, and old films. I have an entire film we did years ago of Terry Sawchuk teaching how to be a goaltender. We want to do something with that some day and share it with the Sawchuks.

Gordie's been using the last skates he wore at Hartford,

and that makes me very nervous. I tried to put them away for posterity, but he got them out to wear for the oldtimer games. He hates to break in new skates. In fact, I had them all photographed, indexed, boxed and stored. He liked those old skates for comfort, so he is still skating on them. When he goes out on the ice, even if his back is bothering him or his knees are hurting him, you'd never know it when you see him skate. It's later he pays the price, because sometimes he can hardly stand up or sit down. He doesn't want to say anything, to admit that he's not feeling well or his knees are hurting. In fact, he has played in two charity games this spring when he should have been in traction the night before. Murray referred him to a specialist in Toledo so he could get treatment before he played a game in Pittsburgh. He could barely walk for two or three days before that game. But the specialist helped his condition, and Gordie scored a beautiful goal in that game on a breakaway. He always amazes me. He has never been a complainer, so it's hard to judge how he really feels. Sometimes you can tell he's in pain, but he doesn't talk about it. It's always "I'm fine, I'm fine." But I see him massaging his knees or favoring his shoulder, and I know he's not fine.

GORDIE: Colleen has saved everything over the years. She's a scavenger. She hasn't missed anything. She has letters, sweaters, pictures, everything. If I get a nice jacket, like the Saskatoon 55s jacket I got on the birthday tour from my old baseball team, she has it in a box, and labeled before I even get a chance to try it on. She labels everything.

The skates I used the last year I played are a good example. She said "They look so bad." I said "Yeah, but they feel like slippers." So I got a new pair, and oh geez, they were terrible! I could hardly stand up in them. I went back to my old skates, and so she saw me skate and said "You do look more comfortable in your new skates." I said "Those were my old skates I used, not the new ones."

The next time I had to play in a game, I said "Where's the skates?" And she said "Use the new ones." I said, "No, I'll die. I'll get killed in those new skates. Give me my old skates." Colleen said "Nope, they've already been put away."

And I went out in the garage, and sure as hell, there was a box with the words "Gordie's last pro career skates written on it, and my old skates in it. I pulled them out of the box and didn't tell her. The hell with posterity. It doesn't make my feet feel good!

GORDIE: There was a lot of publicity when I went out on the road with Wayne Gretzky when he was after my points record a few years back, but I didn't go when he was pursuing the NHL goal mark. There was a combination of things going on at that time, and several reasons why I didn't make that trip, but I took some heat for it anyway.

There was some guy on TV, on ESPN sports. I just happened to be watching the game at home in Traverse City that night. He was talking about Wayne going after the goal record, and he said "And Howe's not with him." He said I was claiming this and that as a reason for not being there, and he said "Come on, Gordie, get off it. Show some class" sort of comment. Something sick as that. He made me madder than hell, so I took down the phone number of his show and I was gonna call him right there. I thought about it, then decided against it. He wasn't worth what I planned to say about him.

Usually when we do things it's a mutual agreement between us. Sometimes I can cool her down, sometimes she cools me down. But she does more things on her own than I do, because she knows that end of the business better than me.

When you have a record broken, you figure that's part of sports. The only thing that bugged me was that guy saying "Come on, Gordie, get off the pot." That was the year when we had just come off our 180-day birthday tour of sixty-five cities, where we raised nearly a million dollars for charity through our Foundation. As Colleen said, there was just so much time. Then, we set aside a month every year to go to Florida with the kids and grandkids. That special time with my family is so much more important than Gordie Howe, Wayne Gretzky, or any damn record. Or hockey itself for that matter. This is prime time in our lives. The hockey goes on forever, time with the kids and little ones is something you can't ever duplicate.

One of the reasons I got so mad at the guy on TV was, I had told the press how sick I was that week. In fact, I had called Wayne to wish him well, and I remember my voice was awful because I was under the weather. I had a hell of a case of flu that had started in Charlotte earlier in the week when we were down to see Cathy and Wade and the kids and complete our tour engagement there. I woke up at three in the morning, and boy was I sick. I was rolling and tossing, I was either in a pool of sweat or chilled to the bone. It was about the worst flu I ever had. Colleen woke up and asked me how bad it was. And I looked at her and said, "Call Dr. Kevorkian." She said, "That's it! You're going to the hospital!"

She called for Cathy and Wade. They put me in a car and Colleen drove me over to the Emergency right nearby in Charlotte. When we walked into the hospital, the doctor looked at me and said "I know who you are. Whatever you've got, I've got to cure you, because I'm skating in your fund-raiser next week in Traverse City." If I'd have felt better I would have laughed. I had to lay down instead. I lost about fourteen pounds in just three or four days. Never ate, never got out of bed. Just drank water. Then that guy shoots off his mouth about something he knows nothing about! Maybe he should go skating with me sometime!

Heck, I had a good time on Wayne's points tour. He's pretty smart, he said "I've been averaging so-and-so per game, so I should be getting the point in Edmonton."

He was right. We ended up in Edmonton, where he got the goal that put him in the lead. He scored the goal to tie the game, then he scored the winner, so you've really got to give him credit. It was a great performance. We ran downstairs to join him on the ice. I remember his wife, Janet, said "Come on!" And I jumped up and bumped my head. And on the record-breaker, he scored on the backhand, which was funny. Because I had talked with him once about developing the backhand, and I think I said he would find that he'd score a lot of important goals that way.

I enjoyed it. It was fun watching him, he's a hell of an athlete. I said the only objection I had to the whole thing was that the media was confusing people. Yes, he was breaking a record. Of regular season points in the NHL, and that is a tremendous accomplishment for him. But counting WHA and playoffs, total goals, I was still ahead. That never was mentioned! It's strange that the NHL doesn't count the WHA goals or points because Wayne started in the WHA and the NHL said when Wayne came to the NHL that he wasn't eligible for the Rookie-of-the-Year award because of his WHA experience. They counted that as legitimate, professional league but they won't give us our WHA points in our totals. Why does WHA play count in one way but not the other? What's the problem? People say "Oh, he broke your career record when he got his 802nd goal." No, he didn't. My career record is 1,071. I showed good faith. I followed him on the tour, Colleen and I respected Wayne and his family enough to join them for that milestone.

When I phoned Wayne the day he broke the 801 record, and I said "Wayne, please get the damn goal and get them off your back and my back. Relieve that pressure." And I wished him luck. He said he knew exactly what I was saying. He told me, hell, he could go half a year without a goal and that could make a long tour.

I know about that. When I was breaking the Rocket's all-time record in 1963, I hit a drought. It was so long the air went out of the balloons at the Olympia. Literally, they had these damn balloons hanging in a net in the rafters of the rink, ready to let them go if I tied or passed the Rocket. The balloons would then come flying down, like at a political convention. It took so many days though, they just came down like "...plop," after I finally scored. I think I went two weeks without getting a goal, and they were all out of air. It looked funny.

GORDIE: People ask do you miss the game, miss the camraderie? I miss the thrill of playing hockey, and I miss the players, but I don't miss all the effort and work it takes year in and year out. Somebody asked me if I feel a diminishment of popularity, now that I'm retired and older. I said, "No." Wherever I go now there's MORE people. I go out to a function, and I'll sit and talk and sign signatures for huge numbers of people. I'm actually getting more attention now than I ever had before.

I said this to my sisters a little while back when I was out in Saskatoon: I've been all over the world, played hockey in Russia, I've played golf with Presidents and visted Prime Ministers, I've been a guest at the White House, I've been on TV and people know me in public and out on the streets. But you know, there's a hell of a price to pay for that. I used to have five

*Mary and Colleen Howe show off their Whalers jerseys at press conference
announcement of the Hartford signing, 1978.*

*Facing off for the March of Dimes in Hartford, Connecticut
at the 1000th Goal Century Walk.*

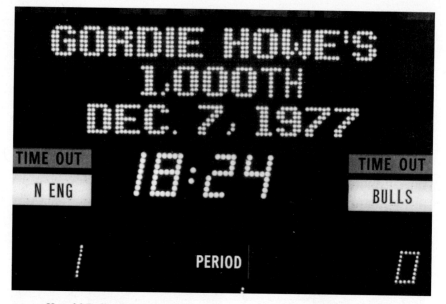

GORDIE HOWE'S
1,000TH
DEC. 7, 1977
18:24

TIME OUT
N ENG

TIME OUT
BULLS

1   PERIOD   0

Harold Ballard wouldn't allow this statistic in Maple Leaf Gardens, but Birmingham, Alabama loved it. John Garrett was the goalie.

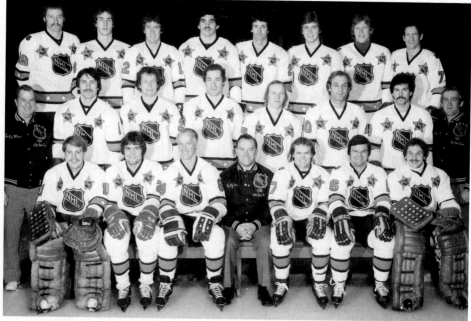

Graphic Artist Photos, Toronto

Gordie's last NHL All-Star game in Detroit, courtesy of Scotty Bowman.

*Murray and Colleen, the senior
Colleen's namesake.*

*Brian Burke and Mr. Hockey.
He gave us another year in Hartford.*

*Mur and Col as
newlyweds.*

Murray says, "I love you, Dad." 1964-65 season.

Murray giving his everything to be a pro hockey player.

Big Bear being hauled into cottage by Murray, Gordie and Meaghan.

Murray stayed in Detroit with Chuck and Jean Robertson to pursue his future hockey career.

Number nine grandchild, Sean Murray Howe.

Rick with his Dad, Chuck Robertson, Murray's second dad for a time.

Murray even dressed like his dad for the Sammy Davis, Jr. Greater Hartford Open, 1977.

Gordie Moore, Meaghan Colleen and Corey Mark Howe.

Mur and little Gordie working out in Florida.

Rafting fun! "Murray will you quit steering us into the rocks!"—Gordie.

*1993—65-City Goodwill fund raising tour climaxes in
Traverse City, Michigan. Home at last!*

*Enjoying the camaraderie of Chris Potter, television star, and Mario
Lemieux at a Celebrity All-Star Hockey Game in Pittsburgh.*

*1980—Our first Traverse City
condo home on
West Grand Traverse Bay.*

*1995—Chuck Robertson and Gordie
showing off grandsons, Travis,
Corey and Nolan.*

*A career highlight—1959! Mum and Dad surprised Gordie in Detroit and
saw him play hockey for the first time ever during his 13th professional season.*

Bobby Lambert finding out, "Where are you now Gordie Howe?" while Gordie plays his Ovation guitar.

1964—Gordie trying to give a thank you speech to 13,000 fans while Murray and Cathy are preoccupied. What control!

Gordie's first sailfish, with Al Philpott and Ed Taube.

Rob Paulsen, Rafael of Ninja Turtle fame, with us in Los Angeles.

sisters, and now I have four. We had just lost Edna to cancer. And the four sisters that I have left I really don't know as much as I should. I feel like I have sacrificed knowing my family as well as I should have because of making a commitment to the game. When I said all this, the girls were all looking at me, and their eyes all filled up like mine. It was very emotional.

Oh sure, I know them as Gladys, Vi, Joannie and Helen, but I don't really know them well enough as members of my family, I don't know their kids. I guess someone might say that's my fault, I should come home more often. That makes sense, but I've had my life to live, too. And that was a life of playing hockey, a job that took me thousands of miles from my home when I was just a teenager. I left home at sixteen to play in Galt. And then my focus went to my marriage, and our four children, and now our nine grandchildren. I have a business, and I'm locked into that life away from my roots and my family. But that was my choice, and I would do it again. I'm just saying that I gave up the closeness, the friendship of my own family, to pursue the life I lead. When I was back home recently, I went to a party where there were forty-five people in this place. And I asked my sister, "Who are they?" And she said "They're all your relatives." I knew maybe six of them.

There's always a sacrifice! When I think about the glory years, no, I wouldn't give them up. Anyone who has done anything with their life, who has accomplished as much as I have, has given up a lot, a whole lot. More than the public can realize at the time.

Often I've asked myself what does being a celebrity mean? Sometimes it's signing autographs for 100 people and then saying "I'm sorry, they're holding up the bus for me, and the guys I play with are waiting to get going. I'm sorry, but I have to go." And somebody in the crowd says "Aw, you've got a big head." There's no way to please people all the time no matter how hard you try.

I was visiting a hospital in Miami a little while back to see a very good friend of ours, Al Philpott, who had contracted polio in his forties. We're visiting, and I looked up at his TV there in the hospital room, and "The Simpsons" show was on. The guy in the next bed was kidding us, he said "Aren't you two a little old to be watching cartoons?" I said "Well actually, I think I was on this program not too long ago. I was supposed to be in an episode where Bart broke some glass with a yoyo and got in trouble, and ends up mailing my picture to his teacher." Then Al says "Hey, this is it." I said "You're kidding, I haven't seen it yet." I knew about it because they had called our office, and Colleen had granted permission for them to use my name and drawing of me in the show. We all sat there and watched it, and were all laughing like hell. The nurses all came in and watched it, too, so it turned into a celebrity TV party just because I was on "The Simpsons."

A lot of things have happened like that. Another production company phoned Colleen to request permission to use my old Red Wing sweater in the movie "Ferris Bueller's Day Off." We saw it when we were in Calgary filming our production "Hockey, Here's Howe" video series, and probably many times afterward with our grandchildren. They loved it and yelled, "Hey grandpa, that's your number.....9 Red Wing jersey!" They watched it so many times they knew all the lines. It a hilarious video. John Hughes did a terrific job!

COLLEEN: One of our pet projects for the future is expand the impact of the Howe Foundation, which was founded to support those causes which improve the quality of life for children, primarily. All the immediate members of our family serve to help give it support. We hope our children and grandchildren will perpetuate the Foundation in the Howe name. Aside from the name, it can serve to continue to offer assistance for others, long after we're gone.

Our inaugural event taking place in August of '95 is the "Riding With The Stars" celebrity rodeo fund-raiser in Winston/ Salem, North Carolina. This is near where our daughter, Cathy, lives and her daughters, Jaime and Jade, are in horseback barrel racing. Many celebrities will be there to help raise money for the North American Riding for the Handicapped. Cathy says it's just awesome when you see some of those handicapped kids around horses. The event is dedicated to Christopher Reeve in hopes of his eventual recovery after his equestrian accident. Cathy said it's amazing how many stars of big screen and TV are excellent riders and love this type of show.

When we held Gordie's 65th Birthday Tour in sixty-five cities, we raised nearly a million dollars. We spread the word of the spirit and name of the Howe Foundation in each city where we appeared, but had each host city designate a local charity that would profit from all our activities and efforts. Cathy helped us and we were able to make all sixty-five cities, but it was like a miracle. After we were half way through Gordie said we should have used his number "9" instead of his age, to create how many cities we visited. There were all kinds of neat events that were used to raise funds. We let everyone get creative. There were large dinners, special hockey games, skates with Gordie, autographing sessions, breakfasts and luncheons, and special visits to hospitals and schools. It was an unprecedented tour that we used as a way to give something back to the fans and teams who welcomed us. It brought us even closer to thousands of people who were awed by the fact we would offer our time and talents without rewarding ourselves. Our reward was that we did it! It would be hard to say what stood out in our minds but the visit to King George School in Saskatoon was very high on our list.

The Howe Foundation may also be a part of the development of the Howe Hall of History museum I think of the day that will open and trust that the good Lord will be there to help us so we can share our artifacts with lots of people. Right now I've just established Power Play Publications, Inc. which has been responsible for this book. And we have so many other book projects to keep us hopping for years to come. We also got involved in doing mail order projects so people can order a variety of items such as books, photos, Northland sticks, pucks and instructional tapes directly from us. We do this because many people don't have any source or method to get these items nearby them.

GORDIE: Colleen's been trying to get me to do things like playing the guitar for forty-seven years. I don't know, I play tunes. I just picked up my mother's guitar one day and she showed me a C chord. I soon learned I could play pretty much anything if I stayed in that range. I memorized tunes, and plucked them out one by one. Those were famous records, old records that I played when I was young.

I used to have a guitar. When Marty and Mark were real young, about four and five, Colleen gave me a Spanish guitar, with a wide neck. The kids thought it was a dang canoe and sunk it in the tub. Then they thought it was a horse, sat on it and flattened that sucker out pretty good.

How many songs do I know? None! I really don't know any of those songs to their completion. I've actually been dinking around with a guitar on and off for a long time. Mostly off. I want to learn how to play that "Where Are You Now, Gordie Howe?" song. Bob says he's going to teach me "Howe." I sure hope so since the family has heard enough of my old tunes.

COLLEEN: I'm often asked how I got the nickname "Honey." Travis was our first grandchild and he spent a lot of time with us when he was real little. Part of that time was during the phase when he was learning to say certain words for the first time. He'd point to things and he would say, "What's that?" And we'd say the word, like "cup," and he'd repeat "cup." At breakfast one morning, he saw one of those small plastic bears with honey in it sitting on the table. So, naturally, Travis points and says, "What's that?" And Gordie said, "That's honey." And Travis said, "honey" plain as could be.

GORDIE: And then I put my arm around Colleen and said, "And this is MY honey." And Travis cheered "Honey, Honey!" He finally had a name for me after calling me "Uh" everytime he wanted my attention. He called Gordie "Pee Paw," Texan for Grandpa, and Ginger's mother "Mee Maw," Texan for Grandma, and he didn't have a name for me because he didn't realize different people could have the same name. Now, at last he created a name for me. From that morning on I've been "Honey" to Travis and all the rest of the other eight grandchildren and even our own kids, especially Cathy because she finds herself making reference to us by the names her children call us.

It was cute one day when Azia, one of the grandchildren, said, "Honey, I can't believe how many birthday cards I saw in the store with your name on it." I told her that was because I had a very popular name. It's interesting, also, when I get these curious looks from other grandparents who hear the kids call me "Honey." It's almost like they wished their family would call them some neat term of endearment. Sadly the sound of being called grandpa or grandma makes some people cringe because it denotes being old in most societies. One day a lady, across the pool from me, was watching and listening to our grandchildren calling out to me "Honey, watch me do this" and "Honey, look how far I can swim under water!" Later she came over to me and asked how I got the children to call me "Honey." I told her the story about Travis and then she started telling me HER story of being a widow who occasionally had some men friends whose company she enjoyed. At various times her grandchildren would come to visit when her boy friends were also there. And, in all cases, when the kids would call her "Grandma" from a distance, in yelling tones, she noticed that these "friends" never seemed attracted to her again. So... she wanted to know how she could go about getting her grandchildren to call her something like "Honey." This was a serious problem for this lady, obviously, so I gave her this advice. #1, be glad you're rid of the guys who acted like that but to treat herself to a wonderful nickname merely gather her grandchildren individually, or in groups, and tell them that she has a very special name that only they will be able to call her... and NO ONE ELSE! Then she should think of what that name would be. She immediately said "Honey" was the one she thought was so ideal. I told her, kiddingly, I'd ask Travis if it was okay.

When she walked away she had a gleam in her eye and a plan in her brain.

In a way it's unfortunate that cherished names like "Grandma" and "Grandpa" scare people and create a stigma about the person. I know some things about maturing—you're wiser, you're more capable and you still like to....as one time Murray asked us if we did...fool around. Our response was "Sure!"

HOWE FOUNDATION

The establishing of the Howe Foundation brings about the opportunity for the Howes and others to perpetuate the philosophy that children are our future and must be coveted. Therefore the mission of the foundation is to assist those organizations who preserve, protect and improve the quality of life of children.

Colleen

A portion of the proceeds from this publication goes to the Howe Foundation.

413

DeLisle's View

A story about the Howes. In March of 1995, as I was about to begin research on this book, my sister was diagnosed with breast cancer and faced emergency surgery. When I informed Colleen of the situation and said it would restrict my availability for a while, she could not have been more solicitous or supportive. She expressed an almost daily concern, making inquiring phone calls from Traverse City as Nancy's operation neared.

On the day after her surgery, I met the Howes in downtown Detroit for the announcement of Marty as the head coach of the Motor City Mustangs. Preliminary reports indicated there was reason for optimism about my sister's post-operative prognosis, but my family had to endure the agonizing waiting period that is required for a lab analysis of the spread of the cancer. We all proceeded with our normal lives and pretended to put our worst thoughts out of our minds.

Colleen and I greeted each other at the entrance of the Omni Hotel on a bright and cold late spring day, and we awaited Gordie, who, because of overflow traffic, had been denied valet parking and was searching for street parking in the area. Present in the lobby were the owners and directors of the new Mustangs—fairly young, very well-dressed and upscale local investors, obviously excited about their new venture. They discussed business and family with Colleen, and the phenomenon of roller hockey in America. Finally, after long minutes, Gordie appeared

414

in the lobby and they moved as a group to walk over and surround Detroit's most storied hero. The sophistication and cool of these guys went out the window the moment Number Nine appeared. They hovered around him, eyes glued, hanging on each word he was saying, as if they were little kids seeking autographs, which doubtlessly, like me, they had been in earlier times. In a short while, Gordie noticed Colleen and me standing across the lobby and excused himself from their midst to walk over to us. Approaching me directly, he said "Tom, give me some good news."

Taking that as a convivial generality and searching for a clever response, I said "Hey, the good news is you've been drafted to play hockey for these guys," which was to be announced that day as a playful public relations ploy by the new team. "No," Gordie said, "tell me everything's okay with your sister."

I had informed Nancy before her surgery of the concern and best wishes Colleen had repeatedly expressed for her over the telephone, and she was impressed and very appreciative. That night I talked to my sister in the hospital, and told her what Gordie had said in the lobby. Nancy, who subsequently received the best possible news about her situation, was as touched as I was about his thoughtful remark. "Well," she said, "that's why he's our hero, isn't it?"

THE END

COLLEEN J. HOWE

Colleen Howe has been active all her life in humanitarian, community and business affairs in Michigan, Texas and Connecticut. Born in Michigan, she spent her pre-school years in the small farming community of Sandusky prior to completing school in Detroit.

Colleen has served for many years on the boards of such deserving organizations as the Michigan 4-H Foundation, March of Dimes of Detroit, Houston and Hartford, the Detroit Junior Wings of the Michigan Amateur Hockey program and the advisory board to the former Colonial Bank of Connecticut. A woman with wide and varied business interests, she spearheaded the formulation of the first Junior A Hockey Club in the United States, the Detroit Junior Red Wings, managing that organization for three years. With this experience, she assisted in establishing a sports medicine council at the University of Connecticut. Colleen is a past director and present coordinator of Newington Children's Hospital. She is also a founder/organizer of the Benzie National Bank of Michigan. In 1987 she completed her first co-executive producer's role in the production of a seven tape video series entitled "Hockey, Here's Howe!", a complete hockey instructional set which was awarded the Premiere Magazine Award of the best "How To" series for 1988.

For the past thirty-two years, Colleen has managed, and currently continues to manage and coordinate, Power Play International, Inc. (formerly Howe Enterprises), which handles all of the functions of the Howe's various business activities. She owns and serves as president of that company developing contracts, projects, investments, financing, marketing, public relations and promotions.

416

Her past business experience spans the range from seed stock breeding of Simmental cattle and Peruvian Llamas to performing as an officer of Howe Travel, Inc. She was a former part owner and developer of the restaurant in her home town of Glastonbury, Connecticut. As contract negotiator, she played a major role in bringing Howes' to the Houston Aeros and the Hartford Whalers Hockey Club of the NHL.

As a licensed insurance agent, Colleen was honored by the Aetna Life Insurance Company for her outstanding achievements in the insurance field. New to politics, she ran for the Connecticut First District U.S. Congressional seat in 1981 which ended for her in a primary election.

Colleen performs as an international speaker on sports, marketing, motivation and being a woman. She has written articles for *Face Off,* a hockey publication, and the New York Times. She is the author of a book entitled, *My Three Hockey Players* and is creator/producer of another book entitled *After the Applause*, featuring ten of hockey's most distinguished retired "couples" which reached the best seller list several weeks in Canada.

She has appeared, nationally in magazines, on radio and on television. Her varied lifestyle, interests and family keep her in demand. In 1972 she was voted "Sportswoman of the Year" by the Sportscasters/Sportswriters of Detroit. In 1979 the Hartford Chamber of Commerce awarded her the Charter Oak Medal for outstanding community achievement. *The Connecticut Journal* publication named her Executive of the Year. In 1997, she and Gordie were awarded the March of Dimes Lifetime Achievement Award for their longevity in fund raising. She attends Faith Reformed Church and is listed in the "Who's Who of American Women". Getting out for a walk, run or a bit of sailing is on her preferred sports list.

Colleen recently developed a sixty-five-city 65th Birthday Tribute Tour for 1993 which served to raise nearly $1 million dollars for various charities. As the tour's spokesperson, she also spread the word of the newly formed Howe Foundation whose mission is to improve the quality of life of children and adults. Always the fighter of injustice and suffering, she also finds time to become involved with the needs of former players and their families.

Colleen's next five-year program will be to establish a Howe Hall of History to include the hundreds of artifacts she has preserved as the family historian. She has recently established her publishing company, Power Play Publications, Inc. which completed the first of their books, entitled "and...Howe." More will follow. She also has some exciting corporate contracts in the works. The first of these is a finalized agreement to establish a "Gordie Howe's Tavern & Eatery" restaurant in Traverse City, Michigan, the Howe's place of residence, and look for a new Howe stick with Christian Stick Company. In addition to men's clothing, Zellers of Canada is planning to announce other new Gordie Howe goods this year.

A people's person, she mainly enjoys her family, friends and meeting new people. In addition to her famous marriage partner, Gordie Howe, she has two sons, Marty and Mark, who also established their own outstanding professional hockey careers. Colleen is equally proud of her daughter, Cathy, and a third son, Dr. Murray Howe. Moreover, she is the grandparent of nine, third-generation children...Travis, Jaime, Azia, Nolan, Jade, Meaghan, Gordie, Corey and Sean. Affectionately they call her "Honey".

Colleen Howe likes who she is and being a vital and productive person.

GORDON (GORDIE) HOWE

To literally millions of sports fans, worldwide, Gordie Howe IS "Mr. Hockey."[®] He achieved one of the most illustrious careers and distinguished records in the history of professional sports. He began his career at the age of sixteen with the Detroit Red Wings and spent twenty-five of his twenty-six years in the National Hockey League as "Number 9" with that organization. During a two year retirement, Gordie served as a Vice President for the Detroit Hockey Club.

Consider the "firsts". In 1973, in an unprecedented return to the ice, Gordie came out of retirement to become a player for the Houston Aeros of the World Hockey Association after already setting eleven NHL records. He was voted the WHA's Most Valuable Player that season. He than took the new position for the Aeros by becoming the first player/president in hockey's history. When his sons, Marty and Mark, signed with the Aeros, it was the first father/son combination ever to play together in a major professional sport. Their four-year, triple contract, negotiated by Colleen Howe, was an unprecedented agreement in the history of hockey or any other sport.

In 1978, Colleen secured a ten-year player/personal service arrangement with the Hartford Whalers of the WHA for the trio. In the first playing year, Gordie lead the team in scoring which includes his 1,000th career goal, making him the only player to reach that plateau.

Gordie and Colleen have been husband and wife as well as business partners, for forty-one years. Colleen, as President of Power Play International, Inc., creates and manages all of its' business interests. Those interests include corporate endorsement programs, public relations, promotions, film and video projects as well as varied investments. Gordie serves as Vice President of public relations for that corporation.

Gordie and Colleen have three sons, a daughter and nine grandchildren.

The following totals demonstrate the remarkable performance of Gordie's active years in professional hockey, not including Omaha in 1945-46.

Most games: 2186
Most goals: 975
Most assists: 1383
Most points: 2358
Most games, including playoffs: 2421
Most goals, including playoffs: 1071
Most assists, including playoffs: 1518
Most points, including playoffs: 2589
Most 20-or more goal seasons: 27
Most consecutive 20-or more goal seasons: 27
Most 30-or more goal seasons: 18

POINTS OF INTEREST

Played defense, center and right wing...6'...205 lbs...Born in Floral, Saskkatchewan, March 31, 1928...Shoots right and left...Brother of former N.Y. Ranger, Vic Howe (played with Rangers in '50-51, '53-54, '54-55 total of 33 NHL games)...Suffered severe head injury during 1950 Stanley Cup Playoffs...Set NHL record for most assists (59) and most points (103) in a season by a right wing in 1968-69 (both broken by Ken Hodge in '70-71)...Had calcium deposits removed from left wrist in June, 1970...Missed part of '70-71 season with a rib injury...Spent 1971-72 and '72-73 season as a Vice President of the Detroit Red Wings...Became reactivated as a player in 1973-74 season with Houston Aeros (WHA)...Became President of the Houston Aeros in June, 1975 and continued to play (resigned, September 1976)...Missed 22 games in 1978-79 season with a hairline fracture of ankle bone...Father of Mark and Marty Howe who played pro hockey with Gordie...Holds the record for career points (2589), goals (1071) and assists (1518) and active seasons as a player (32)...playing 2421 games.

(a) - First Team All-Star (12-NHL, 2-WHA)
(b) - Second Team All-Star (9-NHL)
(c) - Winner of Art Ross Trophy (Top NHL points) (6-NHL)
(d) - Won Hart Trophy (NHL MVP) (6-NHL)
(e) - Leading Scorer in Playoffs (6-NHL)
(f) - Led in Penalties during Playoffs (1-NHL)
(g) - Led in Goals during Playoffs (3-NHL)
(h) - Led in Assists during Playoffs (1-NHL, 1-WHA)
(i) - July 1973-Signed by Houston Aeros (WHA)
(j) - Named as WHA MVP (1-WHA)
(k) - June 1977-Signed by New England Whalers as a free agent.
(m)- Named winner of Lester Patrick Trophy (outstanding service to hockey in U.S.)
(n) - June 1972-Named to Hockey Hall of Fame
(o) - 1972-Named to the Order of Canada, Canada's highest citizen award

Detroit Red Wings have never won a Stanley Cup without a Howe on their team. When they won the Cup in 1934-35, '35-36 and '42-43, Syd Howe played (no relation to Gordie) and when they won the Cup in '49-50, '51-52, '53-54 and '54-55, Gordie was a member of their team.

GORDIE'S STATS

YEAR	TEAM	LEAGUE
1944-45	Galt Red Wings	OHA
1945-46	Omaha Knights	USHL
1946-47	Detroit Red Wings	NHL
1947-48	Detroit Red Wings	NHL
1948-49	Detroit Red Wings (b-e-g)	NHL
1949-50	Detroit Red Wings (b)	NHL
1950-51	Detroit Red Wings (a-c)	NHL
1951-52	Detroit Red Wings (a-c-d-e-h)	NHL
1952-53	Detroit Red Wings (a-c-d)	NHL
1953-54	Detroit Red Wings (a-c-f)	NHL
1954-55	Detroit Red Wings (e-g)	NHL
1955-56	Detroit Red Wings (b)	NHL
1956-57	Detroit Red Wings (a-c-d)	NHL
1957-58	Detroit Red Wings (a-d)	NHL
1958-59	Detroit Red Wings (b)	NHL
1959-60	Detroit Red Wings (a-d)	NHL
1960-61	Detroit Red Wings (b-e)	NHL
1961-62	Detroit Red Wings (b)	NHL
1962-63	Detroit Red Wings (a-c-d-e)	NHL
1963-64	Detroit Red Wings (b-e-g)	NHL
1964-65	Detroit Red Wings (b)	NHL
1965-66	Detroit Red Wings (a)	NHL
1966-67	Detroit Red Wings (b-m)	NHL
1967-68	Detroit Red Wings (a)	NHL
1968-69	Detroit Red Wings (a)	NHL
1969-70	Detroit Red Wings (a)	NHL
1970-71	Detroit Red Wings	NHL
1971-72	Did not play (n) (o)	
1972-73	Did not play (i)	
1973-74	Houston Aeros (a-h-j)	WHA
1974-75	Houston Aeros (a)	WHA
1975-76	Houston Aeros	WHA
1976-77	Houston Aeros (k)	WHA
1977-78	New England Whalers	WHA
1978-79	New England Whalers	WHA
1979-80	Hartford Whalers (age 52)	NHL

National Hockey League Totals
World Hockey Association Totals
MAJOR LEAGUE TOTALS

REGULAR + PLAYOFF TOTALS

GP	G	A	Pts	PIM	GP	G	A	Pts	PIM
-	-	-	-	-	-	-	-	-	-
51	22	26	48	53	6	2	1	3	15
58	7	15	22	52	5	0	0	0	18
60	16	28	44	63	10	1	1	2	11
40	12	25	37	57	11	*8	3	*11	19
70	35	33	68	69	1	0	0	0	7
70	*43	*43	*86	74	6	4	3	7	4
70	*47	39	*86	78	8	2	5	7	2
70	*49	*46	*95	57	6	2	5	7	2
70	33	*48	*81	109	12	4	5	9	*31
64	29	33	62	68	11	*9	11	*20	24
70	38	41	79	100	10	3	9	12	8
70	*44	45	*89	72	5	2	*5	7	6
64	33	44	77	40	4	1	1	2	0
70	32	46	78	57	-	-	-	-	-
70	28	45	73	46	6	1	5	6	4
64	23	49	72	30	11	4	11	*15	10
70	33	44	77	54	-	-	-	-	-
70	*38	48	*86	100	11	7	9	*16	22
69	26	47	73	70	14	*9	10	*19	16
70	29	47	76	104	7	4	2	6	20
70	29	46	75	83	12	4	6	10	12
69	25	40	65	53	-	-	-	-	-
74	39	43	82	53	-	-	-	-	-
76	44	59	103	58	-	-	-	-	-
76	31	40	71	58	4	2	0	2	2
63	23	29	52	38	-	-	-	-	-
70	31	69	100	46	13	3	*14	17	34
75	34	65	99	84	13	8	12	20	20
78	32	70	102	76	17	4	8	12	31
62	24	44	68	57	11	5	3	8	11
76	34	62	96	85	14	5	5	10	15
58	19	24	43	51	10	3	1	4	4
80	15	26	41	42	3	1	1	2	2
1767	801	1049	1850	1685	157	68	92	160	220
419	174	334	508	399	78	28	43	71	115
2186	975	1383	2358	2084	235	96	135	231	335
2421	1071g	1518a	2589p	2419m					

BOOKS TO LOOK FOR

"and...HOWE!" will be a prelude to other Howe publications to be produced in the future. Look for them!

"The Impossible Dream"—The story of Gordie, Mark and Marty Howe's unparalleled father and son adventure on and off the ice.

"Hockey, Here's Howe!®"—The updated version of the Howe's instructional book.

"Teammates"—The story of a selection of the most prominent hockey wives in the games history.

"On Frozen Pond"—The personal, wondrous and intimate account of the pre-hockey, prairie boy years of Gordie Howe and the formation of his native intellect and survival instincts.

"Gordie and Company"—The photographic account of every aspect of Gordie along with those who have been a part of his life.

"The Gordie Howe® Stories"—Gordies favorite hilarious and touching memories, as told by players and others close to him.

"The Powermaker"—Colleen Howe's intimate experiences into the world of amateur athletics, parenting, and women in the corporate, professional and hockey worlds.

"After the Applause II"—A reflection of ten of hockey's most successful husband/wife combinations in retirement.

"Letters to MR. HOCKEY®"—A humorous and touching combination of mail to Gordie Howe, preserved through the years by Colleen, which provide historical insight into what fans mean to the Howe family.

WATCH FOR THEM!

BOOKPLATE OFFER

To get a personally autographed bookplate, signed by both Gordie and Colleen Howe, refer to the information below. This self adhesive bookplate can be placed over the printed bookplate on the first page of this book These signatures will not only give your book added value, but will be our way of saying thanks for letting us share some of our lives with you.

To acquire this bookplate, please write or fax:

Colleen and Gordie Howe
Power Play Publications, Inc.
6645 Peninsula Dr., Dept. 1
Traverse City, Michigan 49686
(616) 947-8585

Please include a self addressed envelope, postage paid.

HOWE TO REACH US FOR OTHER BUSINESS

In order to engage Colleen or Gordie Howe for appearances or corporate programs, the following corporation is the only authorized, exclusive representative.

Power Play International, Inc.
6645 Peninsula Dr., Dept. 9
Traverse City, Michigan 49686
(616) 947-1944 / (616) 947-1948

* No other person or company stating to represent us has any authority to do so.

MESSAGE FROM COLLEEN J. HOWE, "MRS. HOCKEY®" POWER PLAY PUBLICATIONS, INC.

For the past 14 months, Gordie and I have appeared at over 120 unique events. During this process, we helped raise over $350,000 for various charities and non-profit organizations, while traveling from Yellowknife, Canada (there really is such a place, I have a souvenir spoon to prove it!) to Oakland, California. During this odyssey, we've had the pleasure and privilege of sharing our family's historic life story with thousands of wonderful people.

As we enter the second printing (no soft covers here) of our international best-seller, *and...HOWE!* I can now fondly reflect to the time our journey to success started. Beginning in early 1995, and as a neophyte to the self-publishing business, I encountered many obstacles which at the time seemed insurmountable. There were so many decisions that had to be made to produce the book. For example, it was necessary to know and implement what would be the size, format, length, and cost of the book ($100.00, only kidding!). Other questions were, who would be the writer, printer, book distributor, etc? I endured consecutive sleepless nights (where's my Craftmatic bed when I need it), and mind numbing marathon phone calls (thank God for ITS Communications!) to meet the daunting deadlines. Nevertheless, I held firm to my vision and conviction. The reality and gratification of this came to the forefront on November 22, 1995 when Power Play Publications, Inc. was honored at the Canadian Writers & Development Trust dinner for our overwhelming sales and accomplishments. We were really on our way!

Our official book tour began on October 10, 1995 for Zellers of Canada as we launched our quest to sell 100,000 books. After the three week stint with Zellers, we appeared at a few different book

426

stores. Also, along the way we squeezed in a Caribbean cruise book signing for seven days. Even though we had a huge order with Zellers at the time, and were selling books primarily through book stores, we still didn't feel quite right about what our path was. Something was missing. And then, something magical happened.

Soon we engaged an enthusiastic, intelligent person (Hey, did Del's Parent's type this?) Del Reddy, who, coupled with the belief and efforts of principal Neil Thomas and assistant principal Lynn Gregg of John Glenn High School, developed and launched our first non-profit book signing event held at the school on December 2, 1995. It was a HUGE success! For over 5 hours (we felt like the Beatles!), we penned our names on hundreds of books, shook hands with everyone from newborn babies to re-born citizens, and felt terrific knowing we were able to share so much with so many. The school moved over 1,000 books and generated over $16,000 for a variety of school programs. This became the prototype for our on-going mission of utilizing the *and...HOWE!* book to meet the needs of many other non-profit and charitable organizations. Eureka! We had found what we were meant to do!

Fortunately for me, I have a great support team who have helped to make the past 14 months so special and successful. They are: Dawn Blamer-Aspenleiter, Dan Blamer, Kristen Roush, Aaron Howard, Quebecor Printing, McConnell & Associates, Logan & Company, corporate friends, Marty, Mark, Cathy and Murray and their families, the coordinators, Del Reddy, marketing for the U.S., and Lee MacDonald, marketing for Canada, Tom DeLisle, writer, "Mr. Hockey®" (of course!), and you the special fan of the book. Not only are they great teammates, but we also have the greatest of them all on our side—God.

Thank you to everyone who has supported the *and...HOWE!* mission. We look forward to doing a charity event in your hometown soon, and...HOWE!

THOSE WHO MADE IT HAPPEN...

John Glenn High School ✯ L & L Books ✯ Grand Rapids Griffins Youth Fdn. ✯ Borders ✯ Horizon Books ✯ Schulers ✯ Capital Area Charity Hockey ✯ Ultimate Sports Bar ✯ C.A.T.C.H. ✯ MTA Travel ✯ Michigan Farm Bureau ✯ Wendy's ✯ Zellers ✯ Canton Firefighters/Canton Police ✯ University of Michigan Burn Center ✯ Ringette ✯ Easter Seals ✯ Plymouth Canton Jr. Baseball ✯ Bell Celebrity Skate ✯ Building Industry Assn. of S.E. Michigan ✯ Gaylord Grizzlies ✯ Jackson Optimist Club ✯ Crowleys ✯ U.A.W. Teamsters ✯ LumberJack Building Ctrs. ✯ Eastern Michigan Hockey Assn. ✯ Bill Gadsby Golf Training Center ✯ United Fund of Livingston County ✯ AIG Group ✯ Value City ✯ Gene Research Fdn. Walk for Jesse ✯ Dave Coulier Fdn. ✯ McDonald's ✯ Ronald McDonald House ✯ CARD Adv. ✯ Yellowknife Hockey Assn. ✯ Law Auto Sales ✯ Awrey's Bakery ✯ Angela Hospice ✯ Westland Firefighters Public Awareness ✯ St. Clair Art Fair Assn. ✯ Audiovox/Cellular One ✯ Nat'l Kidney Fdn. ✯ Habitat for Humanity ✯ MI K-Wings Booster Club ✯ Crohns/Colitis Tournament ✯ Child Guidance Center ✯ CNIB Celebrity Tournament ✯ Celebrity Pro-Am Classic/Firefighters Fund Charity ✯ Westland Community Fdn. ✯ Red Holman Pontiac ✯ Gordie Howe's Tavern & Eatery ✯ Howe Fdn. ✯ PASS Sports ✯ Italian American Club of Livonia ✯ Hockey Hall of Fame ✯ Lakeview Athletic Boosters ✯ Citizens Insurance ✯ St. Francis Cabrini ✯ MCI ✯ Fantastic Sports Travel ✯ Make A Wish/Joe Louis Arena ✯ The Arthritis Society ✯ AGP & Associates ✯ Dow Corning ✯ The Dallas Stars/The Family Place ✯ Stu Evans Lincoln Mercury ✯ The London Celebrity Classic ✯ Media Play ✯ Livingston County Hockey Assn. ✯ Jacobson's/Livonia Literacy ✯ Fabro & Assoc ✯ JBA International ✯ Gerald R. Ford Museum ✯ Oakland Literacy Council ✯ Michigan Jewish Sports Hall of Fame ✯ Oakwood Healthcare Systems Fdn. ✯ Sterling Heights Betterment Fdn. ✯ Delta College Fdn. ✯ Hamilton Rotary Club ✯ Guelph Minor Hockey ✯ Fergus Minor Hockey ✯ Tim Horton's Fdn. ✯ Davenport College ✯ Children's Achievement Center ✯ Riverview High School Girls Basketball ✯ RTL Adv. ✯ Youth on Ice ✯ Detroit Vipers/Palace ✯ Amer. Lung Assn. ✯ Westland Shopping Center/Friends of the Library ✯ Tom's Collectibles ✯ Gibraltor Trade Center ✯ Kalamazoo Optimist Hockey Assn. ✯

428

ITS Communications
joins in celebrating a
lifetime of achievement.

Congratulations
Colleen and Gordie!